HISTORIC PHOTOS OF
SAN ANTONIO

TEXT AND CAPTIONS BY
FRANK S. FAULKNER, JR.

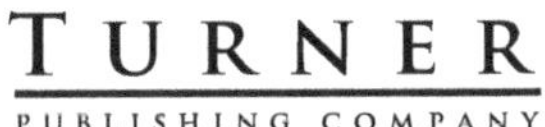

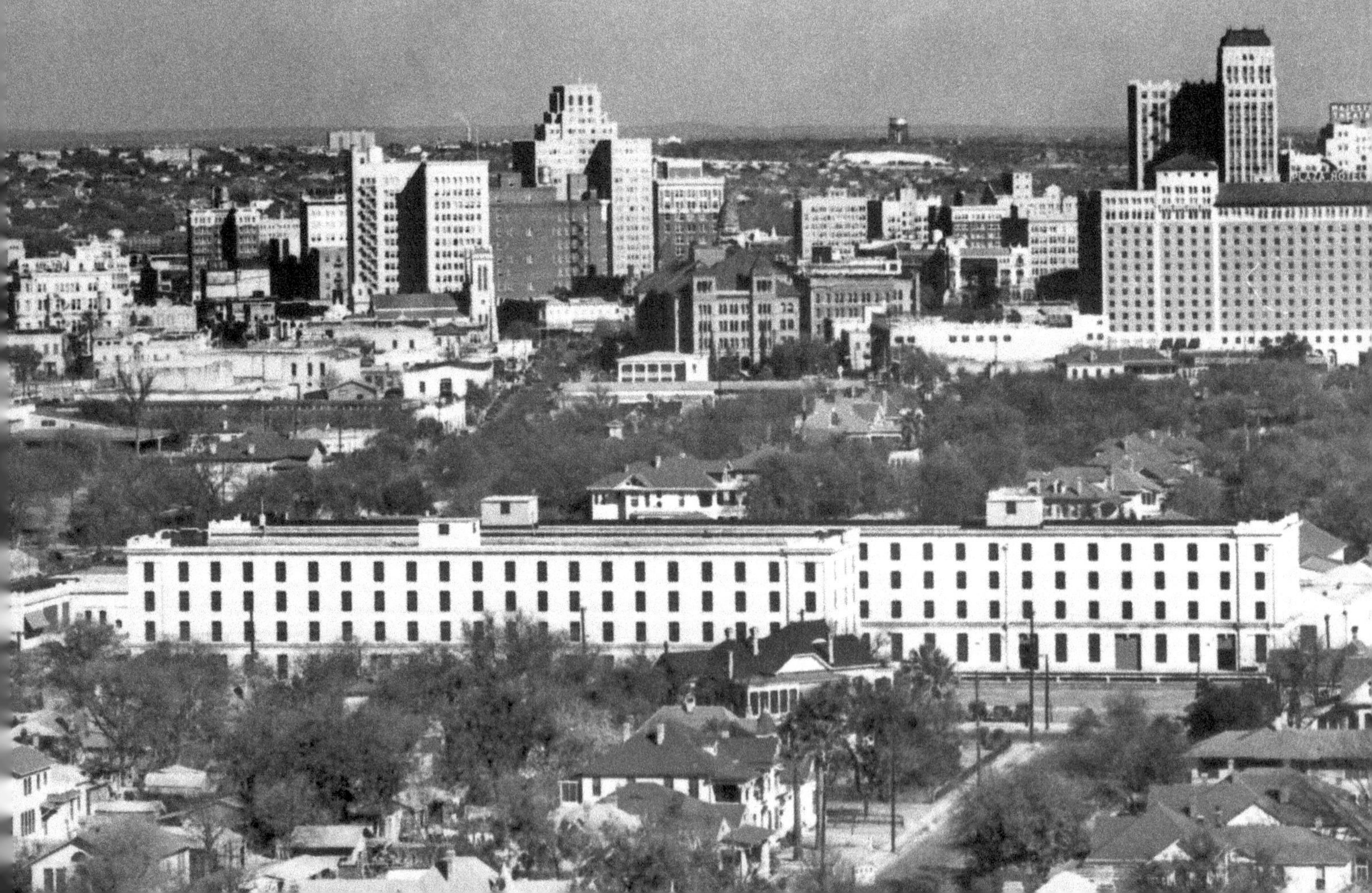

Looking northeast from the top of Pioneer Flour Mills towards downtown in the late 1930s. The town has grown since the early 1920s, and skyscrapers fill the center of the city. The Johnson Street Bridge can be seen in the bottom foreground.

HISTORIC PHOTOS OF
SAN ANTONIO

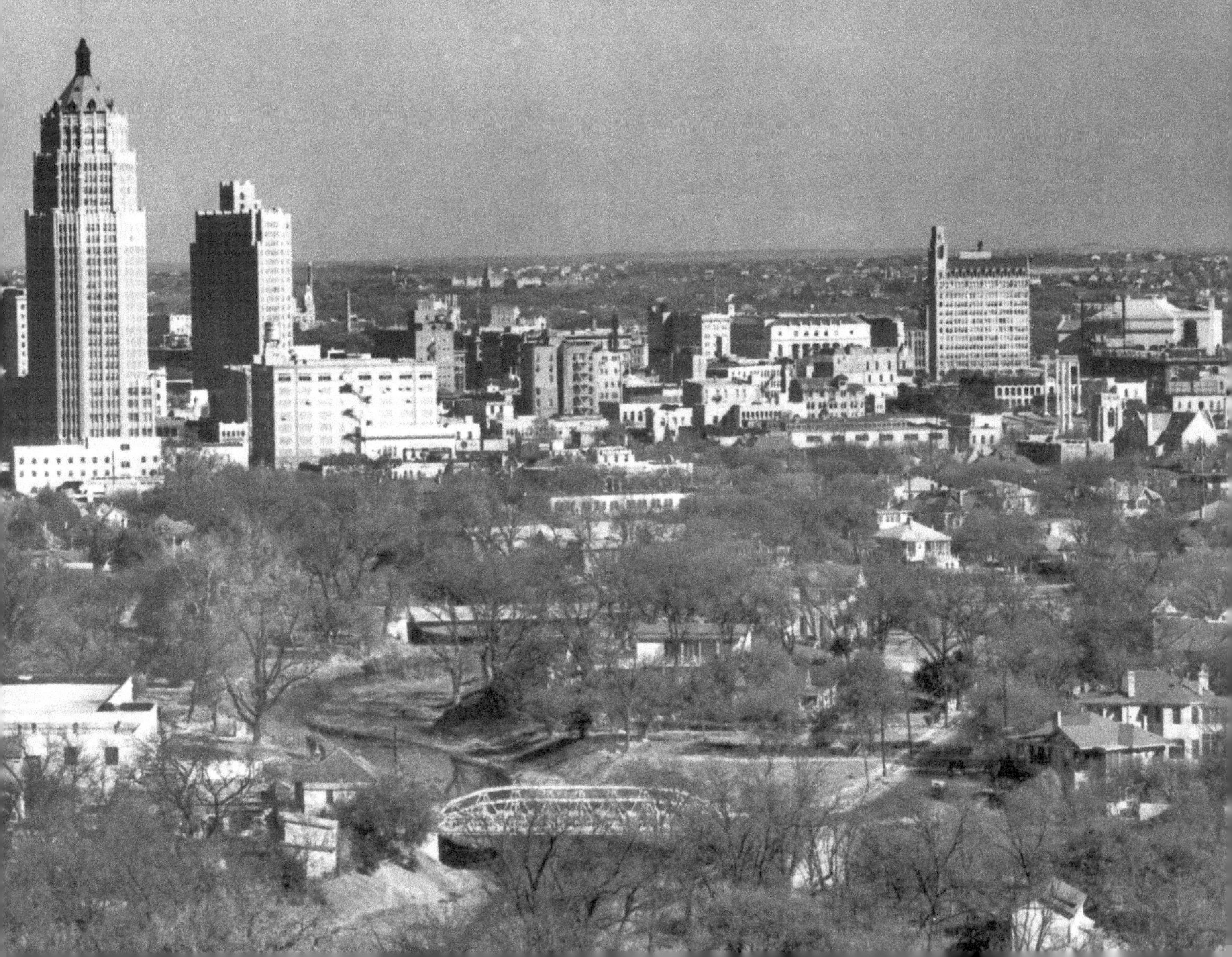

Turner Publishing Company
www.turnerpublishing.com

Historic Photos of San Antonio

Library of Congress Control Number: 2007923677

ISBN: 978-1-59652-378-4

ISBN 978-1-68336-965-3

Contents

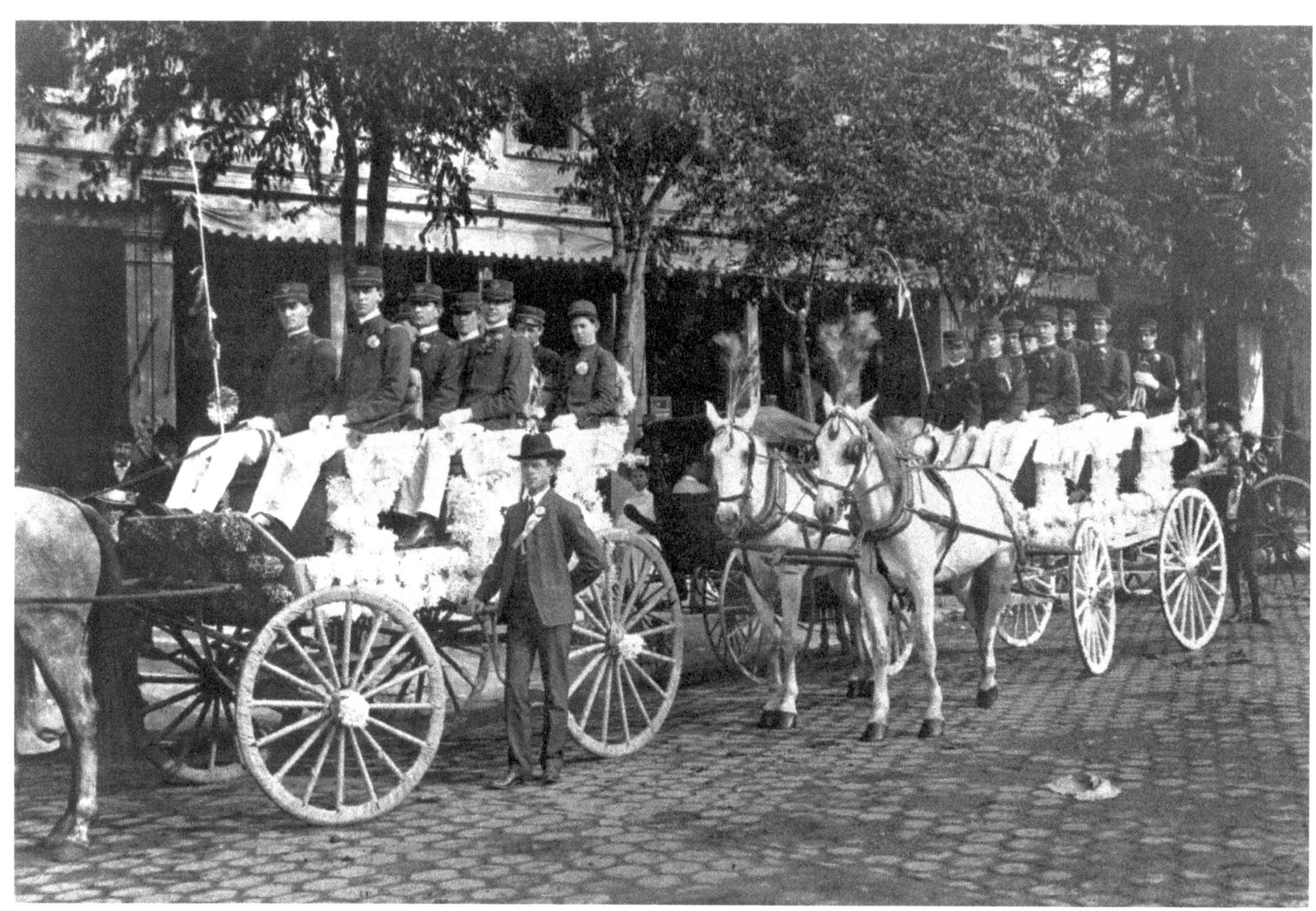

Cadets from Peacock Military Academy seated in decorated carriages in front of the Menger Hotel during the Battle of Flowers Parade, April 1904. Peacock Academy was opened by Wesley and Saline Peacock on September 4, 1894, near West End Lake (later renamed Woodlawn Lake). It was built about three miles from downtown, at the time the area was seeing a real estate boom. Also, note that the street is paved with mesquite blocks.

Acknowledgments

This volume, *Historic Photos of San Antonio,* is the result of the cooperation and efforts of

Library of Congress
Texana/Genealogy Department of the San Antonio Public Library
University of Texas at San Antonio, Institute of Texan Cultures

The author would like to thank the following individuals for their contributions and assistance in making this work possible:

Deborah Countess, Texana/Genealogy, for proofreading and editing
Andrew Crews, Texana/Genealogy, for preparing Texana/Genealogy photographs
Maria Pfeiffer, local researcher, for checking historical data
Thomas Shelton, Institute of Texan Cultures, for helping to identify some photographs
Clarissa Chavira and T. Matthew DeWaelsche, Texana/Genealogy, for watching the reference desk while I took off to do the research
Linda Faulkner, my wife, for everything

Preface

This book begins in the 1860s when photography began to be popular, but the city is much older. It owes its origin and survival to water deep underground to the north and west of the city in what is called the Edwards Aquifer. In prehistoric times, springs bubbled to the ground's surface and, over millennia, created the San Antonio River. Native Americans congregated on its banks long before Mexico, which included present-day Texas, became a Spanish colony.

In 1691, Domingo Teran de los Rios led an expedition that arrived at the river near present San Pedro Park on June 13, the feast day of Saint Anthony. In 1718, Martin de Alarcon received instructions to establish two missions in the area. Villa de Bejar was founded May 5, and on March 9, 1731, sixteen families arrived from the Canary Islands to establish Villa de San Fernando. Three other missions were begun, and a civil government was soon created to complement the ecclesiastical and military organizations. An official census taken in December 1783 shows a population of 1,392.

Over the years, tensions grew between Spain and its Mexican colonists. On September 16, 1810, Father Miguel Hidalgo began a revolution that reached Texas in 1812, when Augustus Magee—an American—and Bernardo Gutierrez de Lara raised a Republican Army of the North. After defeats by Royalists at La Bahia, Rosillo, Salado, Medina, and Alazan, the revolution ended in the San Antonio area, and most of the remaining revolutionaries were put to death. The revolution succeeded elsewhere, however, and Mexico became an independent nation in 1821.

Moses Austin, from Missouri, successfully petitioned the Mexican government to establish a colony in Texas for immigrants from the United States but died soon after it was granted. His son, Stephen F. Austin, carried on the plan and stopped in San Antonio in 1821 before pushing on 175 miles north. Settlers began arriving in 1825, and there were those in the United States who advocated annexing Texas. When Santa Anna came to power in Mexico in 1833, overthrowing the Constitution of 1824 and the colonization laws, unrest escalated to revolution. For thirteen days, ending March 6, 1836, a small band of Texans defied a vastly larger Mexican army under Santa Anna at the Alamo. Their heroic, hopeless stand bought time for the revolutionary army and made San Antonio famous around the world. Texas won its independence and remained a republic through 1845, when it became the twenty-eighth state of the United States.

The majority of Americans who came to Texas were from the South and brought an acceptance of slavery with them. The state sided with the Southern Confederacy in the Civil War, but in the popular referendum on secession held on February 23, 1861, over 40 percent of the citizens of Bexar County opposed leaving the United States. The county, according to the 1860 federal census, had only 1,395 slaves out of a total population of 14,454. Some who opposed the war left, going north or west, including James P. Newcomb, a newspaper editor who went to California. Others left for Mexico or Germany, to return after the war.

During the republic and early years of statehood, a flood of German immigrants created a cultural foundation that dominated the region until their influence was overpowered in the twentieth century by a large influx of refugees from the Mexican Revolution of 1910–1921 and anti-German sentiment during the two World Wars.

At the close of the Civil War, San Antonio was still a frontier outpost, but with a population of about 15,000, an equal number of Americans, Germans, and Hispanics. Within the city were five churches and several schools: a German-English school (150 scholars), a free school (200 pupils), two designated as Negro schools ("one taught by a Northern man and one by a negro," according to *The Texas Almanac* for 1867), and a Catholic College (200-300 students). Between 1866–1867, about 200 new buildings were erected. The city had gas lights, an ice manufactory, five mills, five newspapers, and five bridges. Good land sold for $10 to $50 an acre, and less desirable land from $5 to $10 an acre.

—Frank S. Faulkner, Jr.

With the exception of touching up imperfections caused by the vicissitudes of time and cropping where necessary, no other changes have been made to the photos in this book. The focus and clarity of many images is limited to the technology of the day and the skill of the photographer who captured them.

We encourage readers to reflect as they explore San Antonio, stroll along its streets, or wander its neighborhoods. It is the publisher's hope that in making use of this work, longtime residents will learn something new and that new residents will gain a perspective on where San Antonio has been, so that each can contribute to its future.

—Todd Bottorff, Publisher

Haymarket Square or Plaza (*La Plaza del Zacate*) on a fair-weather day was full of sights, sounds, and aromas. Here, farmers brought flowers, vegetables, and fruit to sell to city residents. At night it would be filled with music, dancing, and food.

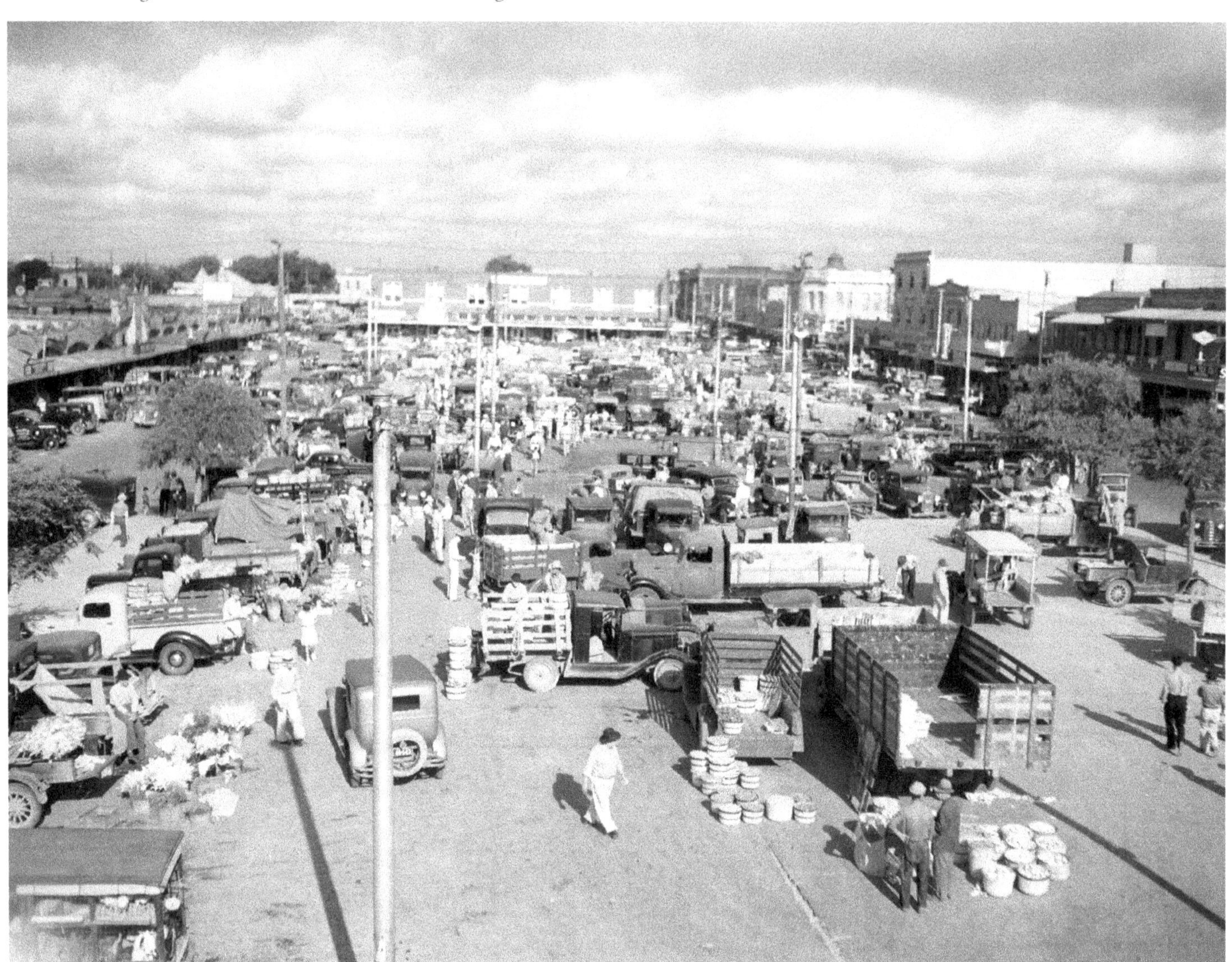

THE BEGINNINGS OF PROSPERITY

(1860s–1899)

Reconstruction was hardly better than the war had been, but progress came on several fronts that would ultimately bring prosperity. Soldiers stationed in San Antonio to protect freedmen of color also protected whites from attacks by Comanches and other native tribes. The city became a supply depot for troops here and in outposts to the west. In 1870 the first forty acres of what would become Fort Sam Houston was donated to the United States government. Educational and social institutions thrived, and churches were built. Public schools, including the Rincon school, the first public school for the children of freed slaves, were constructed. The Casino Association made up of German speakers opened in 1858 for music, literary, social, and athletic activities. Newspapers in English, German, and Spanish met the needs of all readers.

The Market House opened in 1858, and gas lighting illuminated the plazas for the first time in 1869, the same year Santa Rosa Hospital was built. The beef market increased throughout the country as railroads provided a means to ship cattle across the United States. Cattle drives from South Texas to railroad connections helped everyone along the route, including the citizens of San Antonio. The first Agricultural and Industrial Association of West Texas fair was held here during December 1868 to show off local products.

The first train of the Galveston, Harrisburg & San Antonio Railroad pulled into the city in 1877. On February 5, 1881, the International & Great Northern arrived. Soon, San Antonio had several passenger and freight lines. Cattle could now be shipped directly from here, and wool also became a major product sold to northern markets. In 1889, some 84,000 head of cattle were bought and sold, 70,000 horses, 160,000 sheep, and 7,000,000 pounds of wool were traded. In 1875, only 300,000 pounds of wool had come through San Antonio.

On February 15, 1898, the battleship *Maine* blew up in the harbor at Havana, Cuba, killing 260 Americans and resulting in the Spanish-American War. Future president Theodore Roosevelt came west to raise a regiment of cavalry, popularly known as the Rough Riders. Part of the recruiting and training took place in San Antonio.

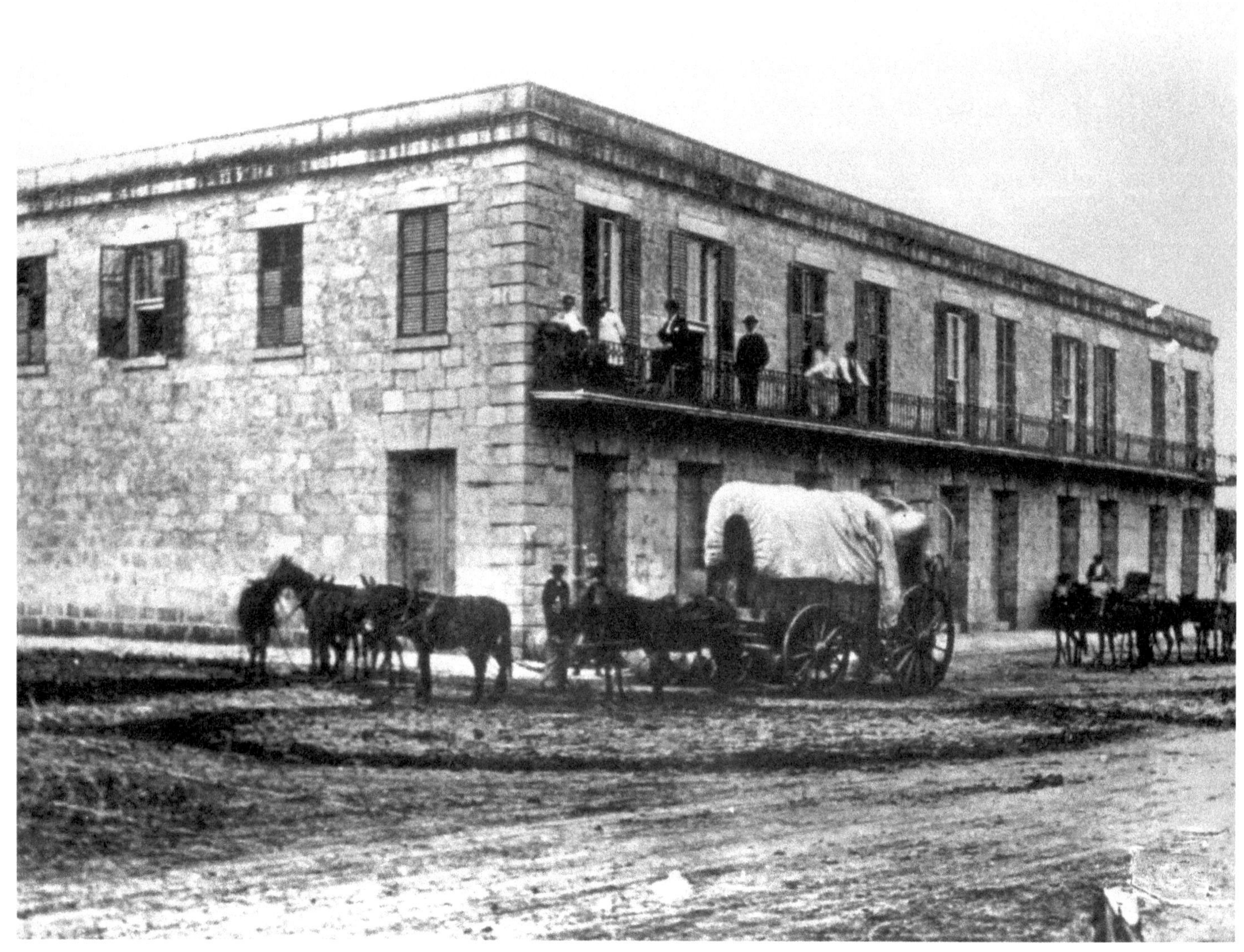

The Vance Building on the northeast corner of Houston and St. Mary's streets, built by John and James Vance, first served as headquarters for the U.S. Army and was occupied by the Confederacy. In 1872, W. G. Tobin remodeled it into the Vance House Hotel, which Ludwig Mahncke renamed the Mahncke Hotel in 1886. It is the site of the present Gunter Hotel.

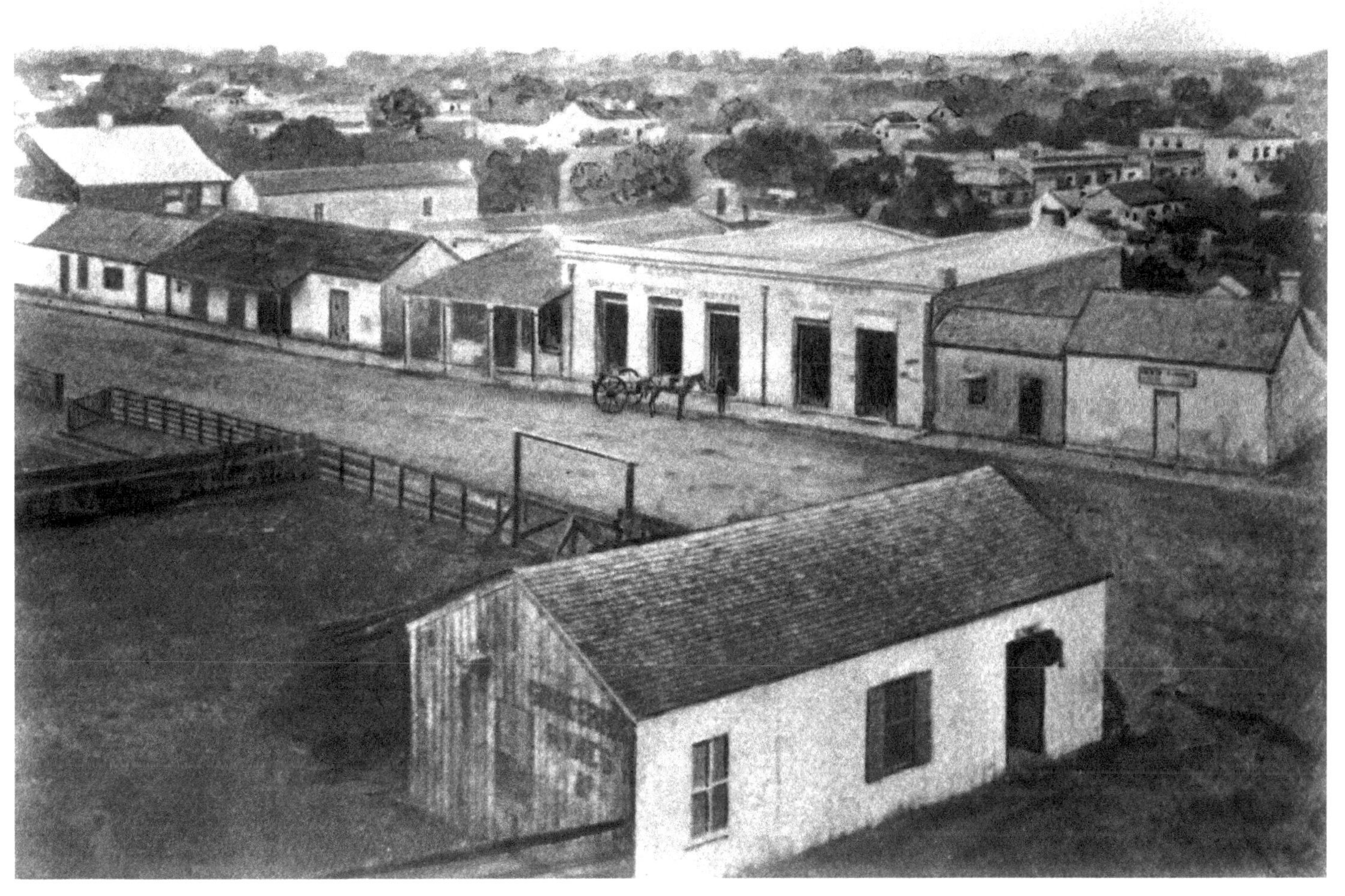

This 1866 view of the south side of Alamo Plaza gives a glimpse of San Antonio as a small, frontier town. The sign on the building advertises groceries and wines. A mule yard is attached.

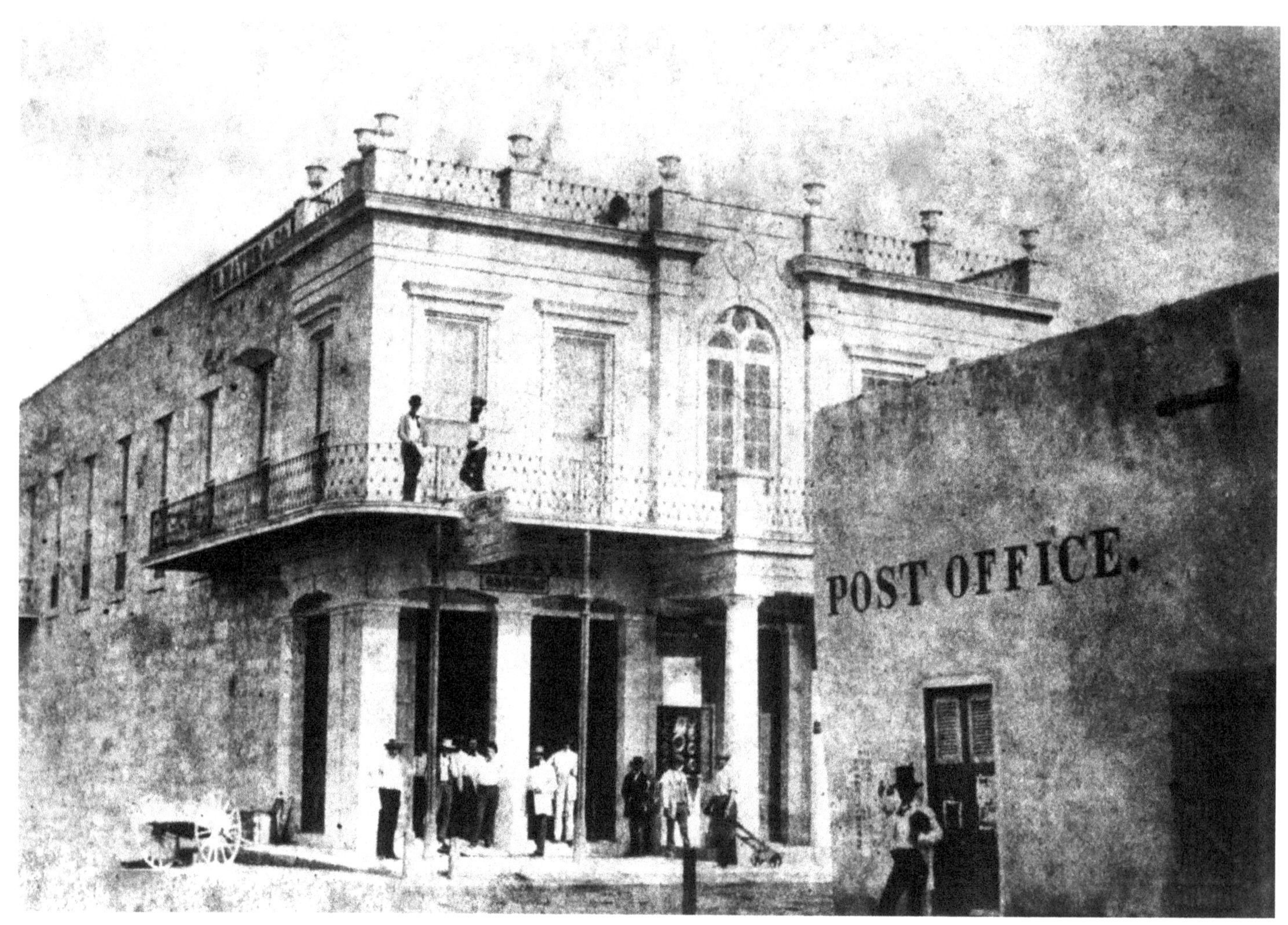

In the foreground is San Antonio's first U.S. Post Office, facing Main Plaza. Facing Dwyer Avenue is the French Building erected at what was then Dolorosa and Quinta streets by John C. French. At various times the building held retail space, a bank, U.S. military headquarters, district and circuit courts, city hall, and a theater where Houdini once appeared.

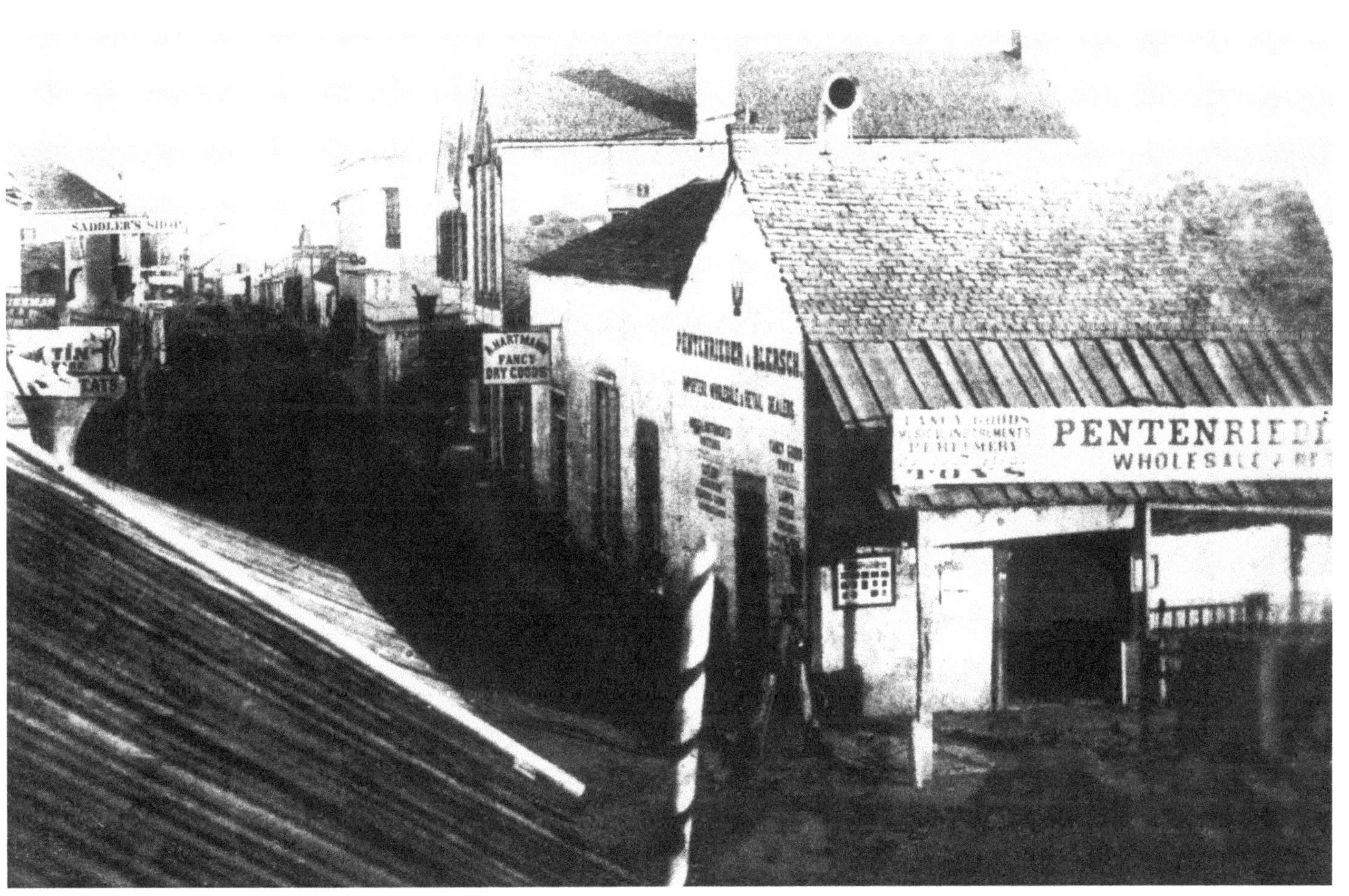

This photograph from the early 1860s, taken from the balcony of the Plaza House on Main Plaza, looks down Commerce Street. On the left is a saddler's shop. On the right are A. Hartman Fancy Dry Goods and Pentenrieder & Blersch general merchandise. During the Civil War, Pentenrieder returned to his home in Germany. He returned in 1866 and reopened his business.

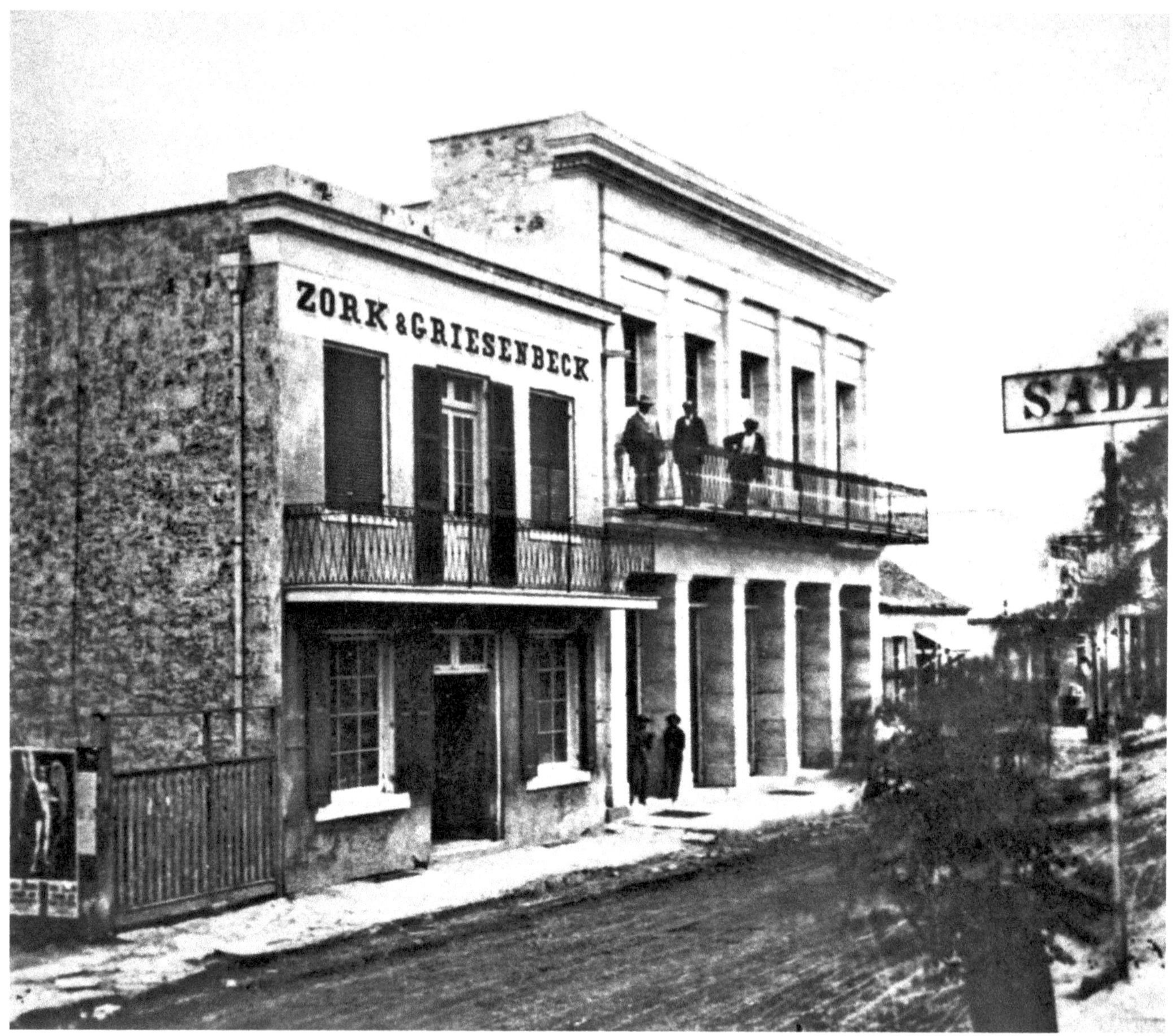

Zork & Griesenbeck moved into this new building at 275 W. Commerce in April 1867, only to dissolve their partnership in January 1869. Zork, believed to be the first Jew to permanently reside in San Antonio, continued in the mercantile business until his death in 1885. Griesenbeck also remained a merchant, eventually owning a prosperous cotton business.

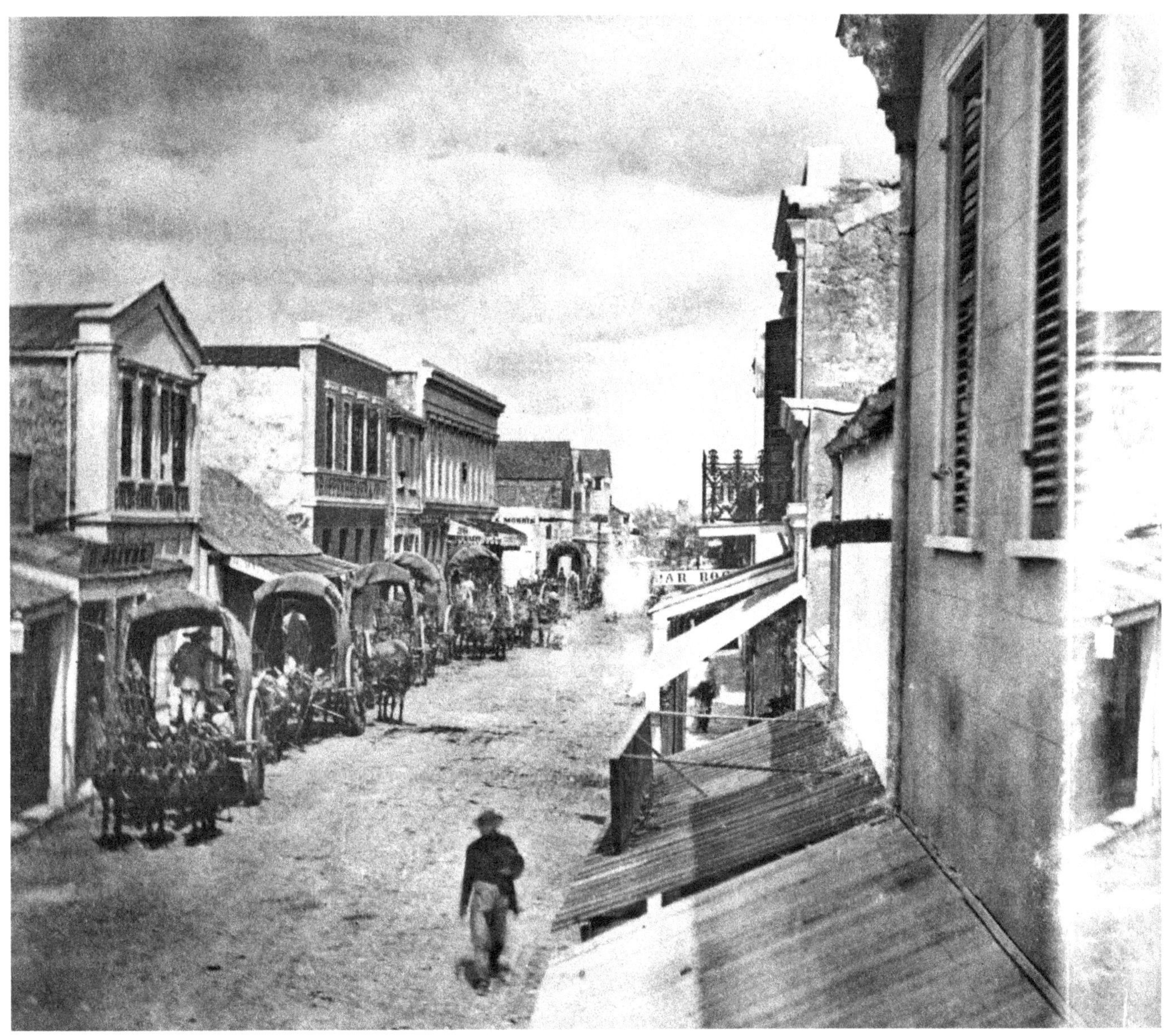

Looking west on Commerce Street about 1870. The wagons lined up on the south side of Commerce may be arriving from the Texas coast with merchandise or headed west to army forts or even to El Paso, a long and dangerous trip.

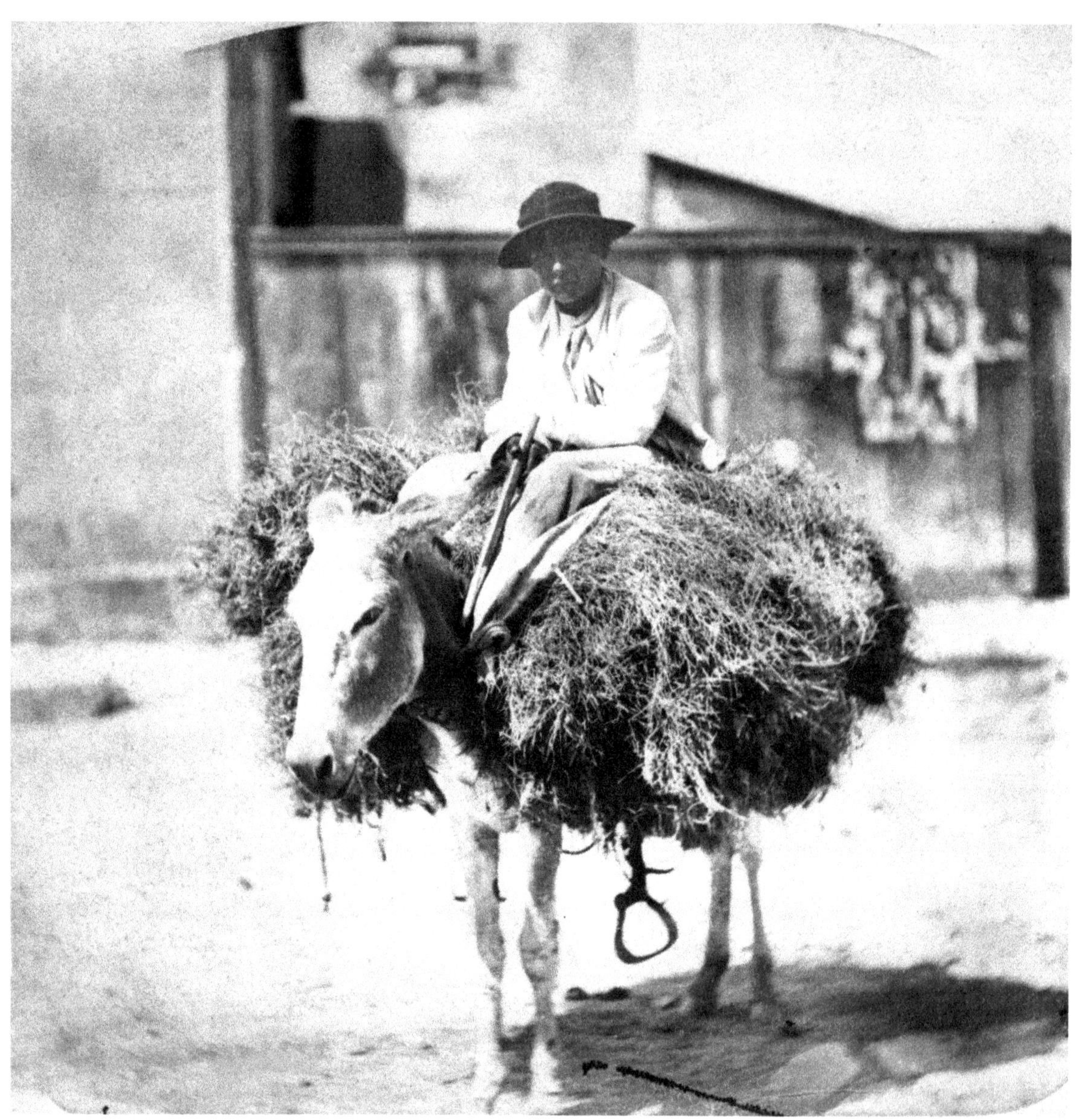

Man on a hay-laden donkey probably on his way to the market to sell the hay.

The Alamo, shown here in the 1870s, was actually the chapel for the larger Mission San Antonio Valero complex. Its cornerstone was laid on May 8, 1744, and the structure was abandoned in 1793. Under the Texas Republic, the Alamo returned to the Catholic Church. After statehood, it was used for quartermaster purposes. The open, bare plaza would have been a dust bowl in summer or a muddy mess in rainstorms.

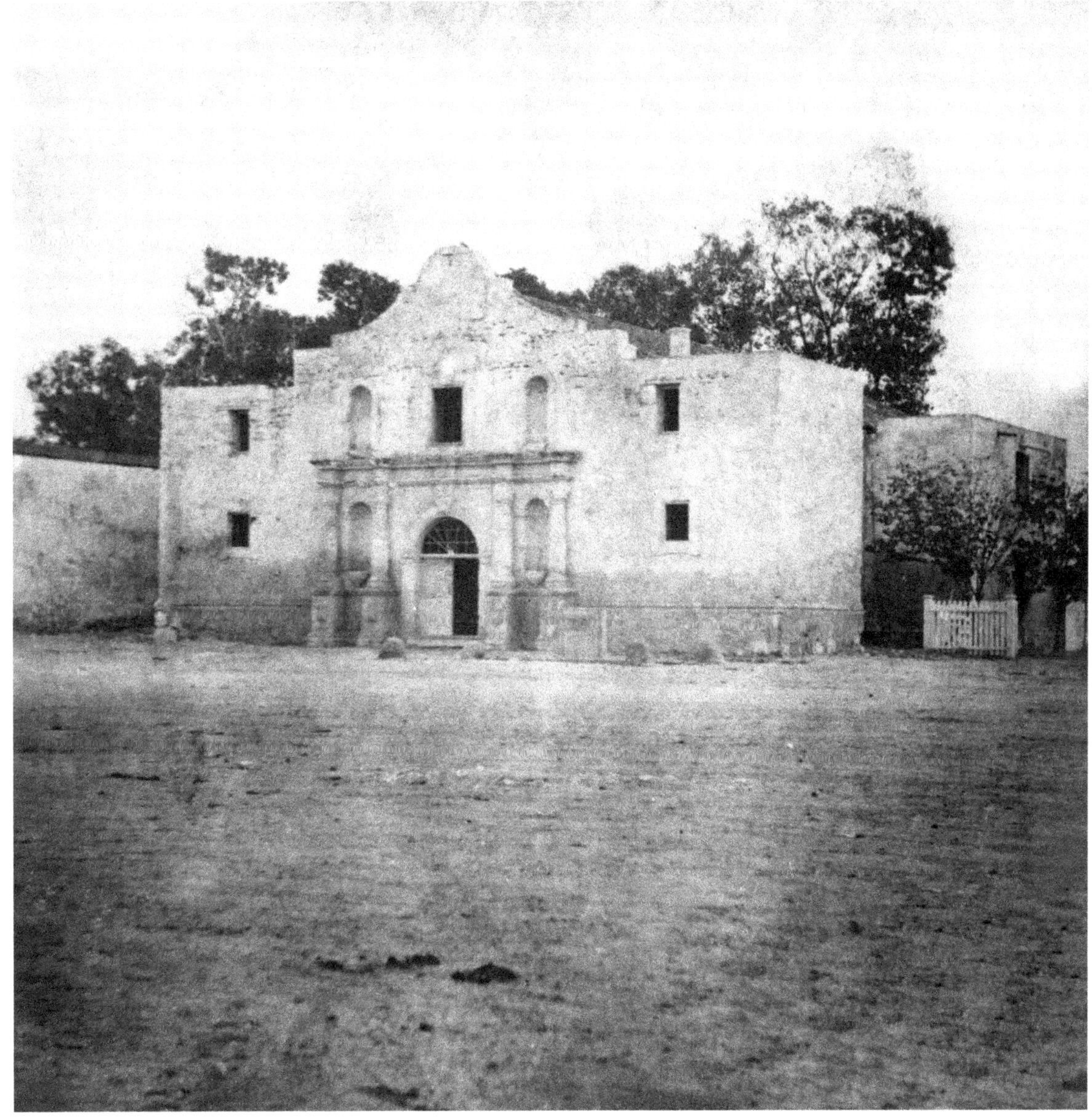

This photograph, taken from Main Plaza at Soledad, looks east down Commerce Street. On the left is Rhodes & Deats Tinware and on the right the entrance to R. Wulfing & Company, commission agents. In November 1872, George S. Deats was elected city recorder.

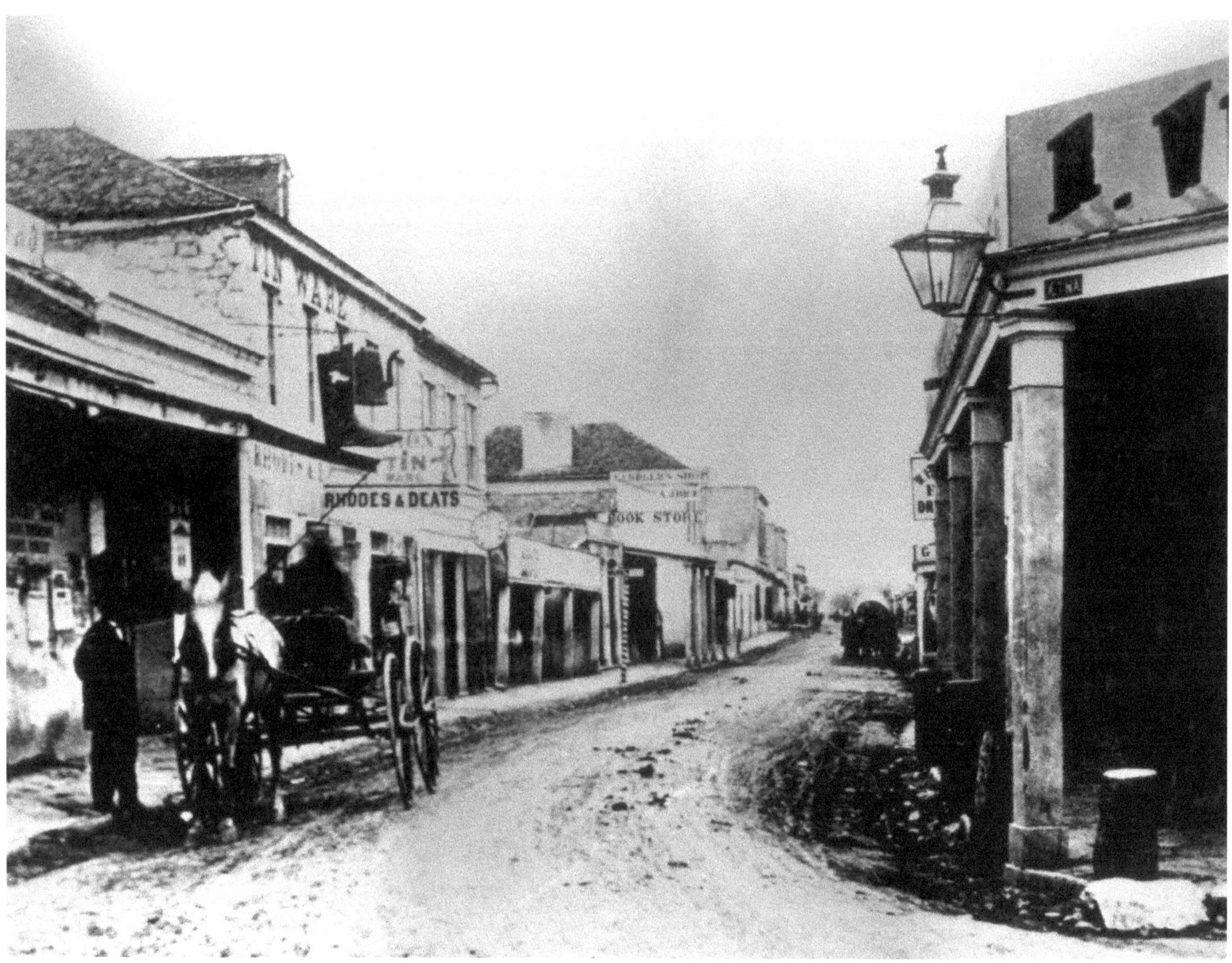

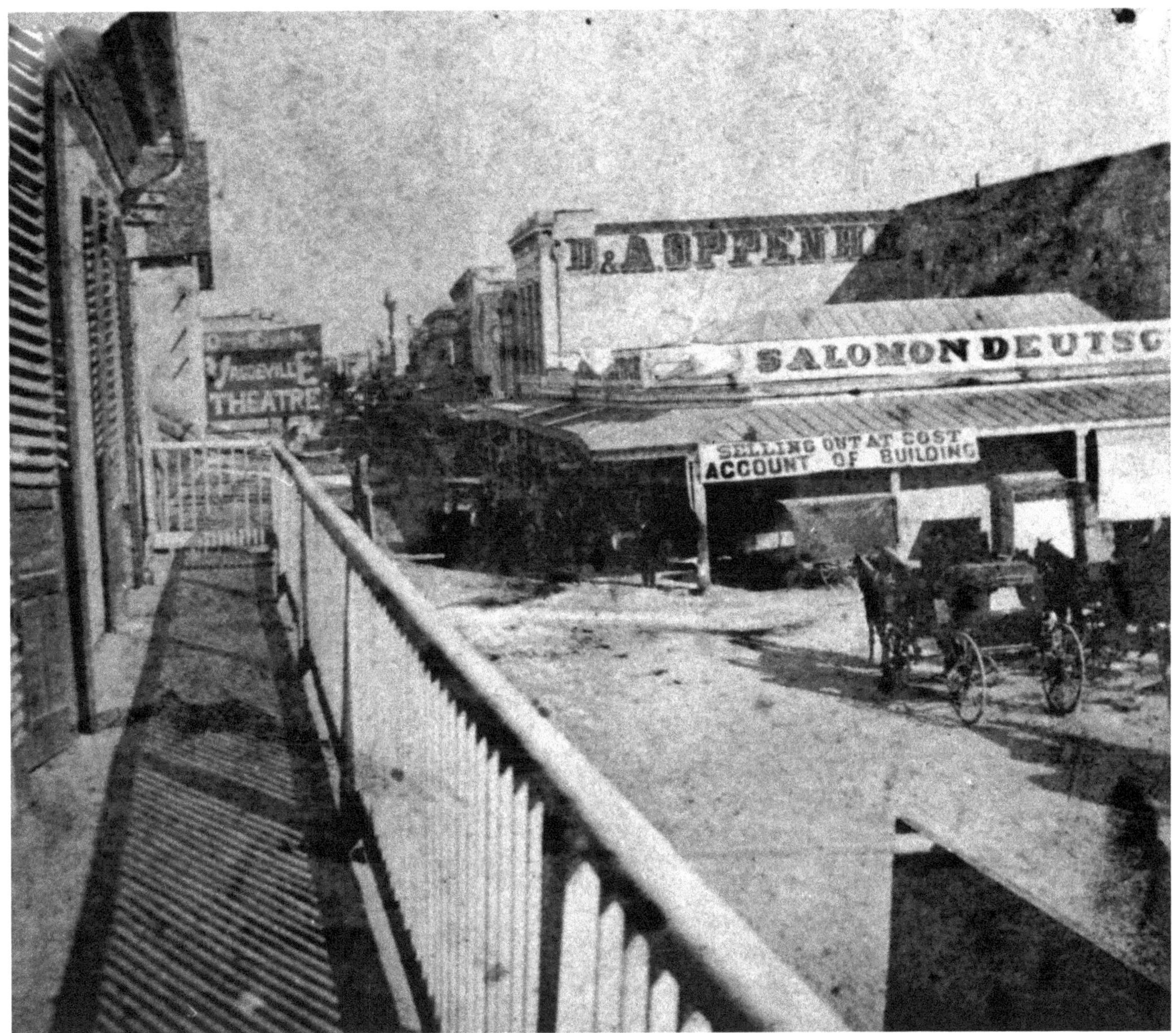

Commerce Street about 1875 showing the Vaudeville Theatre, D. & A. Oppenheimer Store, and Salomon Deutsch Store. The Vaudeville was a notorious saloon run by Jack "Pegleg" Harris, who was killed there in 1882 by Ben Thompson, a gambler and gunfighter who was city marshal of Austin at the time. Two years later, Thompson and John King Fisher were killed in the Vaudeville by Harris' partner, Joe Foster. The corner of E. Commerce and Soledad was known as the "Fatal Corner."

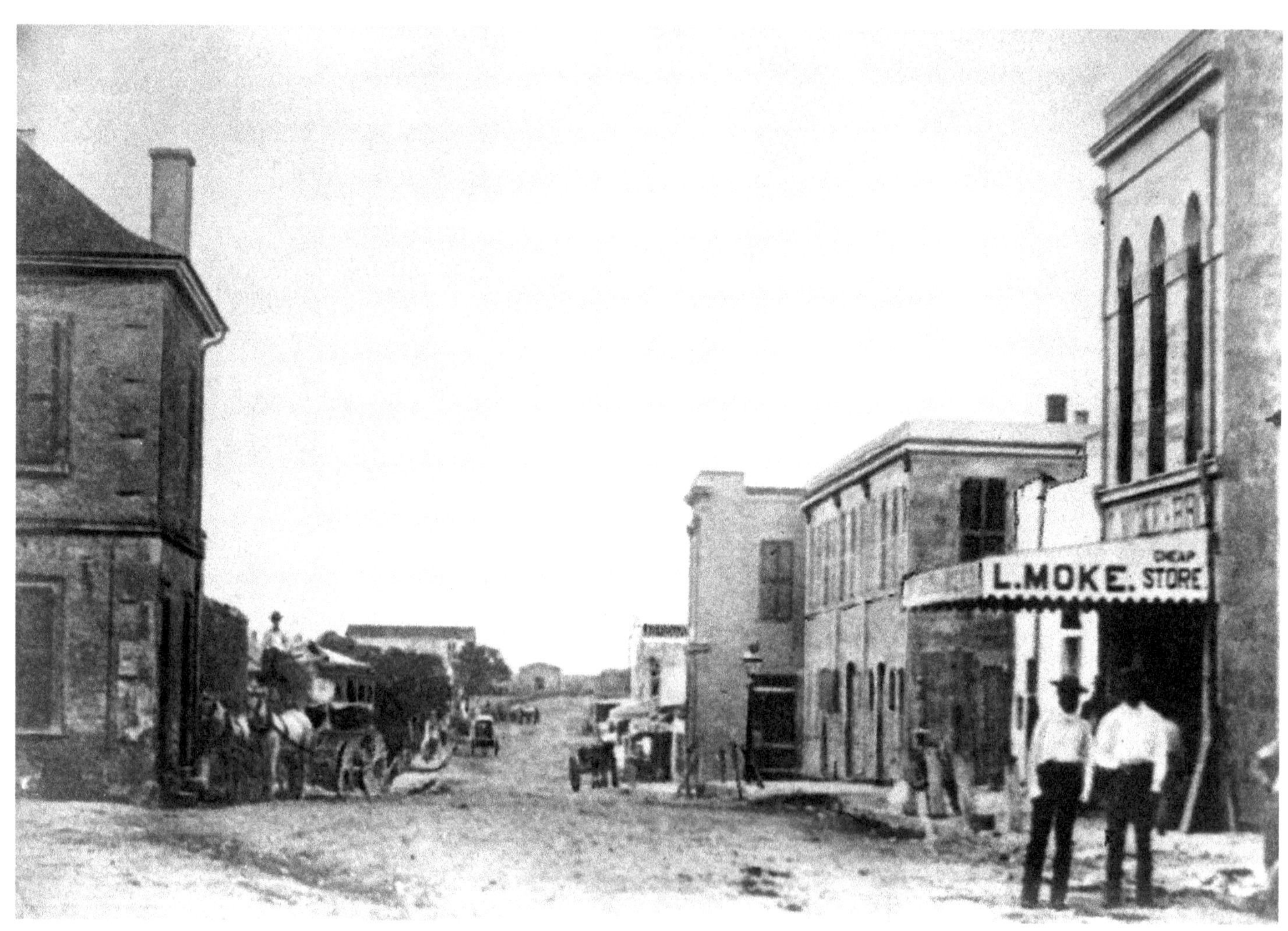

Looking west down Commerce Street from Military Plaza, the "Bat Cave" is on the left and L. Moke and Bros. on the right. Erected in 1850, the "Bat Cave" served as Bexar County jail until 1879, Bexar County Courthouse until 1882, and city hall until 1889. The name "Bat Cave" refers to the many bats that used to roost there. Leon Moke's store sold dry goods and clothing items.

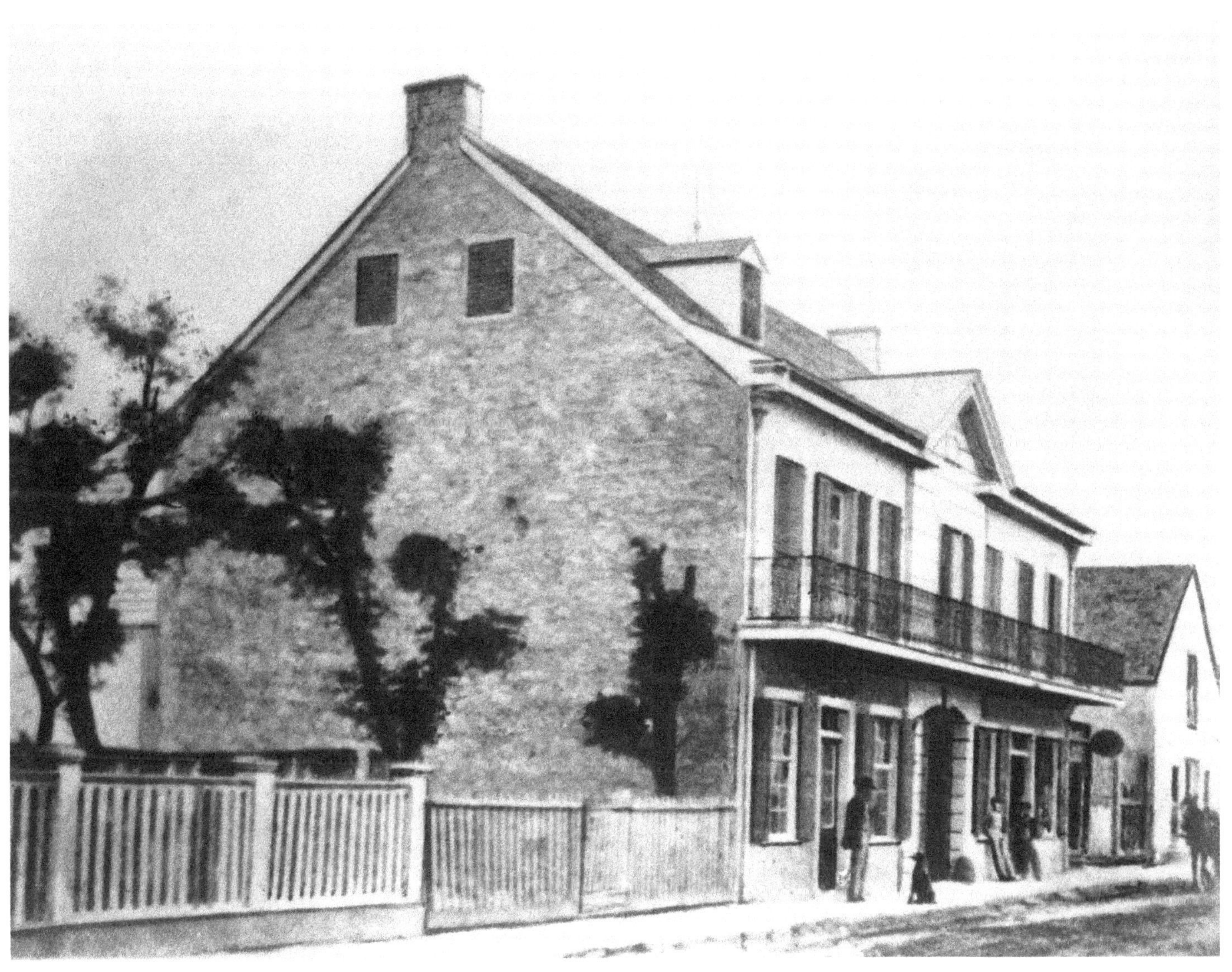

The Charles Hummel residence and business, a two-and-a-half-story rock structure with an iron balcony, located on Commerce Street. He was well known for the fine quality of his hand-made firearms.

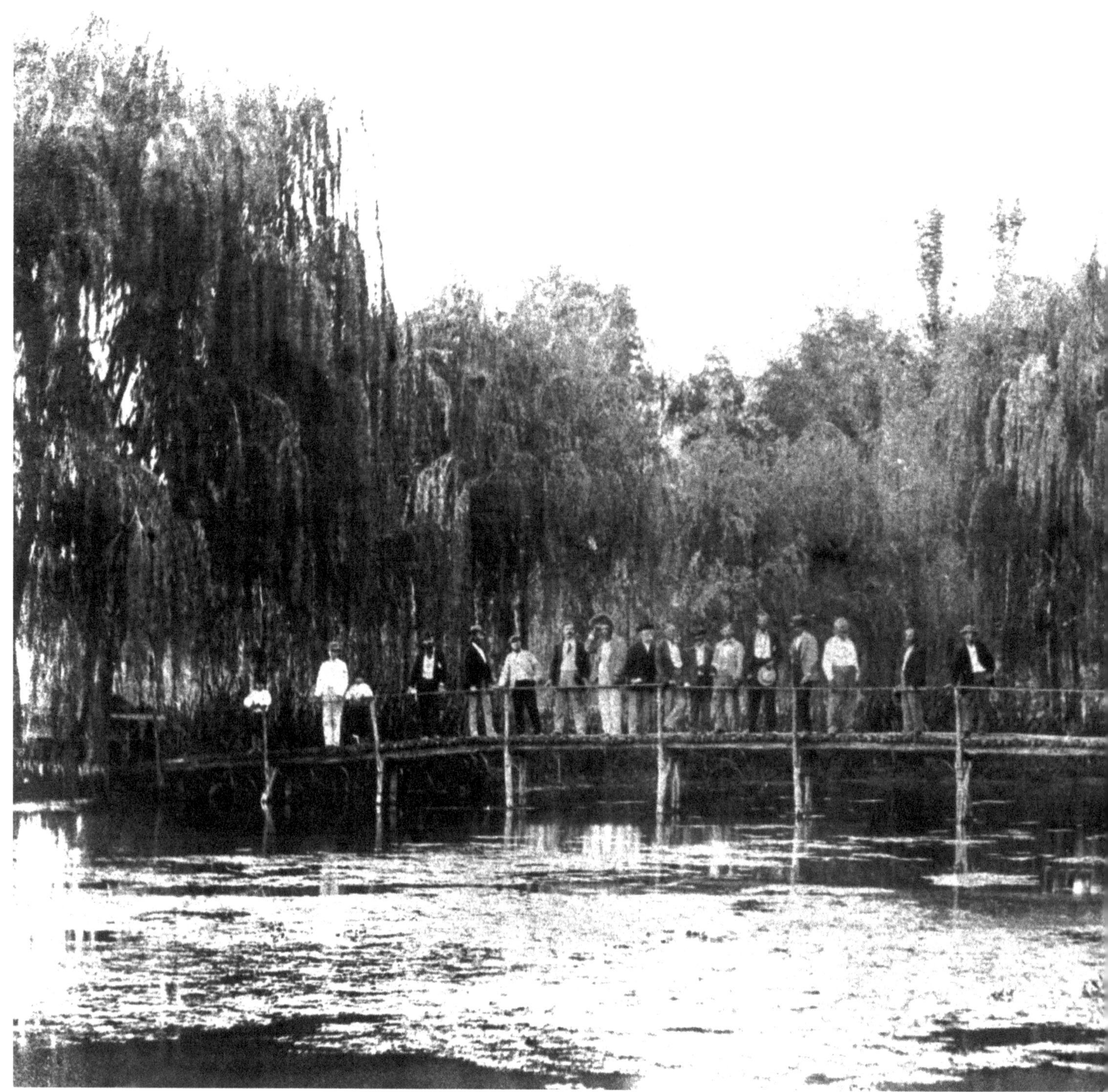

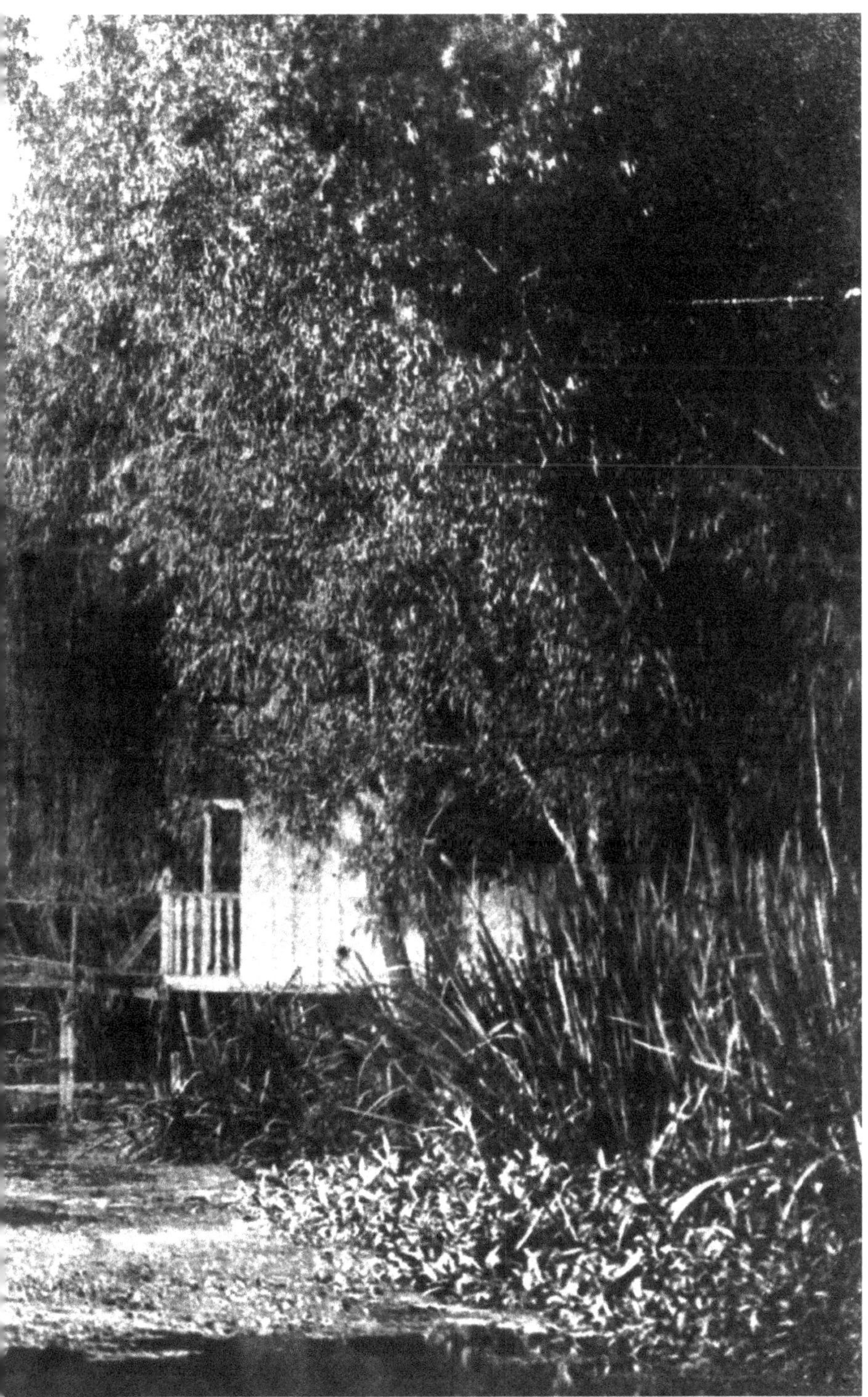

A different San Pedro Park than the one seen today. Said to be the second-oldest municipal park in the United States, San Pedro was dedicated on November 8, 1852. Sam Houston spoke against secession there. Later, it served as a prison camp holding Union soldiers. A museum, bathhouse, and zoo could be found in the park, and musicians and picnics were common. In 1878, the first mule car in San Antonio went from Main Plaza to the park.

A wagon train in front of Hugo & Schmeltzer at the corner of Commerce and Navarro streets. The Staffel and Vogel building is in the background. Charles Hugo and Gustav Schmeltzer, wholesale grocers, started business in 1871, operating from the Callaghan Building until August 1883.

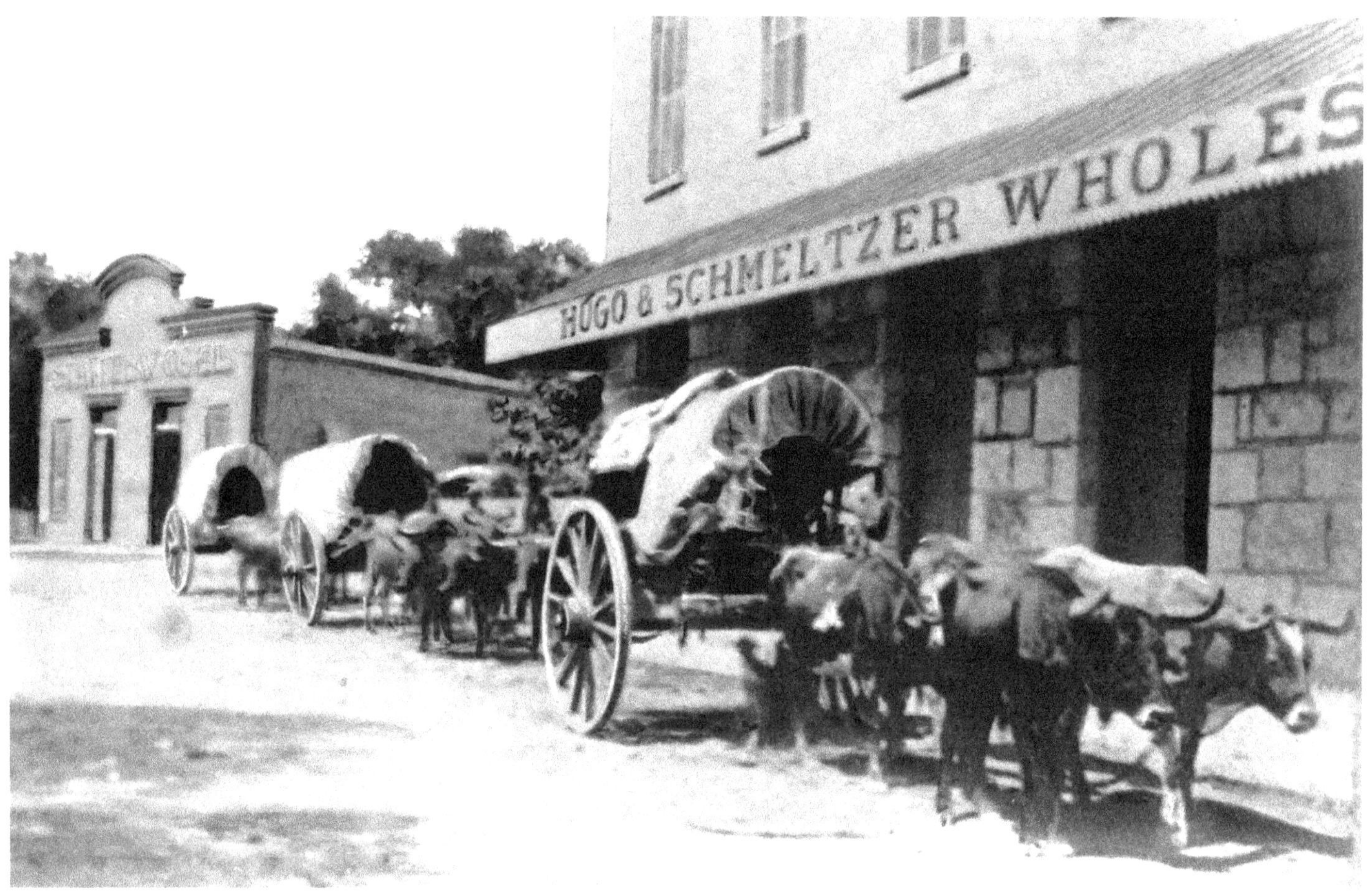

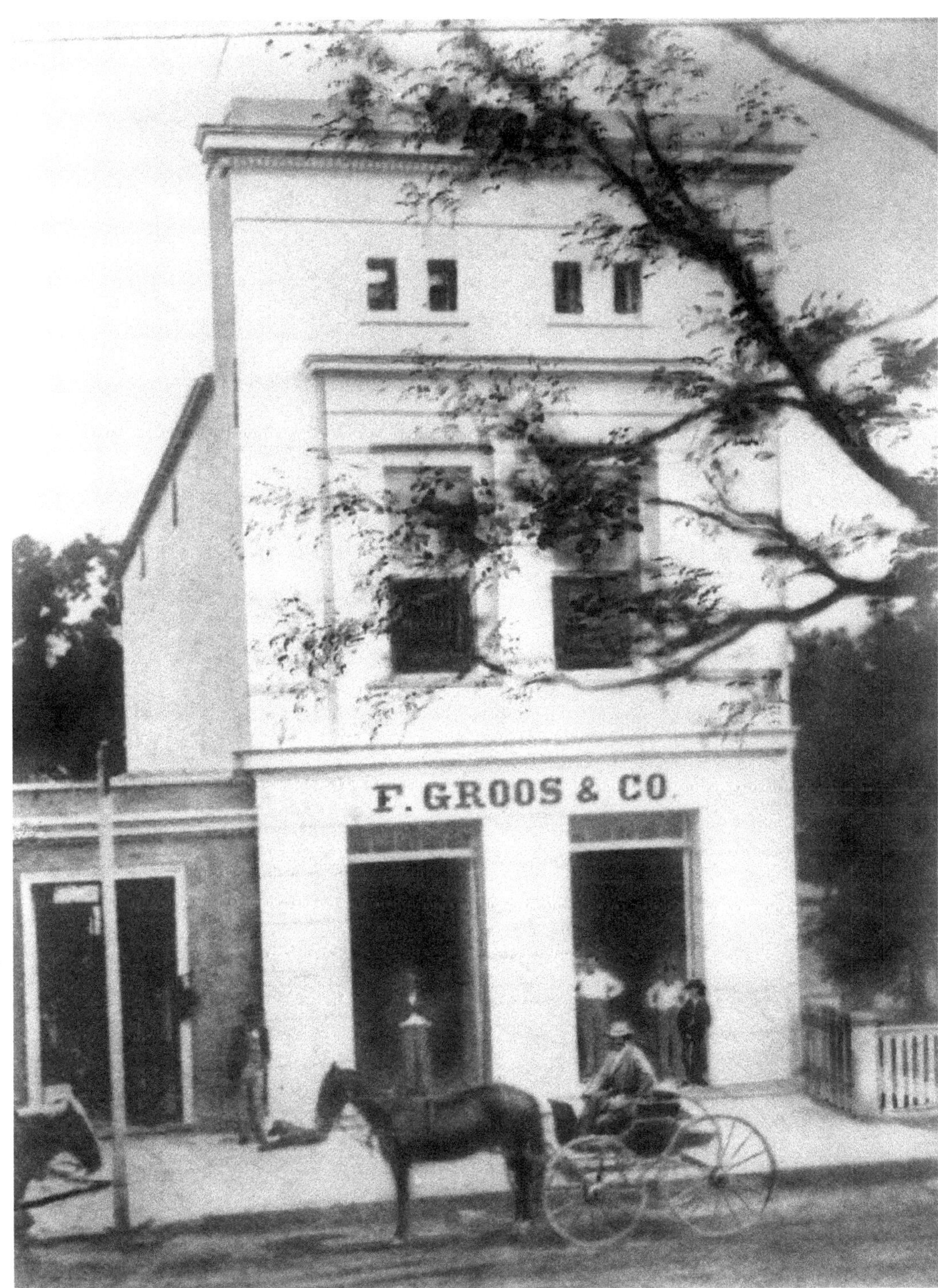

Brothers Frederick, Carl, and Gustav Groos formed a partnership in 1854 under the name of F. Groos & Co. Pictured is the first home of the company in San Antonio, used until 1879. With $2,000 they established a mercantile and exporting firm, with banking as a sideline. Banks were prohibited in Texas at the time. From this beginning, the Groos National Bank served the community for over one hundred years.

A view of Military Plaza looking east, showing the rear of San Fernando Cathedral and the business of Lassner & Mandelbaum, dealers in hides, wool, and cotton. One ox cart appears to be loaded with hides.

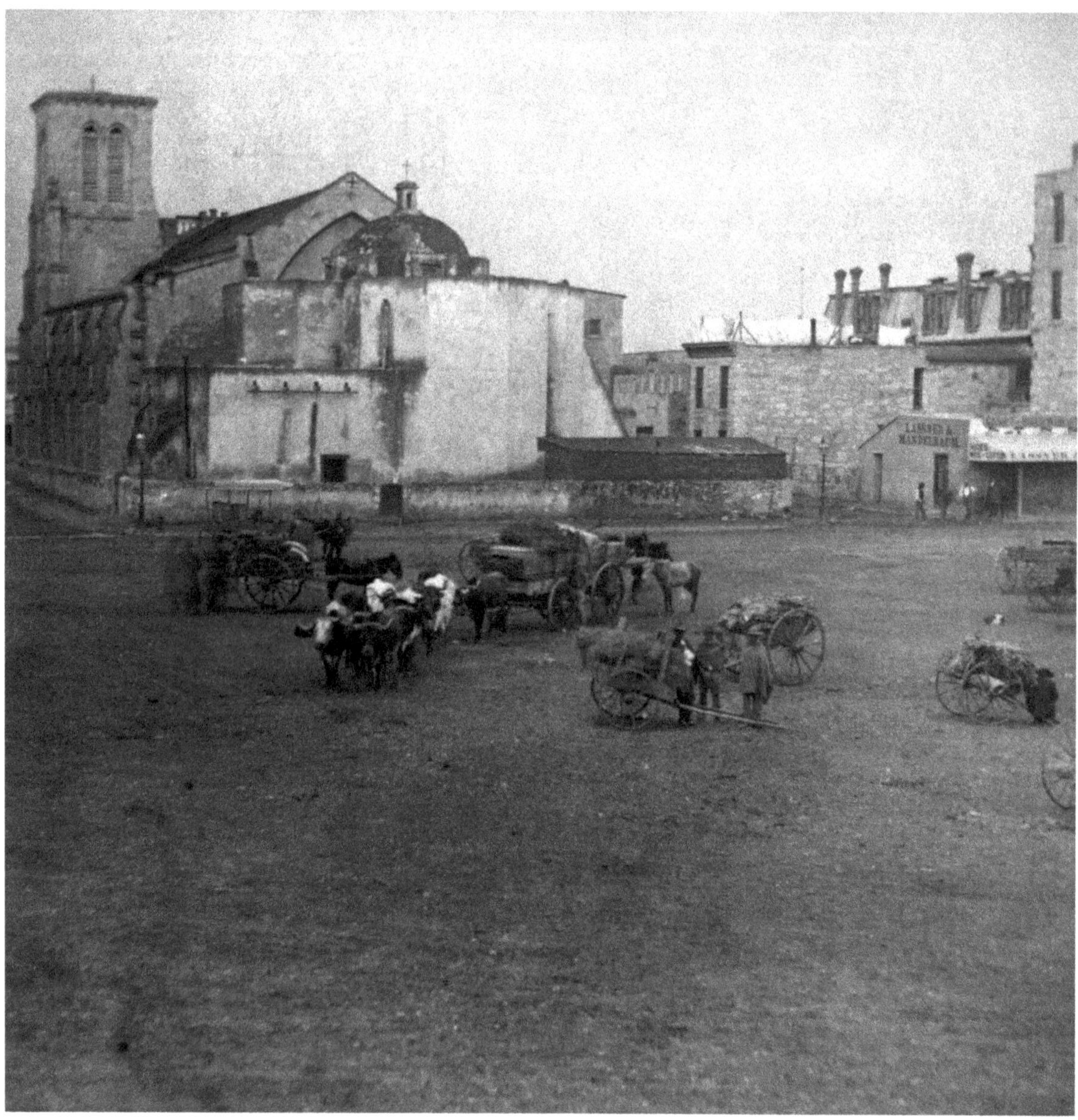

An 1878 picture showing the Mill Bridge crossing of the San Antonio River looking south. La Villita and a public bathhouse are on the left. Bowen's Island is visible on the right. St. John's Lutheran Church appears in the center background.

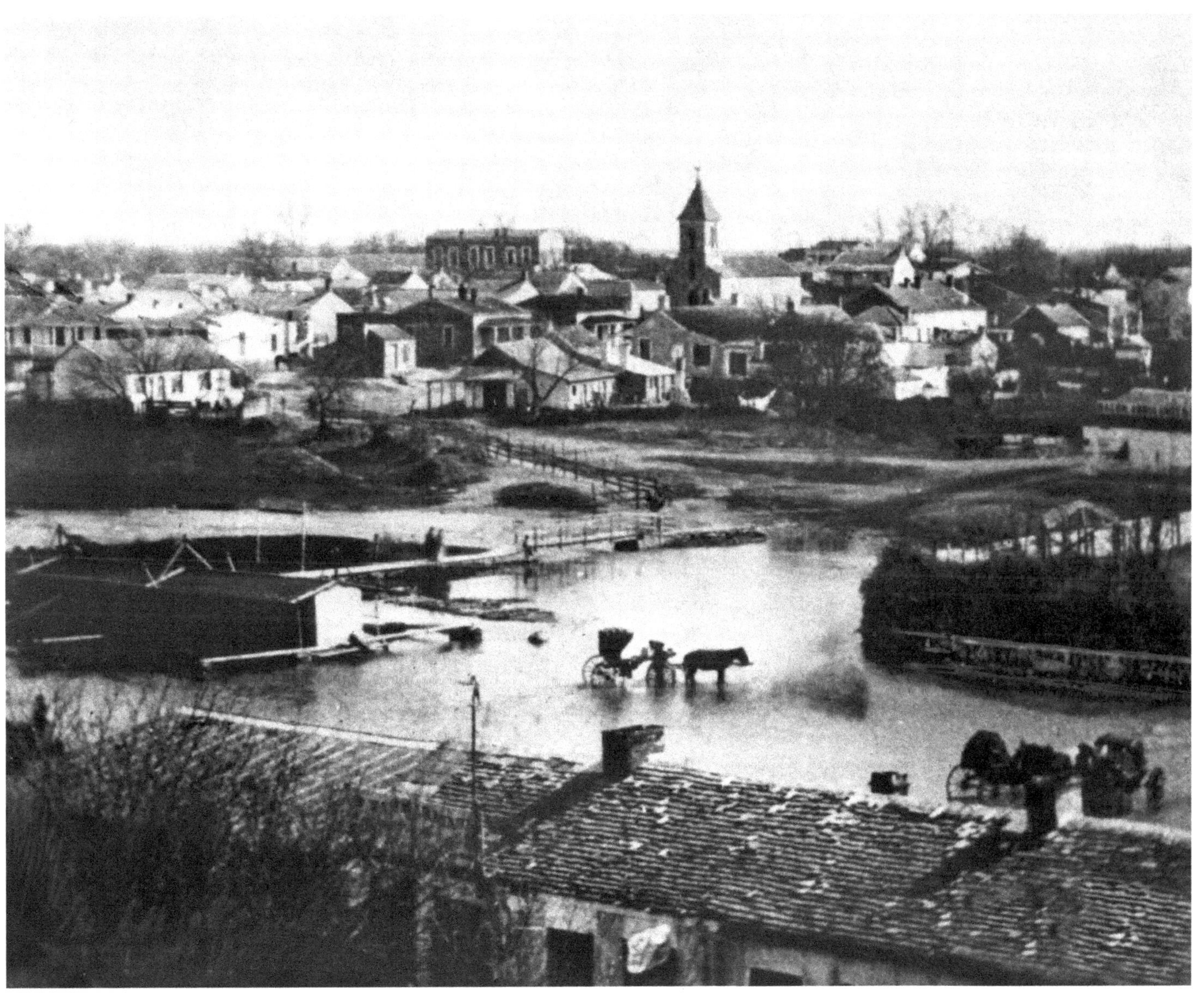

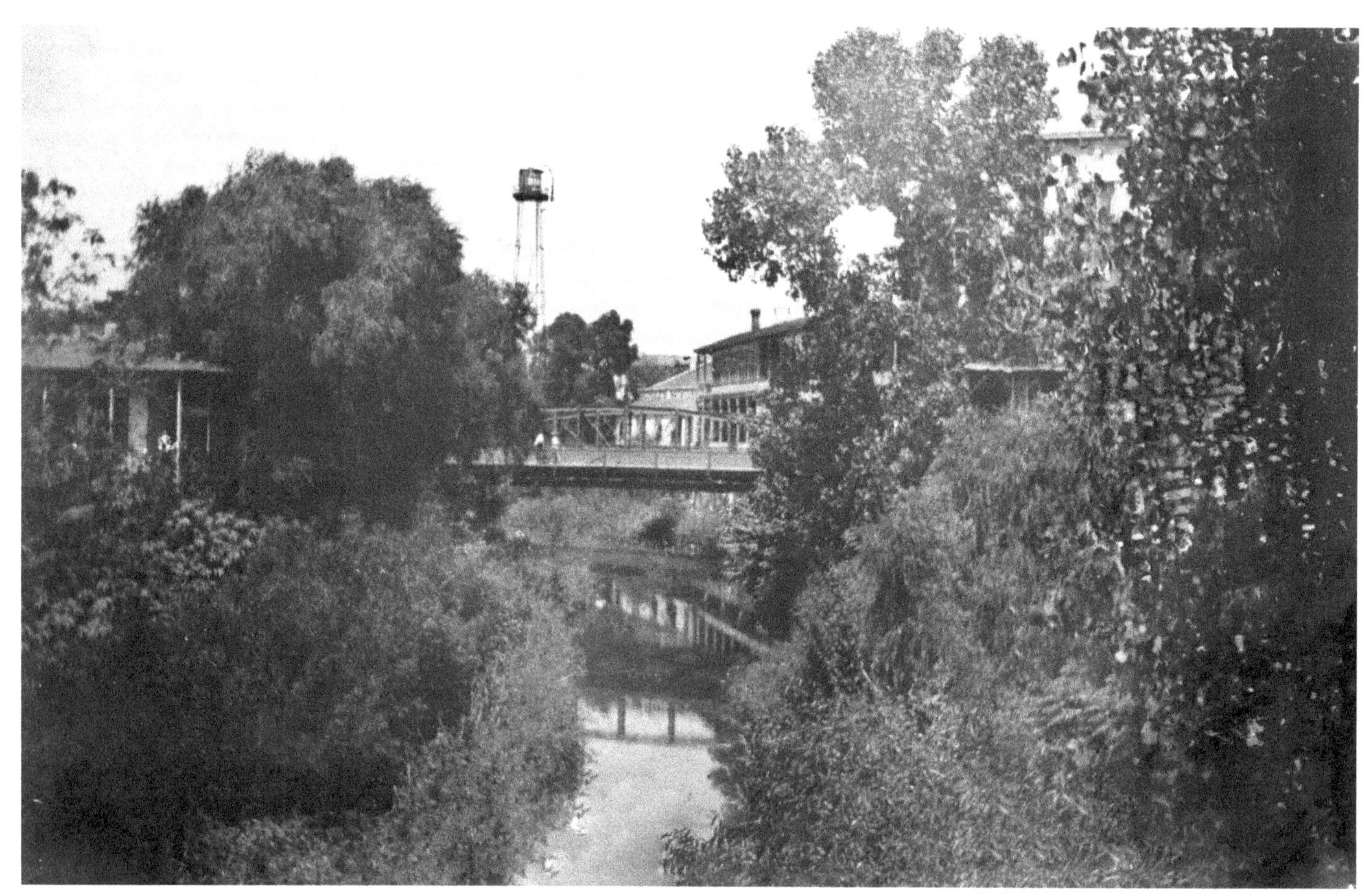

The Commerce Street Bridge is visible at the center rear of the picture. A cast-iron structure, it was brought in by railway and erected in 1880. This was the first iron bridge in San Antonio and probably in Texas. This bridge was later moved and became the Johnson Street Bridge.

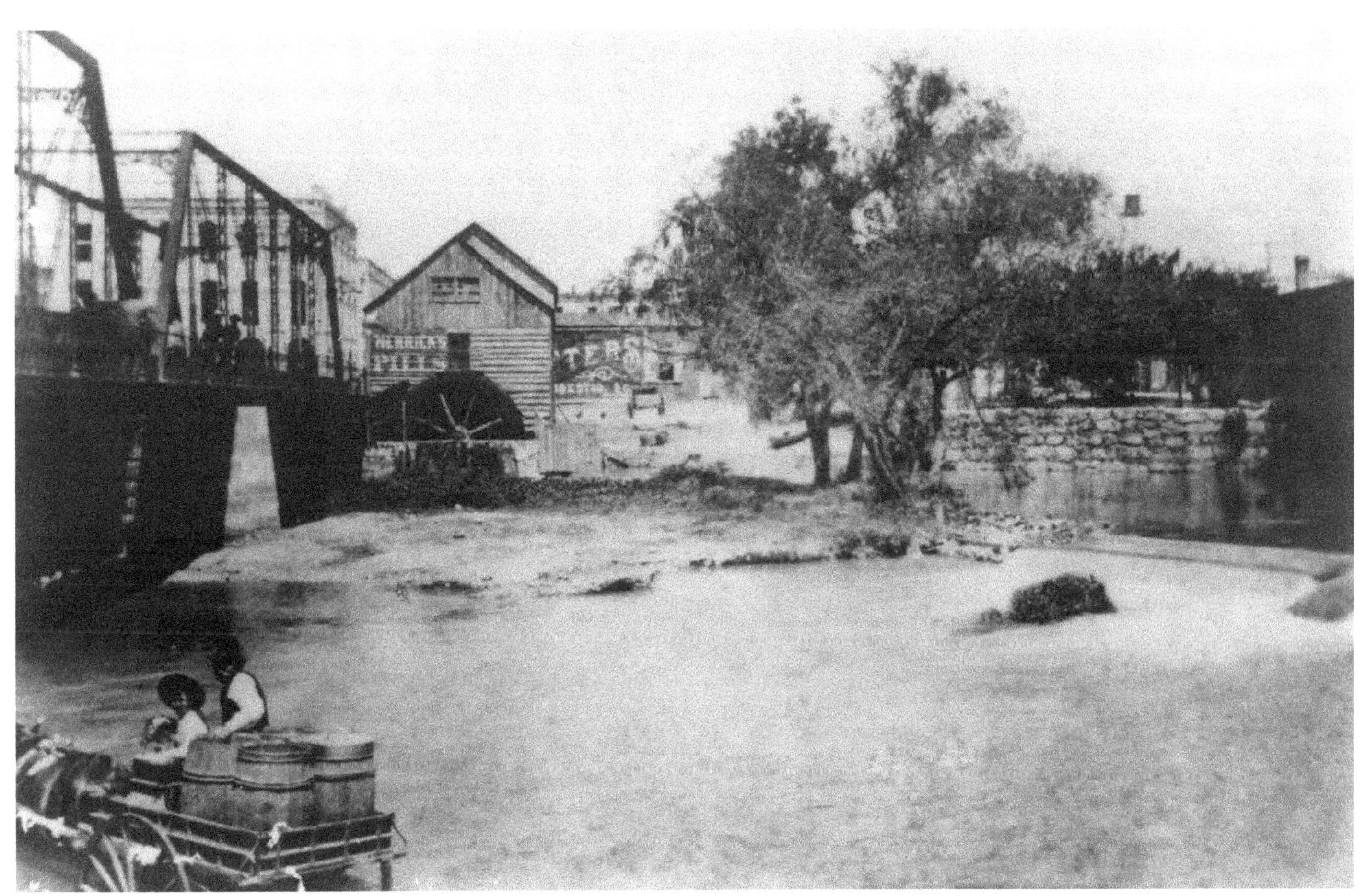

A couple in a wagon cross the San Antonio River while taking barrels to town, as people watch from the old Mill Bridge. An advertisement for Herrick's Pills appears above the mill's wheel.

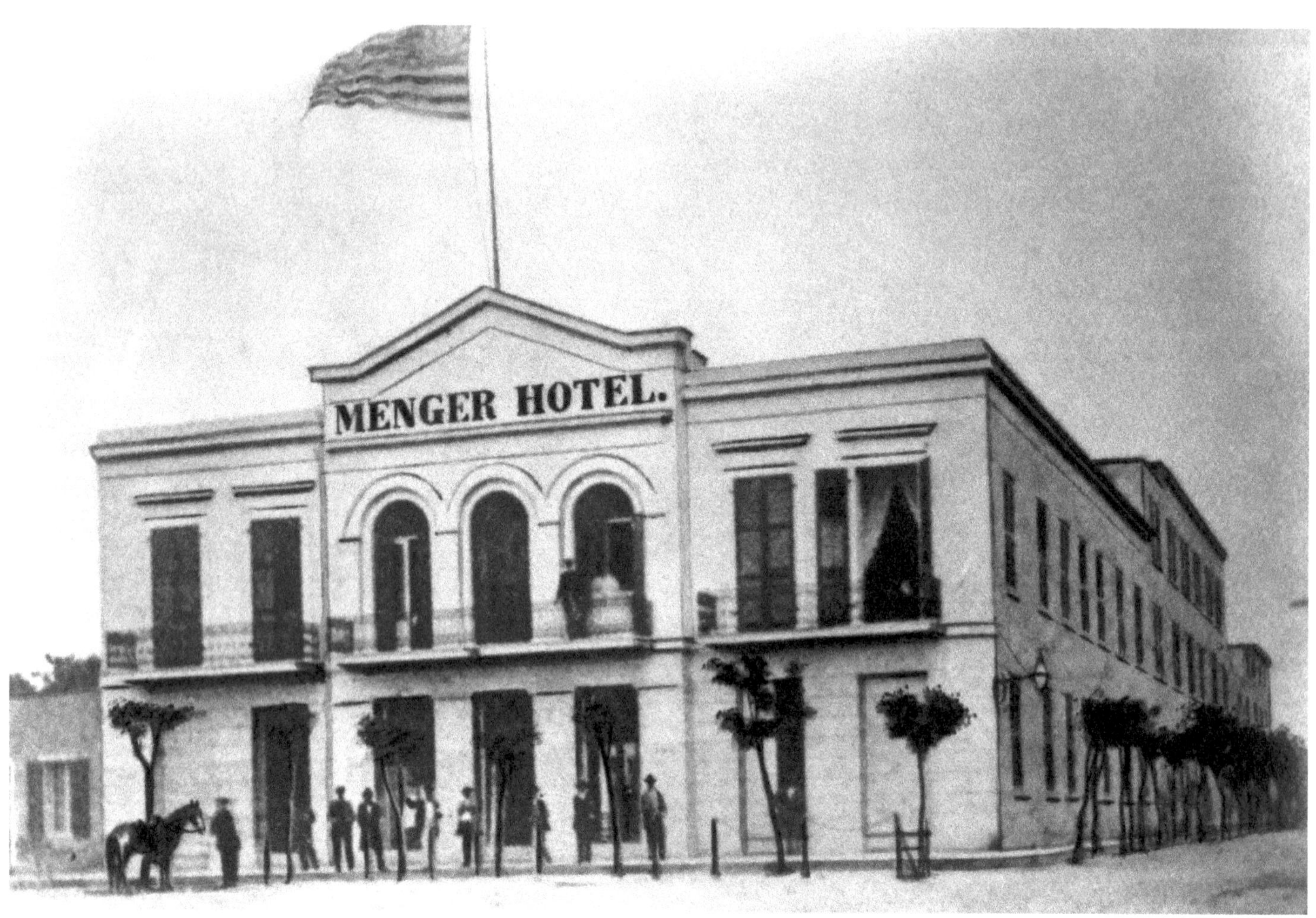

The Menger Hotel as it appeared between 1865–1875. Founded by William A. Menger in February 1859 as the "finest hotel west of the Mississippi," it was also the site of the city's and Texas' first brewery. Theodore Roosevelt, Benjamin Harrison, Robert E. Lee, William Jennings Bryan, John L. Sullivan, and many other prominent people have stayed there.

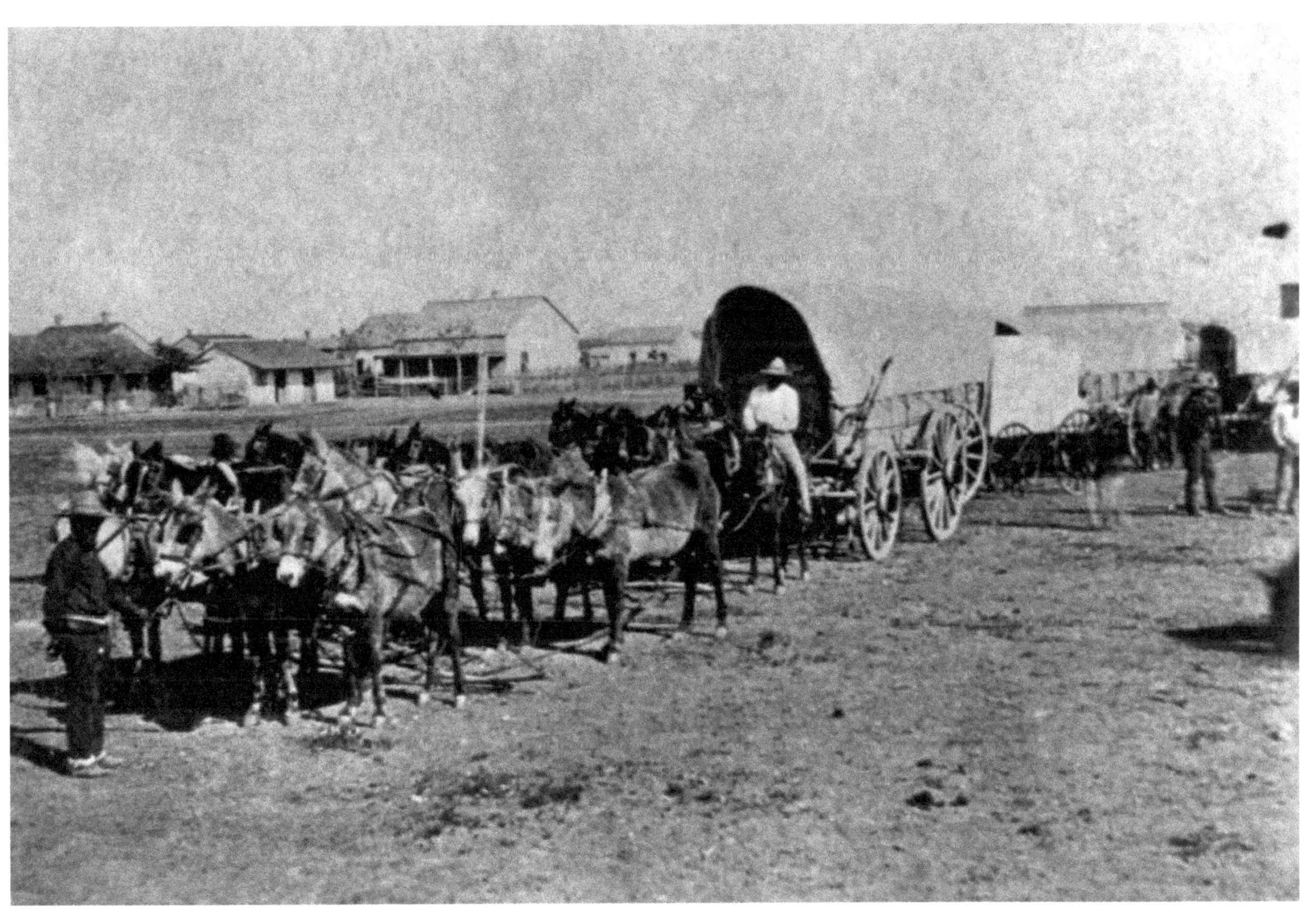

This 1877 photograph shows covered wagons hauling freight at the corner of South Laredo and Arsenal streets.

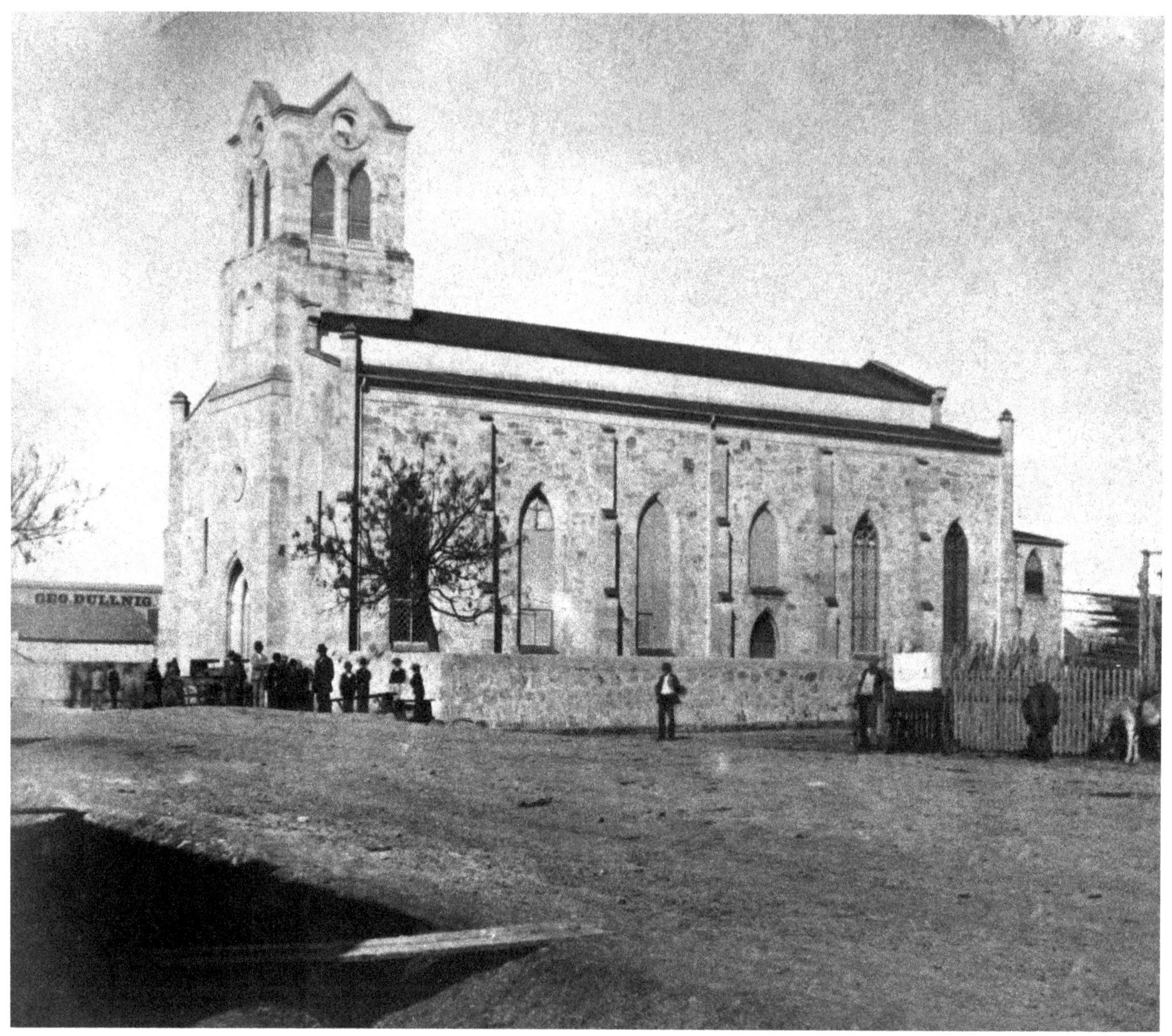

The large number of Germans that came into the city after the Texas Revolution created a need for a Catholic parish that could serve a German-speaking population. St. Joseph's cornerstone was laid November 5, 1868, on Alameda (now Commerce) Street. George Dullnig opened the wholesale and retail grocery shown in the background with his brothers Christian and John in 1864. By the 1880s, it was one of the largest such firms in Texas, with delivery wagons that traveled far beyond the city.

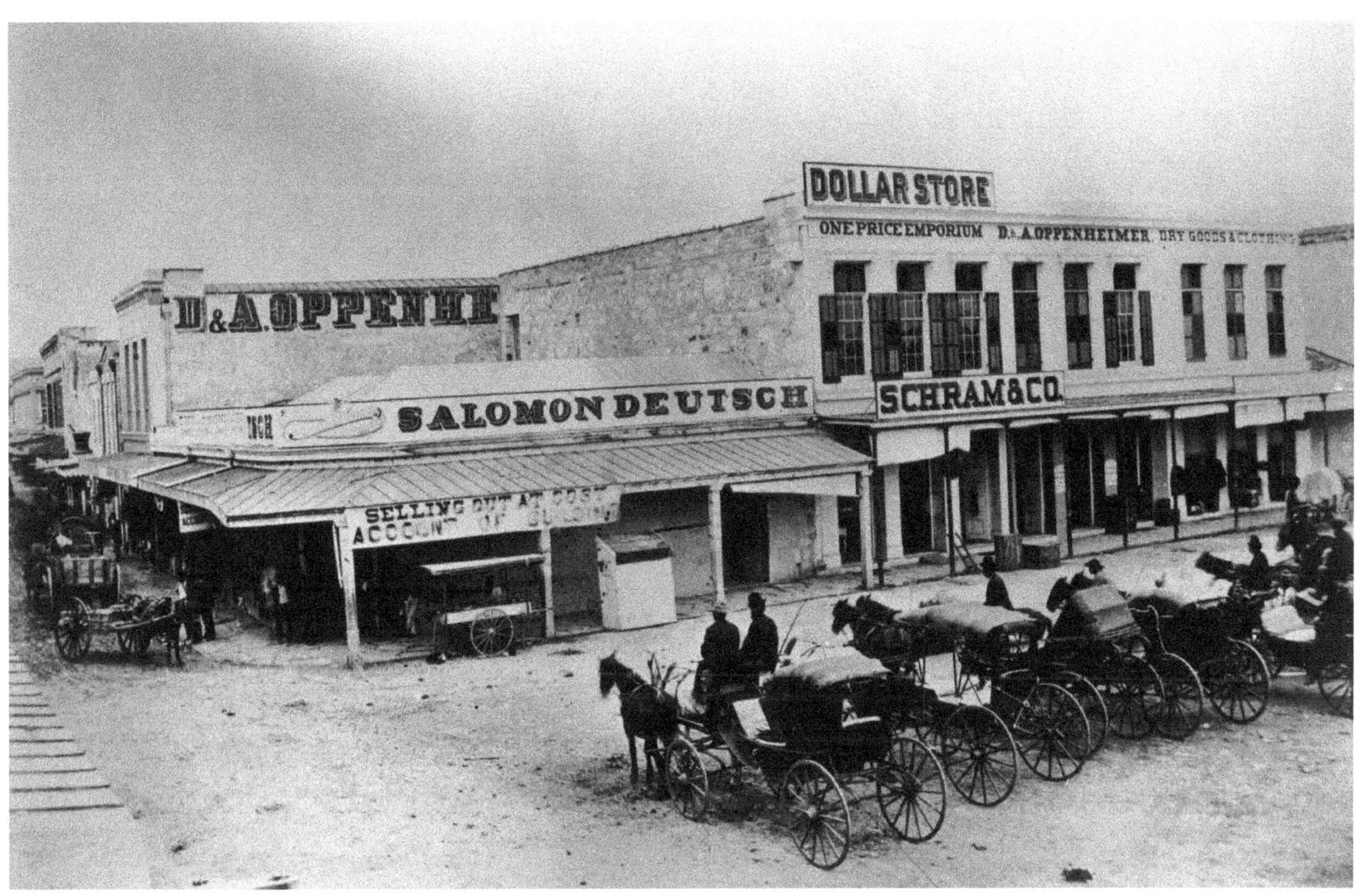

The photograph looks southeast from the Plaza House towards the east side of Main Plaza. Commerce Street is on the left. Salomon Deutsch and Simon Frank dealt in such dry goods as clothes, boots and shoes. Perhaps he was selling out because competing dry goods stores were just a few steps away, including Samuel Schram & Co.'s "one price emporium" dollar store and the firm of D. & A. Oppenheimer (Daniel and Antoine). Like the F. Groos and Co., the Oppenheimers became a banking firm.

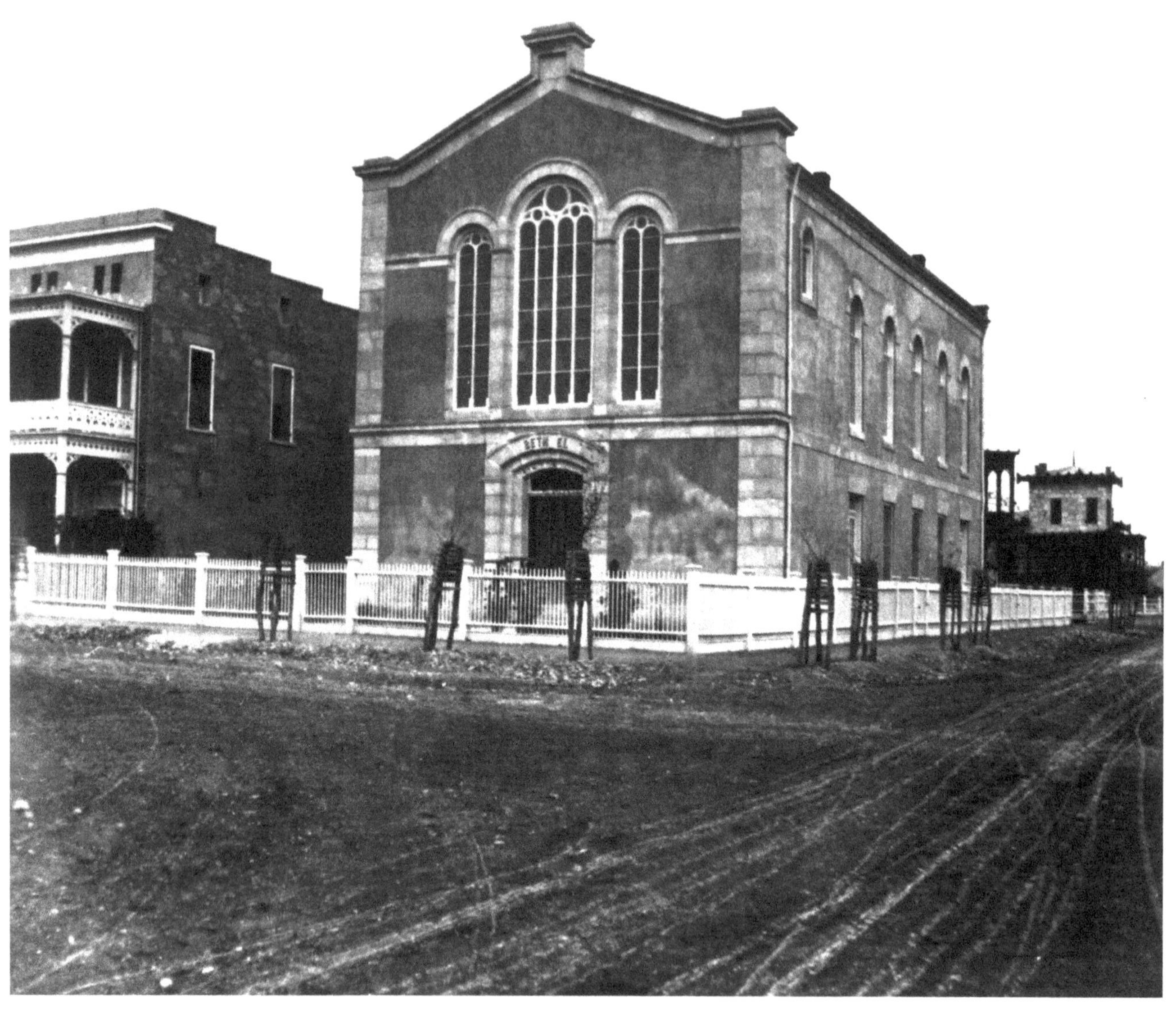

Temple Beth-El, at the corner of Jefferson and Travis streets, was the city's first synagogue. The Congregation was loosely formed in early 1874, and the permanent organization of Congregation Beth-El dates from July 5, 1875. On September 10, 1875, the temple was dedicated. This building was razed, and a new temple was dedicated on the same spot in 1903.

Around 1880, Gustav A. Duerler, a confectioner at 74 Commerce Street (later 222 W. Commerce) advertised his location on his delivery wagon, shown in front of the store. Duerler sold candies, ice cream, cakes, soft drinks, etc., and had his residence above the store. On the right is M. Halff and Bro. (Meyer and Solomon Halff), a dry goods store. An unidentified man in a top hat stands next to a display of photographs.

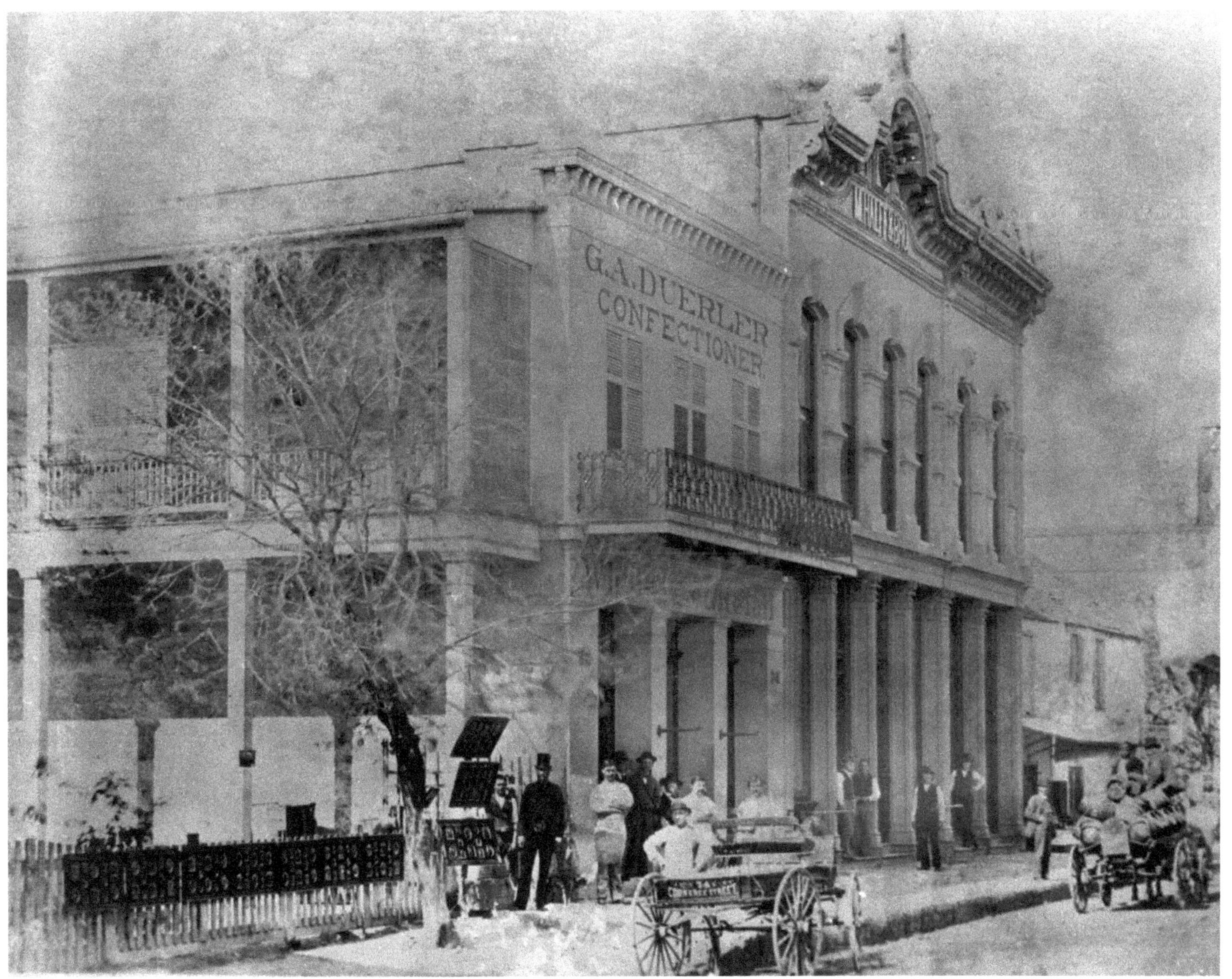

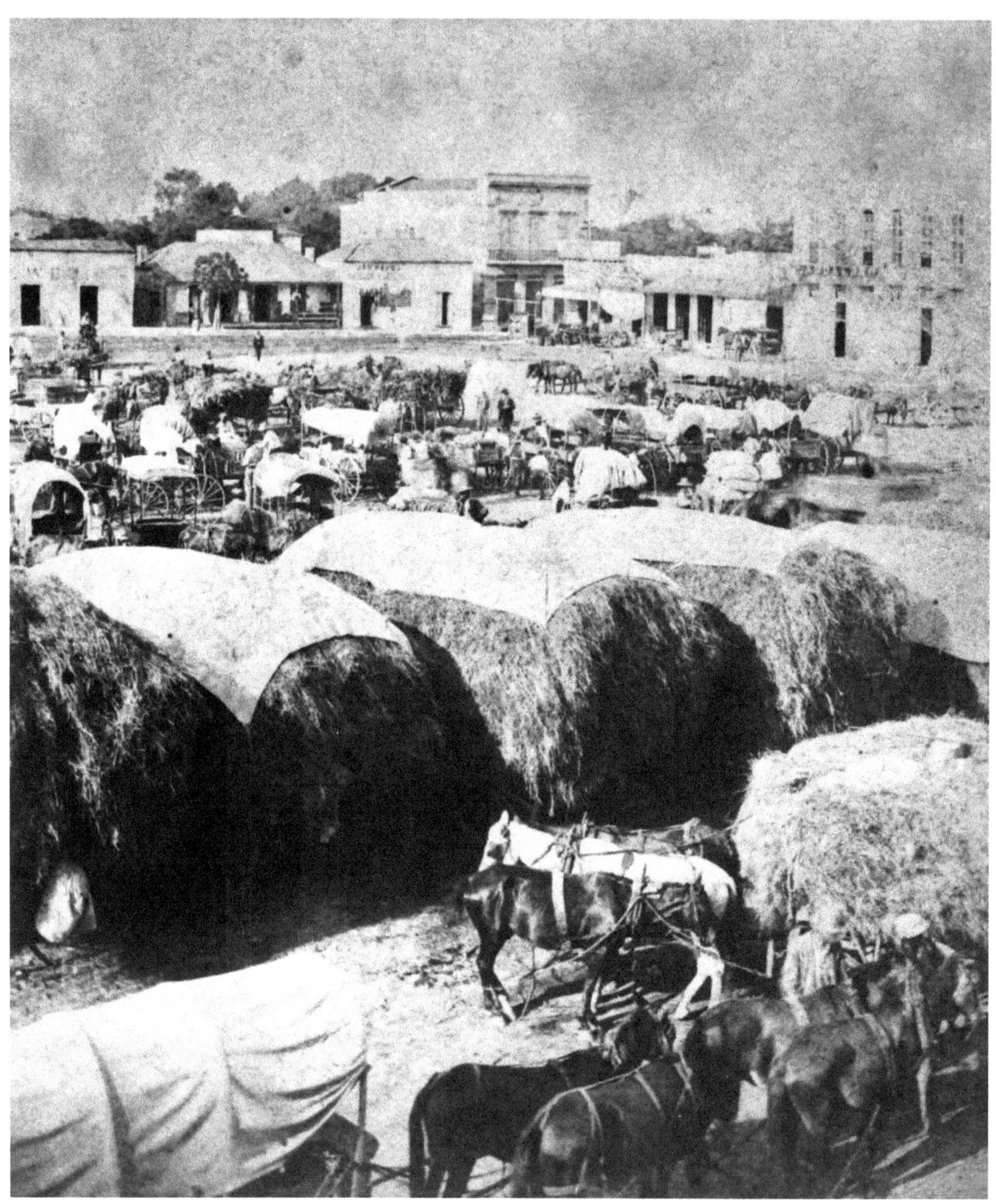

Wagons loaded with hay wait for buyers and sellers on a busy day at Military Plaza in 1883.

Students and teachers sit on the lawn in front of Bishop Elliott's Young Ladies Seminary of Western Texas, officially Saint Mary's Hall. Bishop Elliott, first bishop of the Protestant Episcopal Church in the diocese of West Texas, founded the school in 1879.

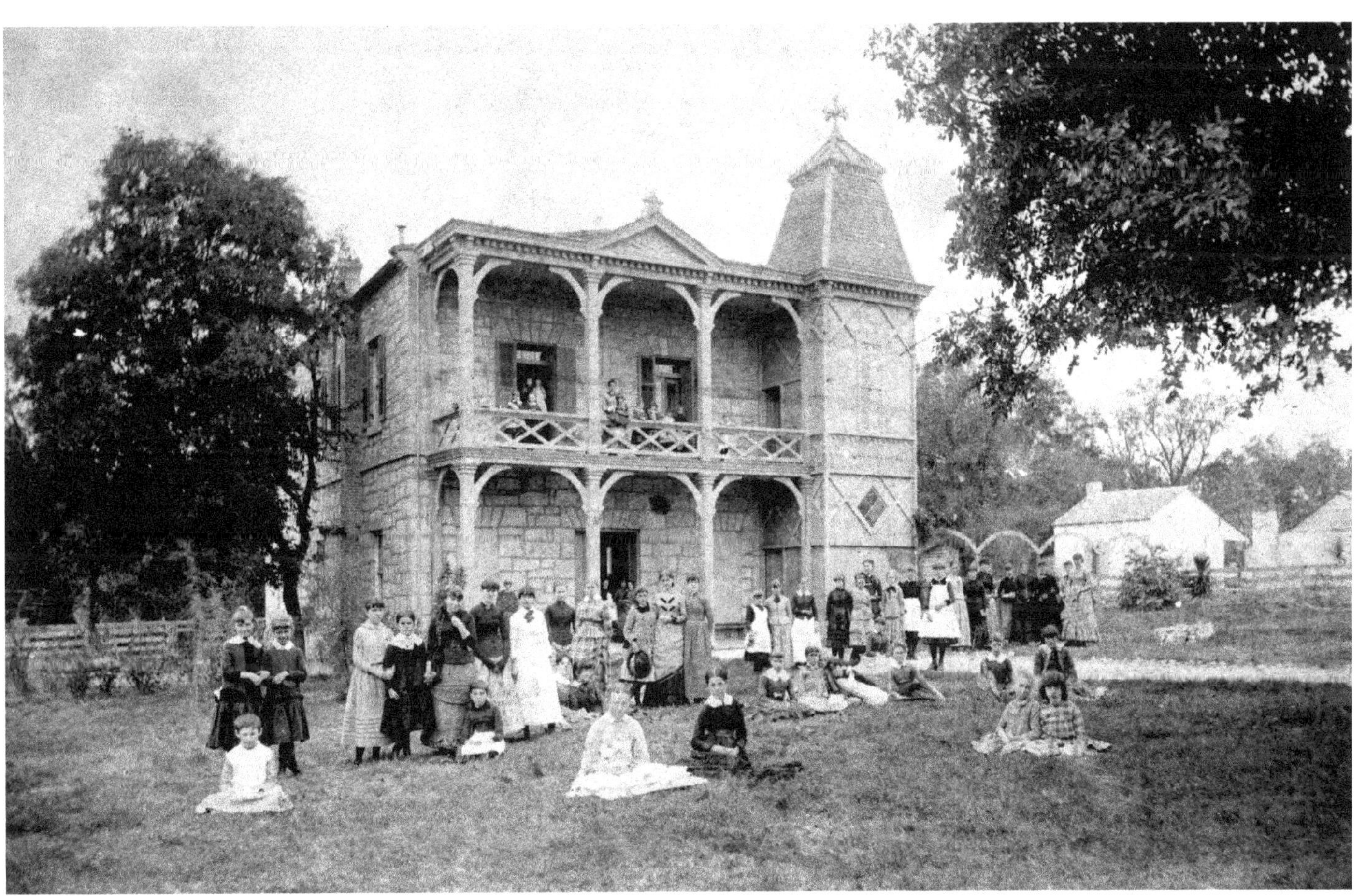

Commerce Street looking west from Navarro Street about 1885. On the left, (Leon) Blum and (Aaron) Koenigsberger, dealers in dry goods and notions, were the local agent for Butterick sewing patterns. The Charles Hummel & Son store, far right, sold guns, ammunition, and sportsmen's needs. Other signs advertise architects James Riely Gordon and Frederick B. Shelton, Cash Grocery Store, an insurance dealer, and a music store.

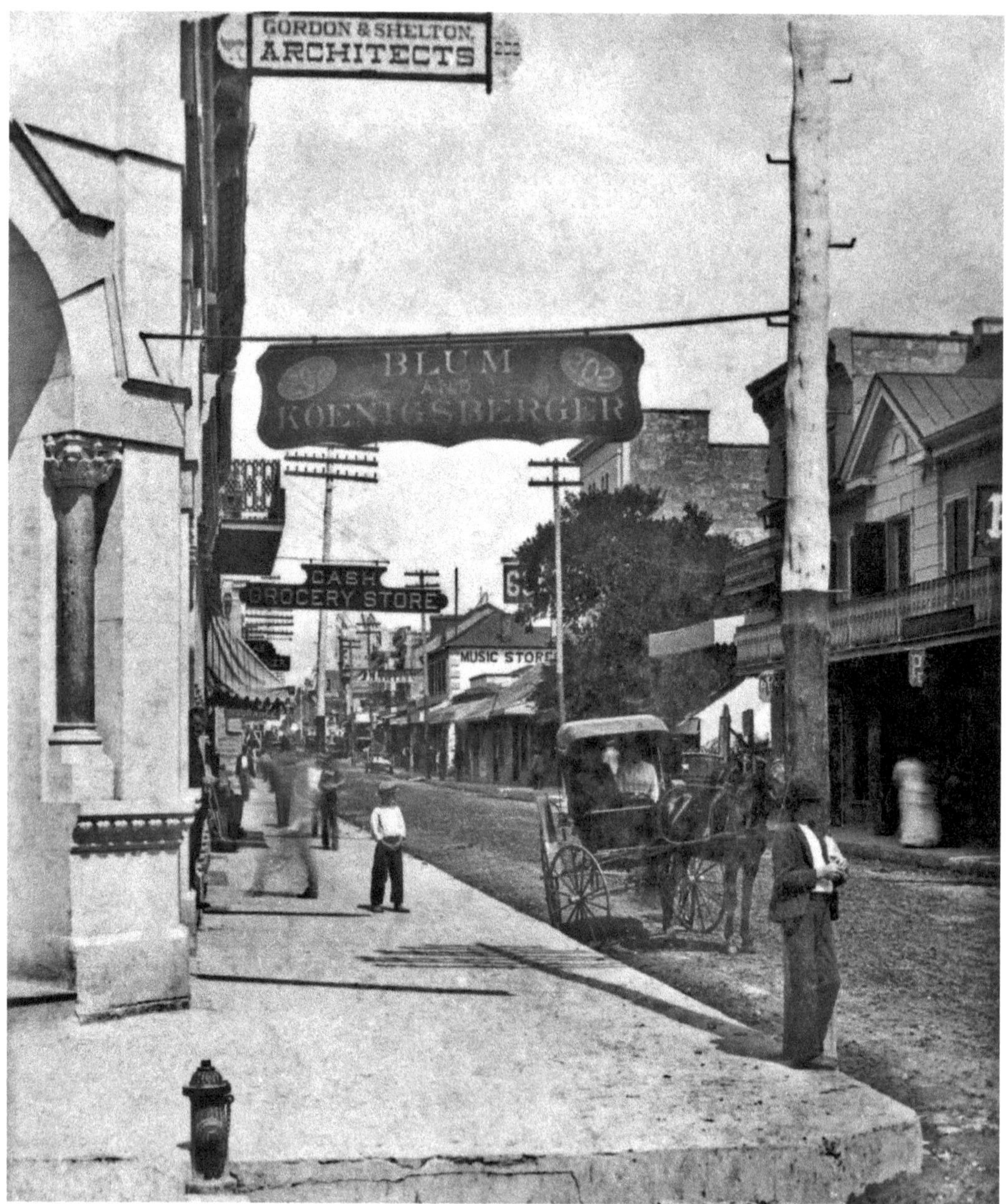

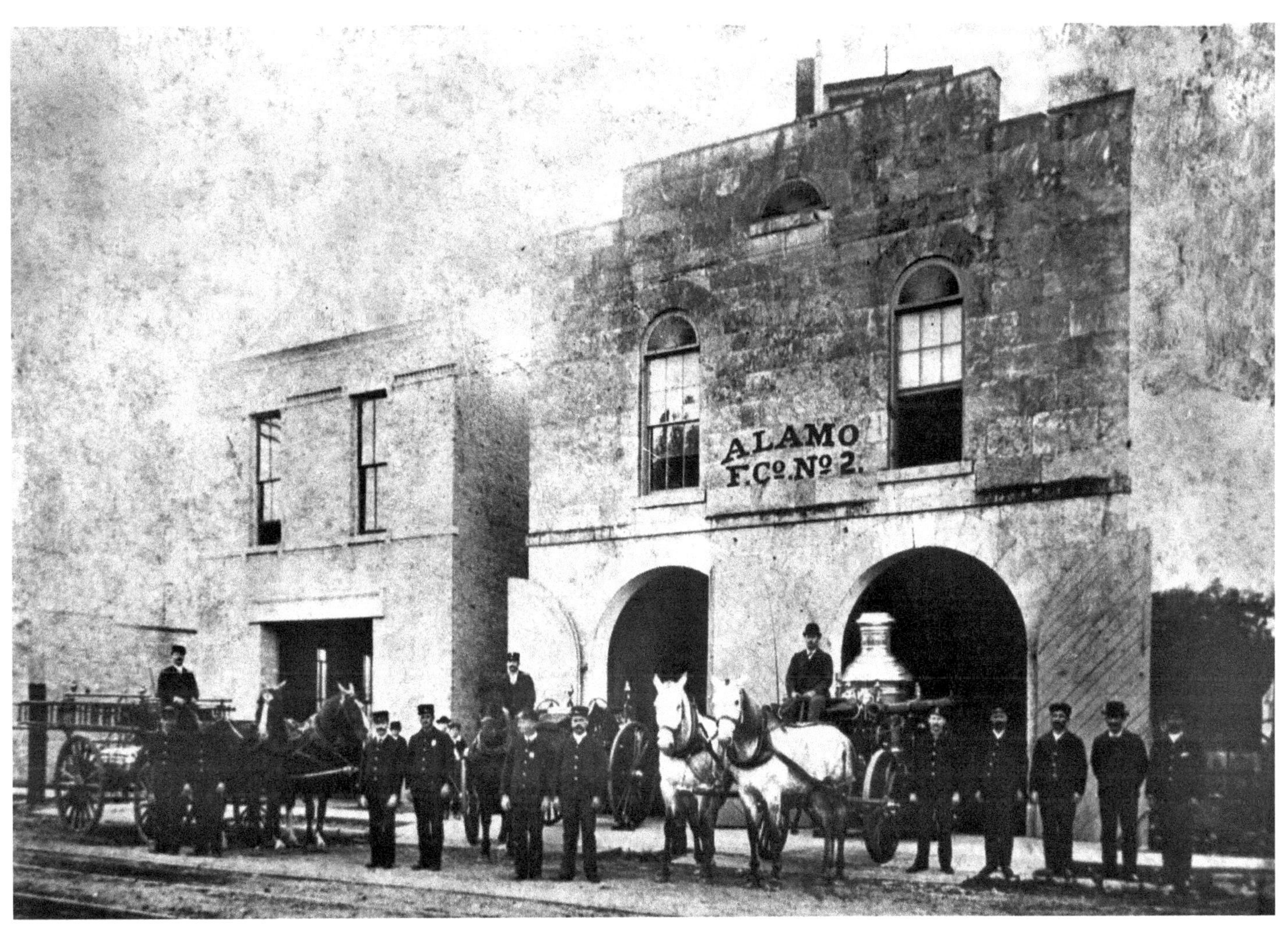

Firemen and their equipment of Alamo Fire Company No. 2 posed in front of their headquarters in the 1880s. The building was located on the west side of Avenue C (Broadway) between Houston and Travis streets. William Menger, C. Byrne, H. D. Strumberg, and D. L. McGary wrote the company's constitution and by-laws. Peter Gallagher was elected chief.

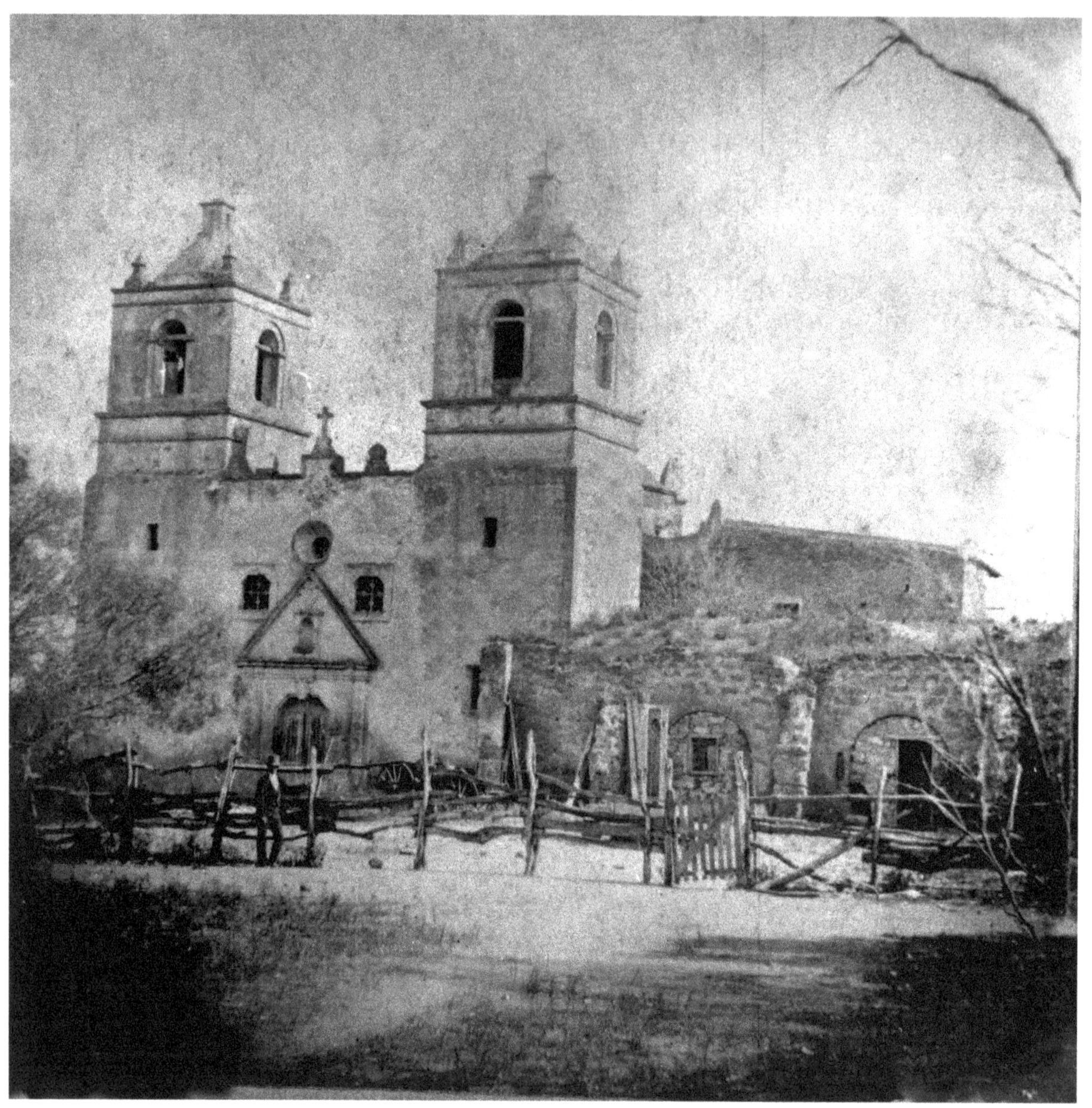

A man stands beside the fence in front of Mission Concepcion. The building of Nuestra Senora de la Purisma Concepcion de Acuna was completed in 1755. Religious services there were suspended shortly after the mission merged with Mission San Jose in 1815. It was damaged during the Texas Revolution but repaired in 1861 and 1887.

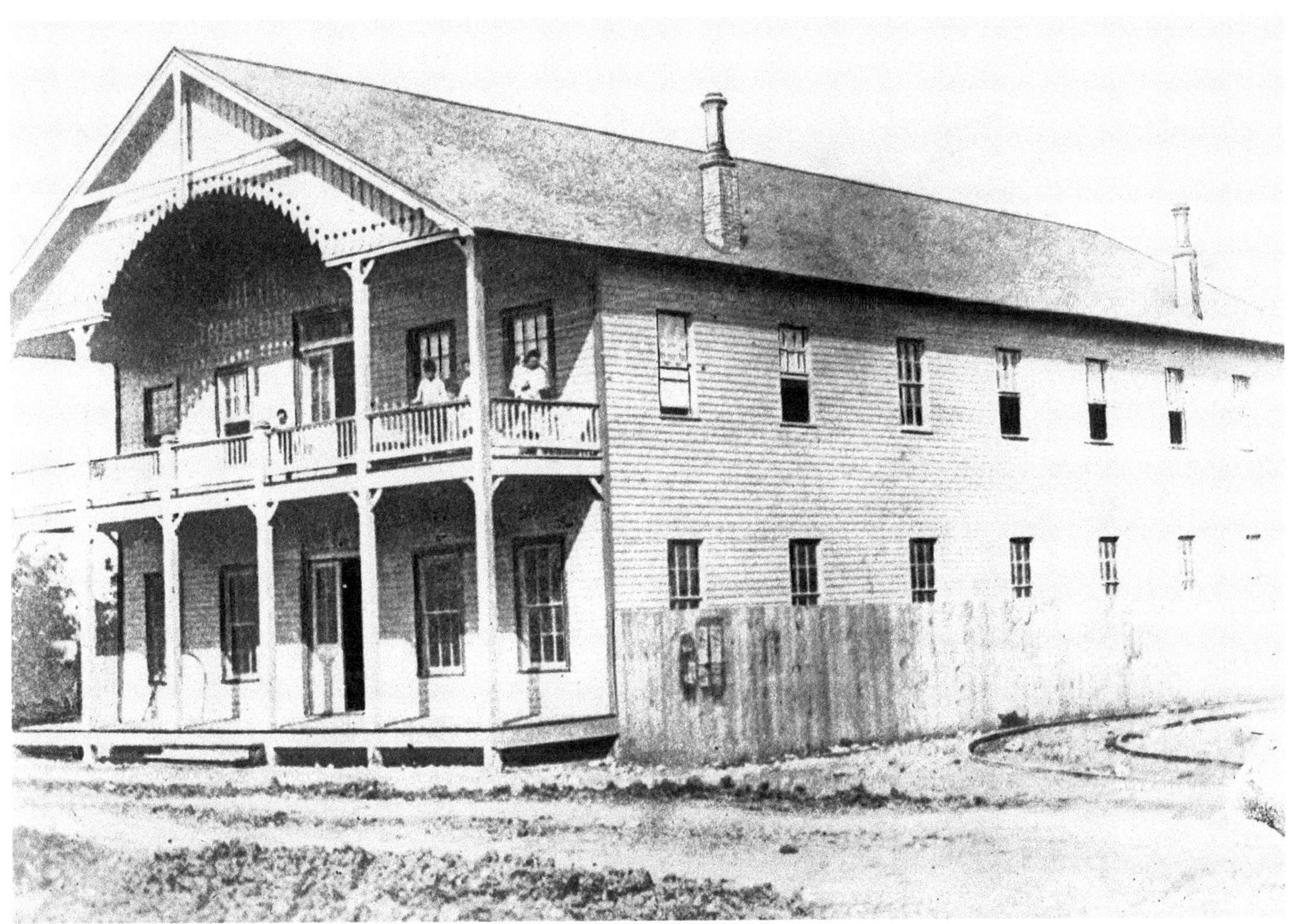

The Immigrants' Home at 327 Austin was at the corner of 10th Street, along the railroad. It served as a temporary residence for immigrants until they either found a permanent residence or moved beyond San Antonio. For a time around 1883–1884, it was managed by Mrs. Theresa Van Dyke.

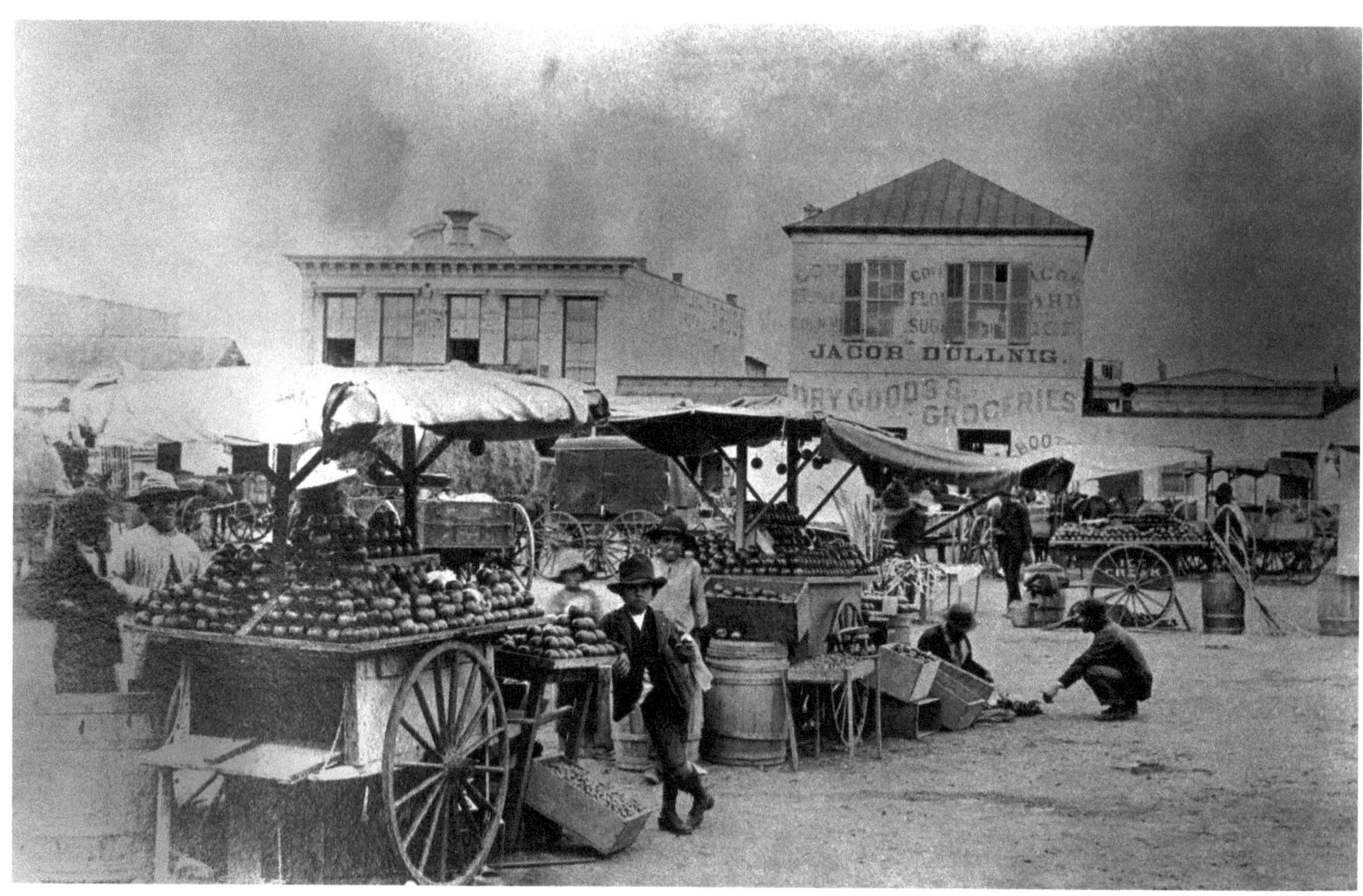

Children and adults stand around vegetable stands in the market on Military Plaza about 1886. On the north side of the plaza, F. Kalteyer Drugstore stands on the left. Beside it, Jacob Dullnig dealt in wholesale and retail "groceries, woodenware, crockery, glassware, cigars, etc."

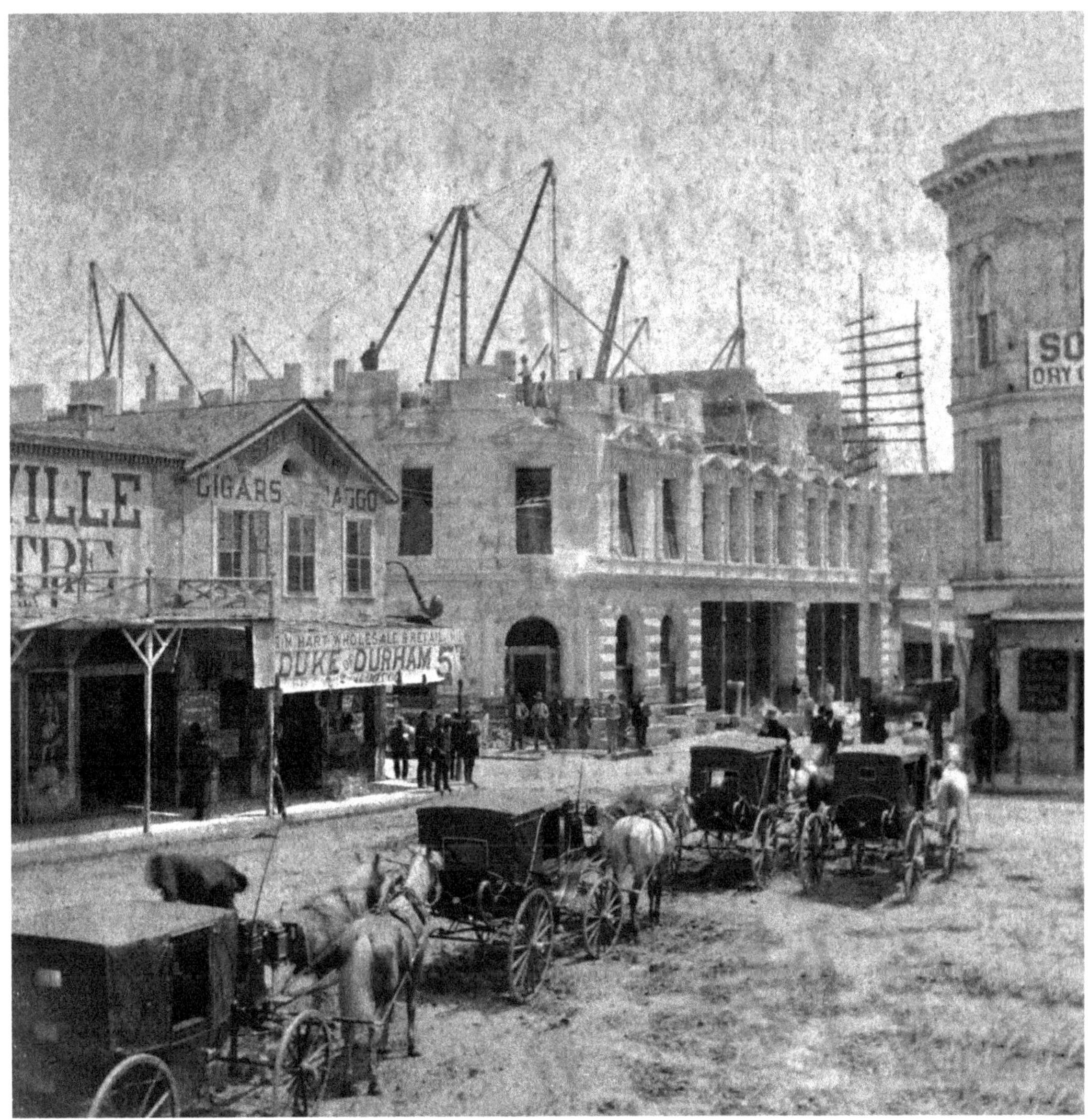

This 1884 photograph of the northeast corner of Main Plaza shows the Kampmann Building under construction. On the left is the "fatal corner" with Jack Harris' Vaudeville Theater and Sim Hart Smoke Shop, which promoted itself with a giant pipe on the roof above its Duke of Durham Tobacco sign.

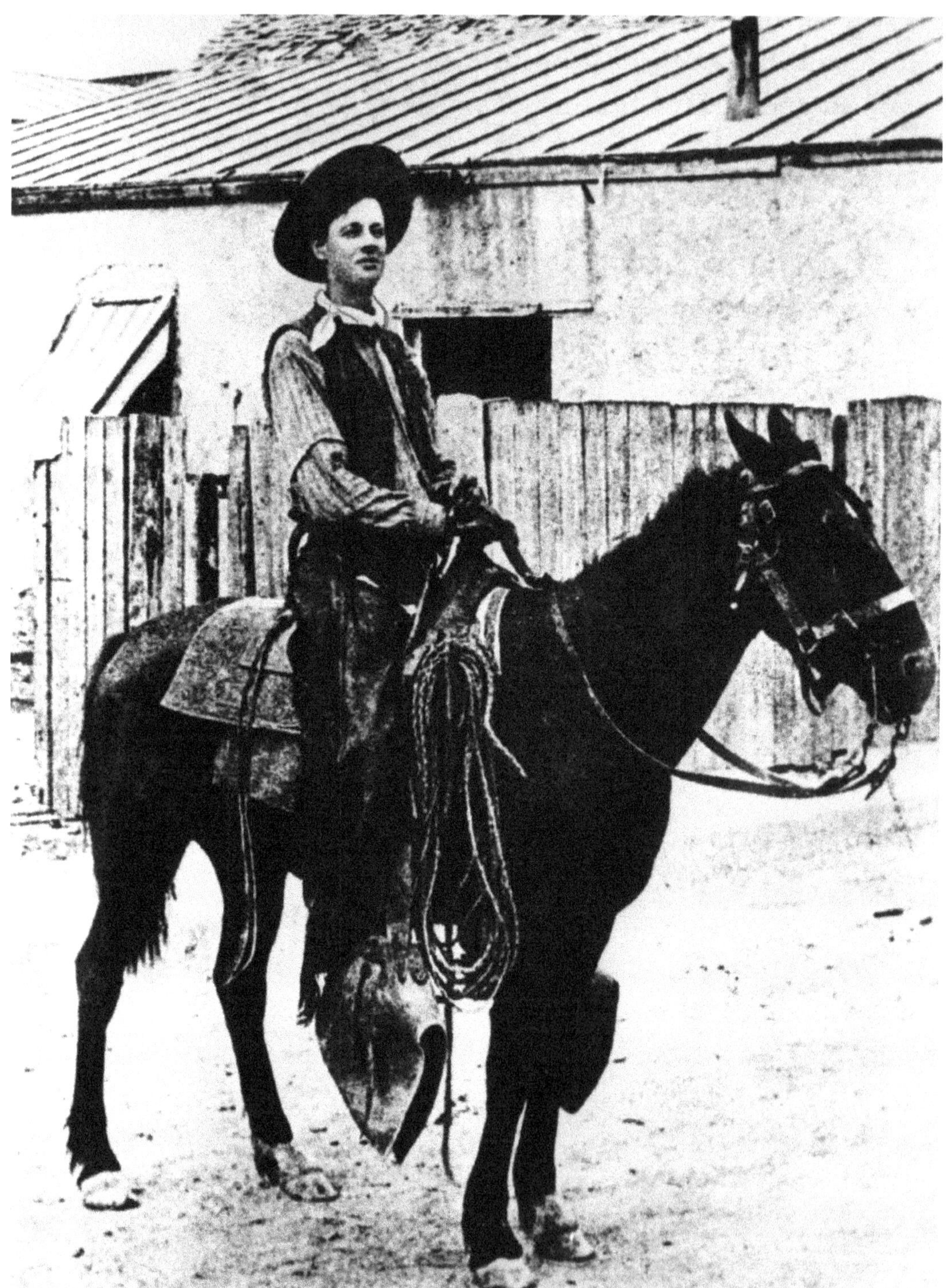

An unidentified cowboy sits astride his horse in this 1880s photograph.

When the Grand Opera House opened in December 1886, it was hailed as the best of its kind in the South. The brick structure on the west side of Alamo Plaza cost $125,000 to build (property included) and seated 1,800. Emma Abbott's opera company opened the theater. The Grand Opera House, which served as a vehicle for vaudeville and motion pictures, was torn down in 1948. Shown to the left is Ed Rische and Sons, offering stationery and cigars. A piano and organ store occupies the bottom right of the building.

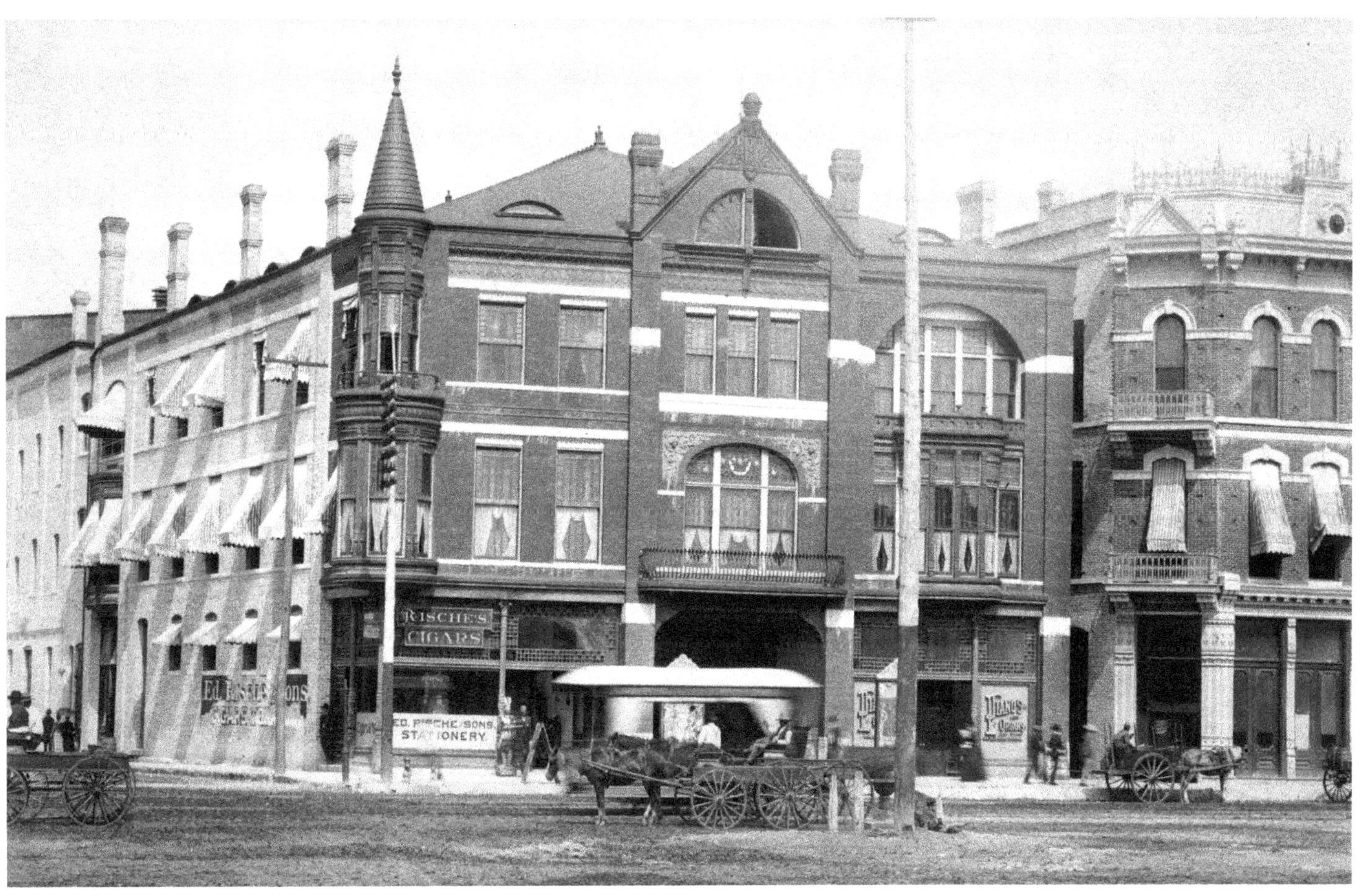

This annual reunion of Terry's Texas Rangers was held at Turner Hall on Houston Street, November 13-14, 1889. Officially the 8th Texas Cavalry Regiment, this unit fought at Shiloh, Murfreesboro, Chickamauga, in the Atlanta Campaign, and many other battles during the Civil War. Of over 1,100 men that enlisted in Houston in 1861, only about thirty surrendered in 1865.

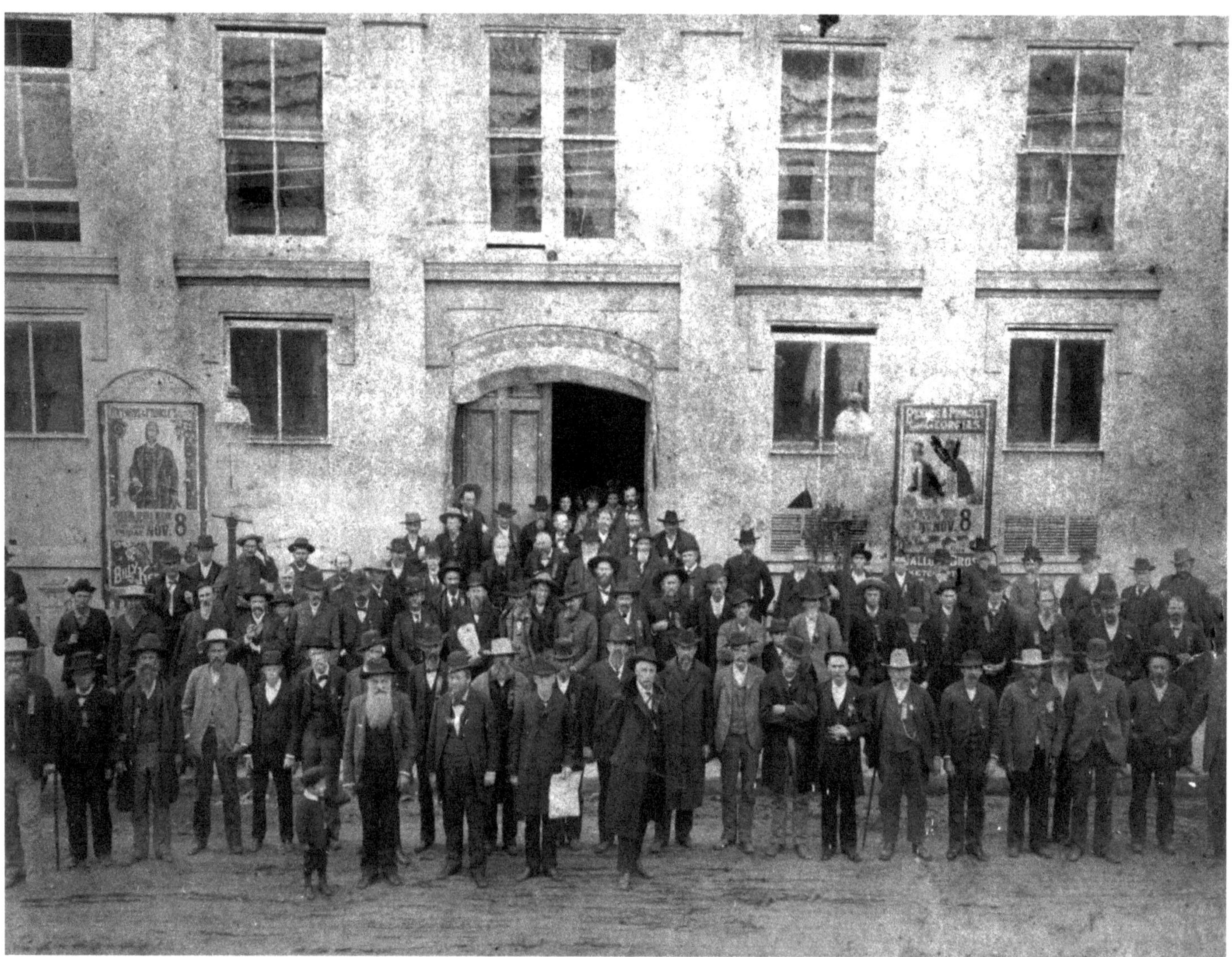

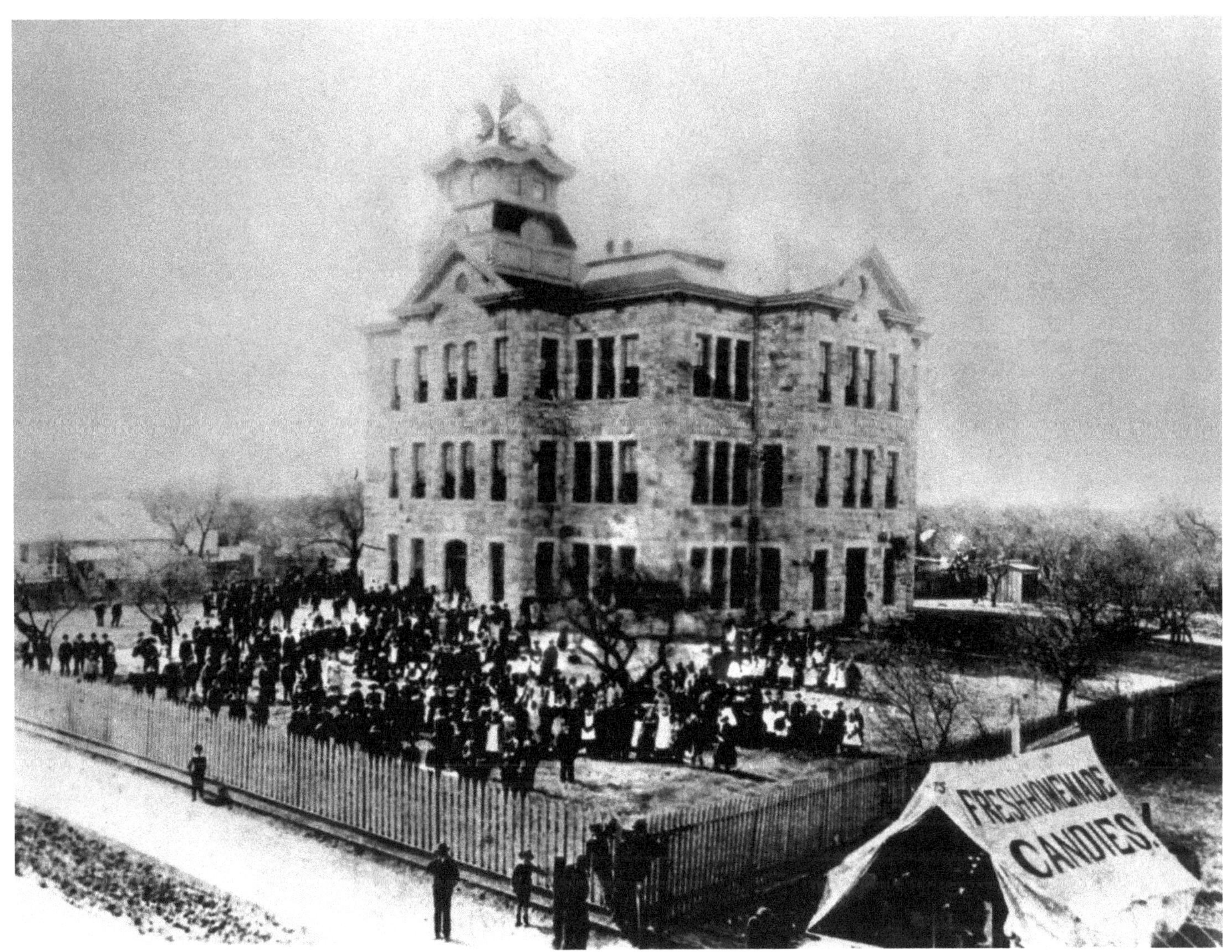

Students gathered in front of the Central Grammar and High School at 463-467 Acequia Street. Soon, it would become Main Avenue High School when the street changed names. A 1924 Sanborn's fire insurance map identifies it as San Antonio High School, with the address of 637 Main Avenue. Today, it is the site of Fox Tech High School.

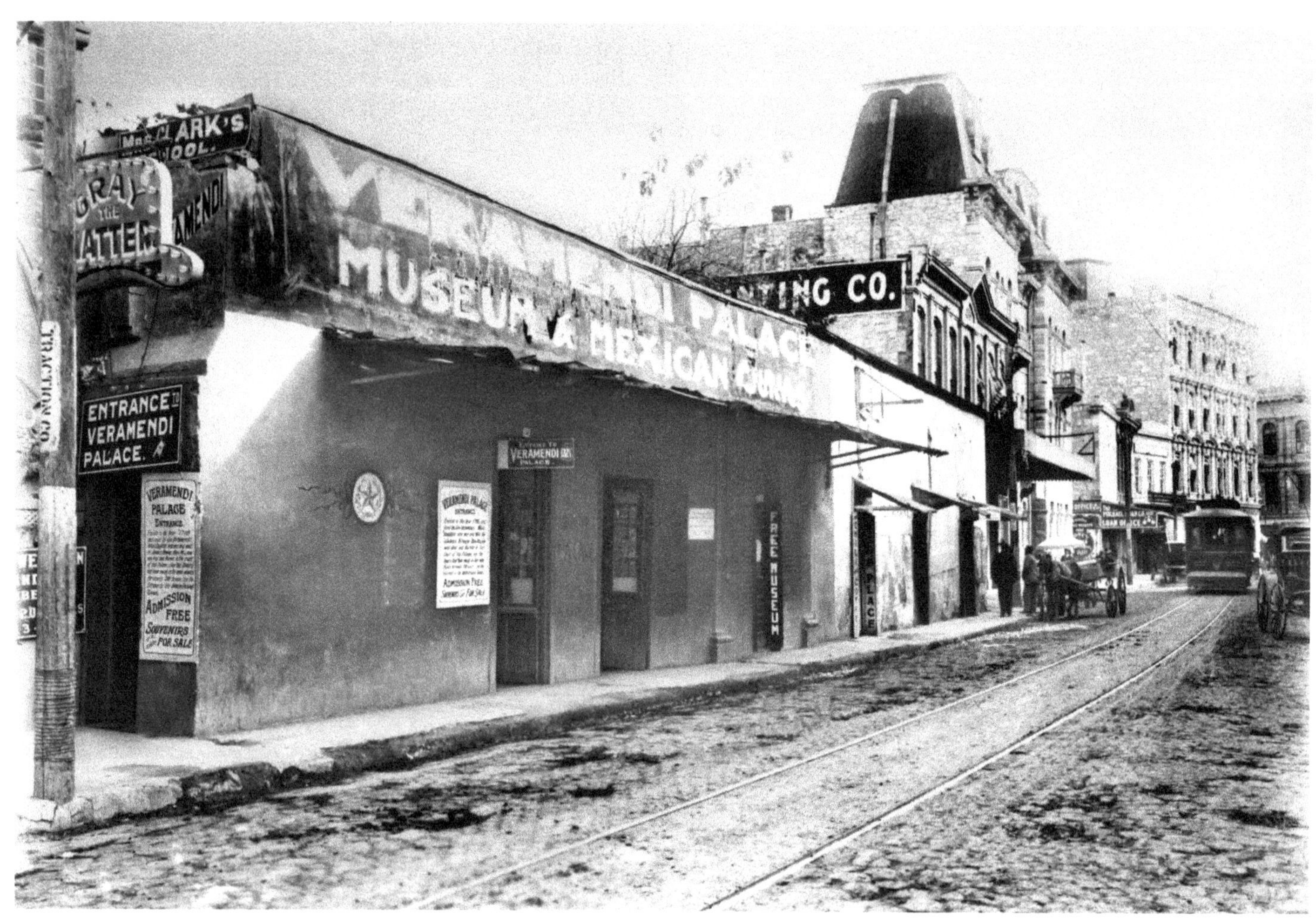

The Veramendi Palace in the 1890s. This limestone and adobe building was built by Don Fernando Veramendi in the early 1700s. His son, Don Juan Martin Veramendi, was appointed vice-governor of the Province of Bexar in 1830, and the structure became known as the Veramendi Palace. Don Juan's daughter Ursula wed James Bowie, who later was one of the officers at the Alamo. The poster at the museum entrance urges visitors "See the entrance to the under-ground tunnel." The building was destroyed for street widening in 1910.

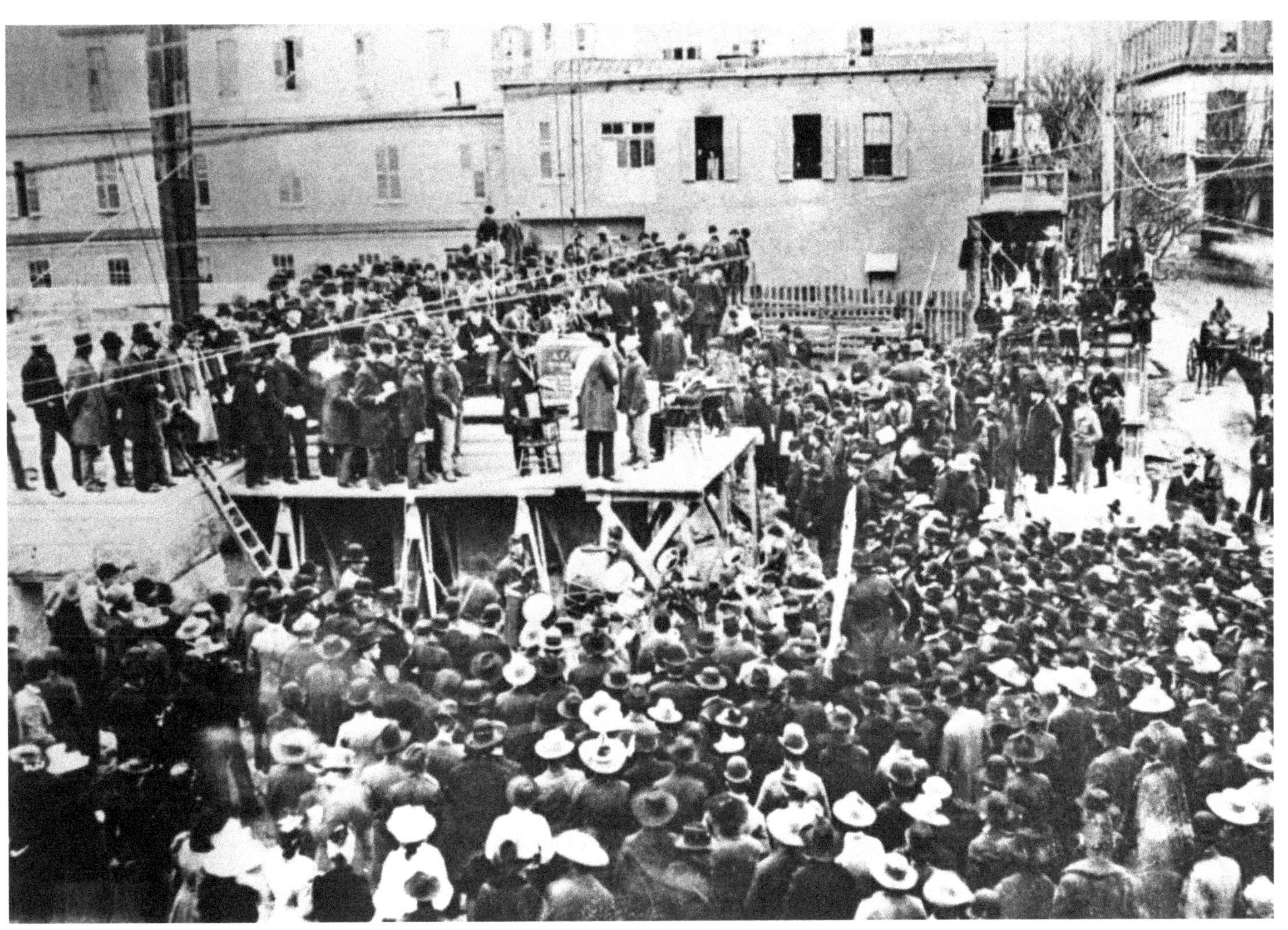

Laying of the cornerstone of the current Bexar County Courthouse on December 17, 1892, by the M. W. Grand Lodge of Texas, A. F. & A. M (Ancient Free and Accepted Masons).

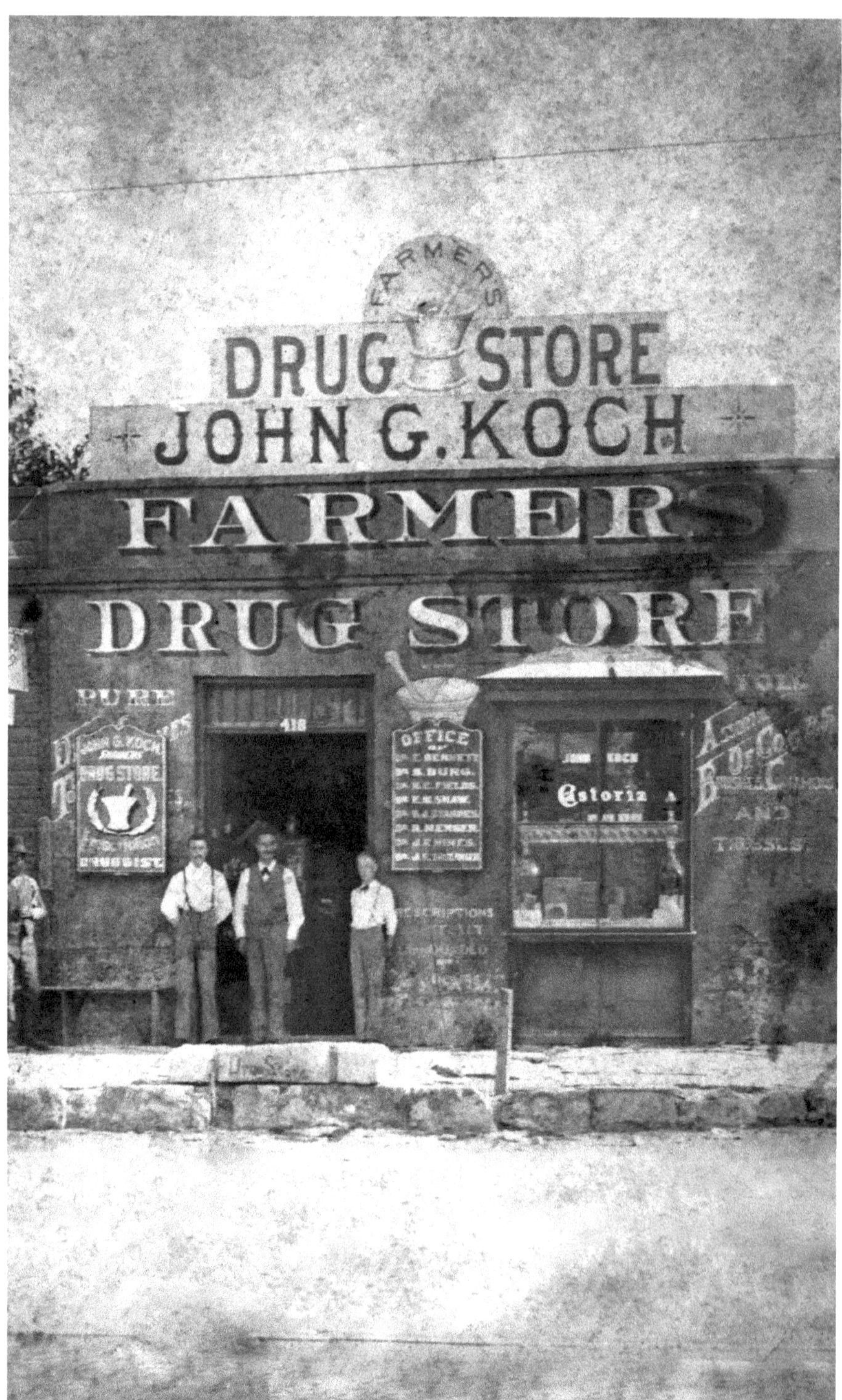

Men pose in front of John G. Koch's Farmers' Drug Store, 418 E. Commerce at Water Street, around 1892.

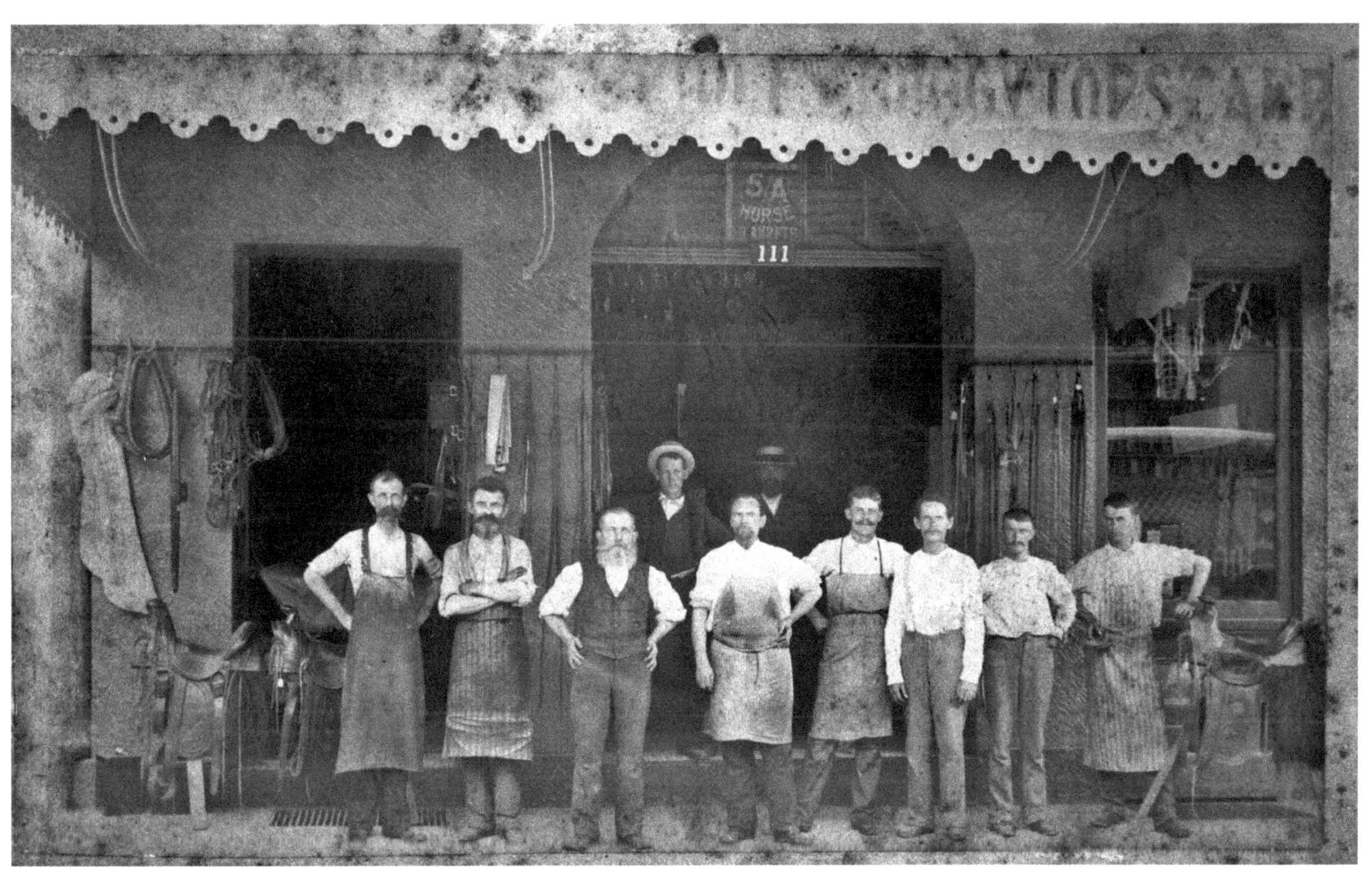

Men standing outside the entrance to Diedrich Heye's Carriage Trimming, Harness, & Saddlery Company at 111 West Commerce in the 1890s. These men were the auto mechanics of their day. Transportation by horse and buggy required saddles, bridles, seats, and trim made by their professional hands.

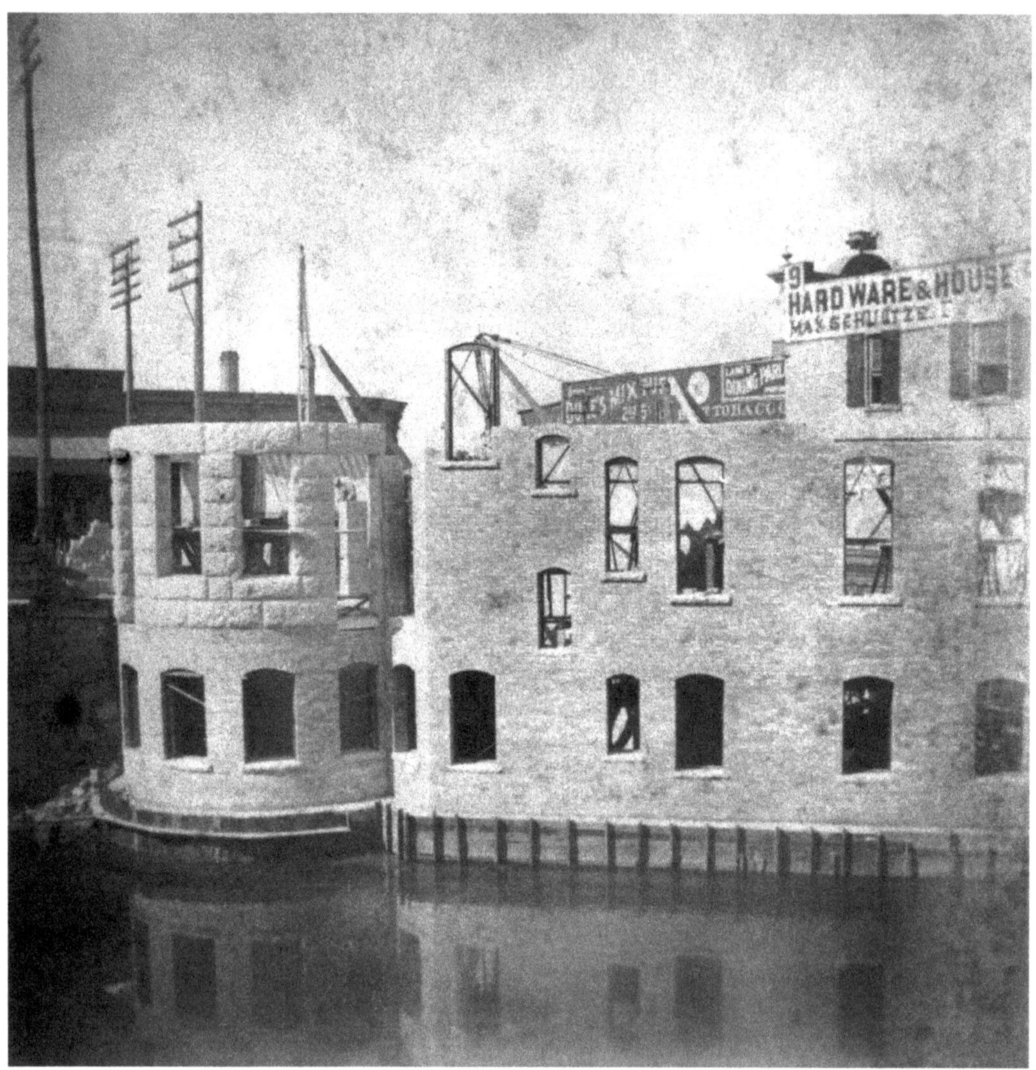

The Clifford Building under construction in 1892–1893. J. Riely Gordon designed this building with its round tower for a local attorney. Its base sits at river level and housed one of the earliest River Walk restaurants. The upper levels consisted of offices, artists' studios, and apartments.

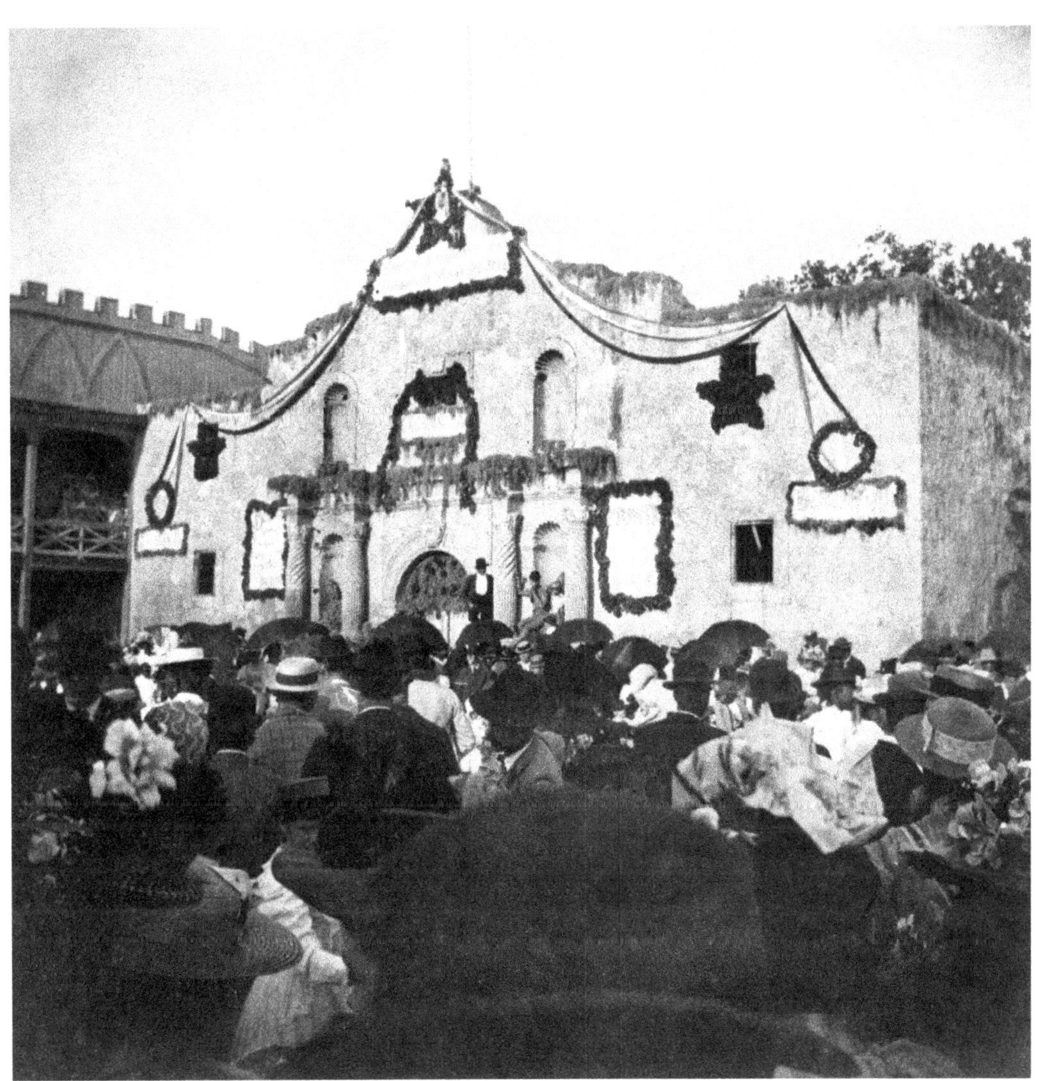

The 1893 Fiesta celebration in front of the Alamo. To the left is the castle-like façade of Hugo and Schmeltzer, a wholesale groceries and liquors warehouse built around the ruins of the mission's *convento.*

People enjoying a good meal at a chile stand, the original "fast food," on Military Plaza. Residents and businessmen would fill the plaza during lunch and supper. In the evenings food and fandangos were common entertainments.

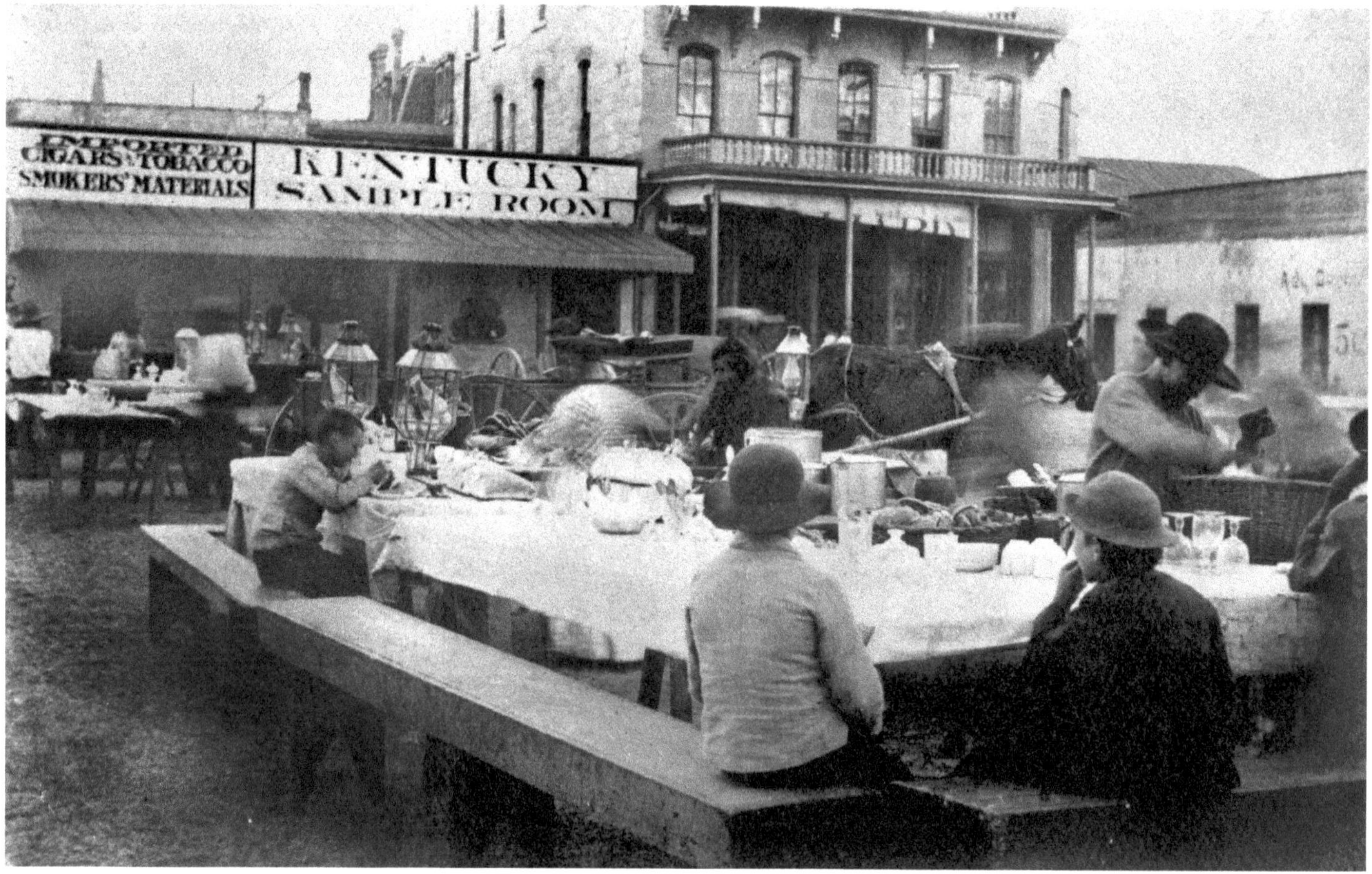

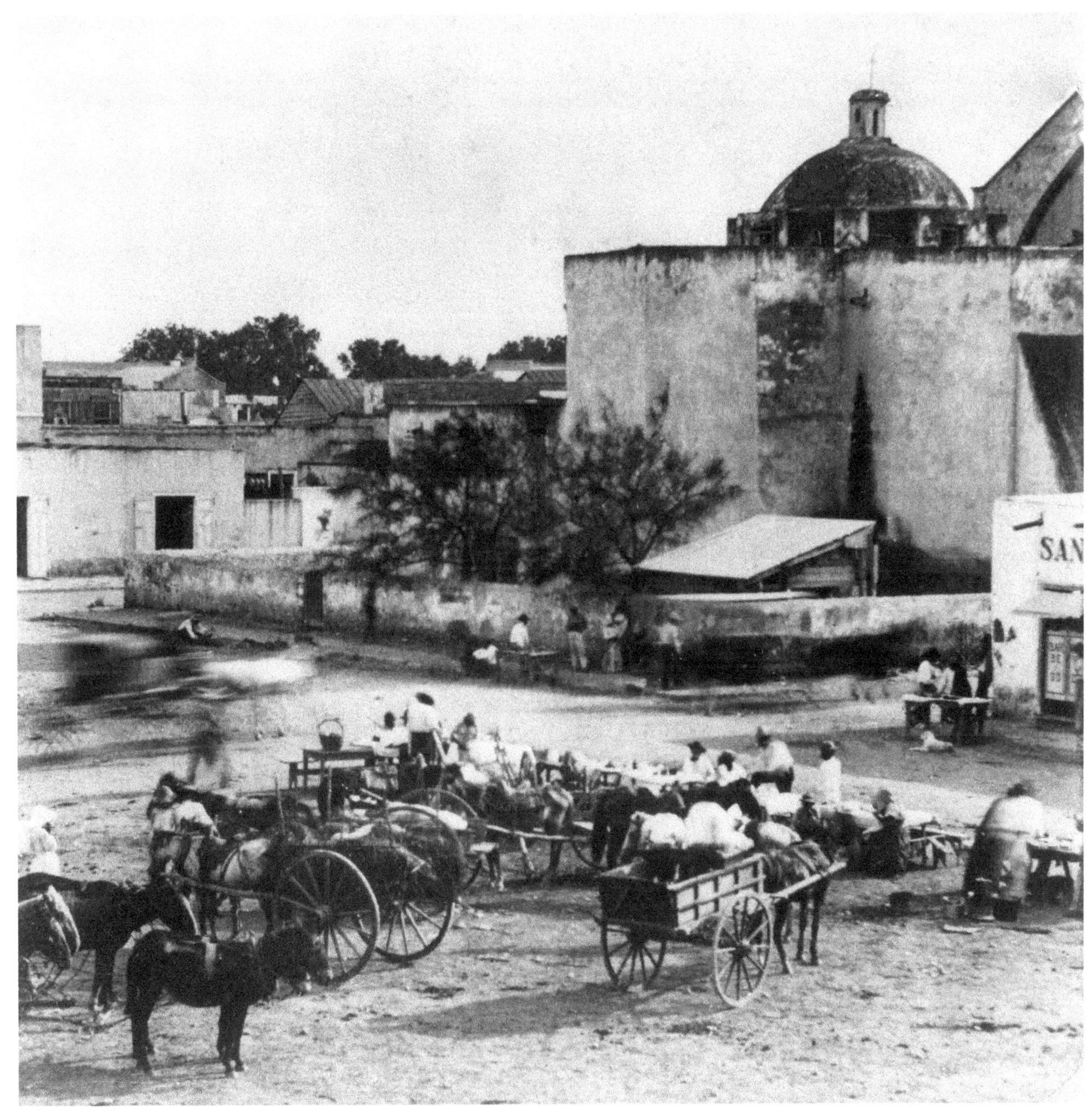

Military Plaza showing the back of San Fernando Cathedral and a busy chile stand. Small horse-drawn carts haul freight.

The old Market House on Market Street, constructed in 1858, was designed after a model of a Greek temple by John Fries and David Russi, leading city builders and contractors. It was torn down, but in 1929, replicas of its columns were created for the San Antonio Little Theater to use in the San Pedro Playhouse, the first city-built, city-owned and city-maintained community theater in the United States. Gutzon Borglum, later the sculptor of Mount Rushmore, was a consultant on the theater project.

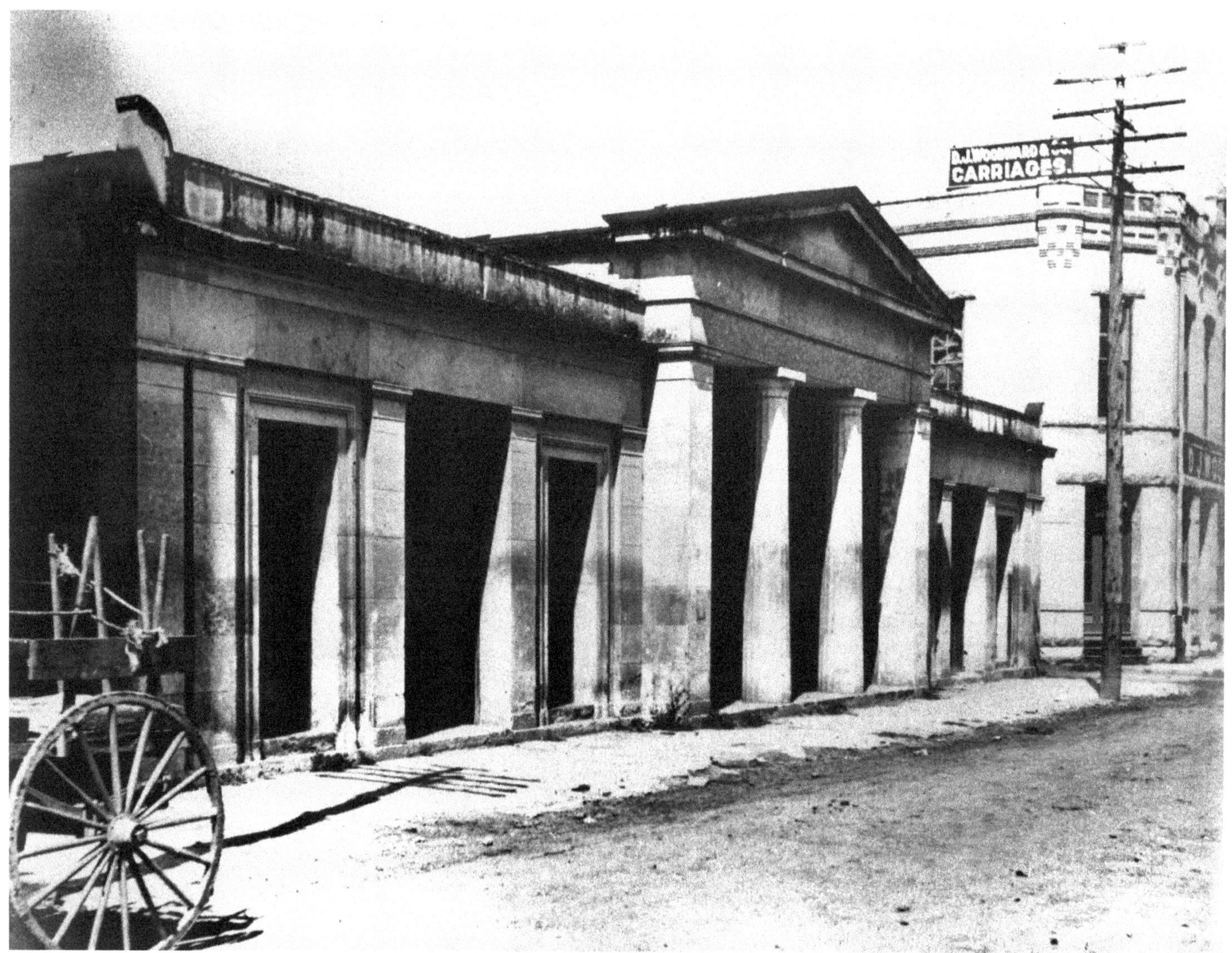

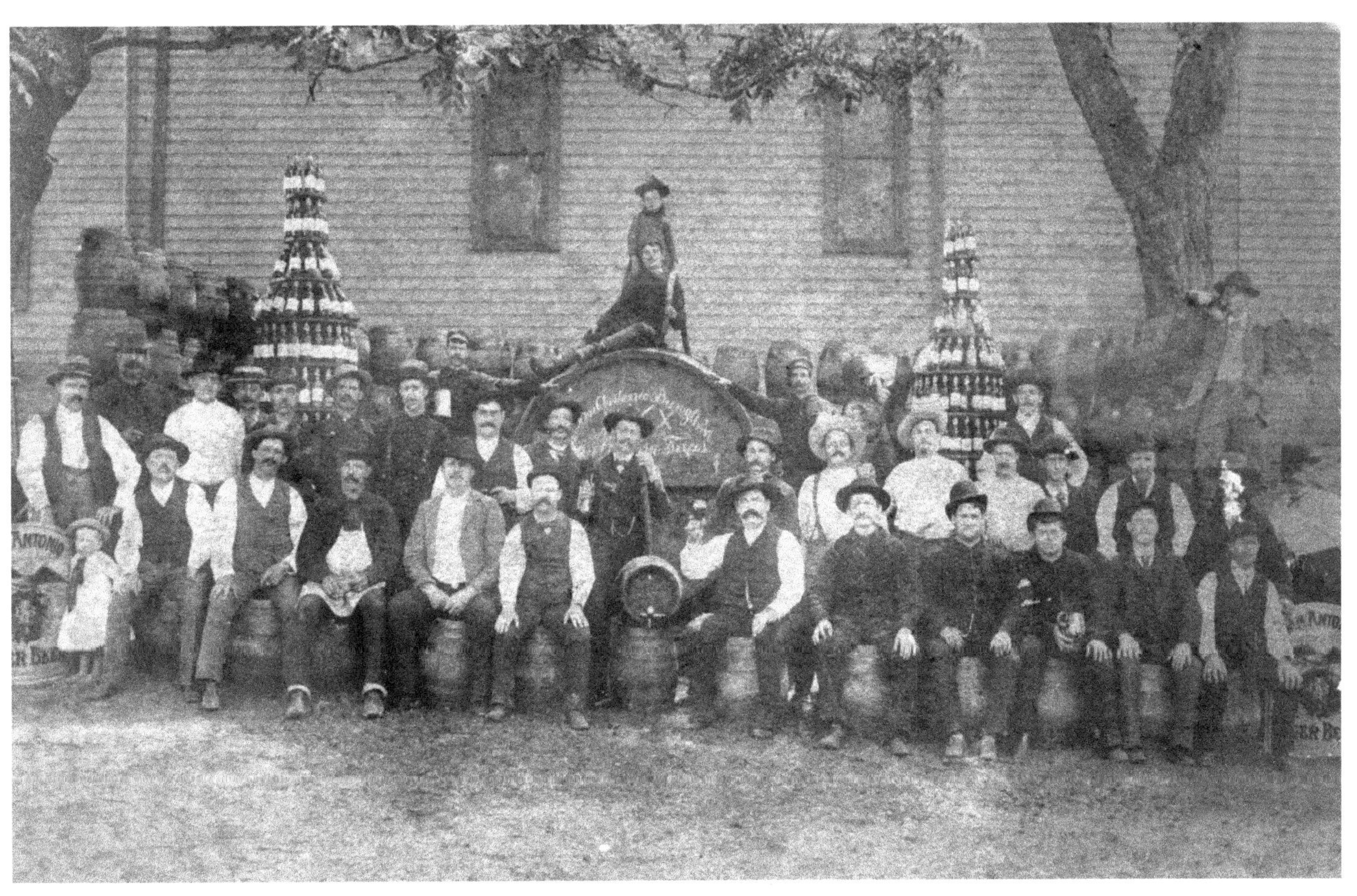

A group of men from Pearl Brewery pose by the brewery with products of their labors, in kegs and bottles.

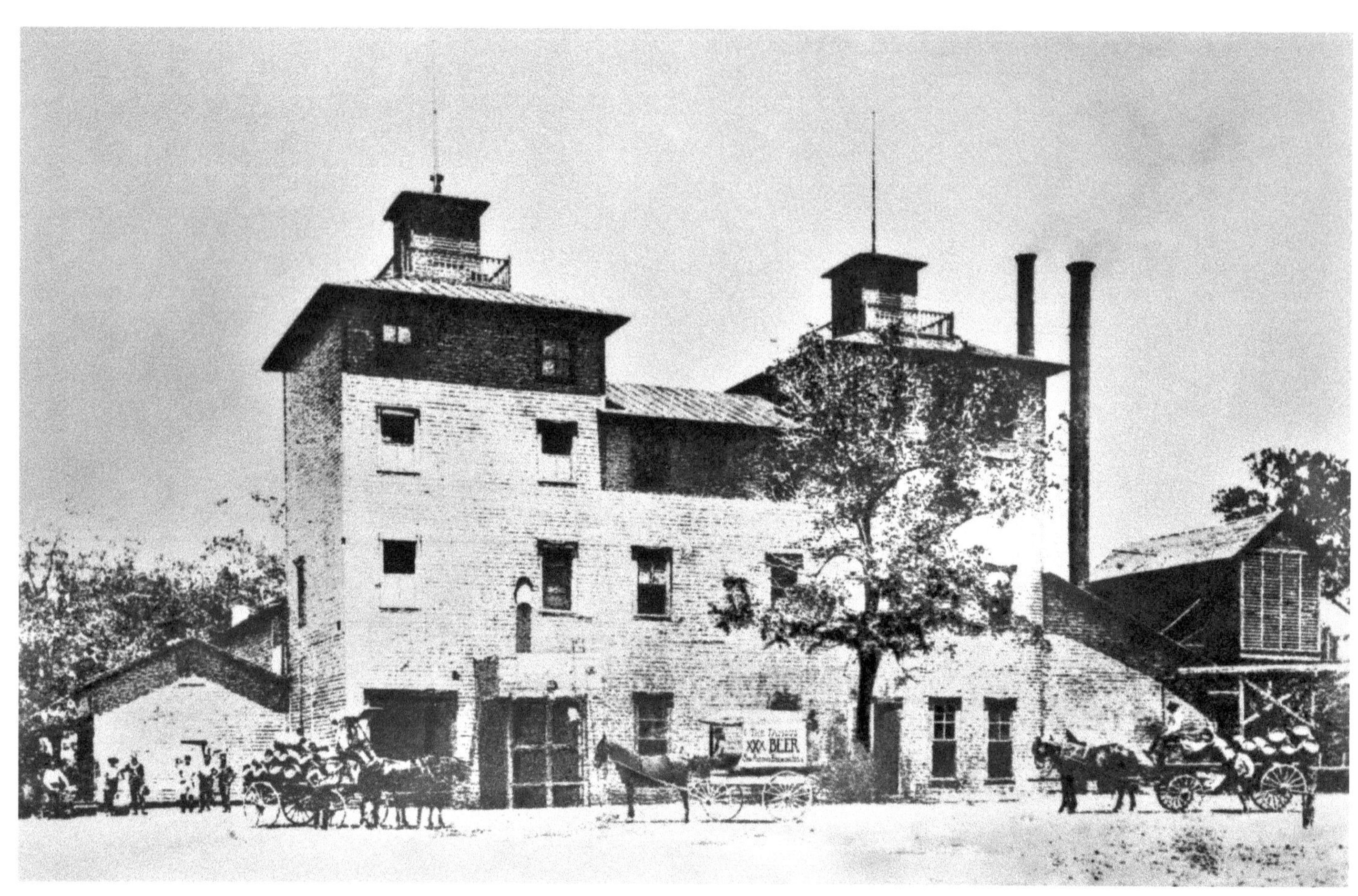

Pearl Brewery came into being when, in 1886, the San Antonio Brewing Association took over the City Brewery and bought the name and formula from Kaiser-Beck at Bremen, Germany. Pearl claimed to have produced the first lager beer in the city and state. This building and Pearl brewing are gone, but Pearl beer is still manufactured at the Miller Brewing facility in Fort Worth.

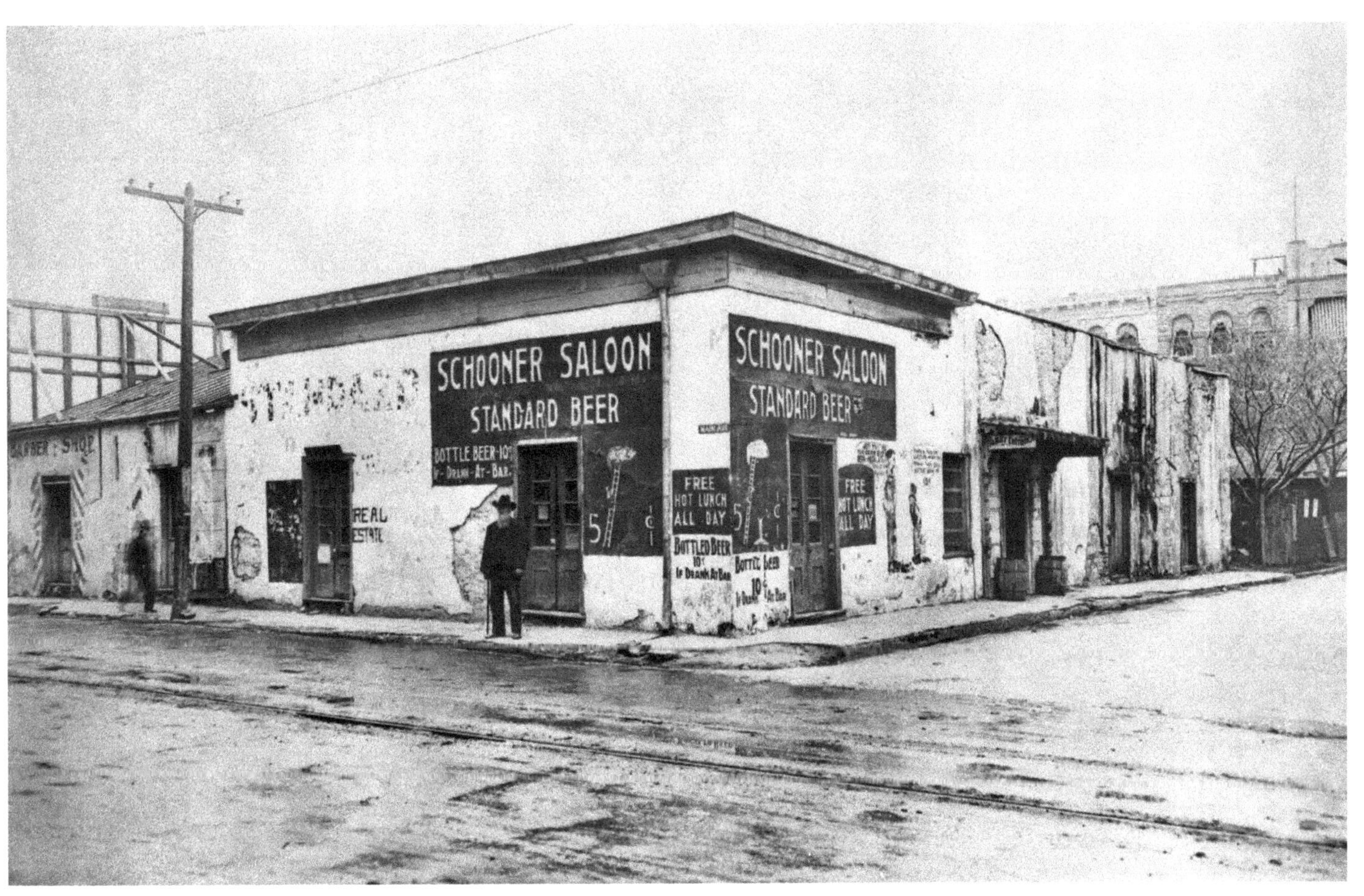

The "Schooner Saloon" name hides the history of this building. Known as the Garza House, it was built by Geronimo de la Garza in 1734 with thick walls and a vault, which local merchants used as a bank. In 1818, Antonio de la Garza received permission from Spain to mint a coin for local use. The house was demolished in 1912 and replaced by the Rand Building.

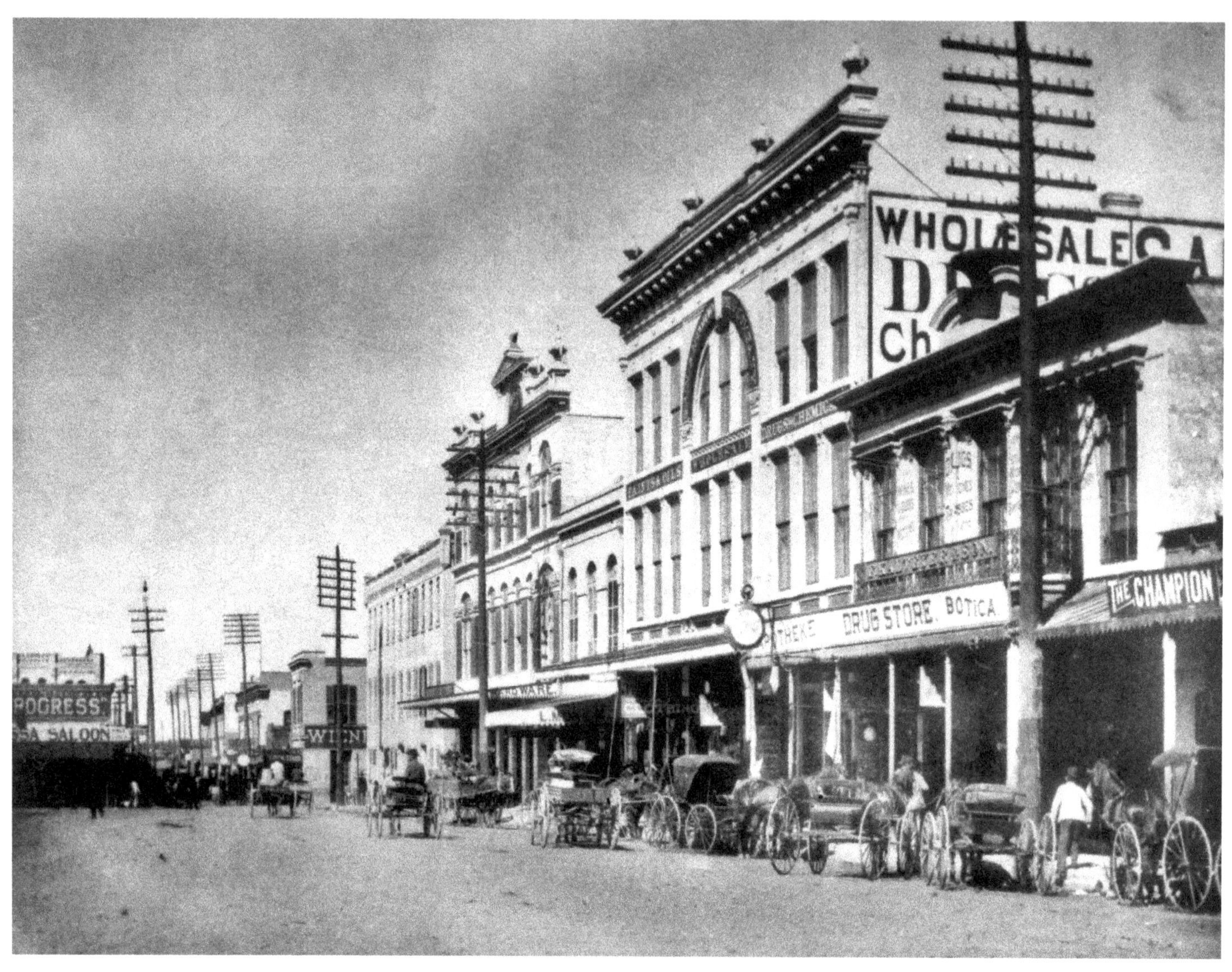

A street scene from Military Plaza showing the F. Kalteyer & Sons Drug Store, the largest building on the right. Frederick Kalteyer, a German native, opened the business, originally called Eagle Drug Store, on Military Plaza in 1854. His son and partner, George Henry Kalteyer, became the state chemist in 1871. The Kalteyer Building seen here was built in 1877. The company eventually became the San Antonio Drug Company.

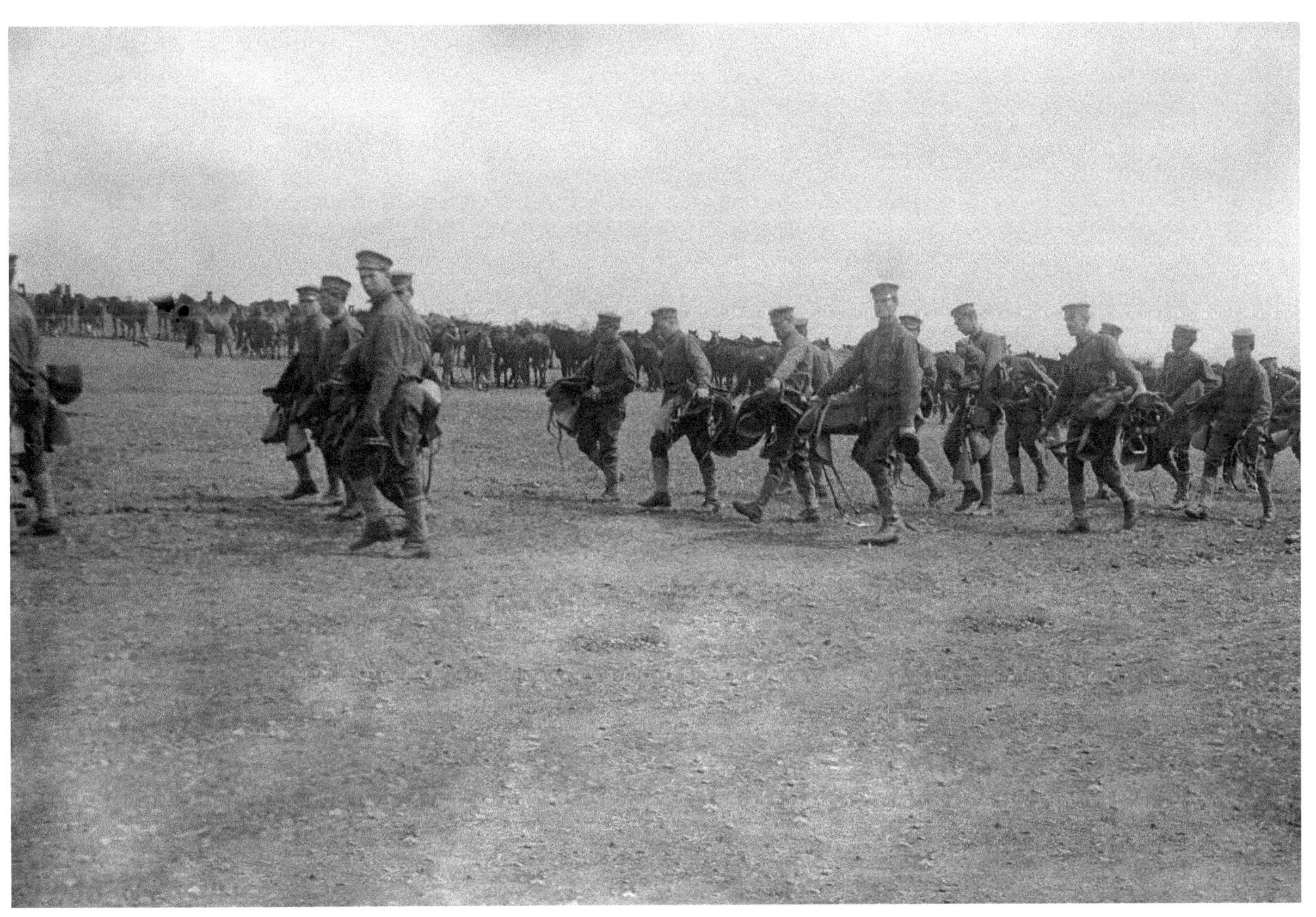

Cavalrymen at Fort Sam Houston unsaddle their horses after a long, hard day. Before they can rest, however, they must first take care of the needs of their horses.

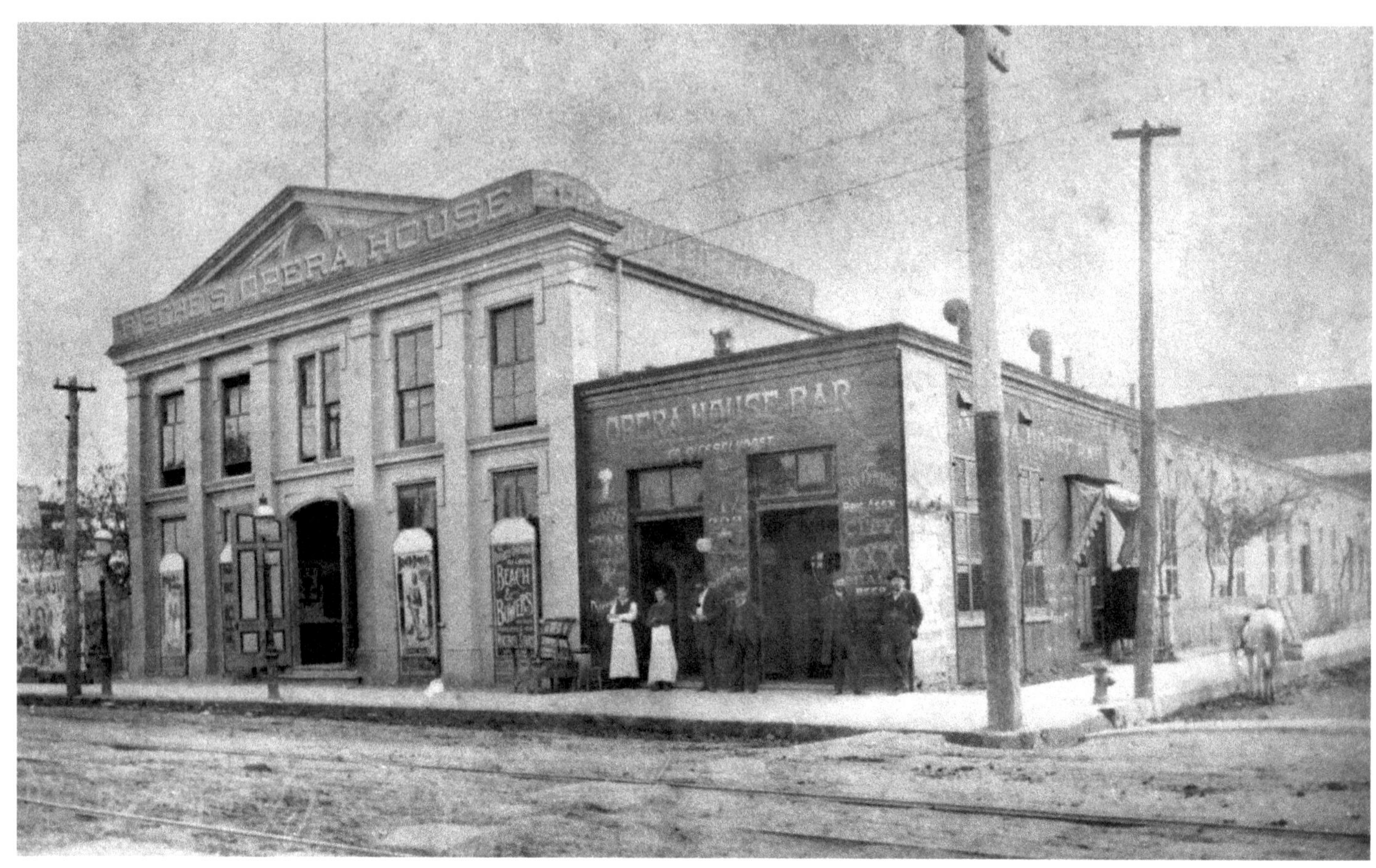

Ernest Rische was the first manager of the Grand Opera House (1886–1888). About June 1890, Rische announced he was remodeling the Turner Opera House, on the southeast corner of Houston and St. Mary's streets, and adding electricity. It reopened as Rische's Opera House and Opera House Bar. Things did not go well, and by the end of 1892, Rische sold out. The poster advertises a show by (Bobby) Beach and (Otis) Bowers' minstrel performers.

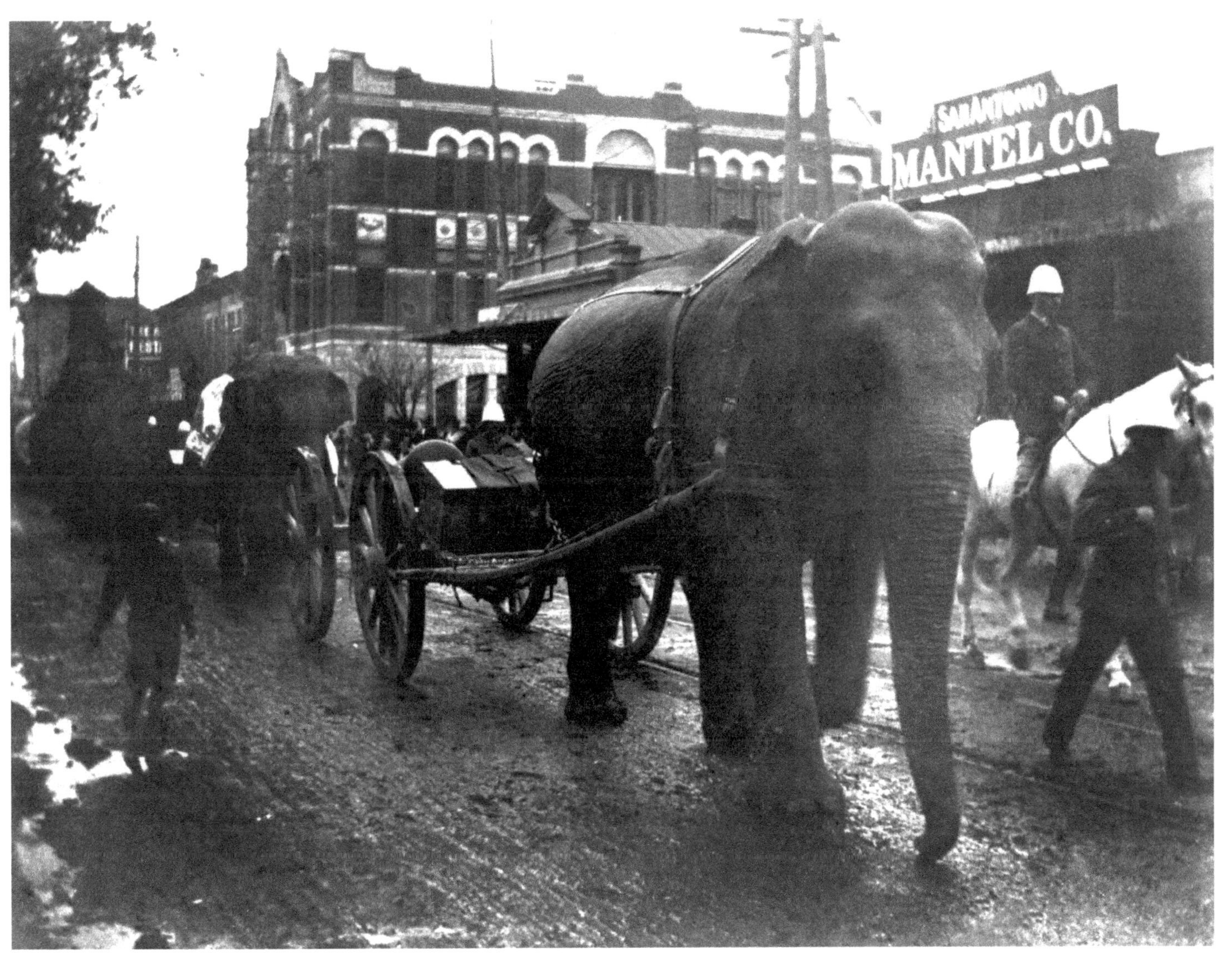

The Ringling Brothers Circus paraded through the streets in November 1898. The arrival of the circus was a major event in every town's past.

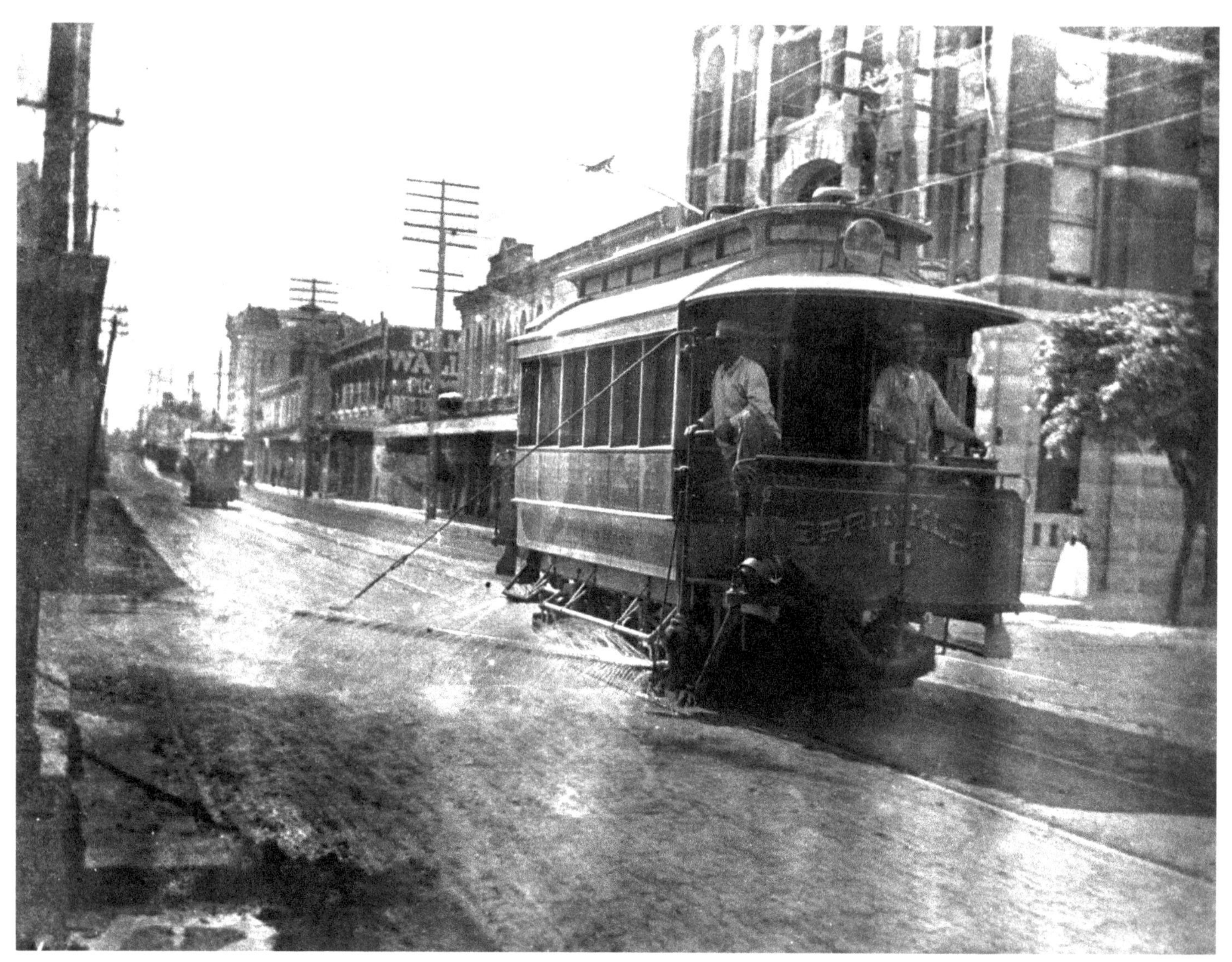

This is San Antonio Electric Tramway Sprinkler No. 6, a streetcar in 1897. Replacing mule-drawn streetcars, San Antonio's first electric streetcar began operation on September 26, 1890. The first electric streetcar line traveled from Navarro Street to the International Fair Grounds.

From Town to City

(1900–1919)

In the first decades of the twentieth century, San Antonio became a bona-fide city. Between 1900 and 1920 its population tripled to over 160,000. People came to Texas for the warm climate and expanding business opportunities. Entire excursion trains were hired to bring prospective businessmen or settlers to visit San Antonio and South Texas.

Hot Sulphur Wells and Terrell Wells provided a spa-like atmosphere for bronchial sufferers and tourists alike. Private sanitariums sprang up across town, especially for tubercular patients. Near Hot Sulphur Wells, a few miles south of town at the time, some of the earliest motion pictures were filmed.

Nearer downtown, Fort Sam Houston's mission continued to grow. The earliest experiments with military aviation began in 1910 when Lieutenant B. D. Foulois unpacked seventeen boxes containing the Army's first airplane, which he assembled and successfully flew. On May 10, 1911, Second Lieutenant George E. M. Kelly, a native of England, suffered a fatal crash, becoming the first American military aviator to die while flying. When the United States entered World War I in 1917, the number of military personnel in San Antonio exploded as trainees from all over Texas and Oklahoma came to Camp Travis. Flight training moved to what became known as Kelly Field.

Several tragedies marred these two decades. On March 18, 1912, the boiler on Southern Pacific passenger locomotive No. 704 exploded at the roundhouse on North Olive Street, killing twenty-six and injuring forty more. In both October and December of 1913, the San Antonio River rose from its banks, as it had in the past, and flooded the city. The Spanish influenza pandemic attacked in the latter part of 1918. World War I touched the lives of the entire city as everyone became involved in the war effort, with many losing husbands, sons, and fathers. When the Municipal Auditorium was dedicated in 1926 to those who lost their lives in the war, 195 names were listed in the official program.

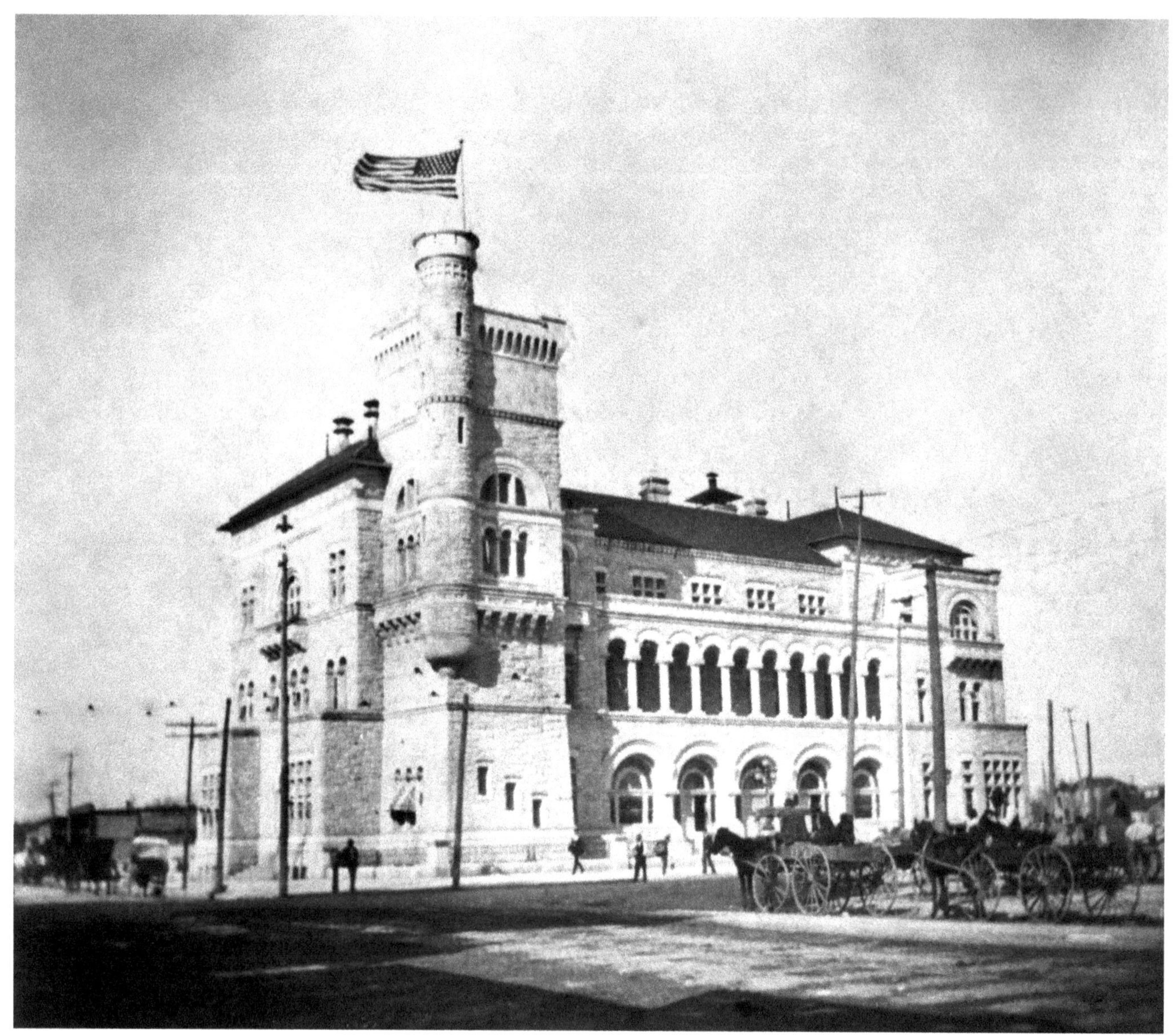

The Federal Building and Post Office, located on the north side of Alamo Plaza, was built in the late 1800s at a cost of $1,864,000. Except for an ox team and a few dray wagons, the plaza appears almost empty.

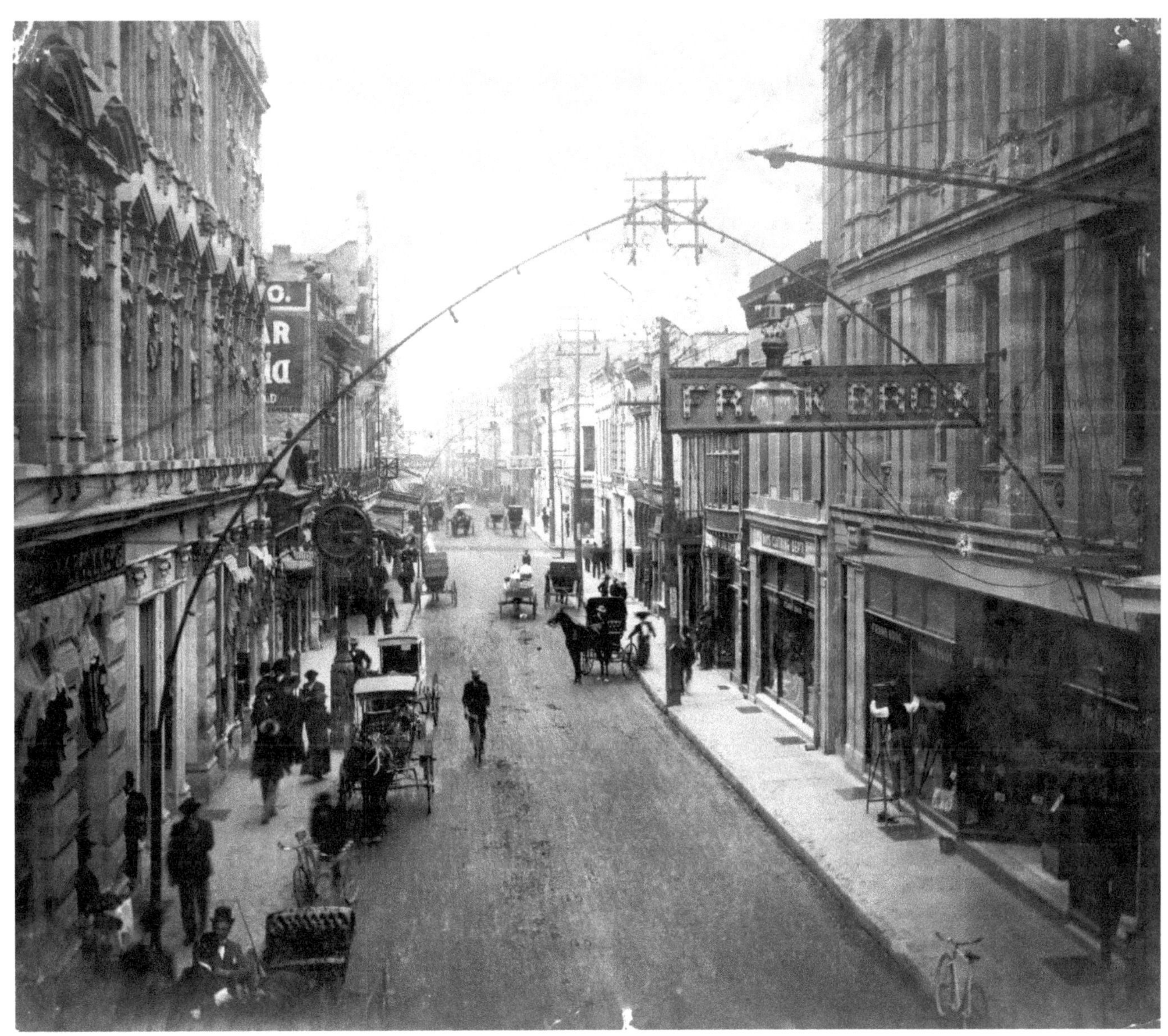

A busy Commerce Street, looking east from Main Plaza in the early 1900s. The curved piping over the street is lighting. To the right is Frank Bros. (Gerson, Emil, and Sol Frank), established in 1868. Known for its fine men's clothing, it was sold in 1963 and ceased operations in 1995.

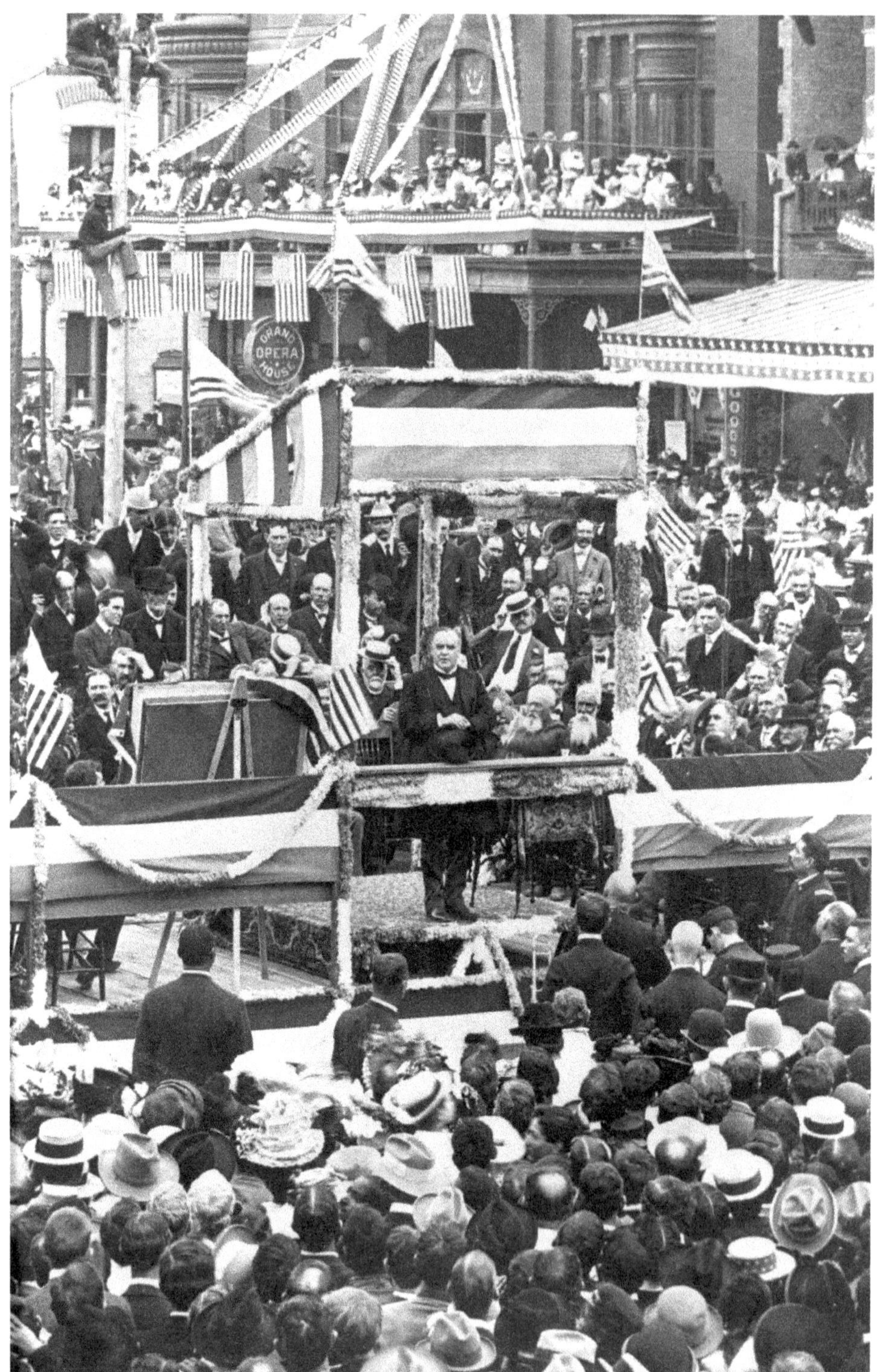

President William McKinley spoke to a crowd in Alamo Plaza during a visit on May 4, 1901. Photograph is looking southwest from the second floor of the Hugo-Schmeltzer Building. In the background, people are seated on the balcony of the Grand Opera House.

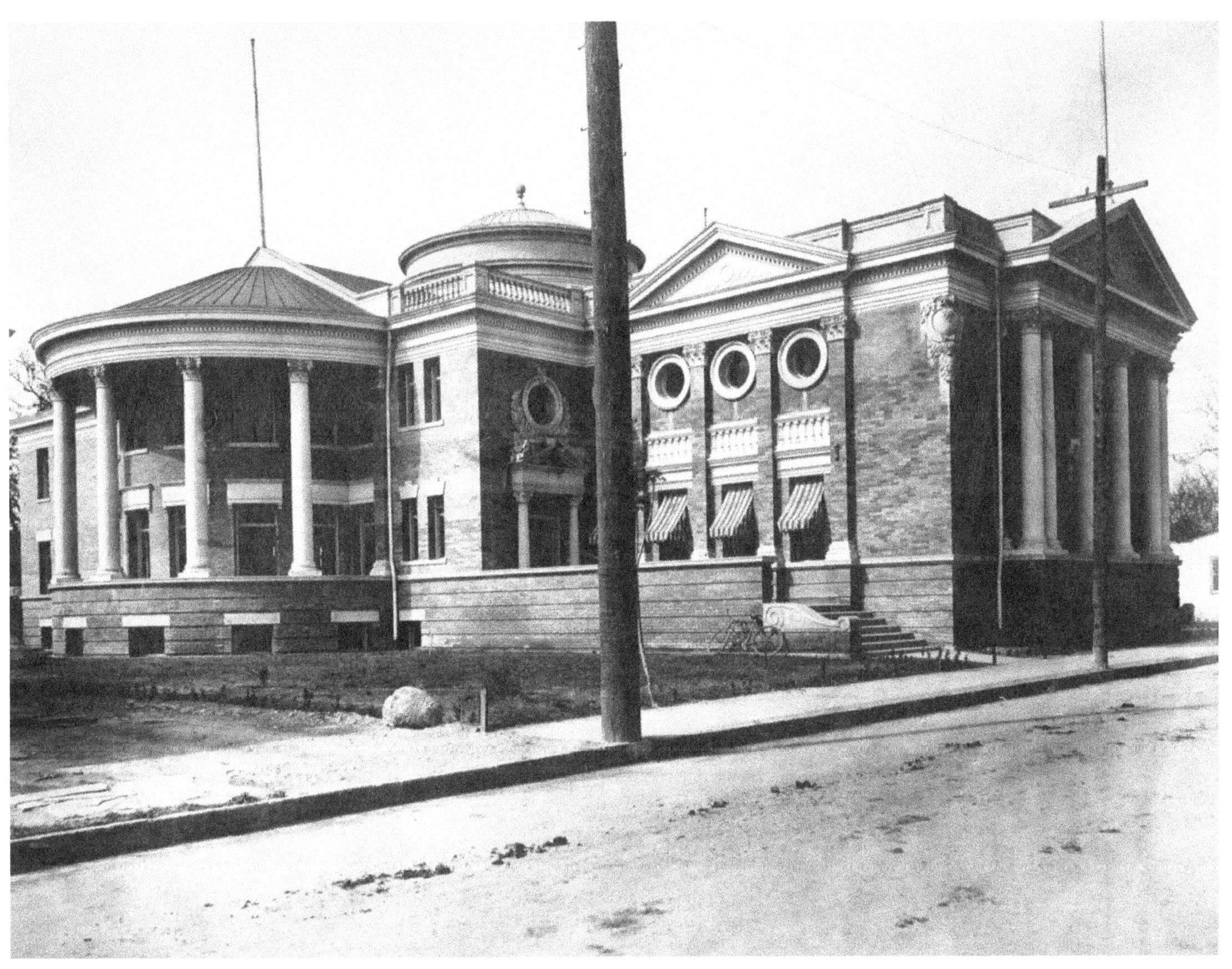

The Carnegie Library of San Antonio, built in 1903. Many organizations and people helped bring about the library, including Caroline Kampmann who donated the land. The building was designed by J. Riely Gordon. In 1909, an auditorium was added. Ultimately, it was razed and a new library erected in its place, opening on August 1, 1930.

Delivery wagons loaded with flour in front of Pioneer Flour Mills on Guenther Street carry signs advising, "Eat Texas Pioneer Flour." Carl Hilmar Guenther established his first mill in Fredericksburg in 1851. Because of drought, he moved his operation to San Antonio in 1859, where it has remained.

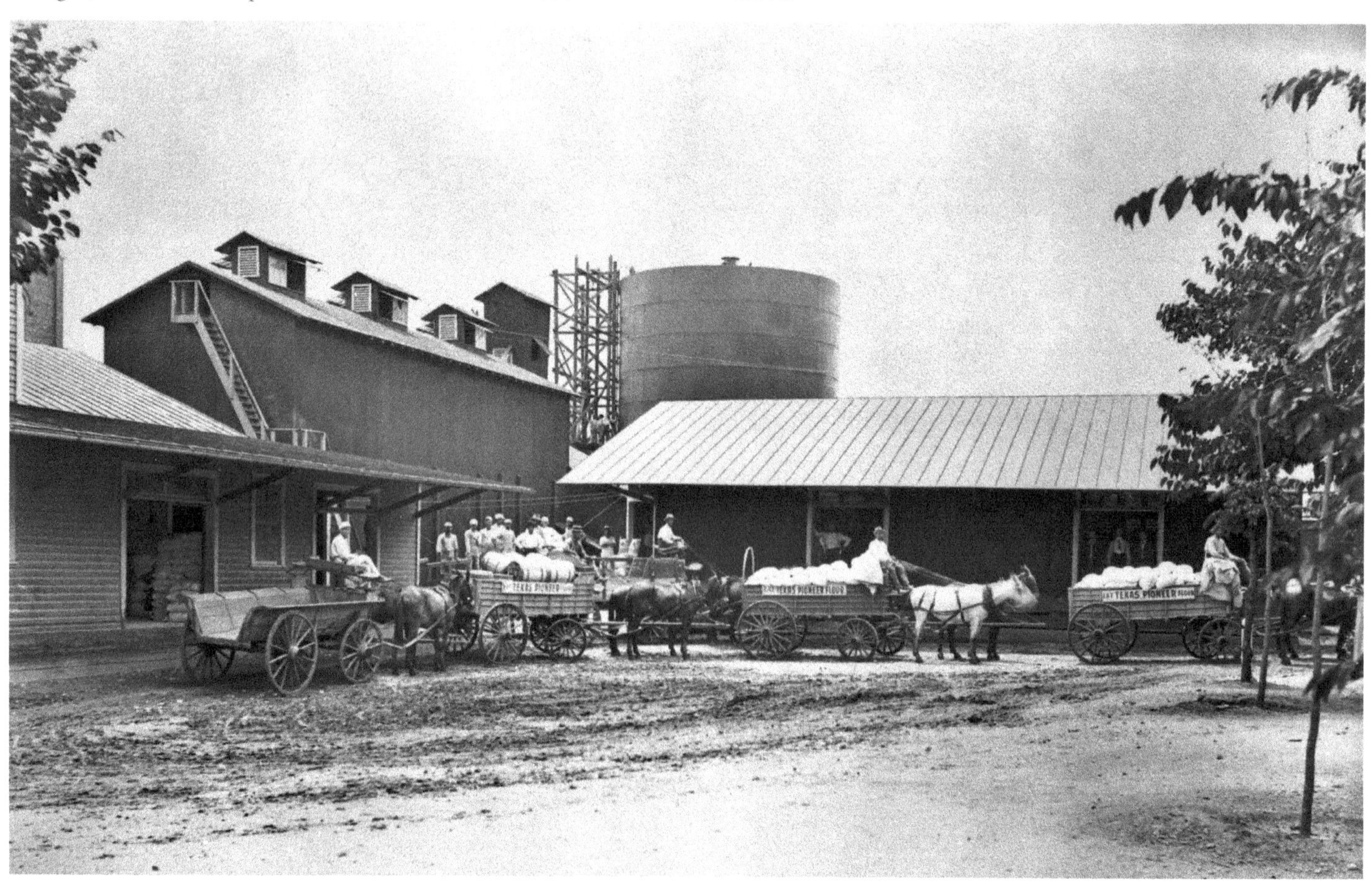

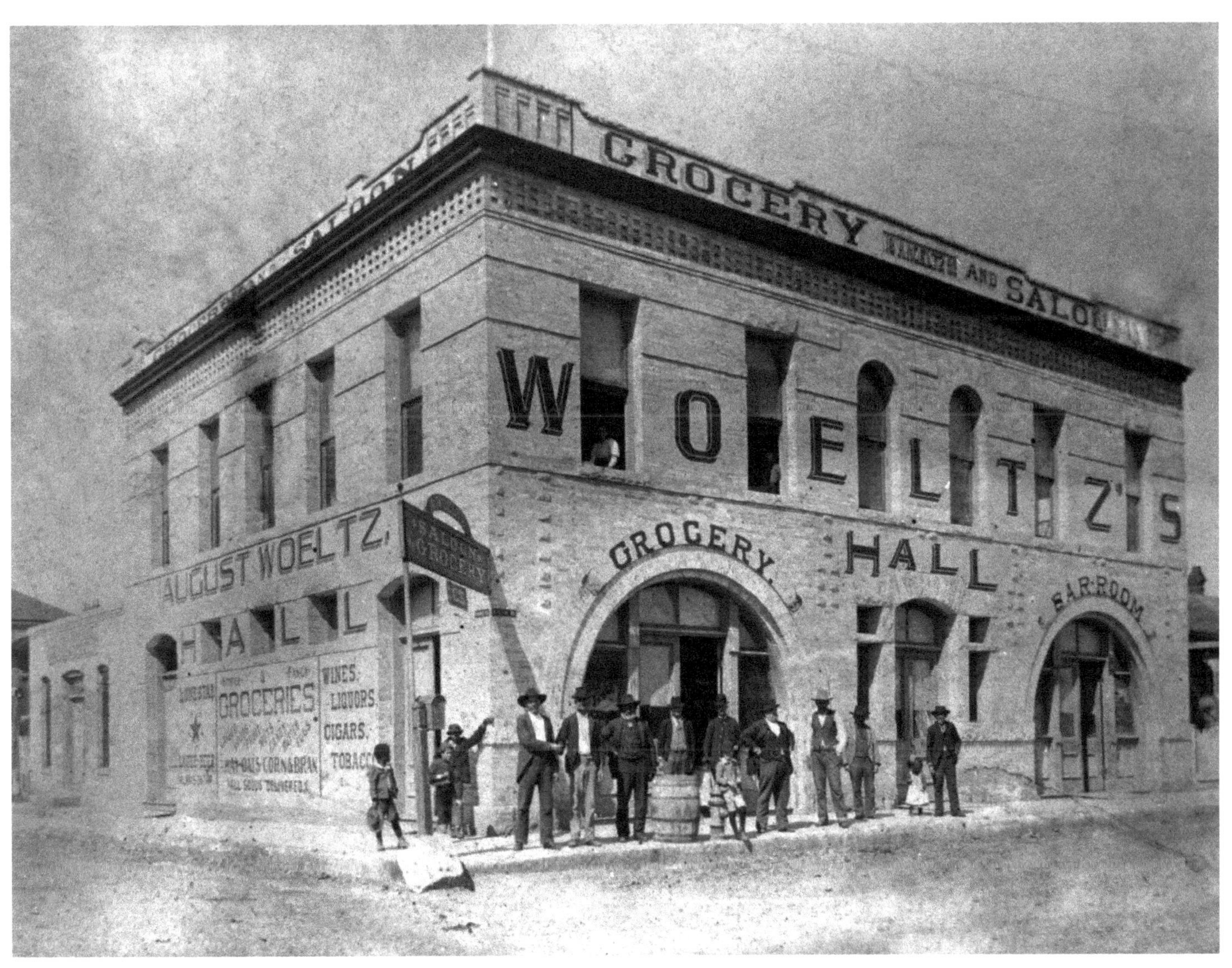

The August Woeltz building had a saloon and grocery on the first floor and a meeting hall on the second. Located at 401-405 N. Pecos Street (northwest corner of Pecos and Salinas streets), it was used by Finck Cigar Co. in the 1910s. In the late 1890s the Bakers' Union No. 10 met there.

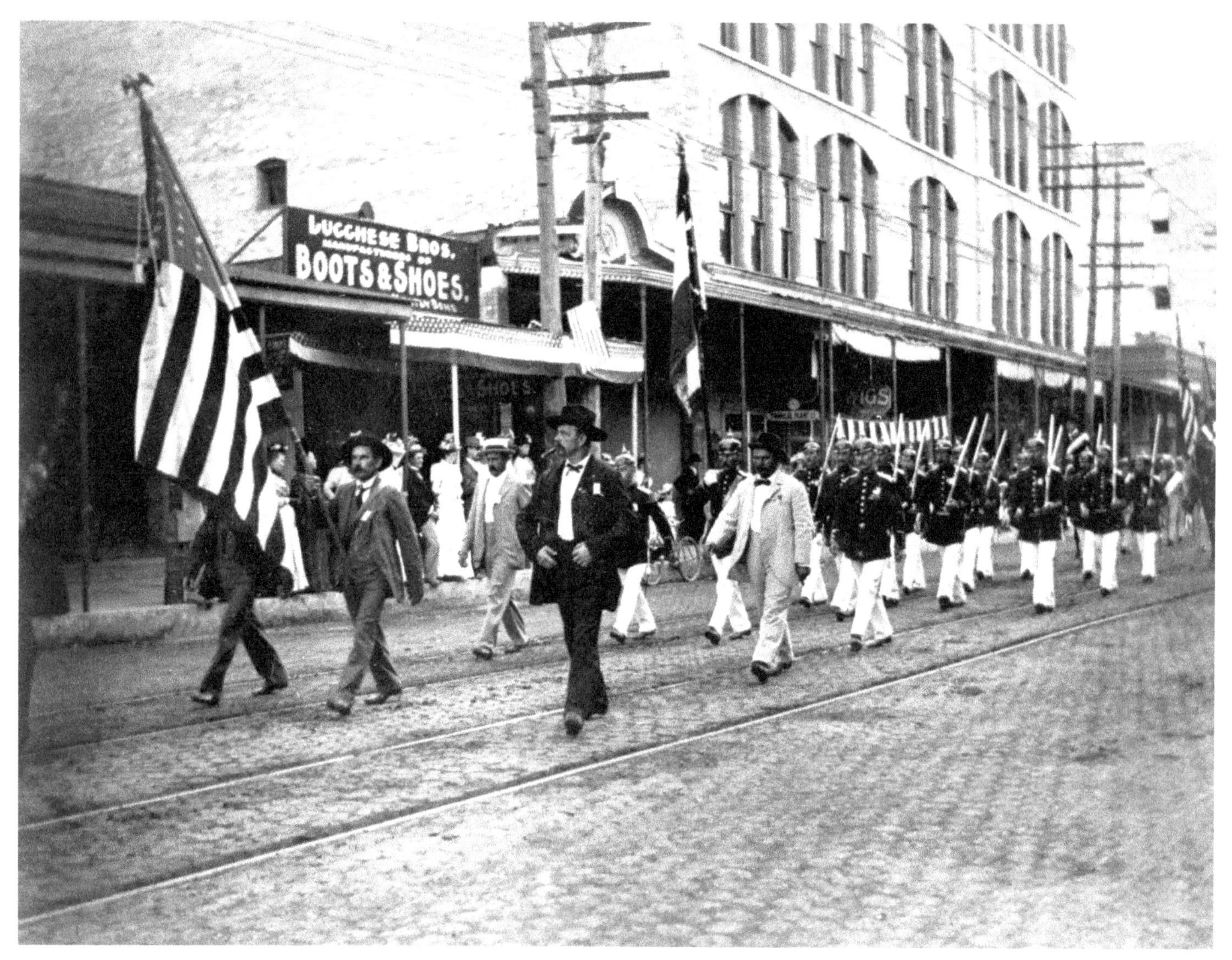

A Fourth of July parade on Houston Street. Lucchese Bros. Boots & Shoes seen near the United States flag, was then, and continues to be, famous for its hand-made boots. Salvatore "Sam" B. Lucchese, who was from Palermo, Italy, founded the company in 1883. Acme Boot Company acquired Lucchese in 1984.

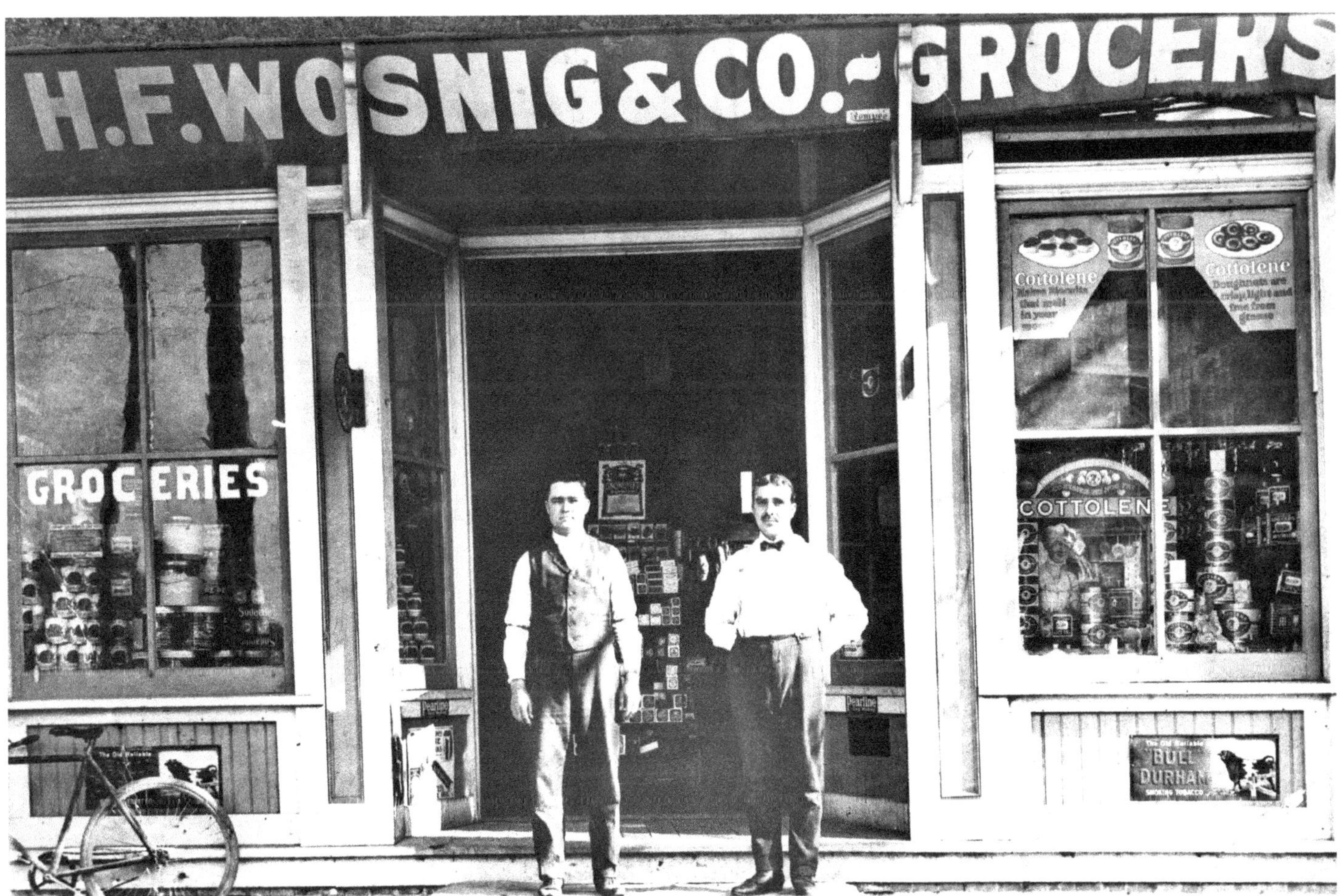

H. F. Wosnig & Company was located at 623 E. Commerce. Henry F. Wosnig and Peter H. Jud, probably the two men shown here, operated this grocery store together from about 1907 until 1925 or 1926. Around 1926, Wosnig became an insurance agent, and Jud continued the grocery store into the 1940s.

The first chapel of St. John Berchmans, on the south side of Brady Avenue, was built by Stephanie Hooge in 1903 for the religious instruction of Belgian children. San Antonio was the primary area of settlement for Belgians in Texas. Pictured are (left to right) Peter Hooge, two unidentified men, Seraphin Hooge, and Henry Grothues. The women in the doorway are also unidentified.

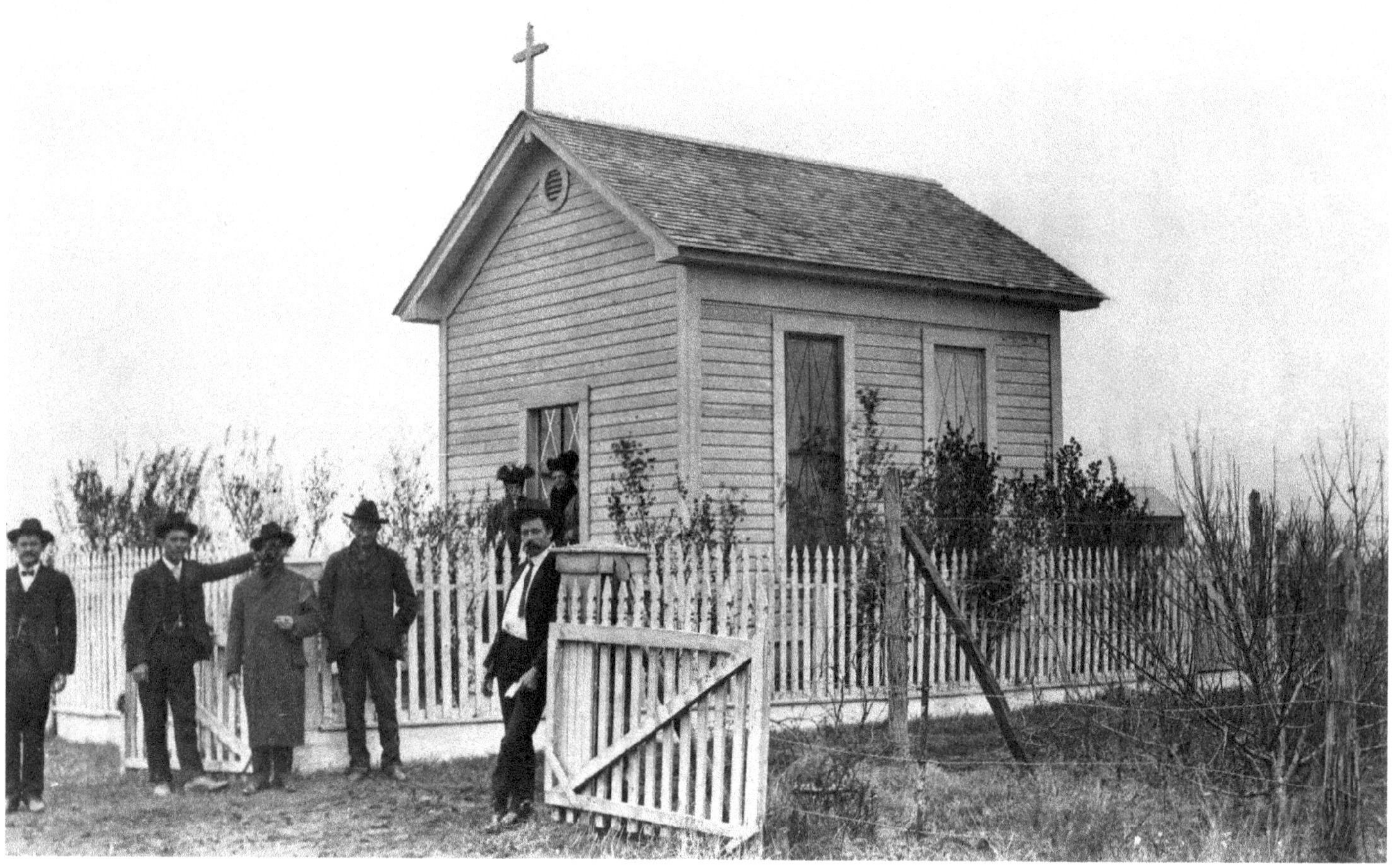

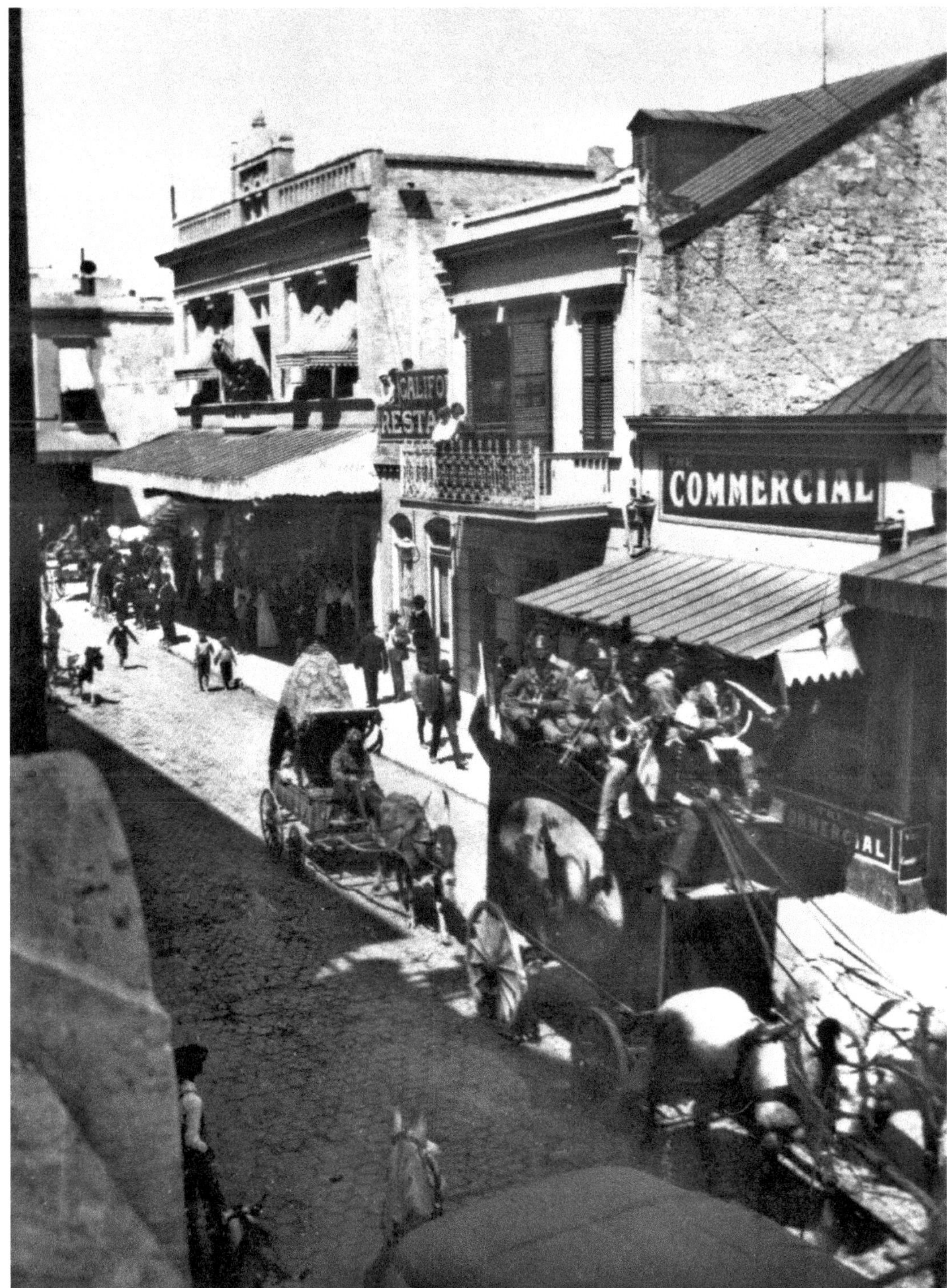

Atlee B. Ayres took this photograph from his office in the Oppenheimer Bank building on Commerce Street about 1910. People on the street watch as circus wagons rumble down the street. The building at the far back was the Sullivan Bank. The California Restaurant and surrounding buildings were replaced by the Aztec Theater.

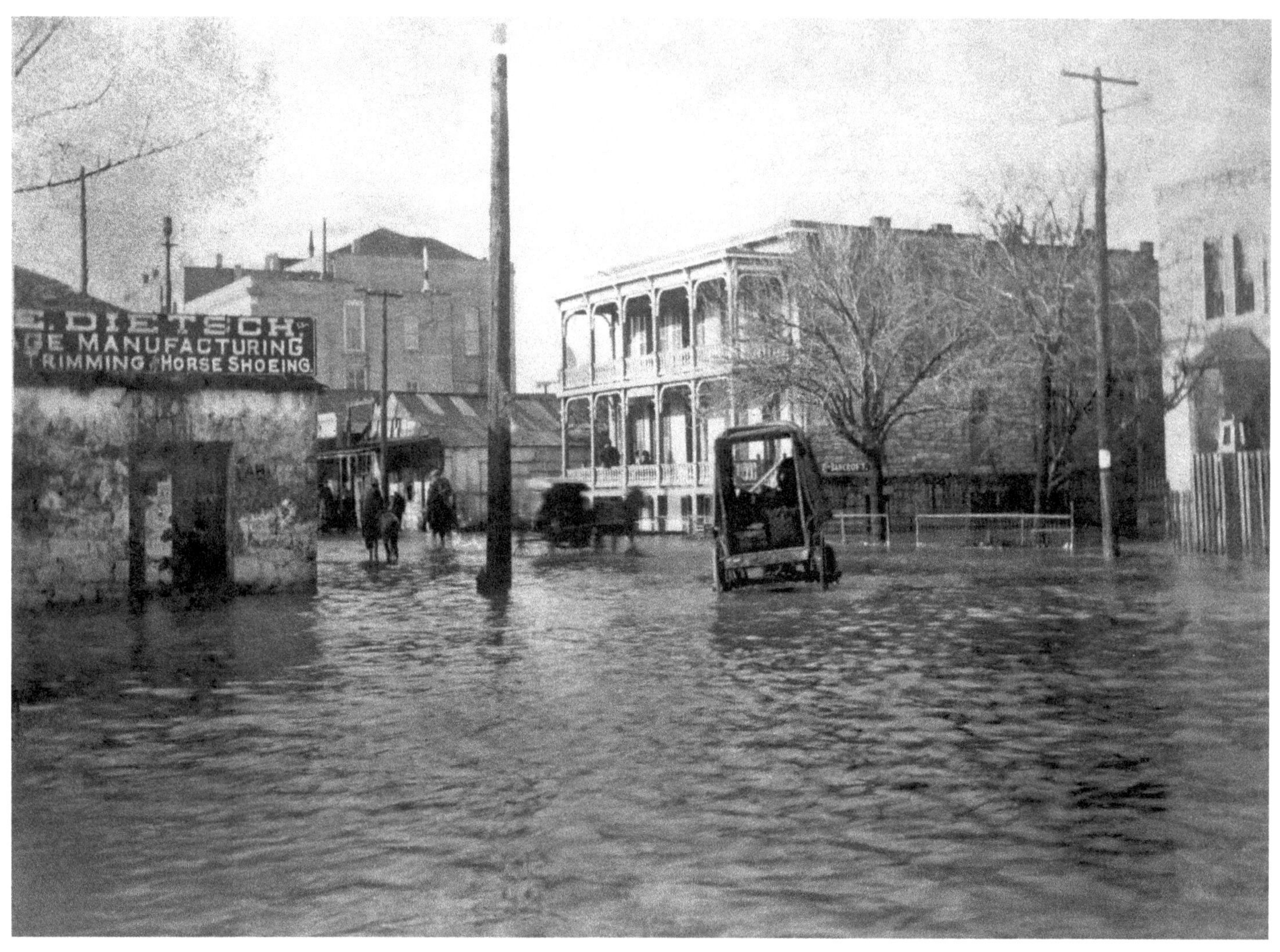

Wagons and men on horseback splash through the flood waters of 1903 at the corner of Travis (left) and St. Mary's streets. At the left is Joe F. Dietsch, blacksmith, at 326 St. Mary's Street.

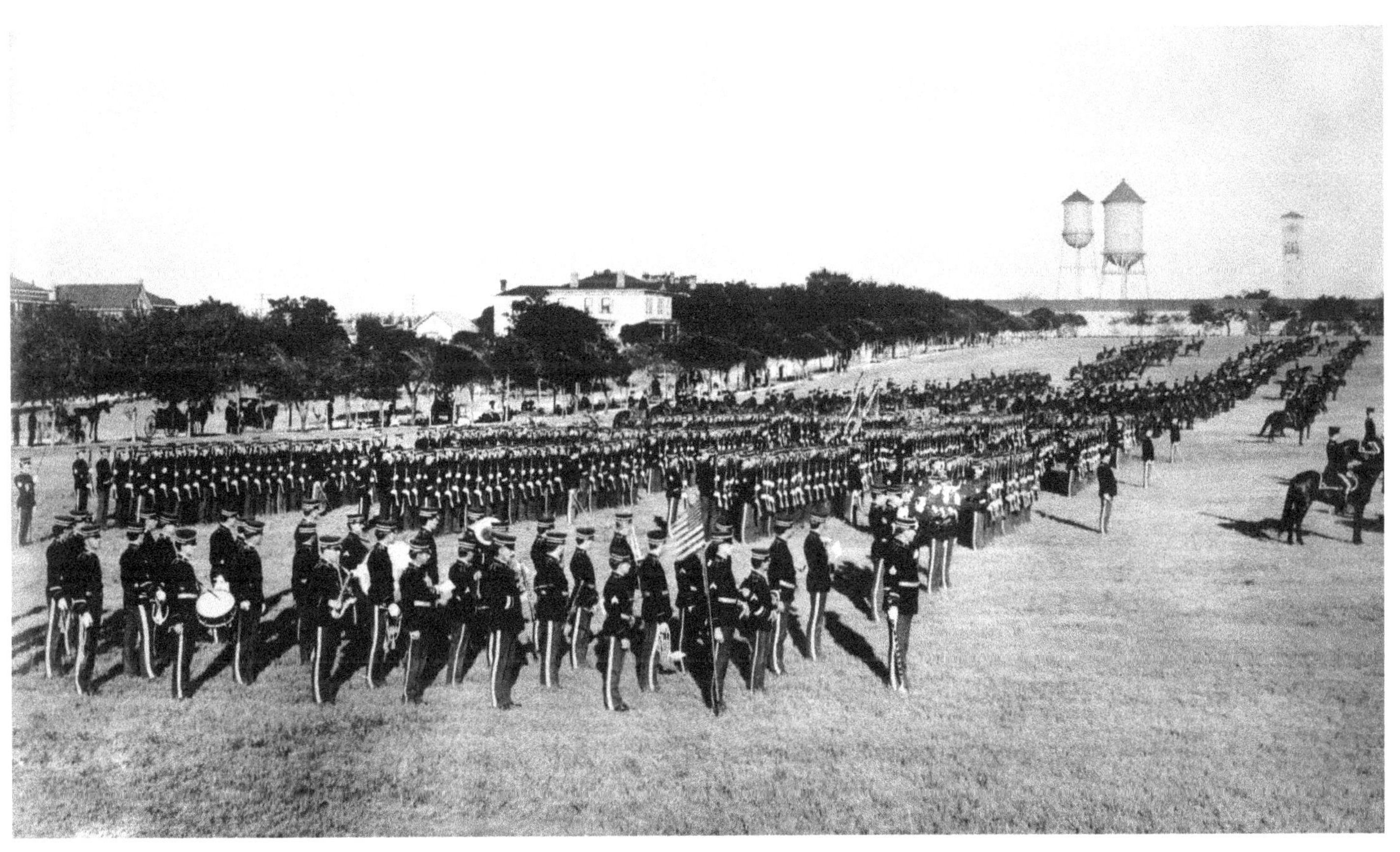

Troops on parade or "review" at Fort Sam Houston in 1906. This photograph looks southwest toward the water towers and tower clock in the distance. Visitors can be seen along the tree line.

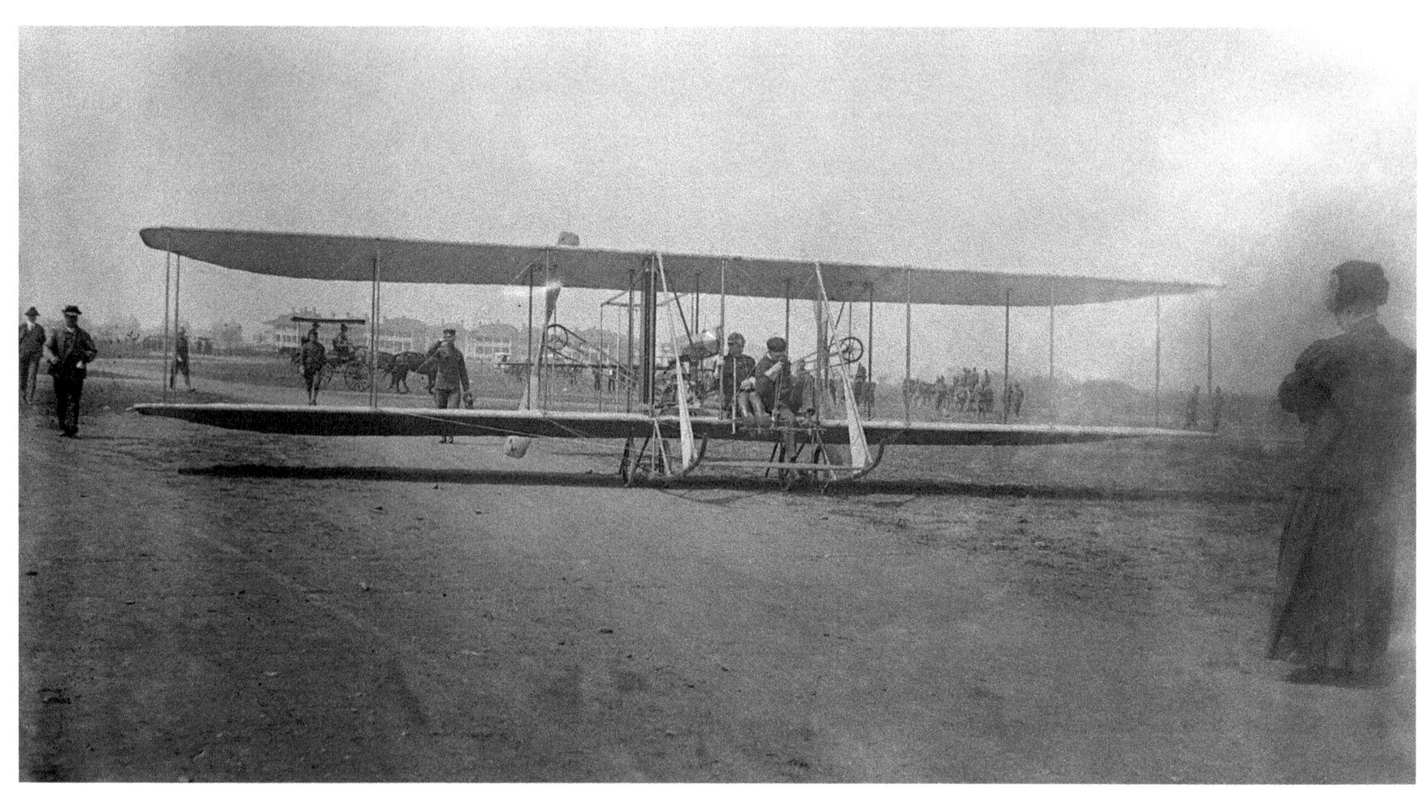

Two early aviators, possibly De Lloyd Thompson and C. M. Vought, at Fort Sam Houston. They made several exhibition flights during 1913. In 1914, it was announced that a flying school had been authorized by officials in Washington. It would consist of eight squadrons of eight airplanes each. These would be trained at the nation's first Army Flying School, Kelly Field.

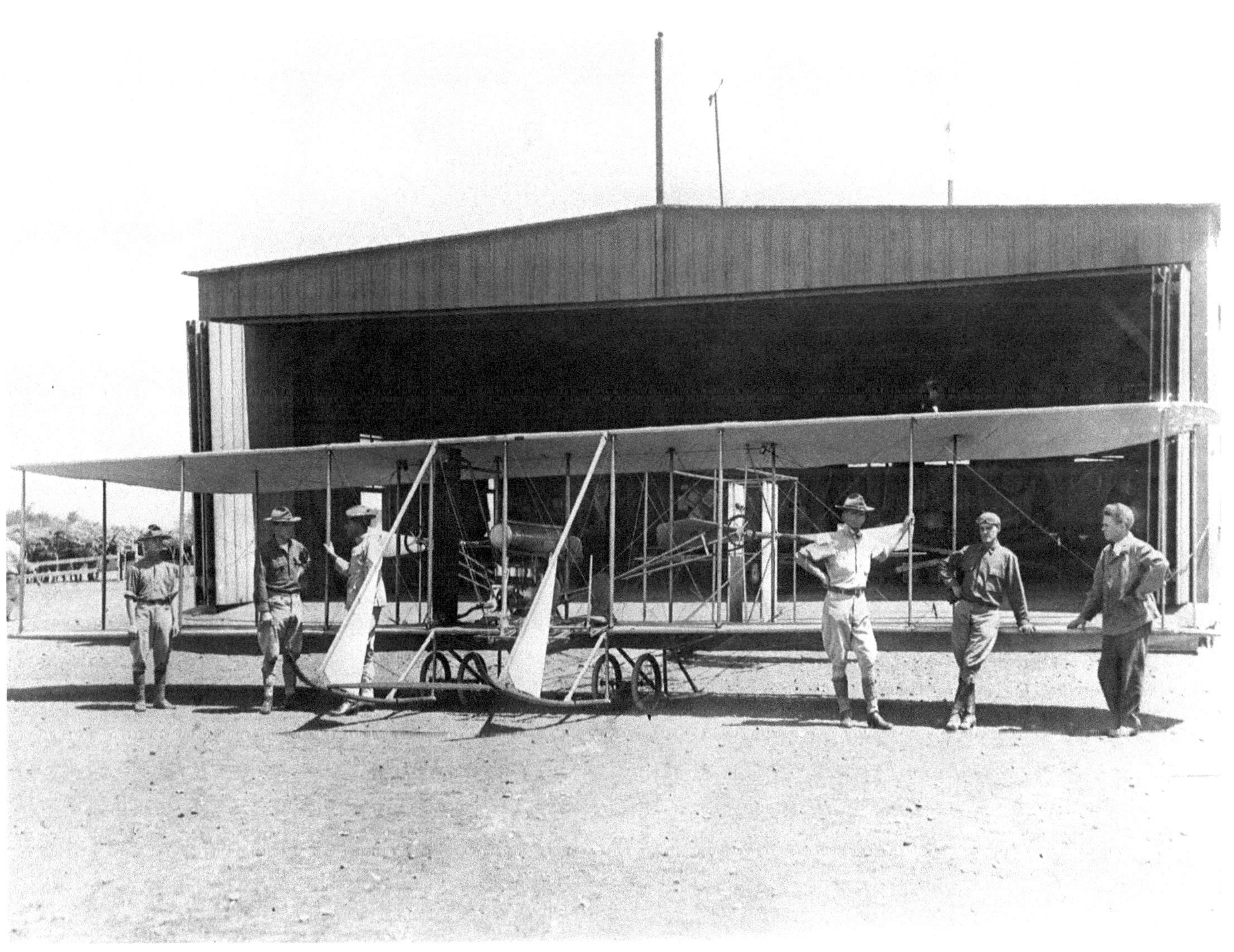

The first airplane owned by the U.S. Army, the Wright Pusher. Lieutenant Benjamin Delahauf Foulois is wearing the helmet. The plane and Foulois, named by the Army as its first pilot, arrived at Fort Sam Houston in 1910. The plane weighed 800 pounds, with a wingspan of forty feet. Army Airplane No. 1 took off on March 2 at fifty miles an hour and rose to one hundred feet. Foulois claimed he was a "mail-order pilot," who received his only flying instructions in letters from the Wright Brothers.

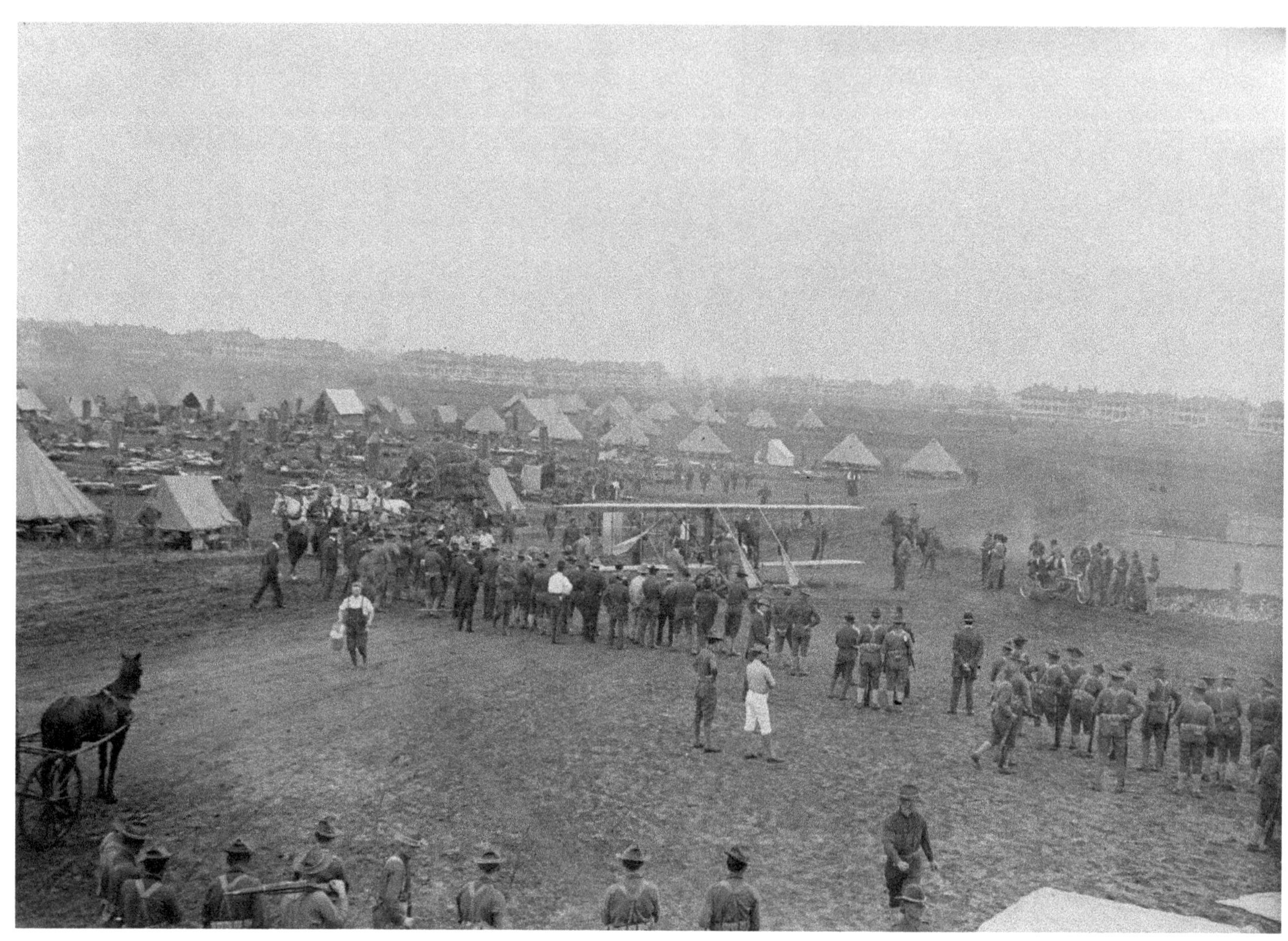

Another view of air training at Fort Sam Houston. In 1916 the entire United States Army Air Corps of six airplanes took part in the United States invasion of Mexico. They served primarily a reconnaissance mission in efforts to capture Pancho Villa.

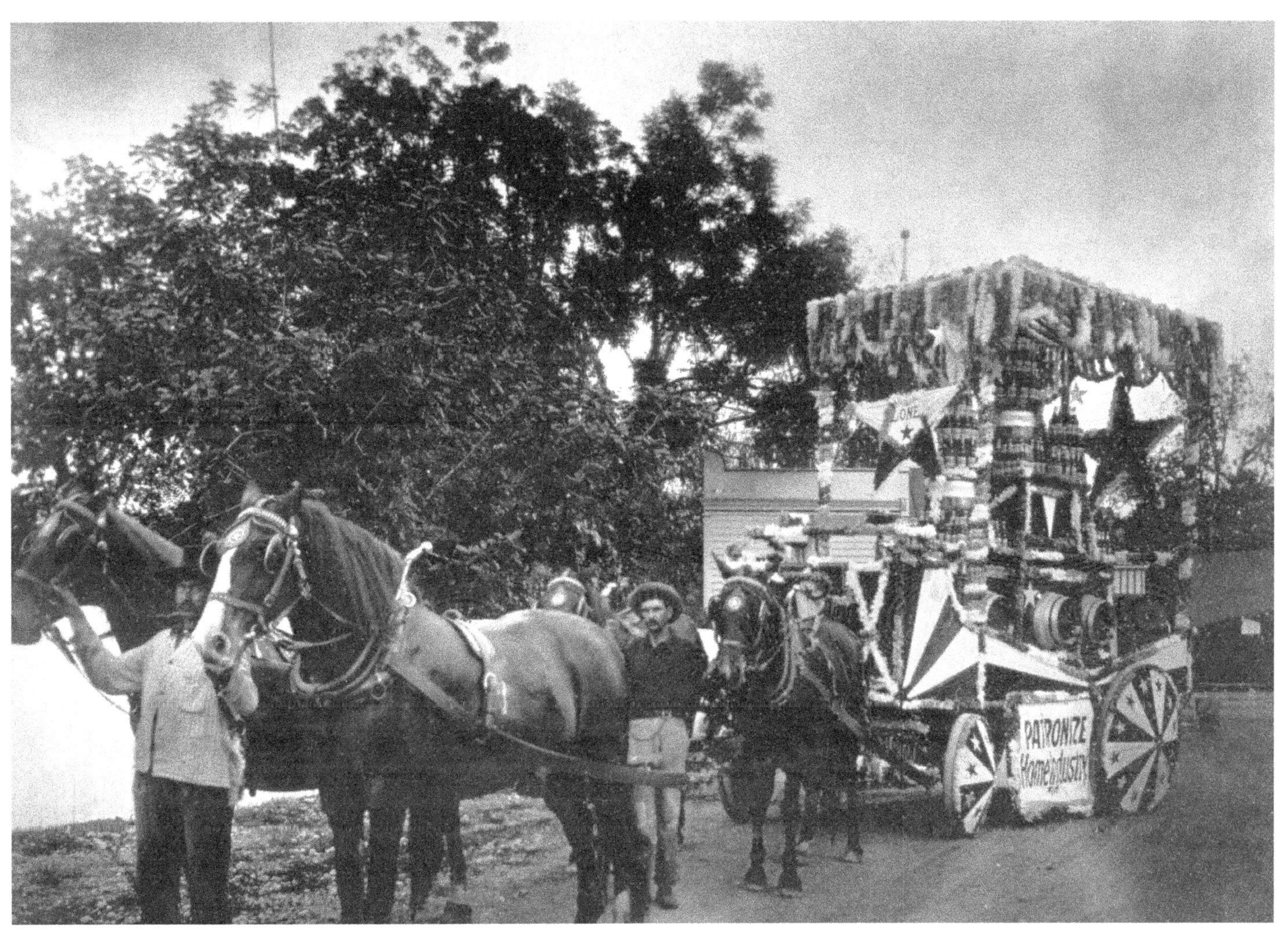

The Lone Star Brewing Company's float in the 1906 Trades Parade, part of Fiesta San Jacinto. The sign on the wagon reads "Patronize Home Industry."

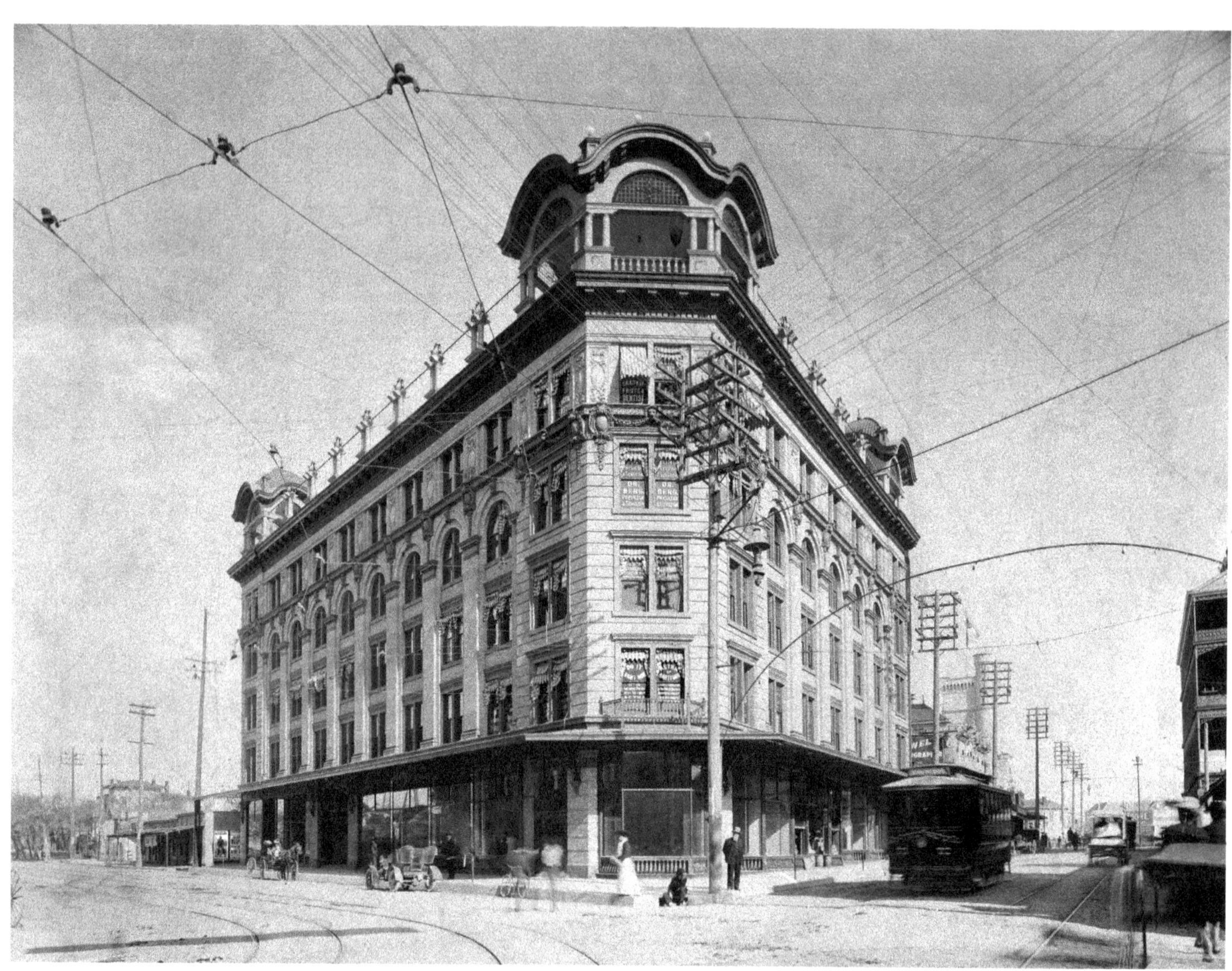

The Moore Building designed by Atlee B. Ayres and C. A. Coughlin was the first large fireproof building with a roof garden. Houston Street is on the right and Broadway on the left. In this photo taken about 1904, a sign in the second-floor window says, "Do It Right Now," get an accident insurance policy from Aetna of Hartford. The floor above has the life insurance office of K. J. Kinhair, and Dr. Berg, physician and surgeon, was on the fourth floor. The auto in the photograph was the eighth car in San Antonio.

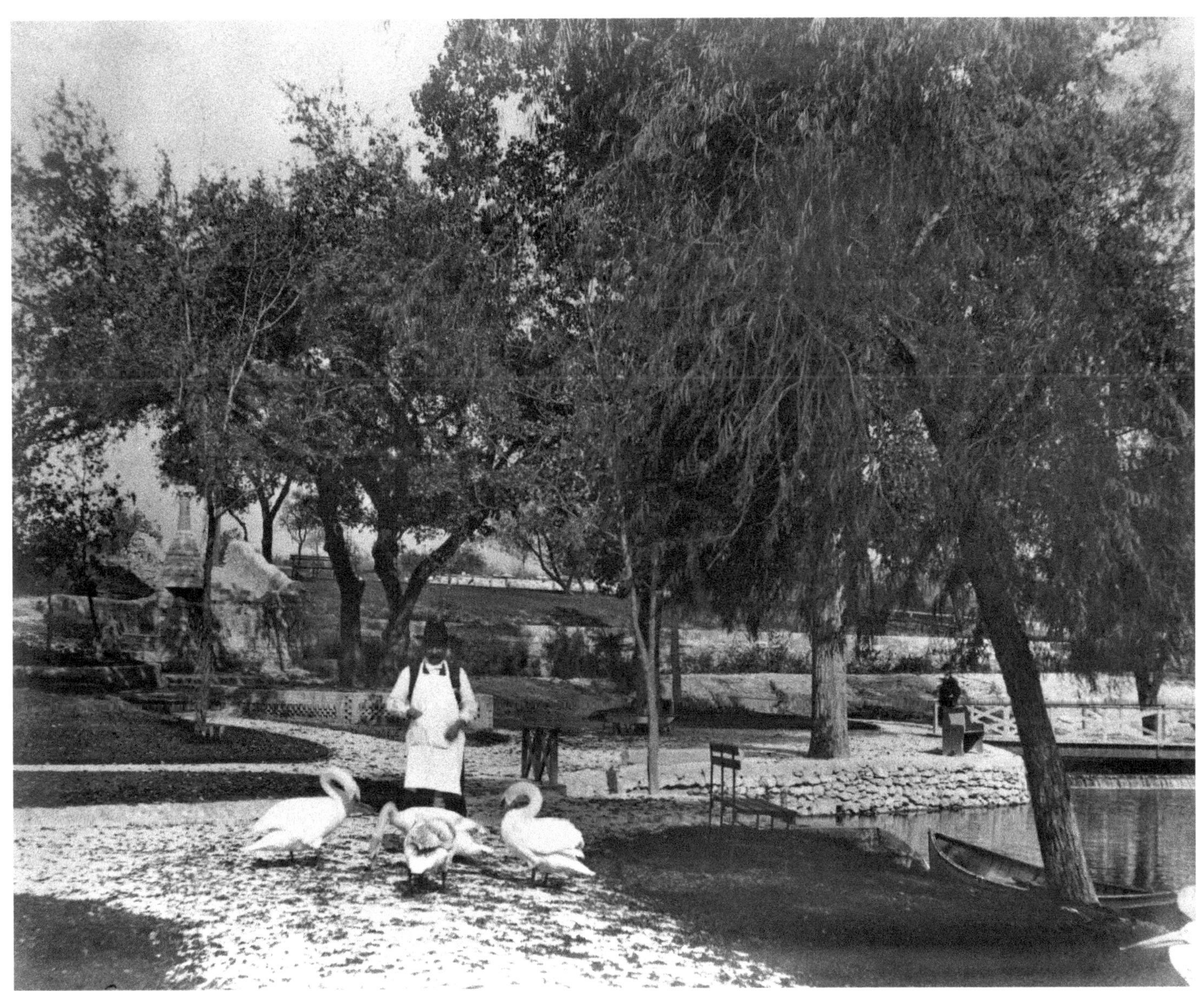

A view of San Pedro Park as a man feeds swans, taken about 1902.

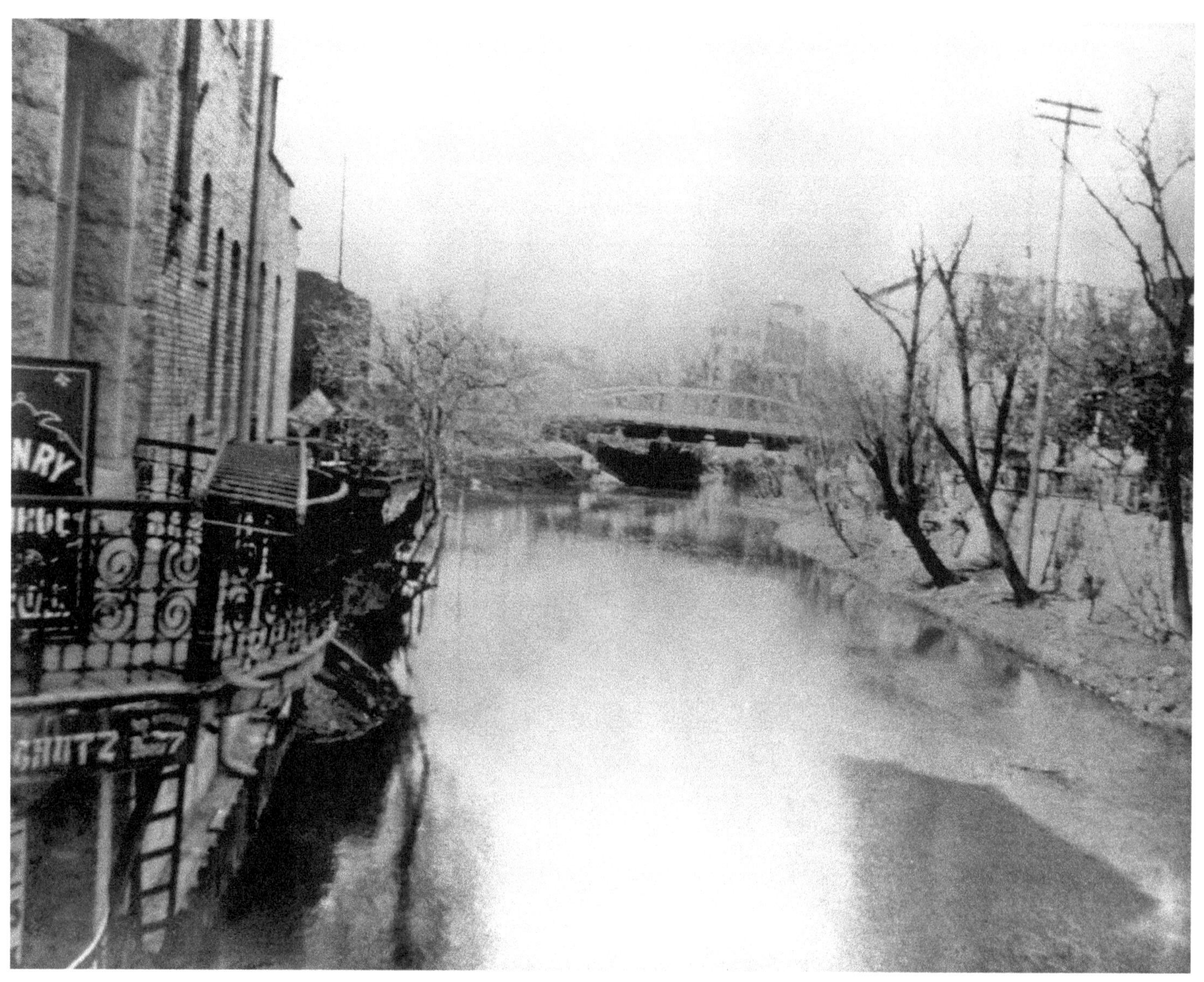

Looking upstream on the San Antonio River from the Commerce Street Bridge toward the Crockett Street Bridge. This 1901 or 1902 picture shows a river side far different from today's River Walk.

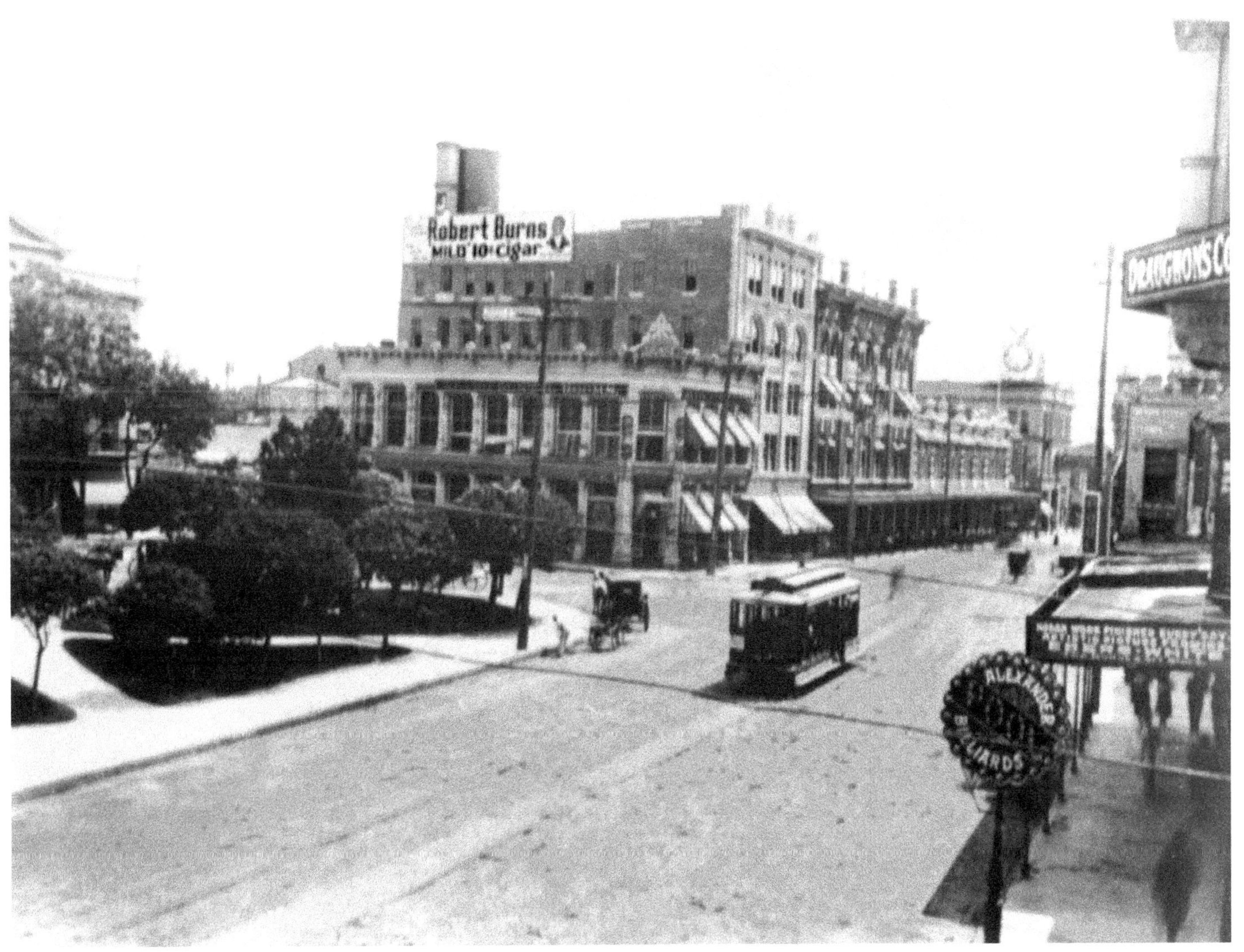

The southwest corner of Alamo Plaza. A streetcar is heading north on a wide Alamo Street. The first building on the left, past the park area, is Joske Bros. Department Store. It later moved to the south end of the same block where it was a long-time fixture.

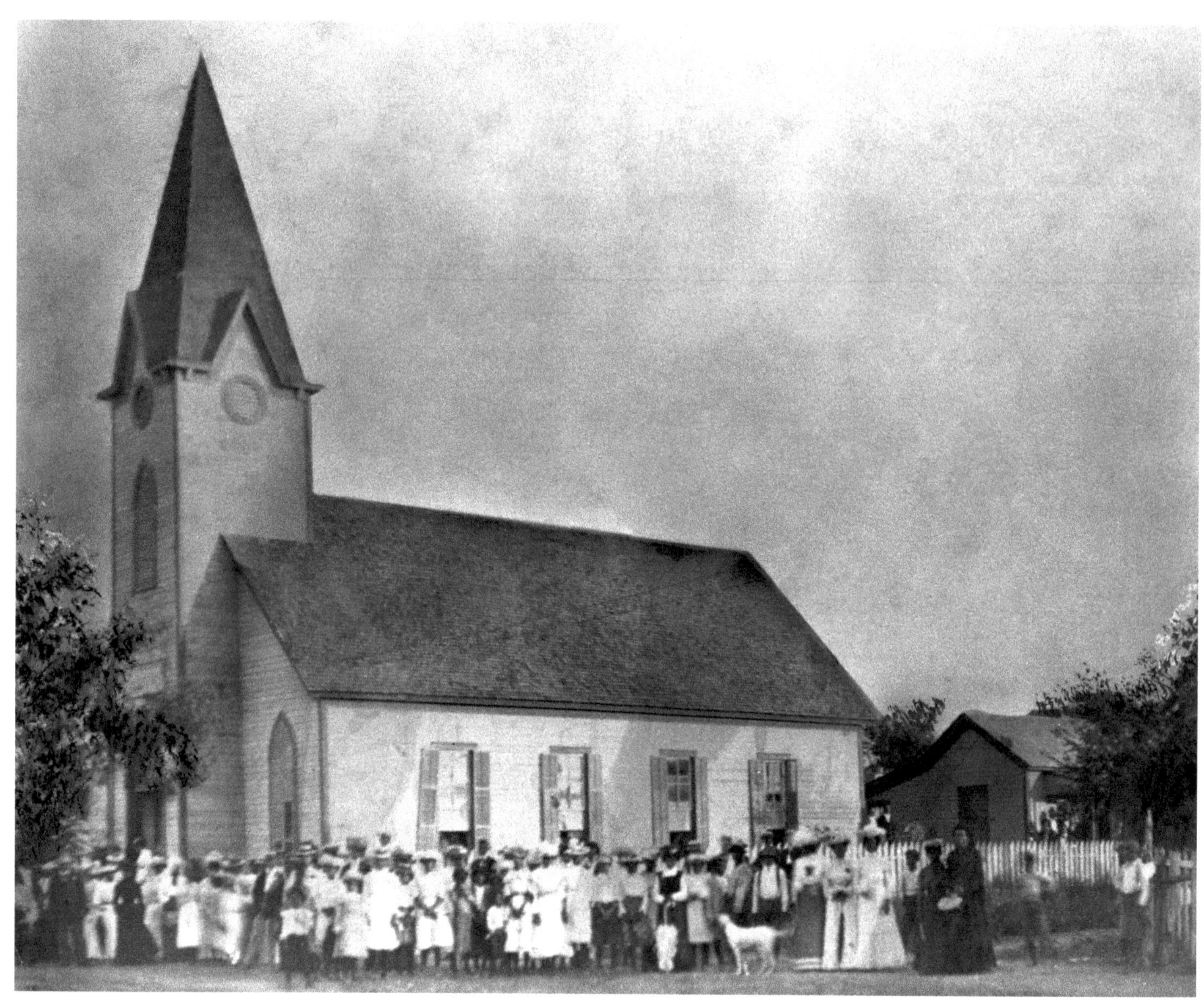

Congregation is posed outside Mount Zion Baptist Church at 210 Santos Street. Mount Zion has had to rebuild its church three times over its lifetime. The first church was built in 1871 and destroyed by flooding in 1886. The second and third were destroyed by fire in 1890 and 1974. Despite this, the church has remained a vibrant part of the community.

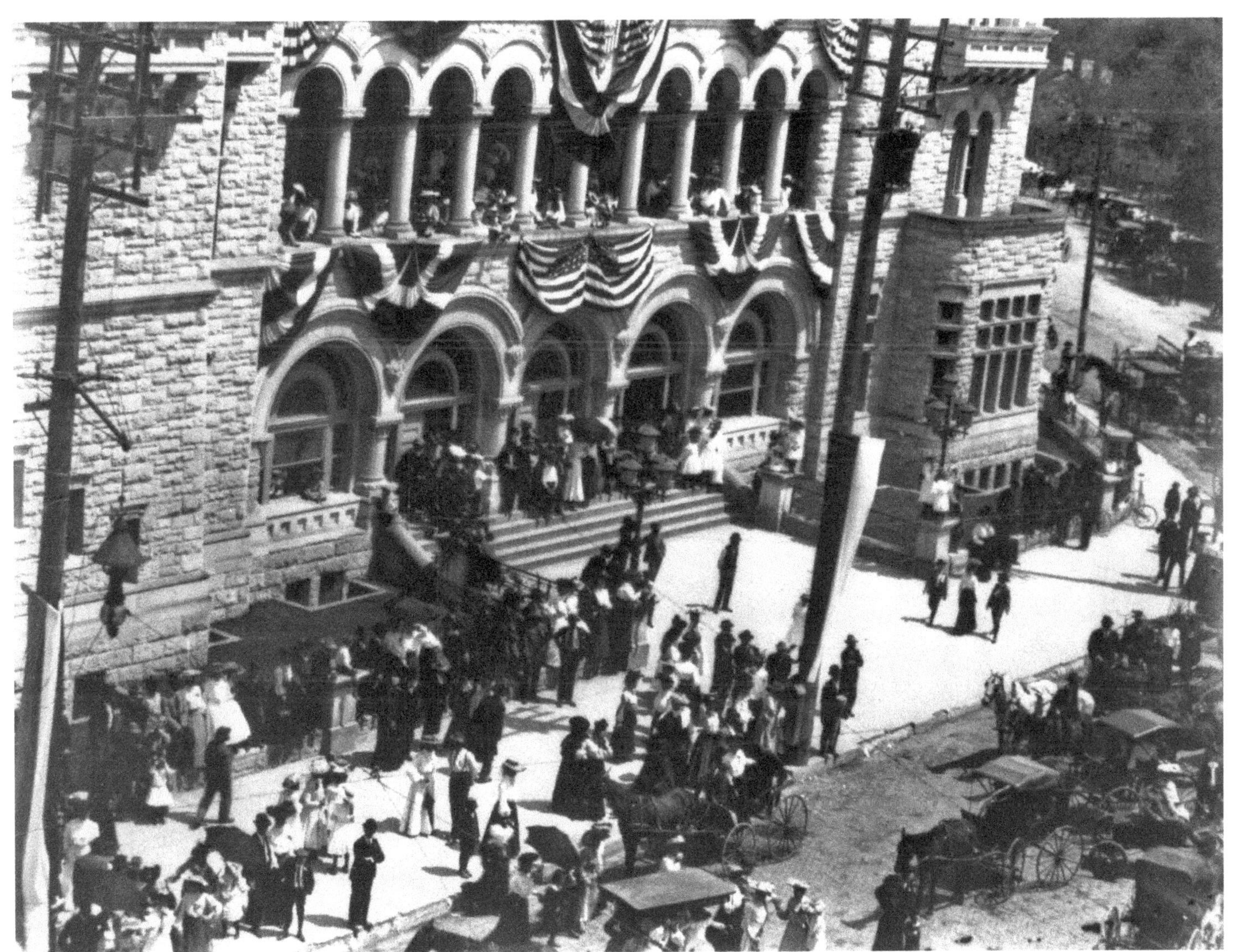

This photograph, taken from the Maverick Bank building, shows crowds gathered at the post office for some auspicious event in the early 1900s.

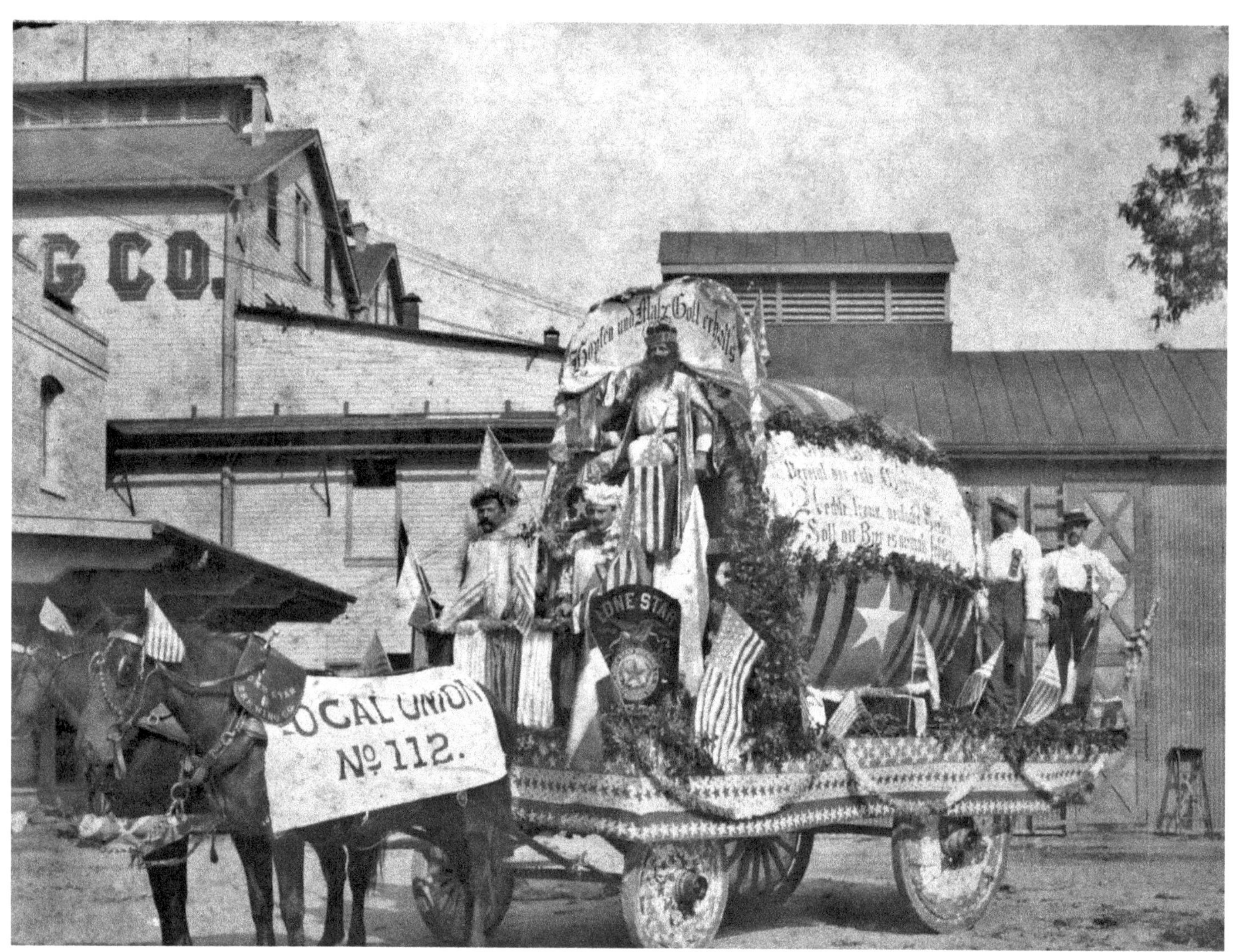

Horse-drawn float, perhaps for Fiesta, for "Local Union No. 112." This was the United Brewery Workmen's Union, which met on the first and third Saturday nights of each month at the Trades Council Hall, 114 ½ South Alamo Street, at 8:00 p.m. The flags on the float are American, but the signs are in German, reflecting the continuing influence of German settlement in San Antonio.

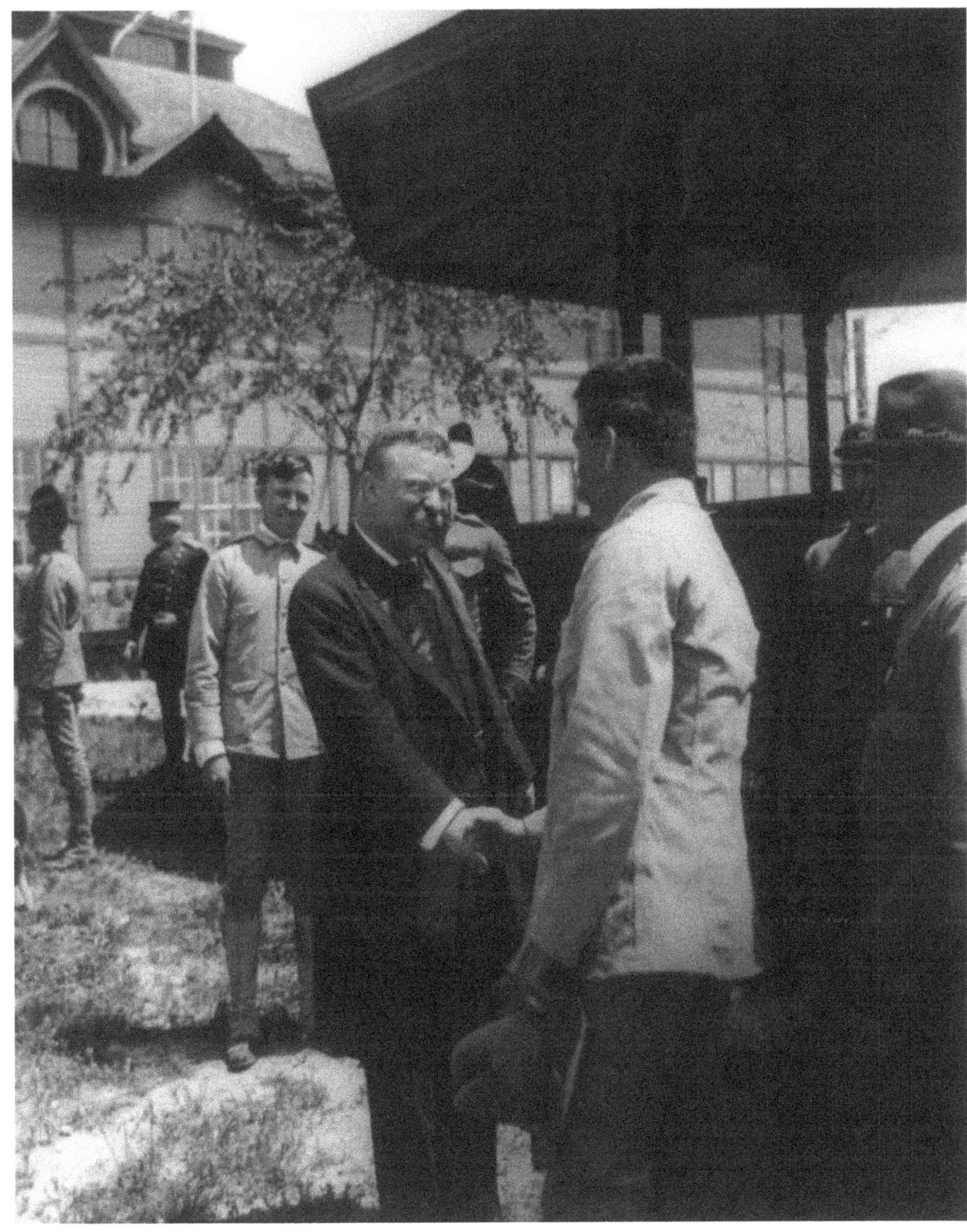

President Theodore Roosevelt visited San Antonio in April 1905. Twenty-five Sibley conical tents, each holding eight cots, were set up for the reunion of Roosevelt and his Rough Riders at the International Fair Grounds, then about three miles south of town. Roosevelt stayed in an officer's tent furnished exactly as it had been in 1898 when he and his men trained nearby for the Spanish-American War. The building in the background is the Exposition Building.

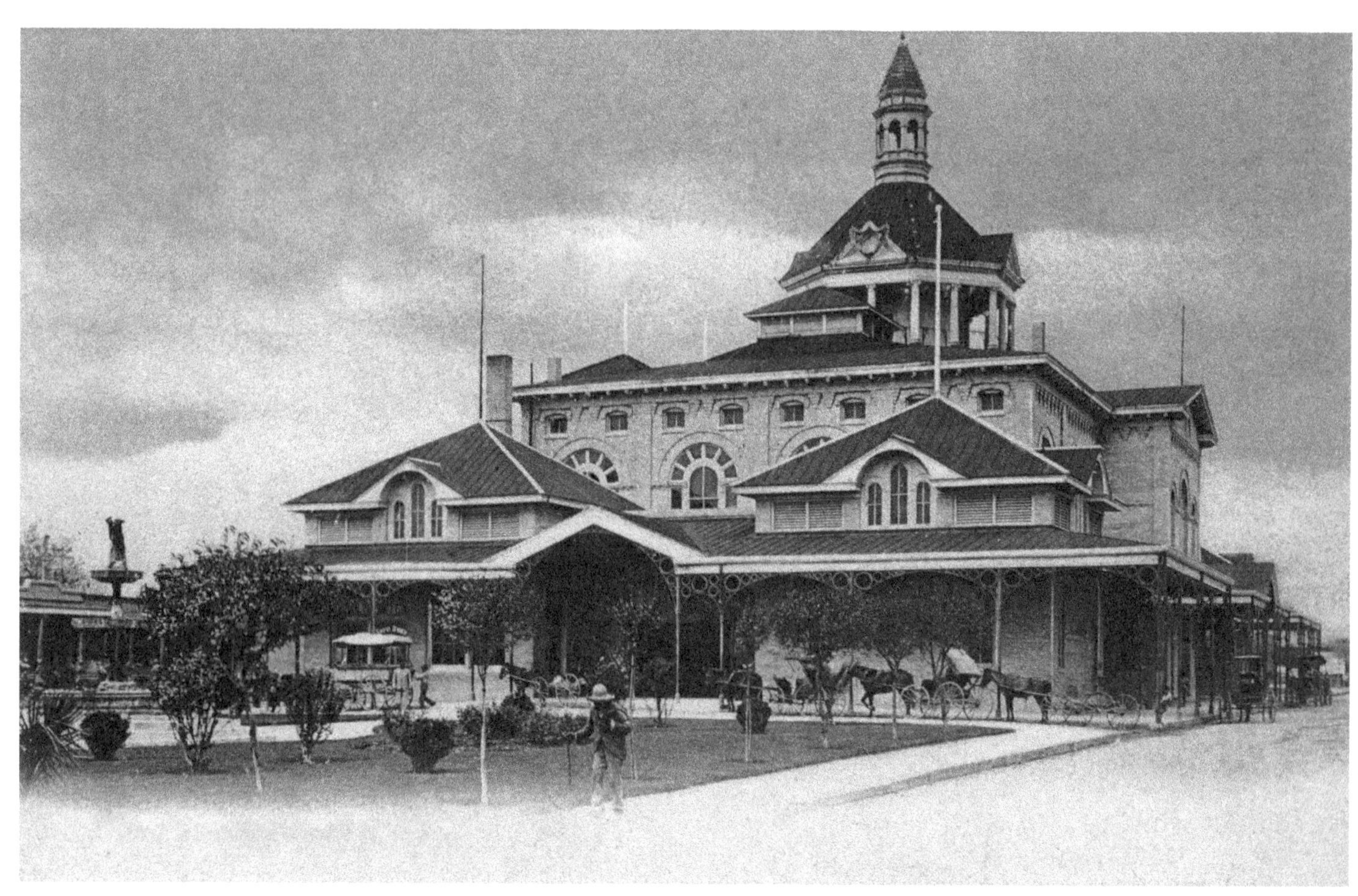

The City Market designed by Alfred Giles, after the previous one had fallen into disrepair. It was completed in December 1900 at a cost of $45,000. The second floor was used as an auditorium. It was later demolished and a new market house constructed on the same site in 1938.

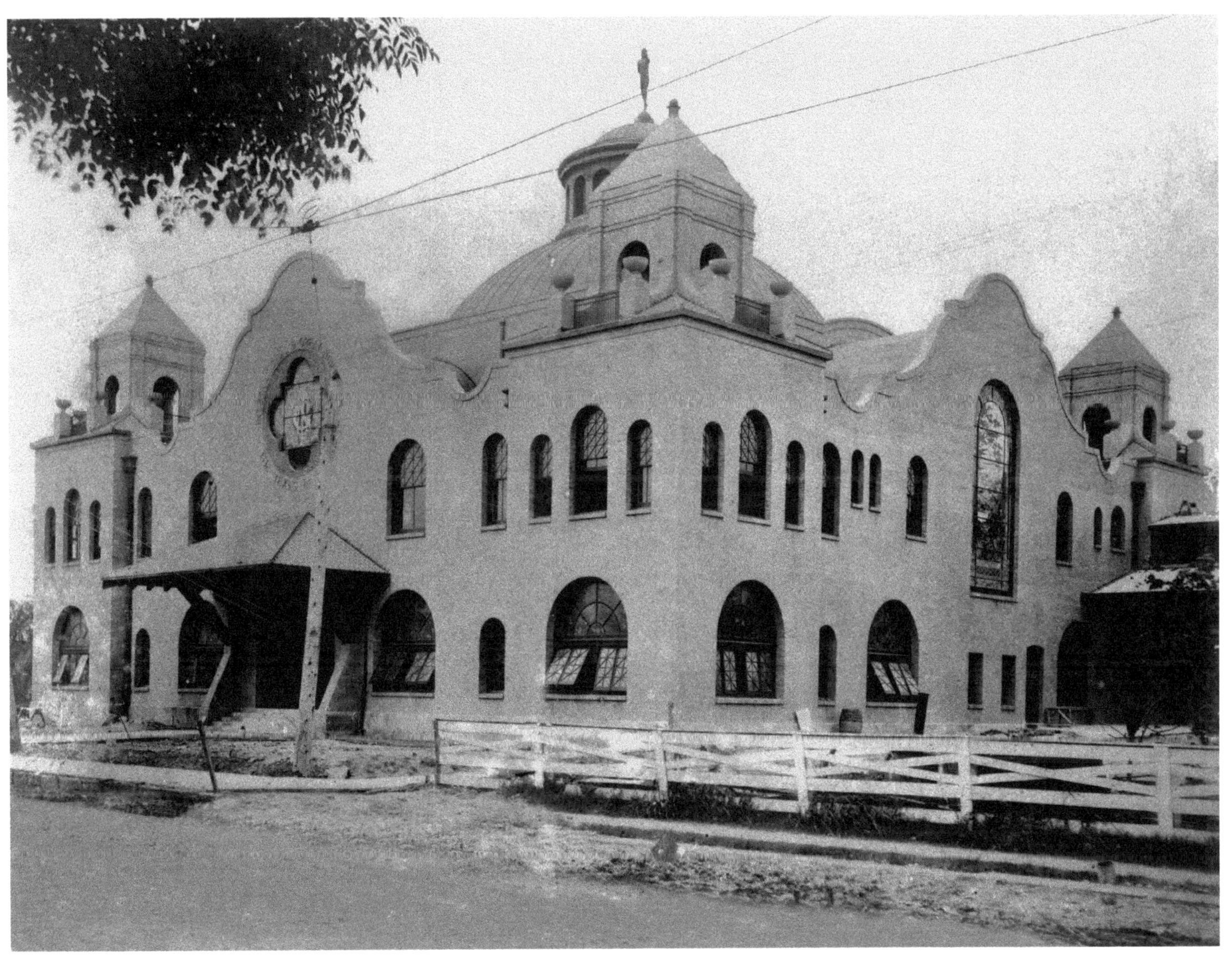

Passenger station for the International and Great Northern Railroad, listed at 1521 W. Commerce Street when this photograph was taken on June 8, 1908. The architect was Harvey L. Page. The building is now the San Antonio City Employees Federal Credit Union.

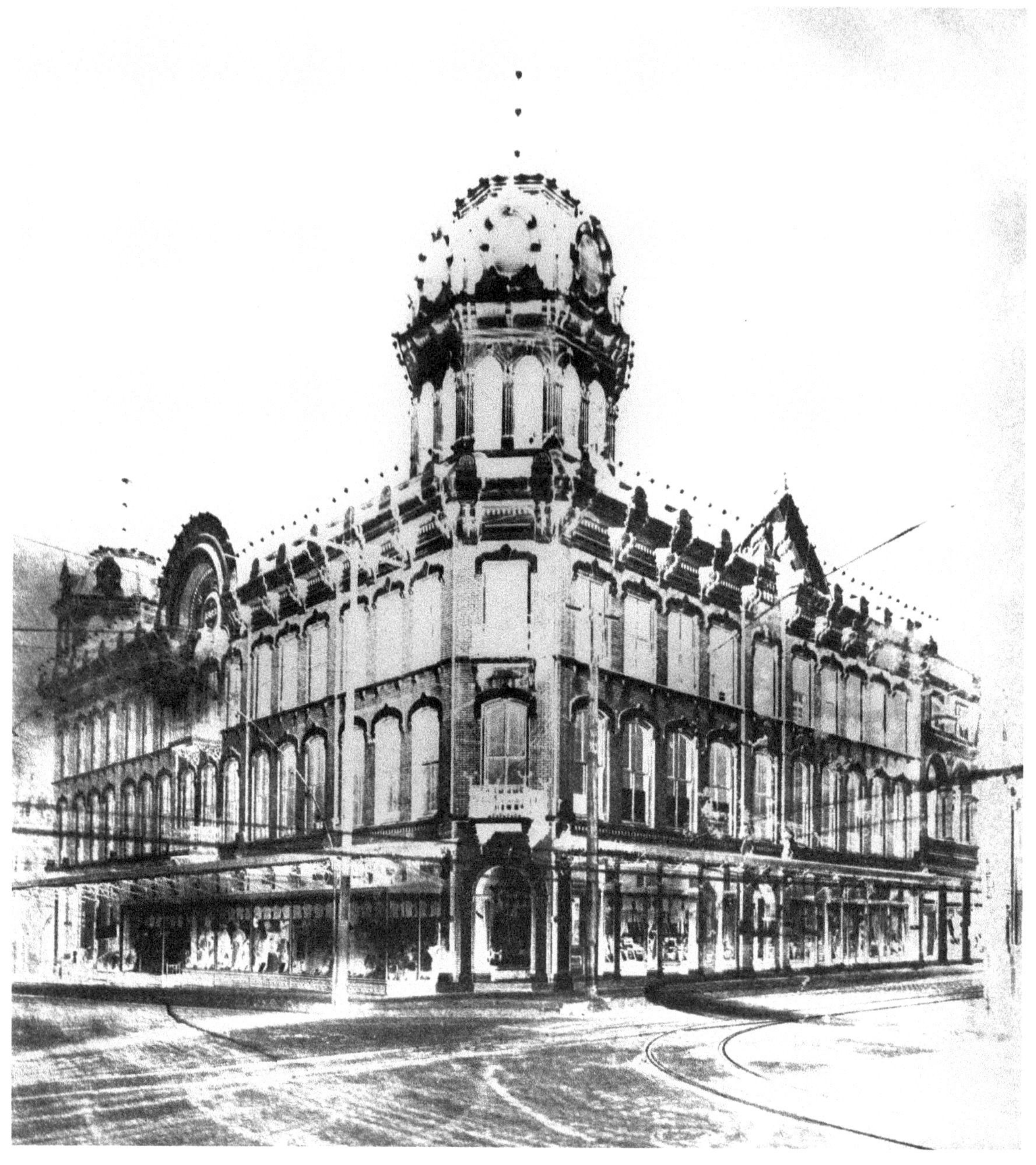

Architect James Murphy designed this three-story, red brick building for George Dullnig, local wholesale/retail grocer. Erected in 1883, it had one of the city's first elevators and steam heating systems. Originally incorporating Victorian, Italianate, and Gothic Revival styles, the building has been altered many times.

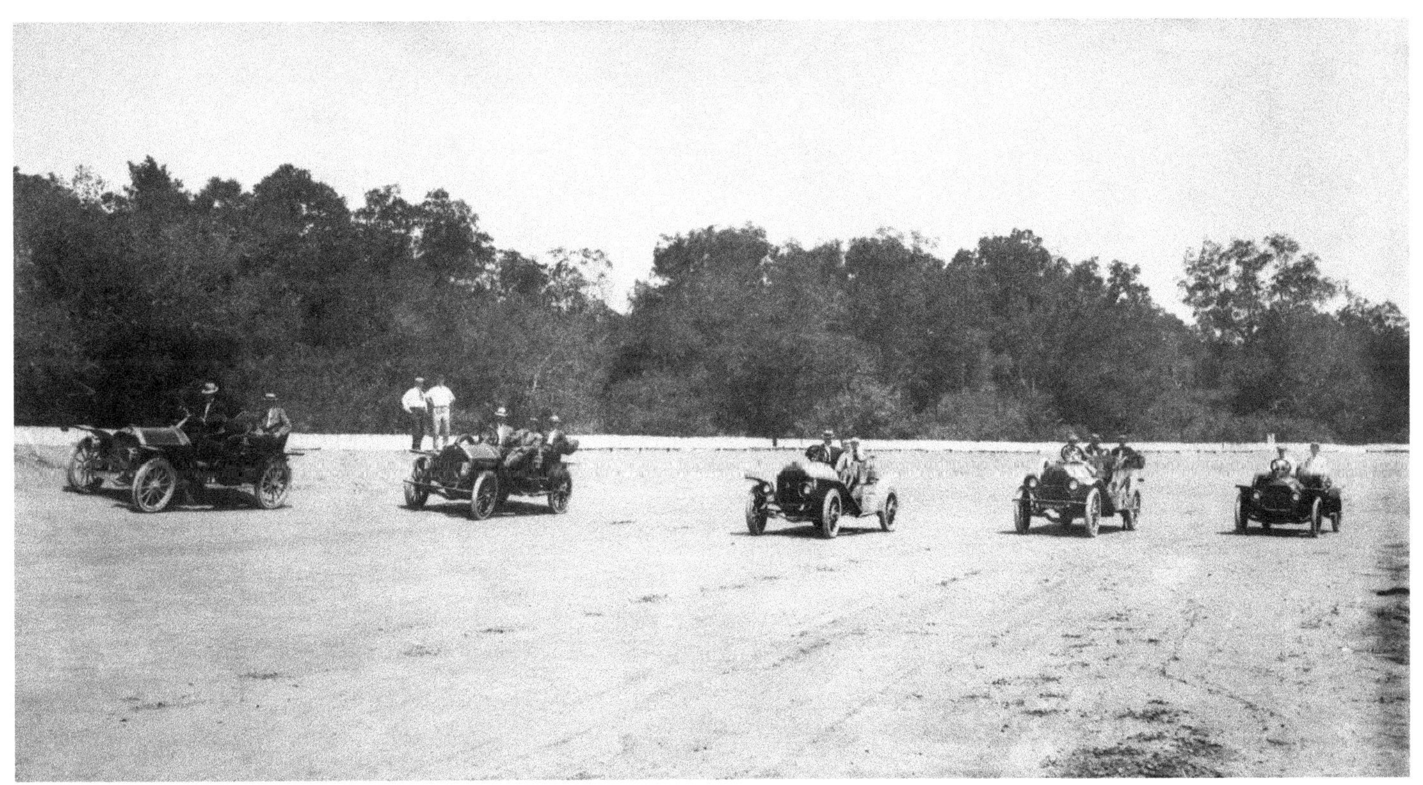

Automobiles lined up for a Sunday morning meet about 1906, including those of Atlee B. Ayres and his sons, Robert (left) and Atlee T. (third car from the left). The Ayres were prominent architects in the city.

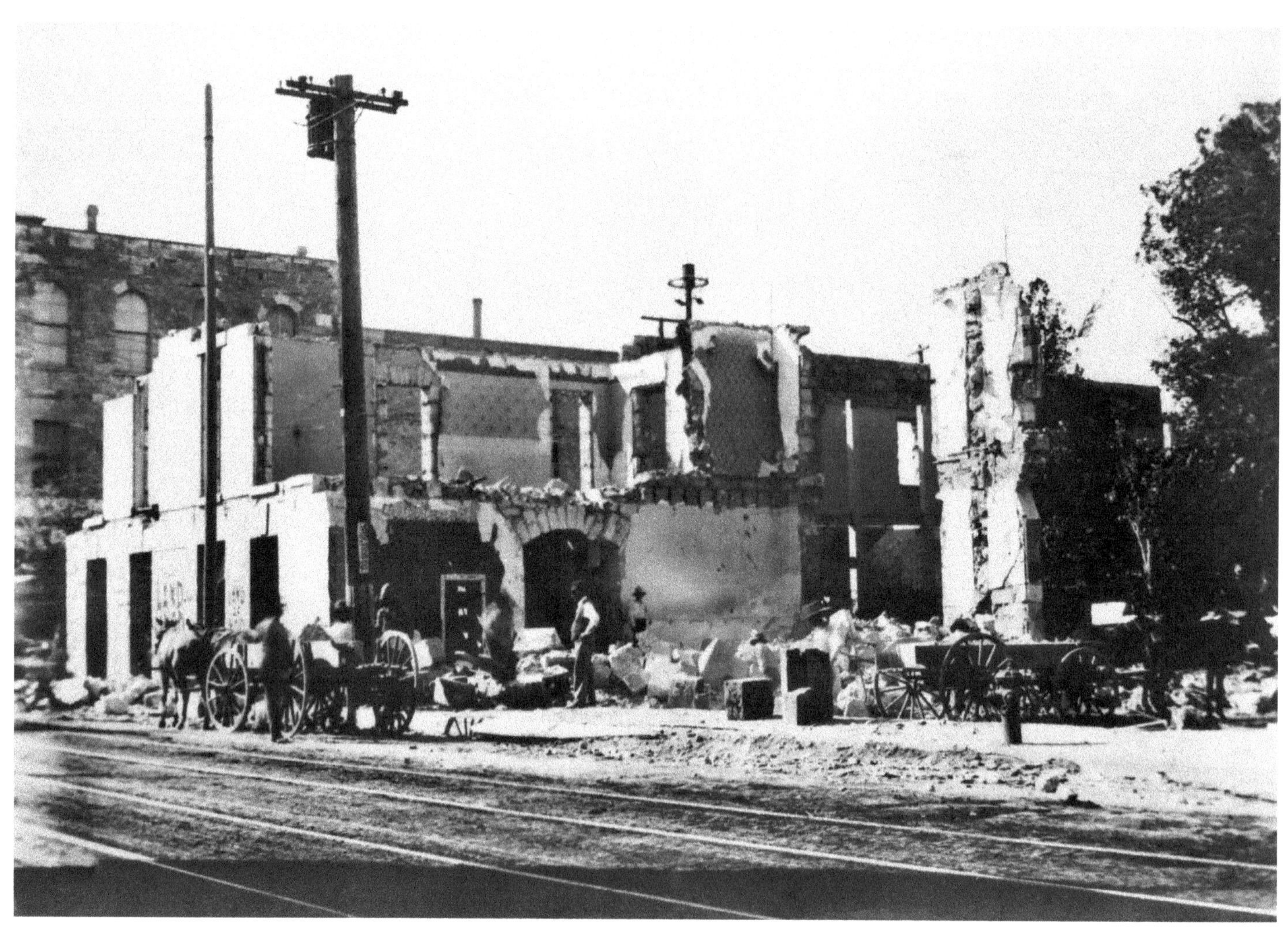

Demolition of the Mahncke Hotel on Houston Street in 1907. The limestone structure was formerly the Vance Building, and the later site of the Gunter Hotel.

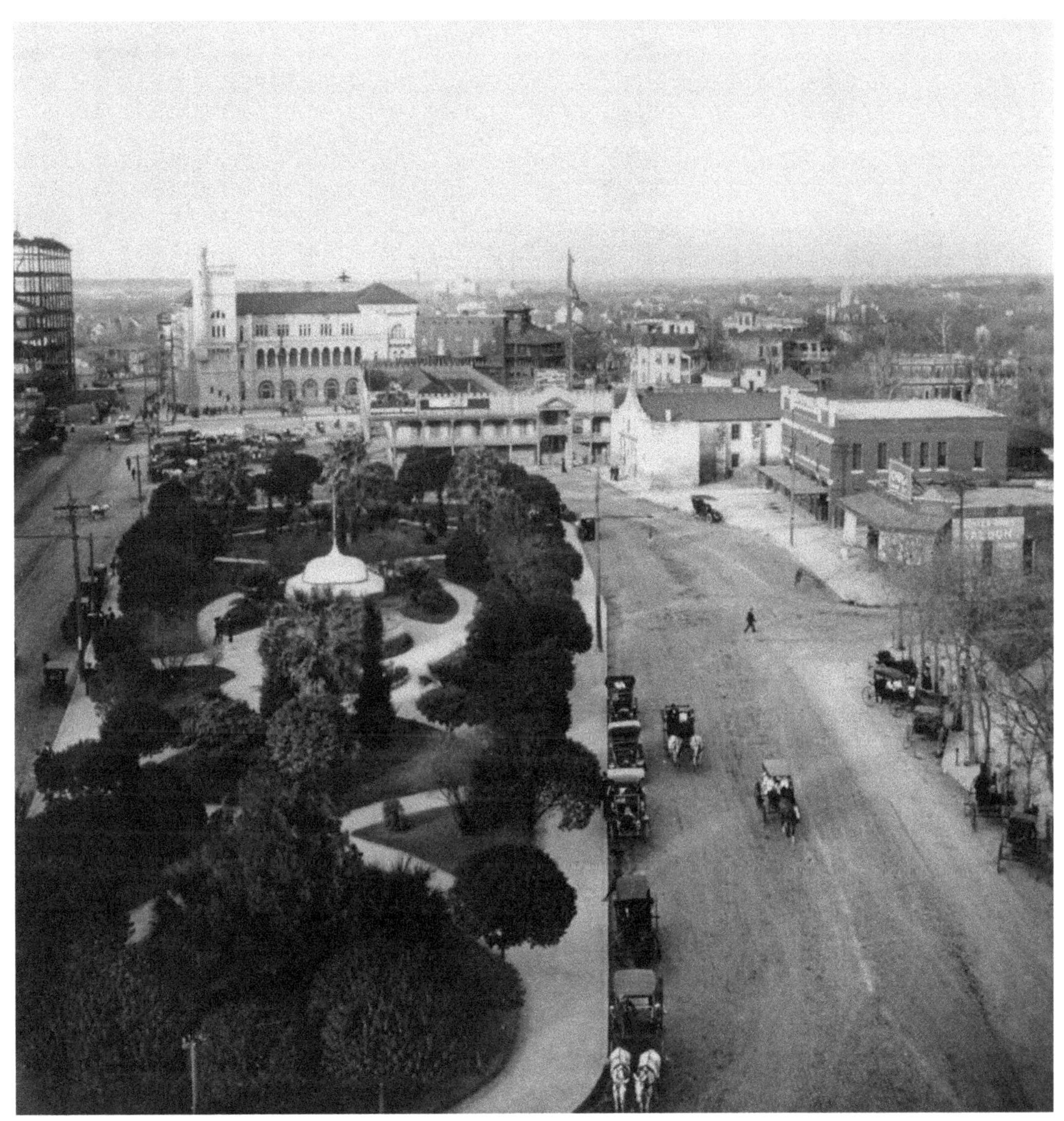

Alamo Plaza in the early 1900s, a beautiful garden area with a bandstand in its center. Beyond the plaza stands the Federal Building.

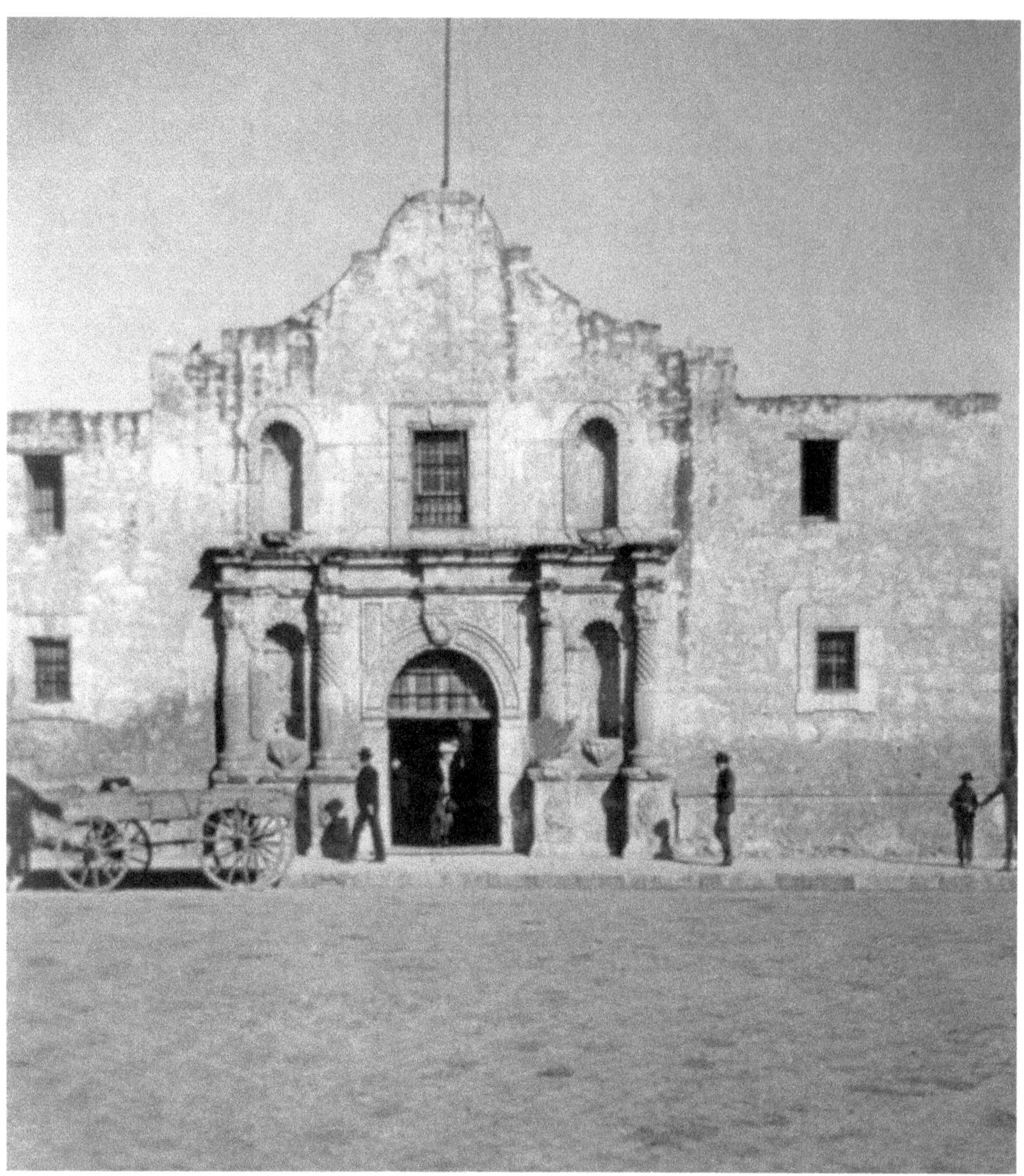

A 1909 view of the front of the Alamo, hardly the tourist attraction of today. In 1883, Texas purchased it from the Catholic Church and placed it in the custody of the City of San Antonio, but little was done with it. In 1905, the Texas Legislature placed the Daughters of the Republic of Texas in charge of the state's most famous building.

During the day, Commerce Street was one of the busiest in town, but night was very different, even though Commerce and other streets were well lit with these electric-light arches.

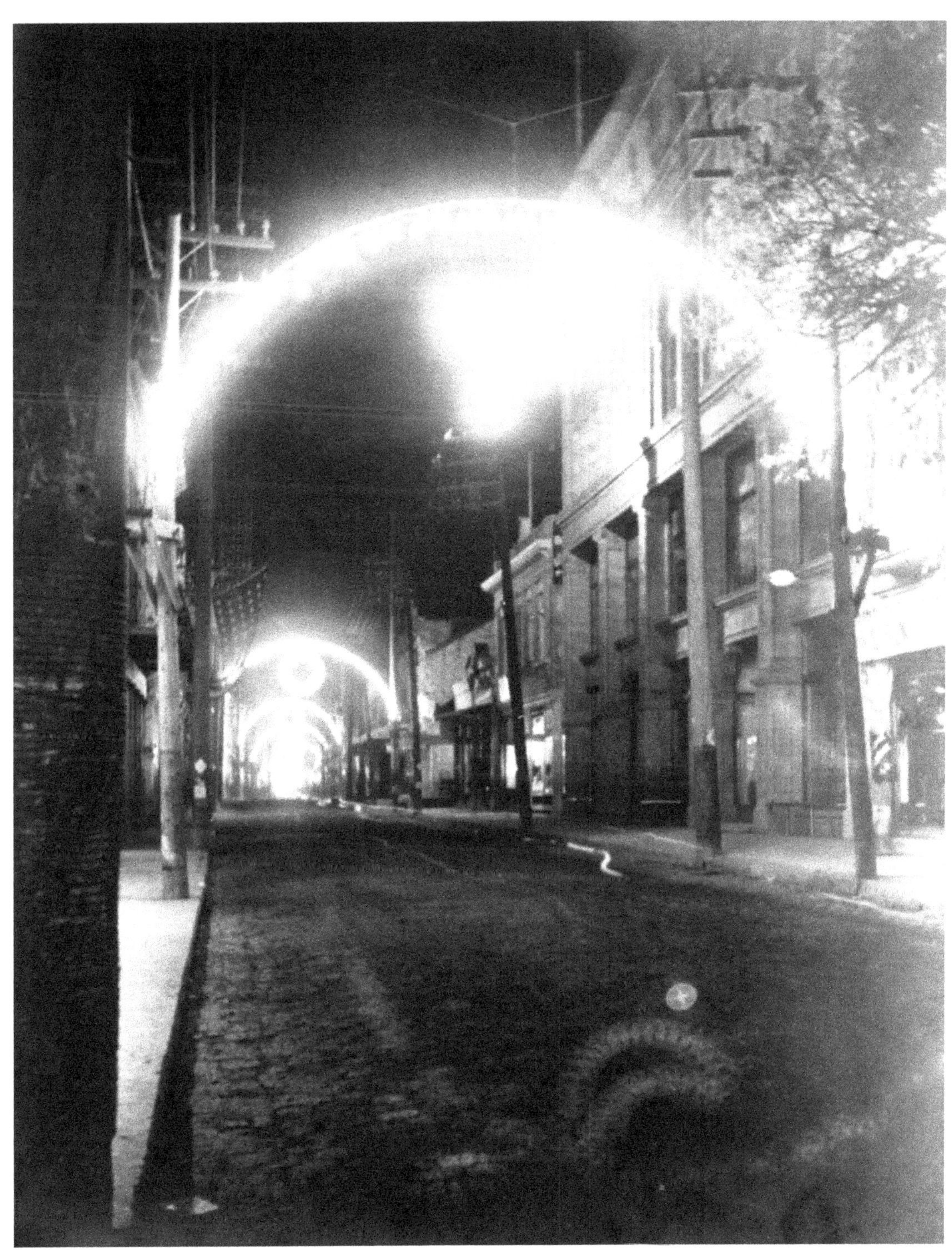

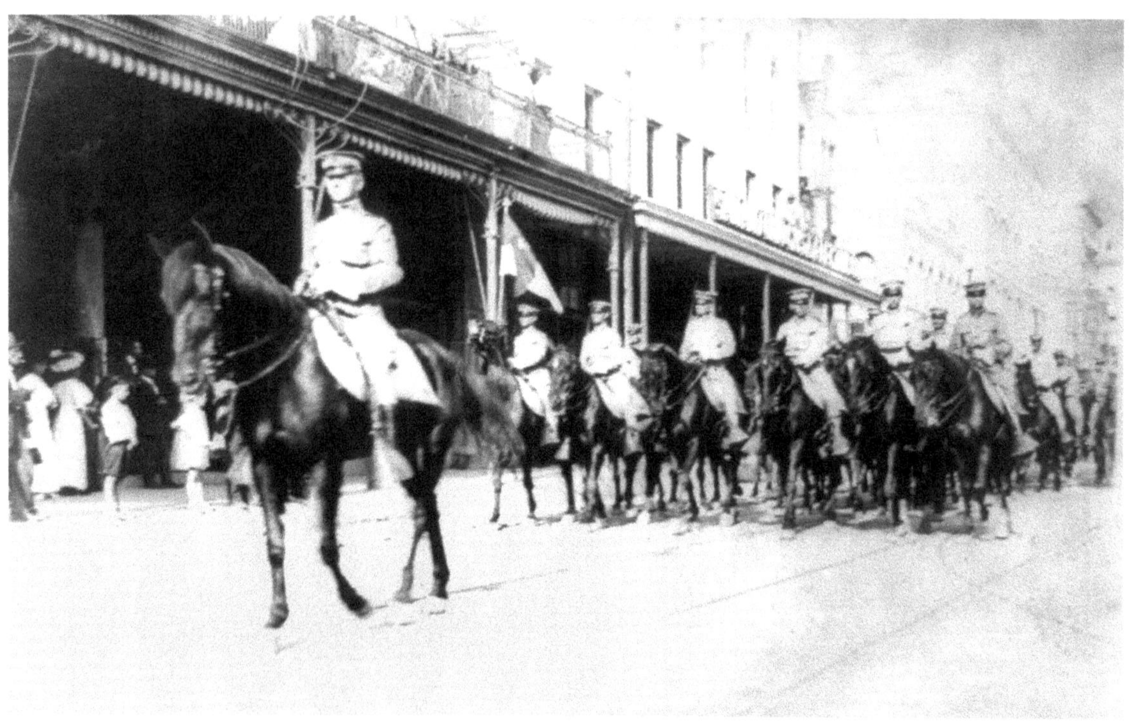

With unrest and revolution in Mexico, the United States Army held maneuvers in Texas. This photograph shows elements of the 17th Infantry arriving on horseback in San Antonio on March 14, 1911.

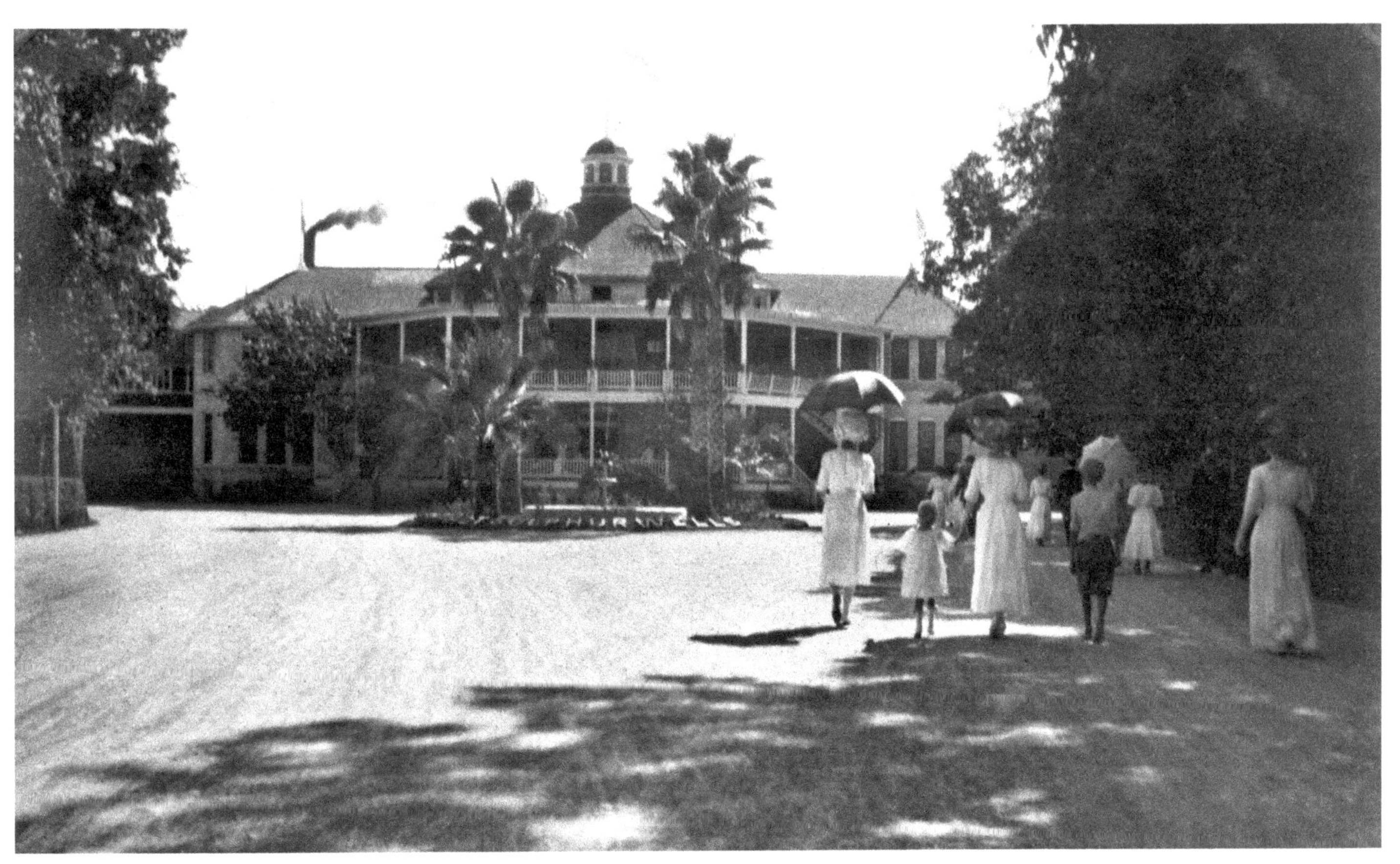

A group walking towards the bath house at Hot Sulphur Wells about 1911. Sitting on about thirty acres, this health resort acquired world-wide fame for its healing hot sulphur waters. Its daily output was about 30,000 gallons with a temperature of 104 degrees.

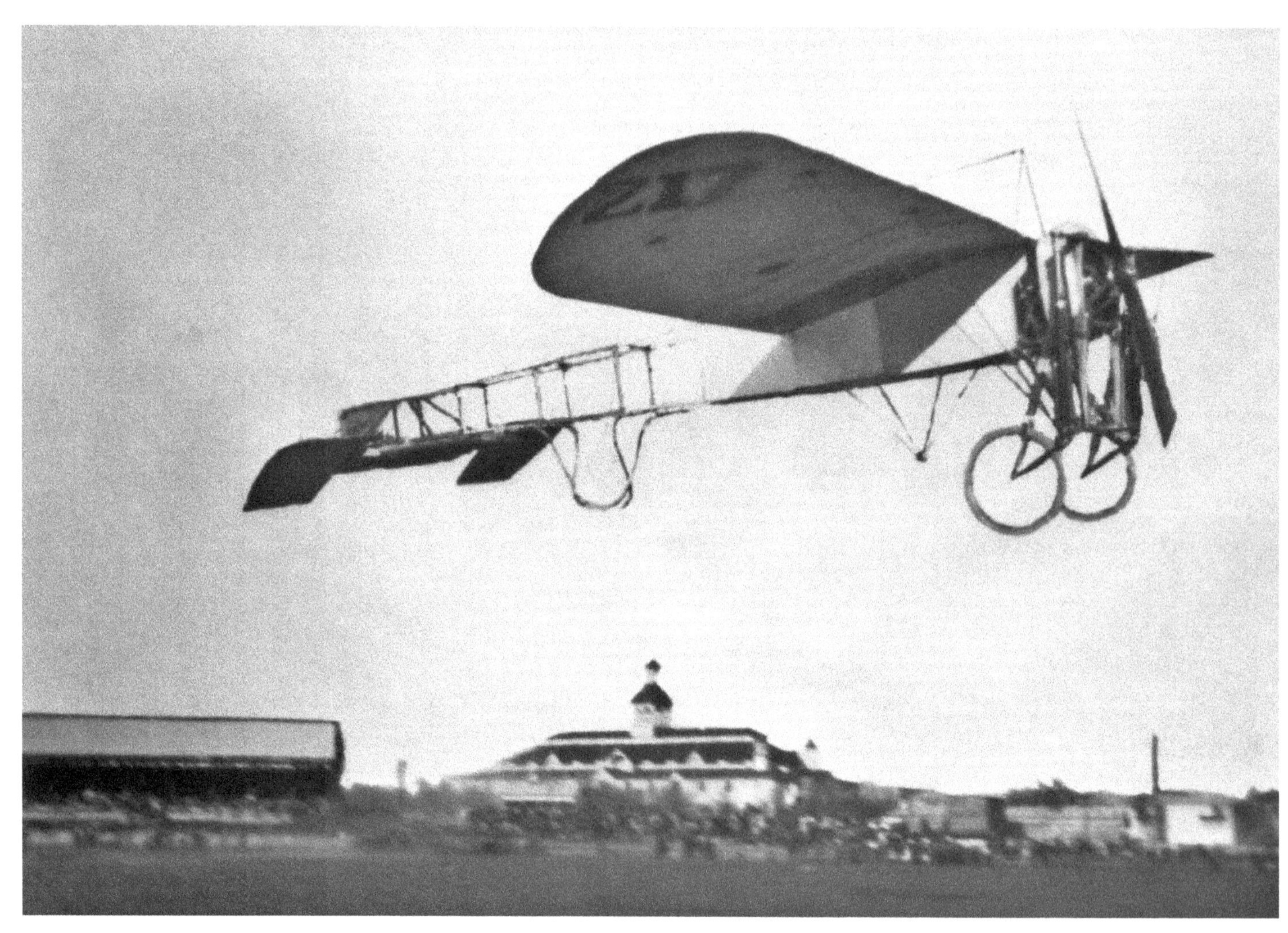

A Bleriot-type monoplane flies above the Exposition Building at the International Fair Grounds in the early 1910s.

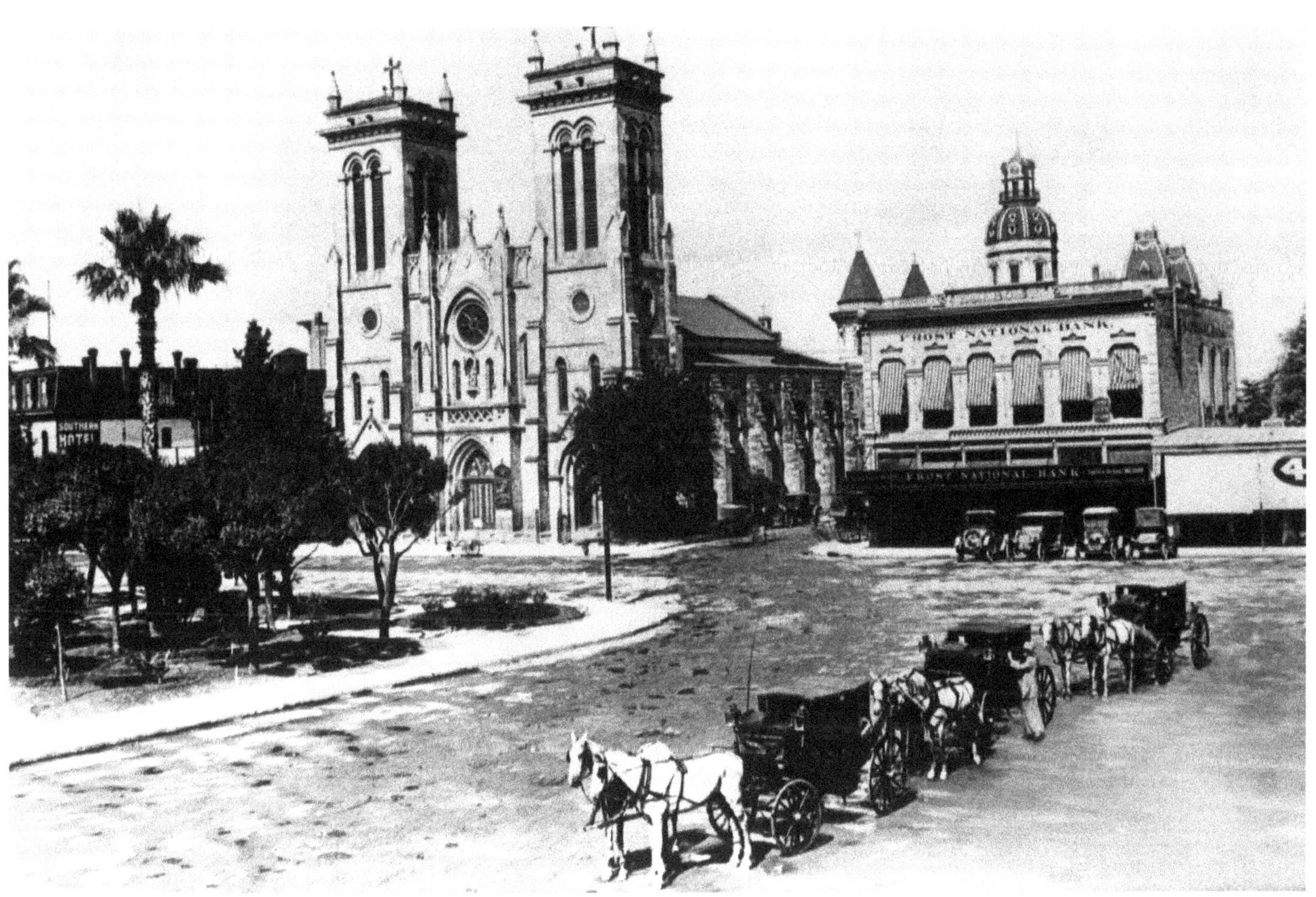

In 1914, San Antonio stood part-way between its frontier past and industrial future. Horse-drawn carriages share the street with automobiles that are parked in front of the Frost National Bank. To the left of the bank is San Fernando Cathedral.

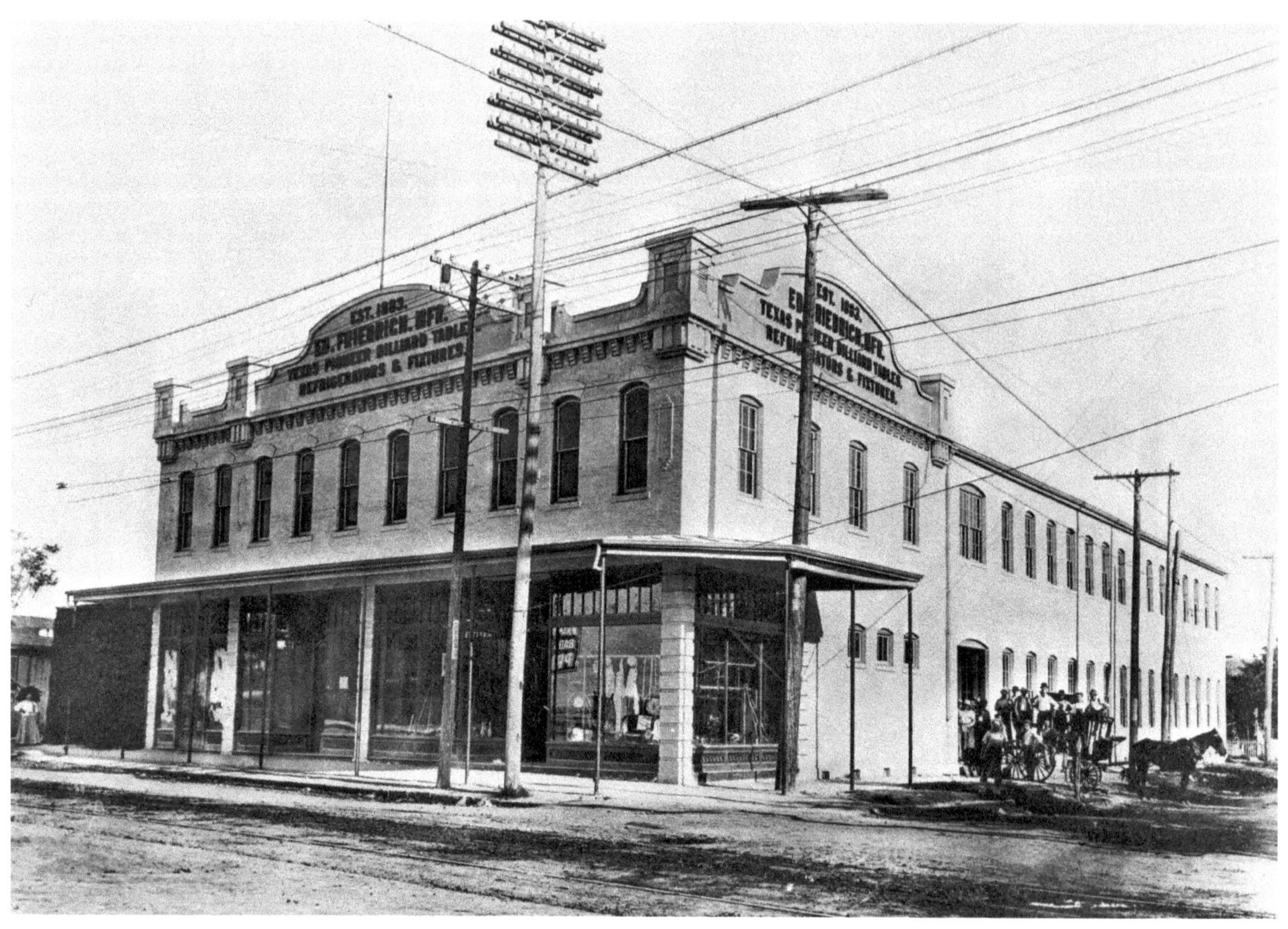

Ed Friedrich started his business in 1883, producing fine, handcrafted wood products. This building, located at 802-804 E. Commerce on the corner of Cherry Street, was constructed in 1907 and was destroyed by fire in 1925, just as the company was moving to a new facility. Friedrich later became a major air conditioning and refrigeration company.

The Belgian gardeners float in the Battle of Flowers parade, 1910. Seated on the float-wagon decorated with vegetables is Peet Calle. Smartly dressed boys stand at the rear of the float.

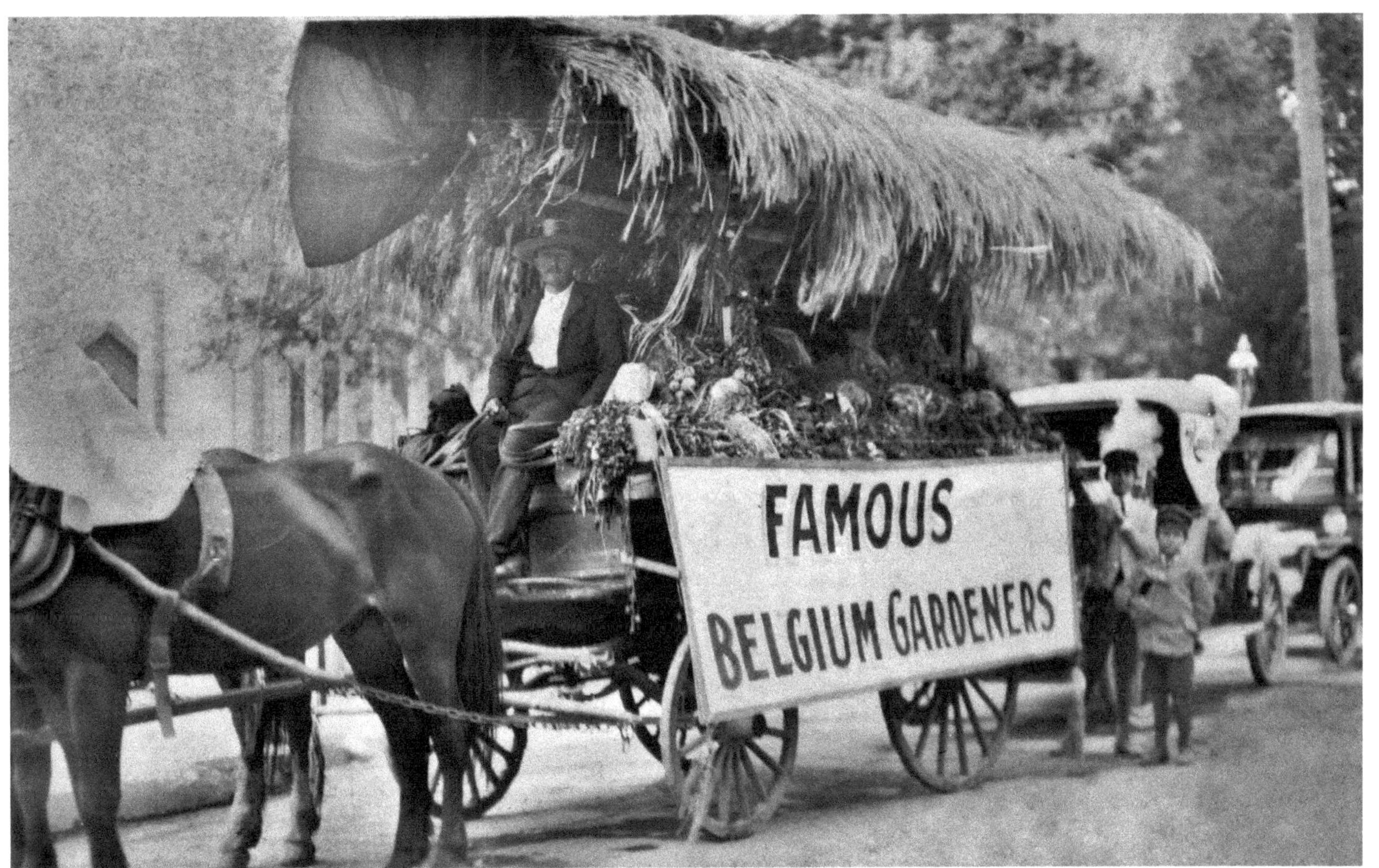

This October 1910 photograph shows several men standing around a steam shovel that has dug a ditch for sewer pipe. The operator of the steam shovel is listed as Ed Edmunds.

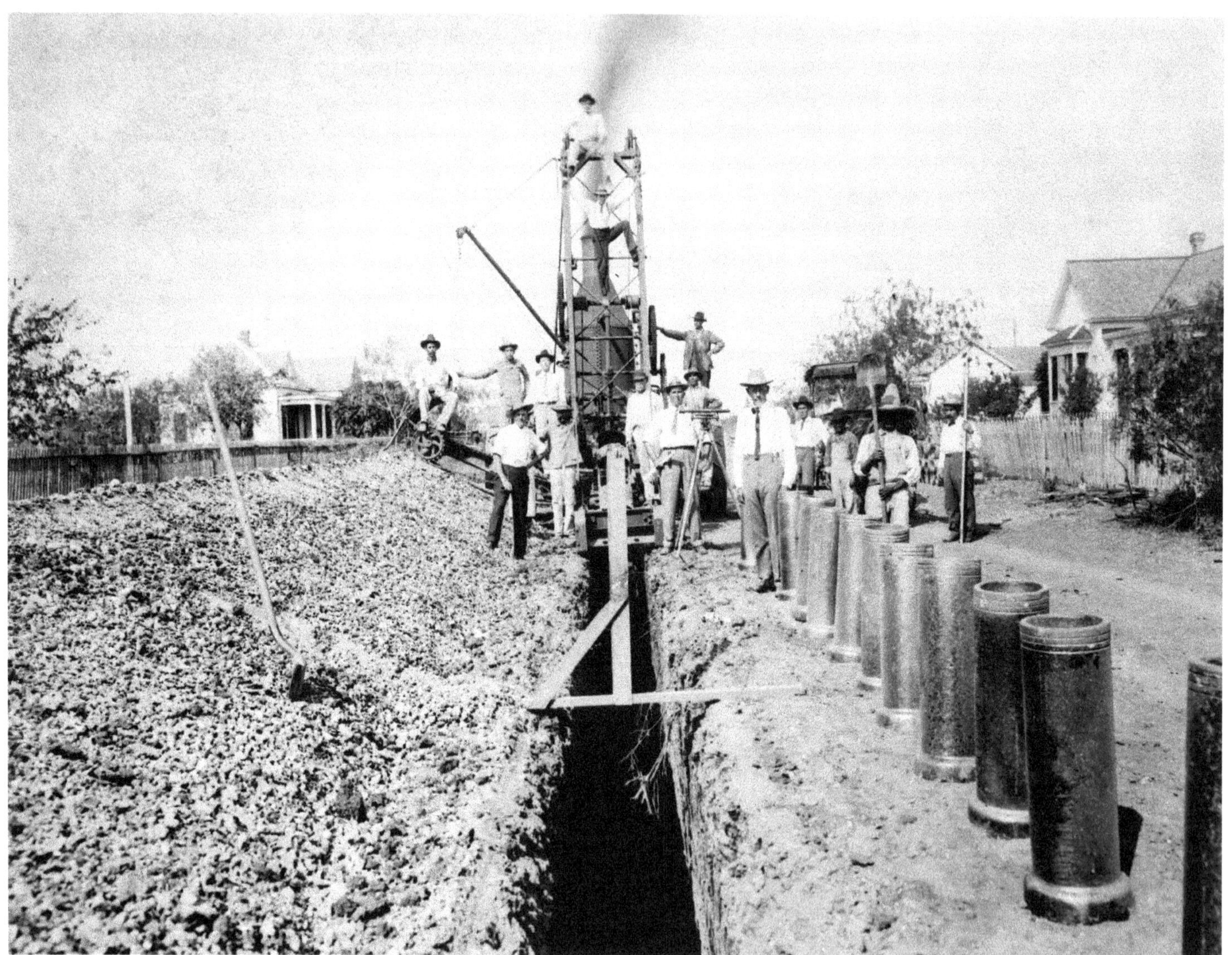

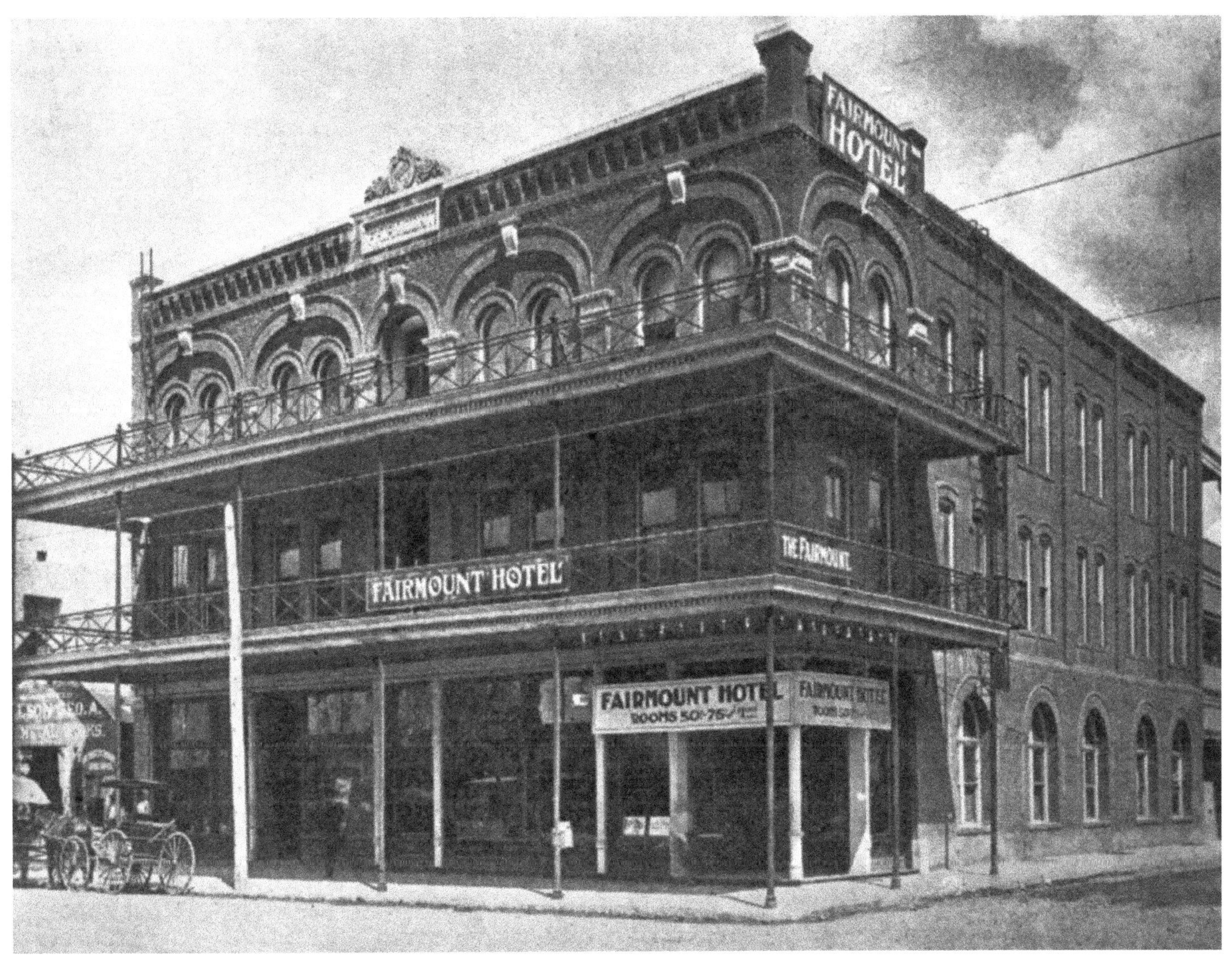

The five-story Fairmount Hotel, 357-361 E. Commerce Street, as it appeared about 1914. Built in 1906, the Fairmount was abandoned by 1968 and scheduled for demolition by 1980. A startling series of events led to the hotel being lifted and moved six blocks to a new location in 1985. The cost of the move was $1.2 million, and an additional $3.1 million was spent on renovation and expansion. The shop that appears next door belonged to George A. Stillson, who sold tin roofing, cornice, steel ceilings, etc.

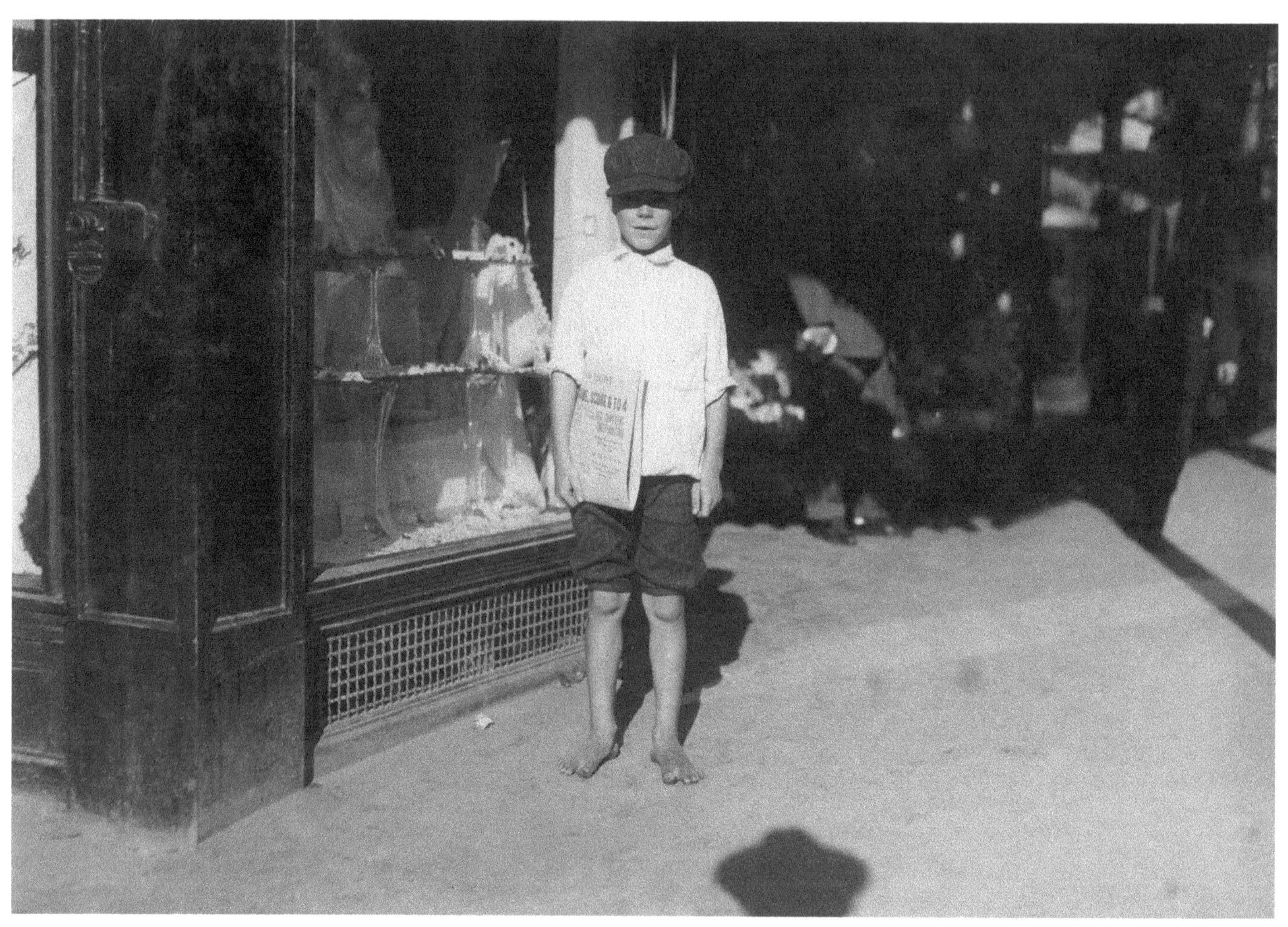

This photograph, taken in October 1903, shows Lionel Perry, a nine-year-old newsboy, who began his day at 5:00 a.m. on weekdays and 4:00 a.m. on Sundays. He sold newspapers after school.

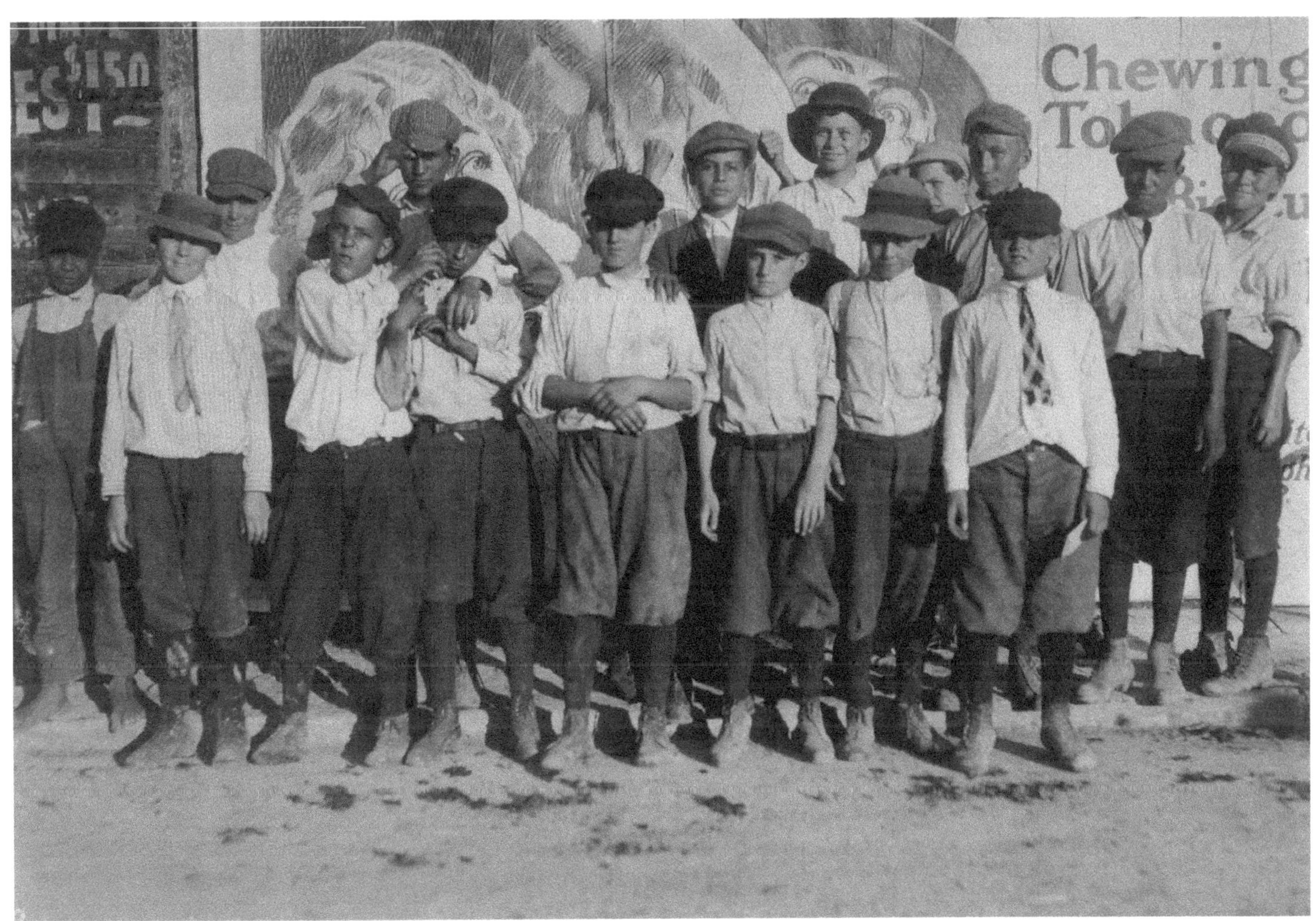

A photograph of a few of the San Antonio messengers. Their contact with the Red Light district was considered one of the worst phases of child labor. This photograph was taken by Lewis Wickes Hine during October 1913 while touring for the National Child Labor Committee. Hine spent years documenting poor labor and living conditions, especially for women and children.

Workmen are lifting the Alamo National Bank to place it on rollers and move it backward for the widening of Commerce Street. Most buildings on the south side of Commerce were partially demolished and rebuilt so that the street would be a uniform sixty-five feet wide, to accommodate automobiles and streetcars. The widening of Commerce began during the later half of 1913 and was completed in 1915.

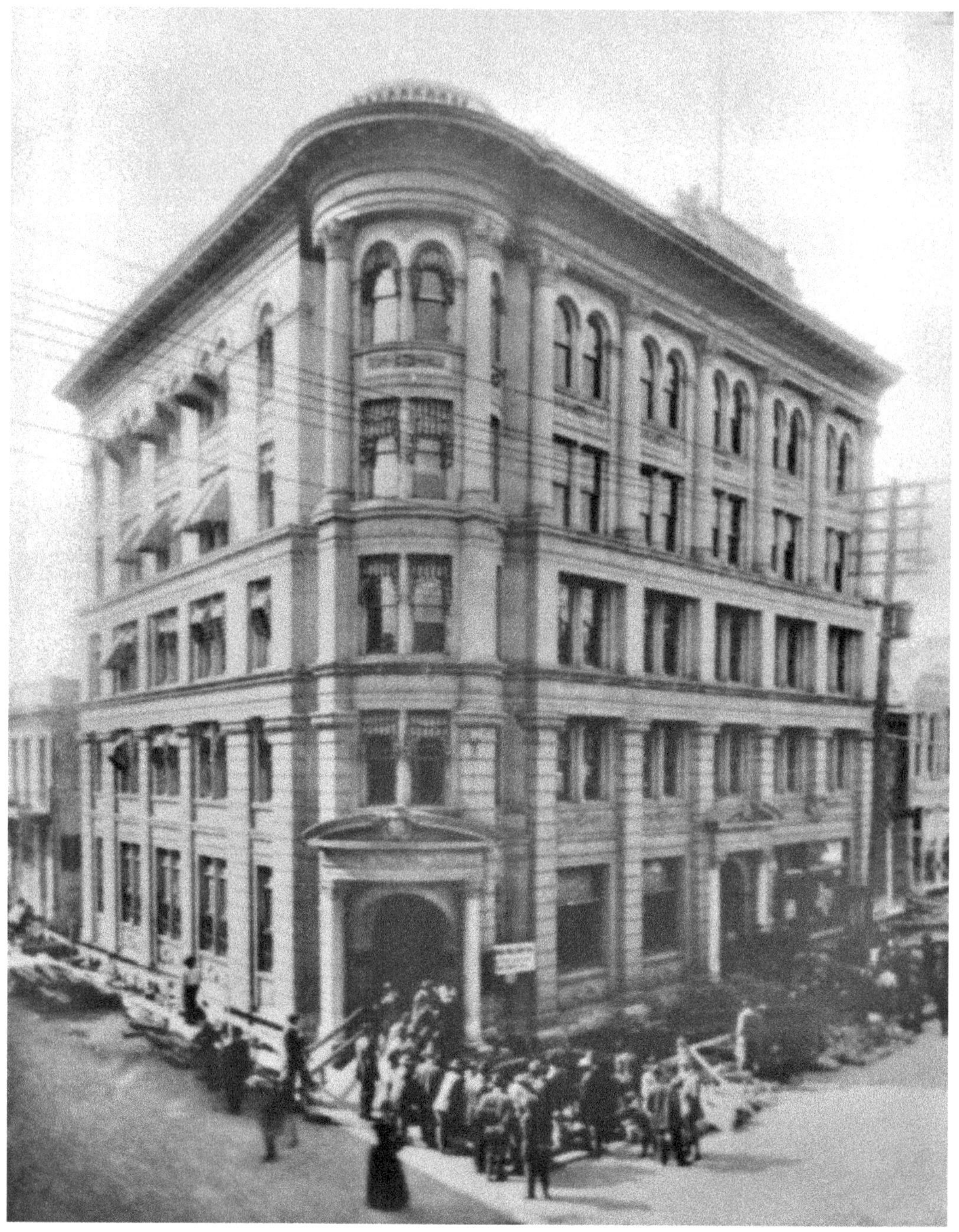

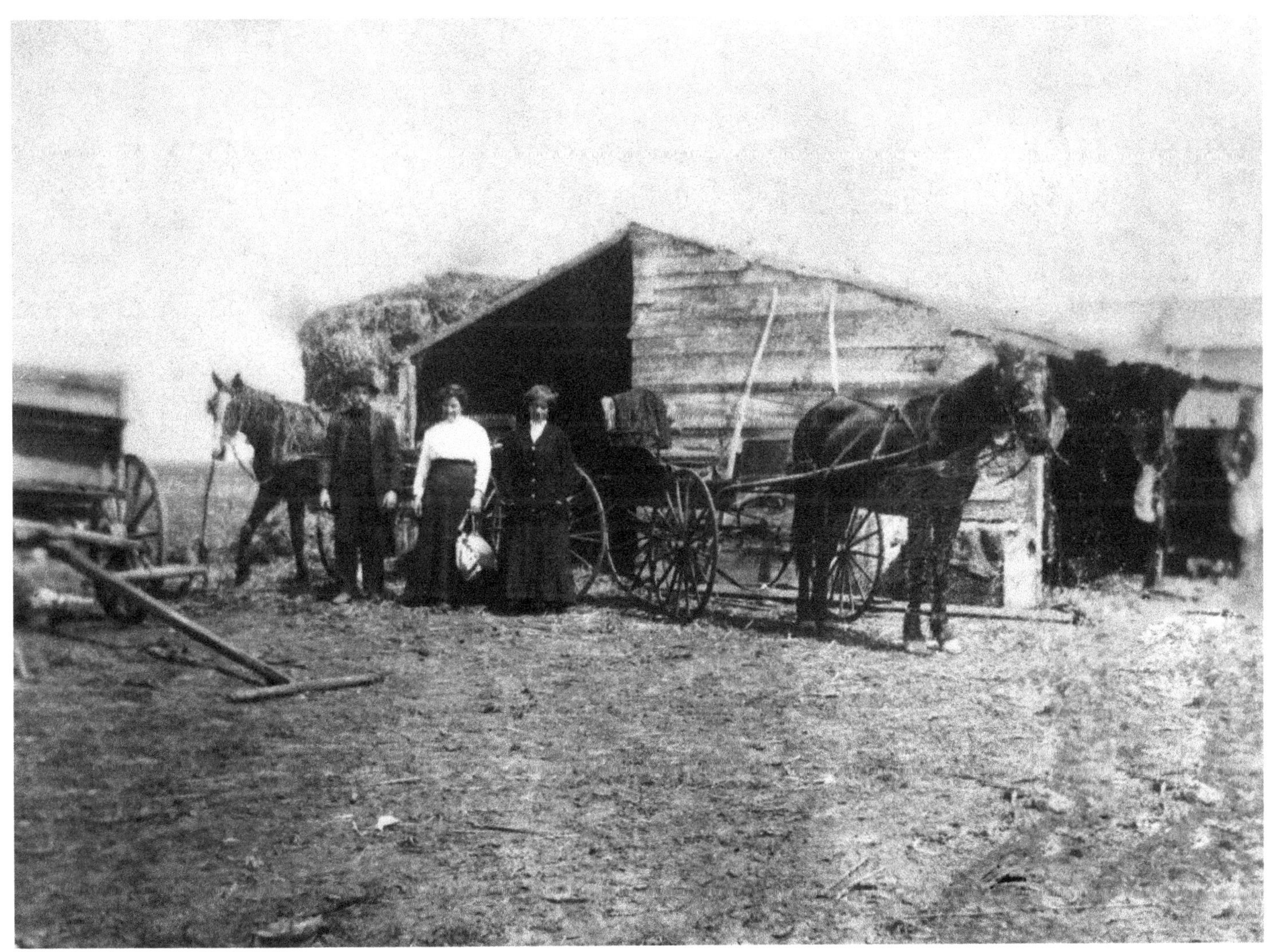

Man and two women standing outside Peet Persyn's barn about 1915. The Persyn family was one of several Belgian farming families to establish vegetable farms on the southwest side of San Antonio. Descendants of the Persyns and other Belgians continue to farm in the area known as the "Belgian Gardens."

Exterior of the Princess Theatre built in 1911 for W. T. Fenstermaker, and designed by Atlee B. Ayres. The upper floors were occupied by offices, the Powers School of Expression and Dramatic Art, and the Consolidated Film and Supply Company. It was razed in 1929 for Blum's Department Store, later known as Frost Brothers. The theater's attraction the day this photo was taken was "The Snake."

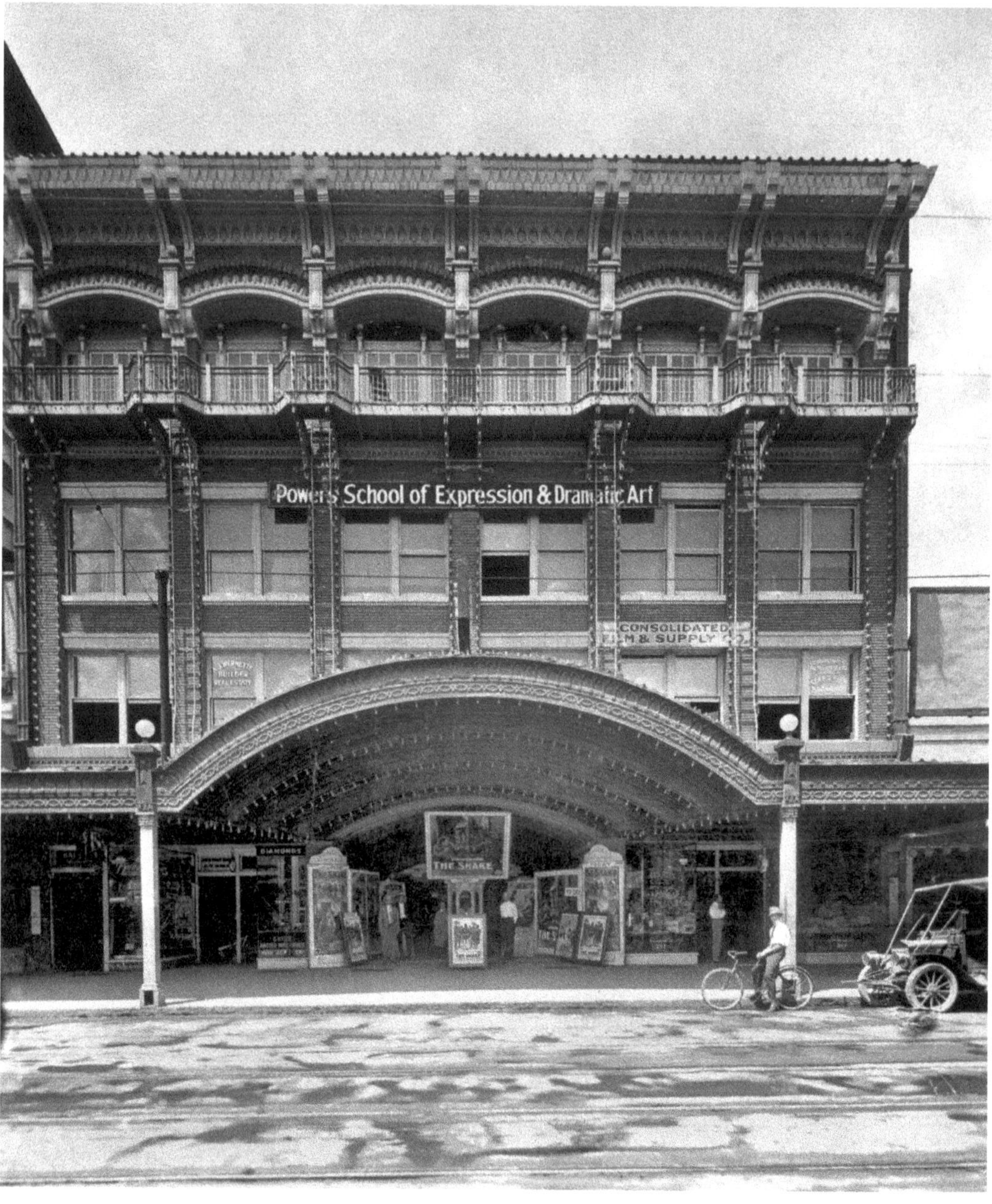

A view from Alamo Plaza looking west down Houston Street about 1912. On the left is the Swearingen-McCraw (formerly Maverick Bank) Building. On the far right is the Federal Building, and next to it the Hicks Building. Notice the wide open space with horse-drawn wagons, automobiles, and trolley cars going down Houston Street.

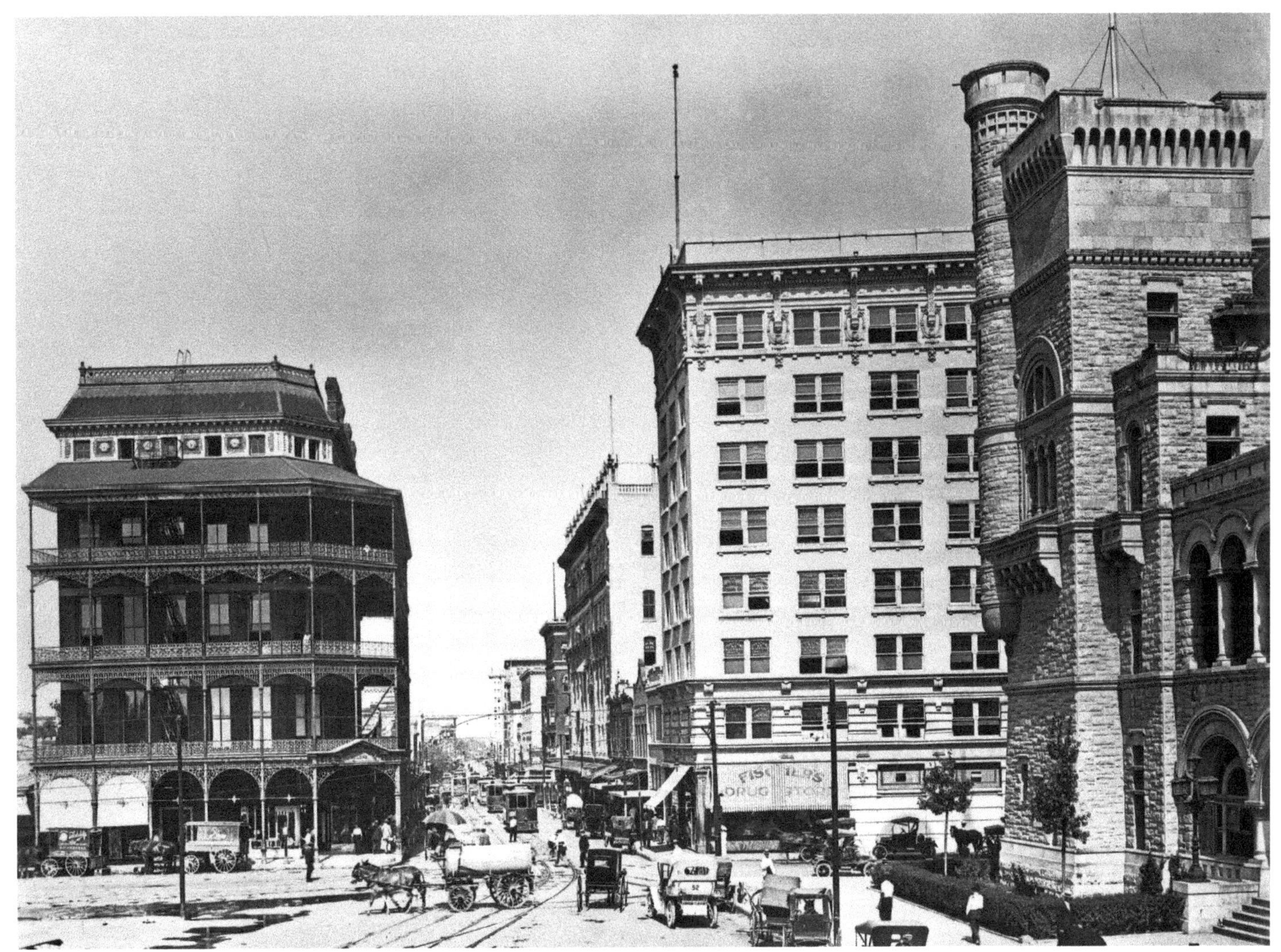

On October 2, 1913, a flash flood filled San Antonio's streets with 7.08 inches of water in twenty-four hours. Here is Travis Street with several horse-drawn carriages caught in the flood waters.

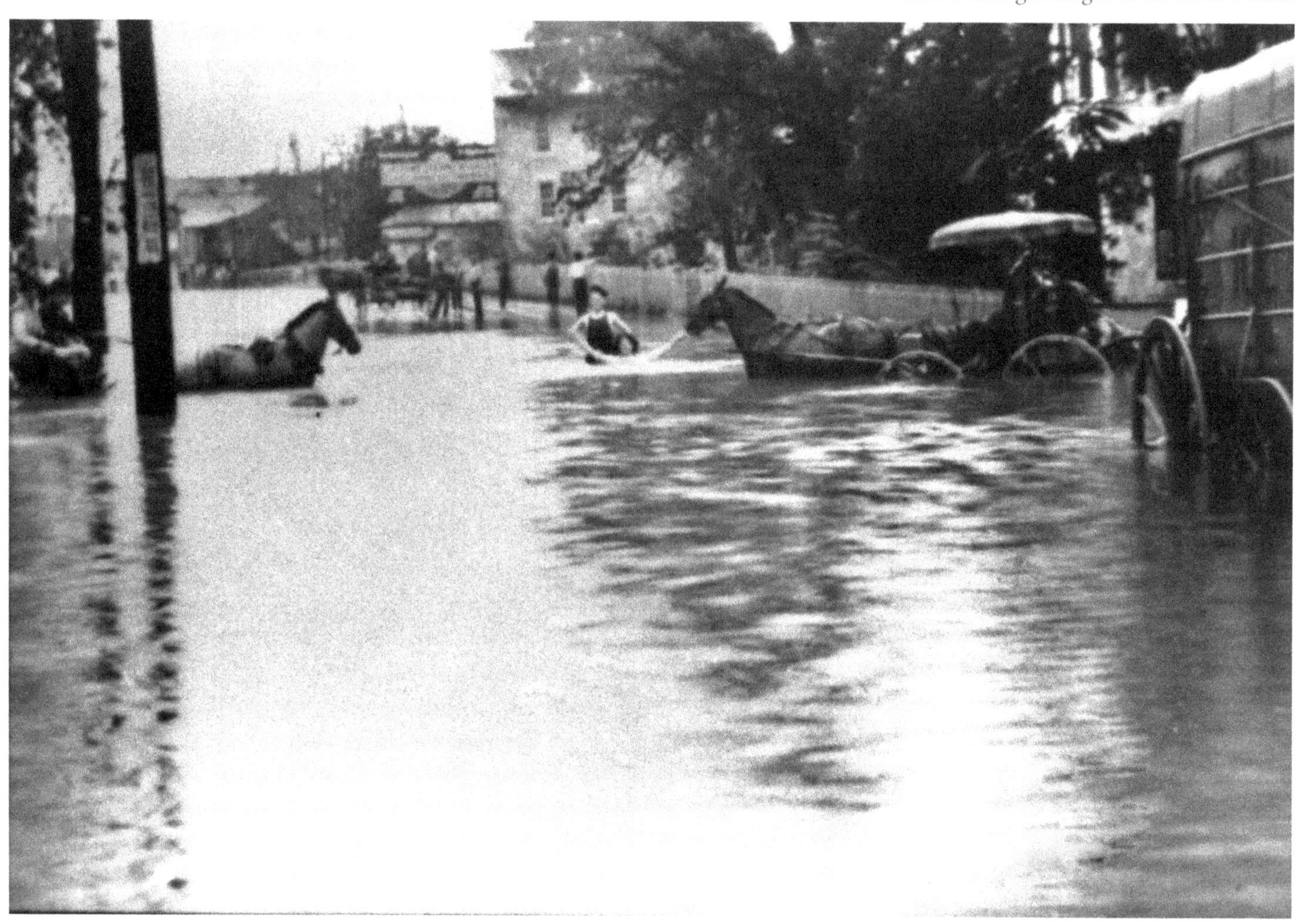

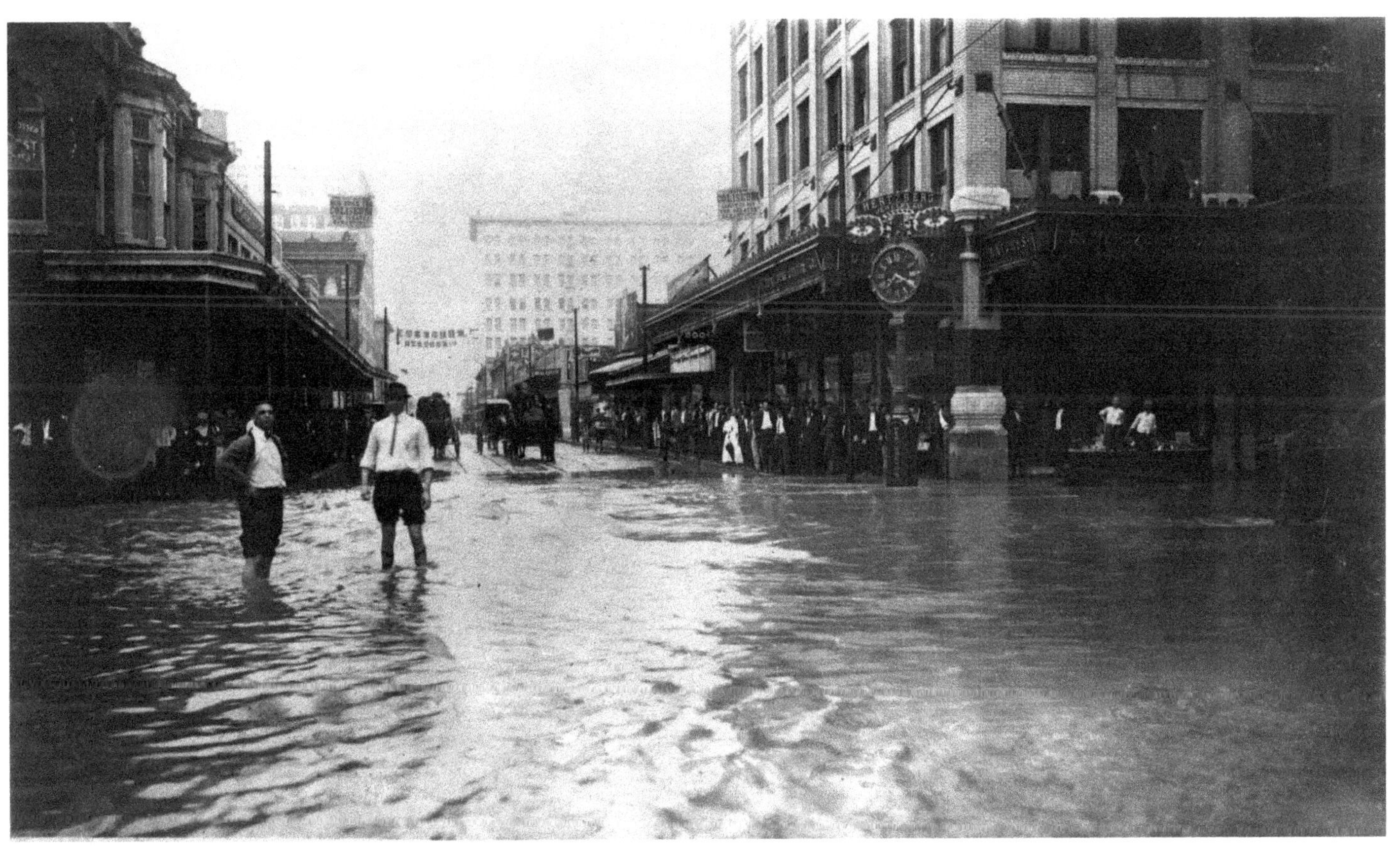

Another view of the October 1913 flood, looking west on Houston from the corner of St. Mary's Street. Note the people on the sidewalk near the Hertzberg clock looking on as others wade in the water-filled avenues. Signs along the street call for construction of a coliseum, but it was not built, probably because the proposed riverside location flooded in December. After the river was rerouted following the 1921 flood, the Municipal Auditorium was built on the same location proposed earlier.

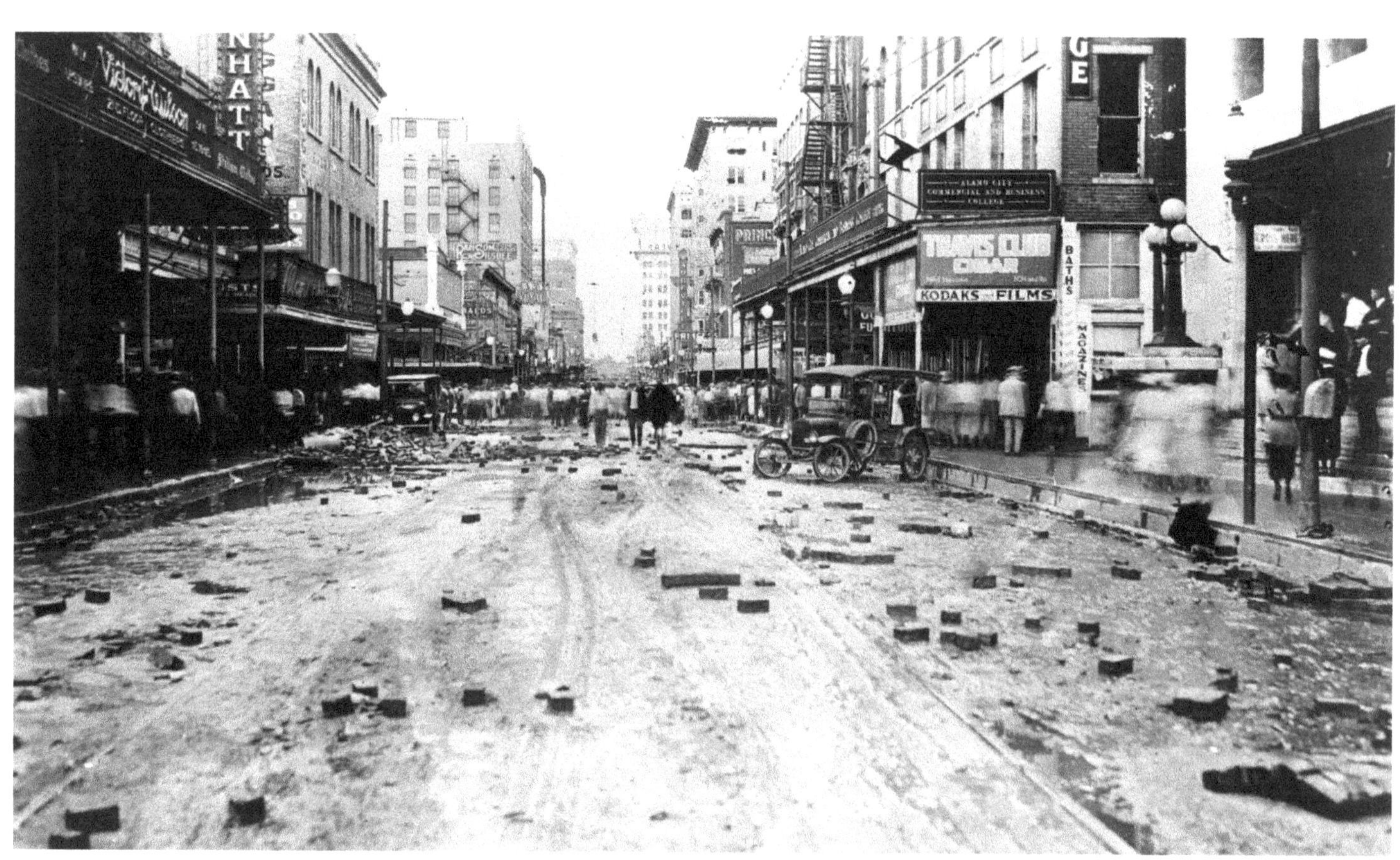

A scene near Houston and Navarro streets after a flood on December 4, 1913. Water was two- to three-feet deep in the downtown area. Among a population of just over 120,000 at the time, 15,000 were homeless and fifty people died.

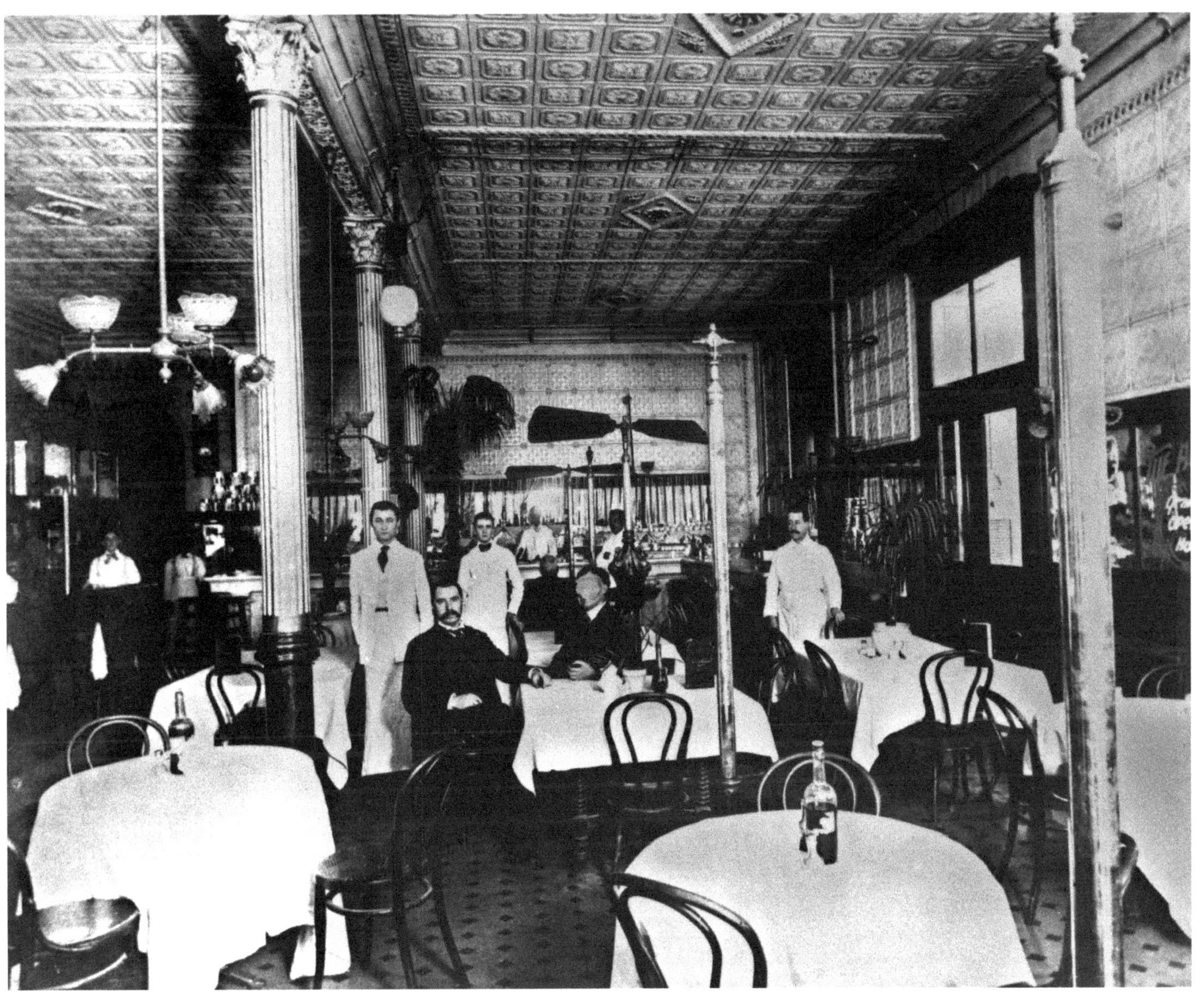

Interior of Bull Brothers Saloon on the first floor of the Reuter Building at 217-219 Alamo Plaza. The building was designed by James Wahrenberger for William Reuter in 1891. The saloon was on the first floor, the second and third floors housed offices, and the fourth was the lodge hall for the Knights of Pythias. Billy Reuter had a bandstand built for Alamo Plaza; a replica of it still stands there today.

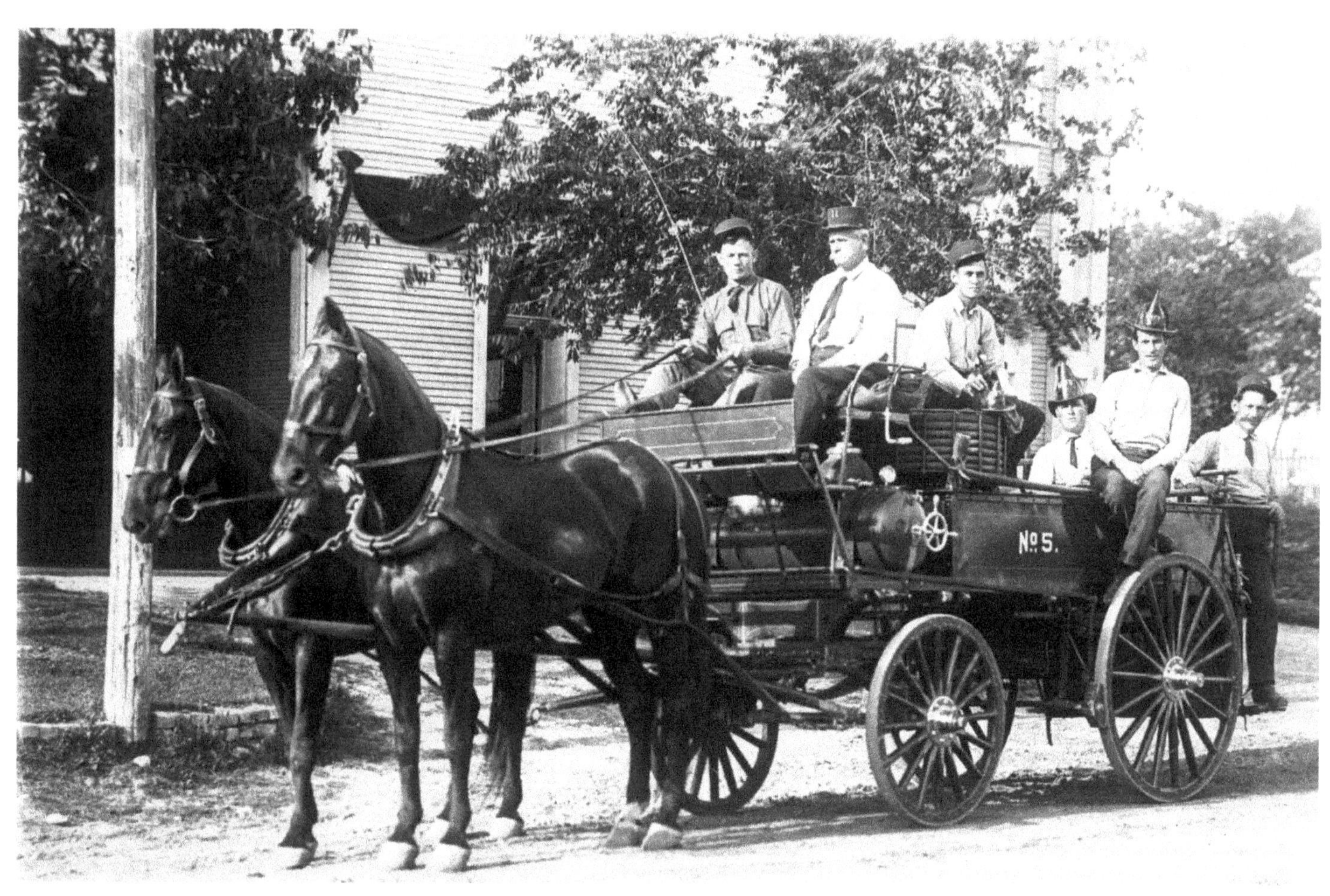

Members of Fire House No. 5 at 1015 Mason Street posing on their horse-drawn wagon. On April 4, 1927, Fire House No. 5 became the last to cease using horse-drawn apparatus.

A bird's-eye view looking west, southwest, towards the San Antonio River and the Navarro Street Bridge. The old San Antonio Express Building (northeast corner of Crockett and Navarro streets) is on the left.

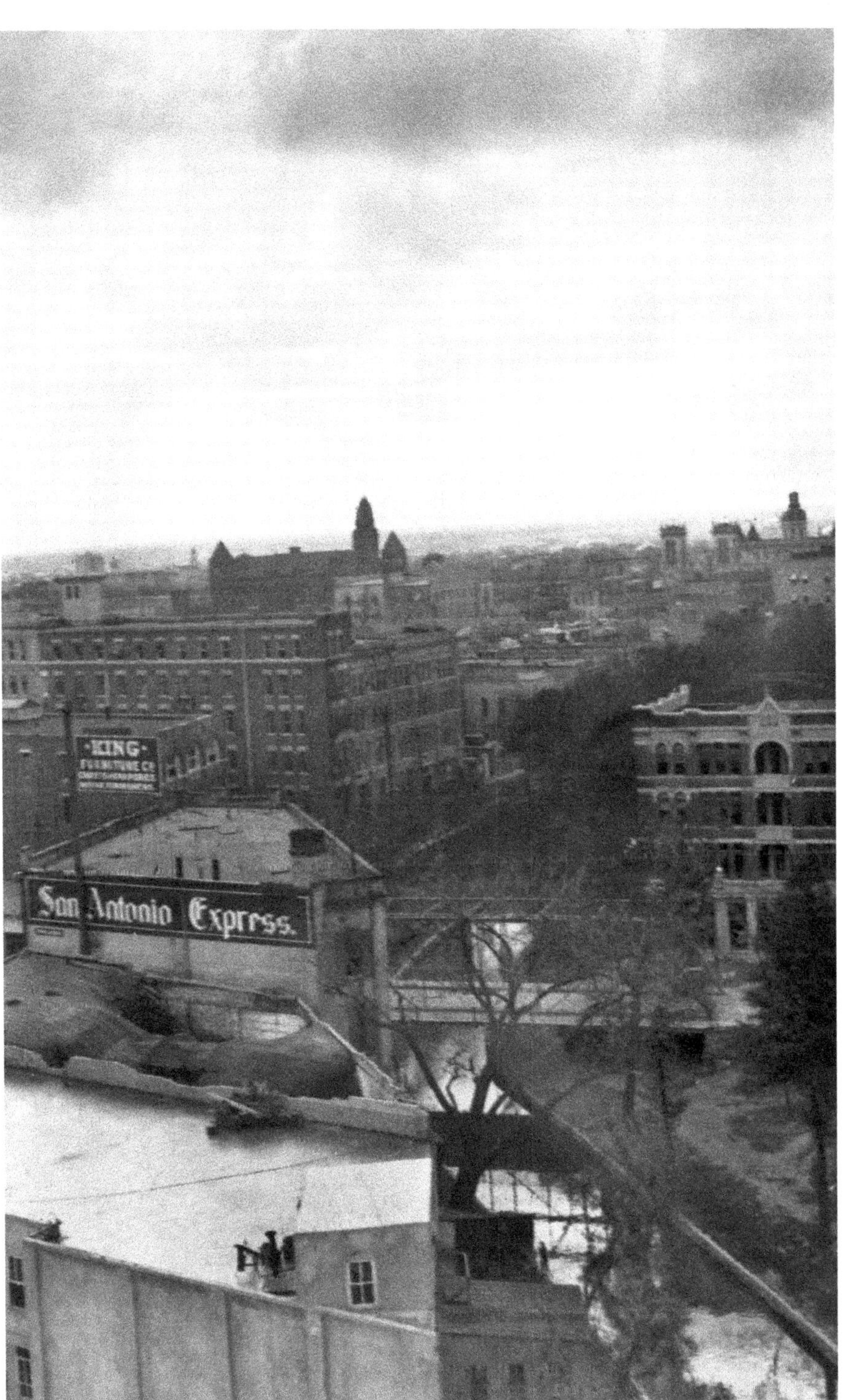

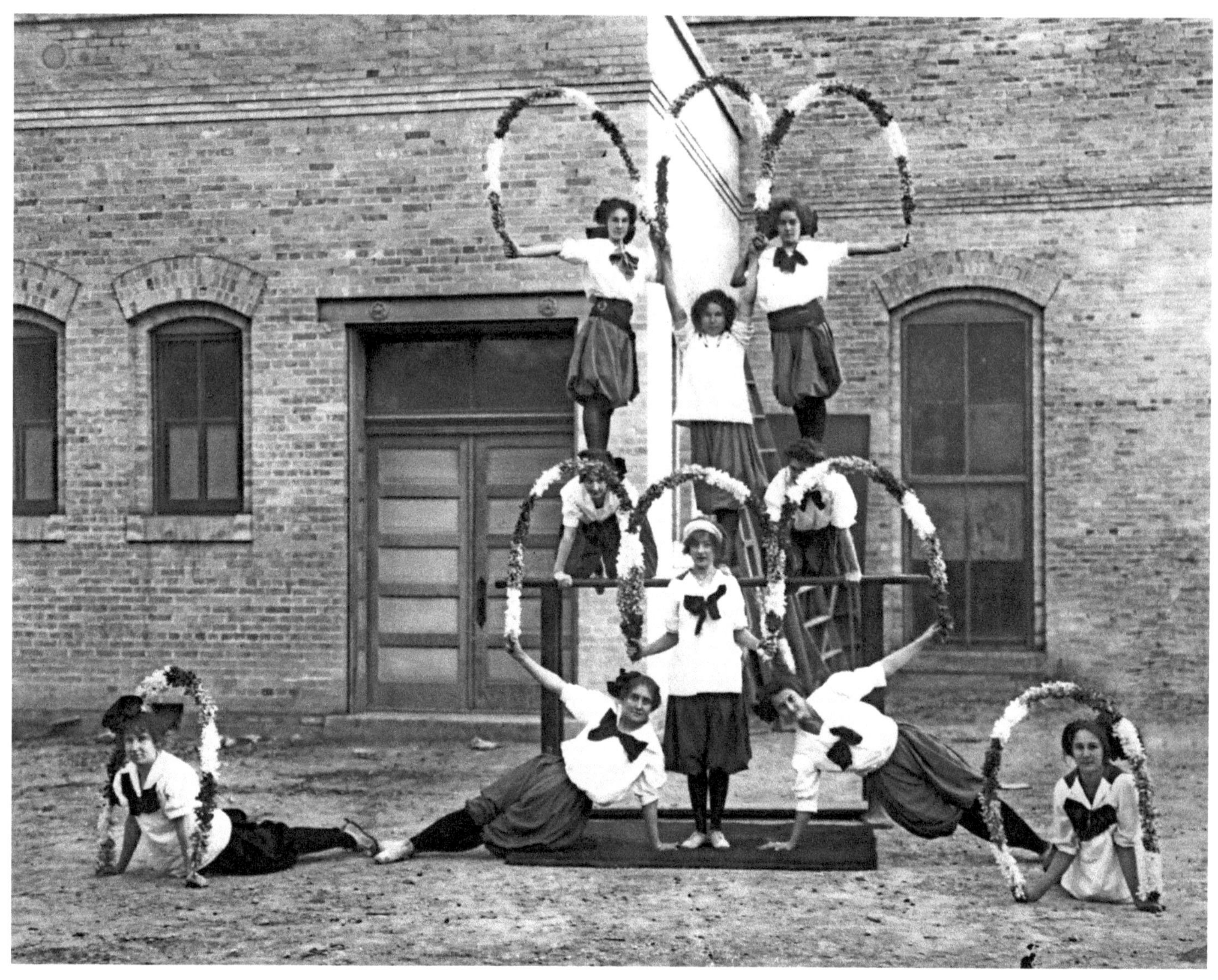

San Antonio's Turnverein girls' team posed in a pyramid with hoops about 1915. The Turnverein, or athletic club, was an early German institution in San Antonio, and its members were involved in athletics, music, civic, and social activities.

This 1917 photograph shows boys washing buggies in the San Antonio River near the Navarro Street Bridge. Buildings in the background front on Market Street.

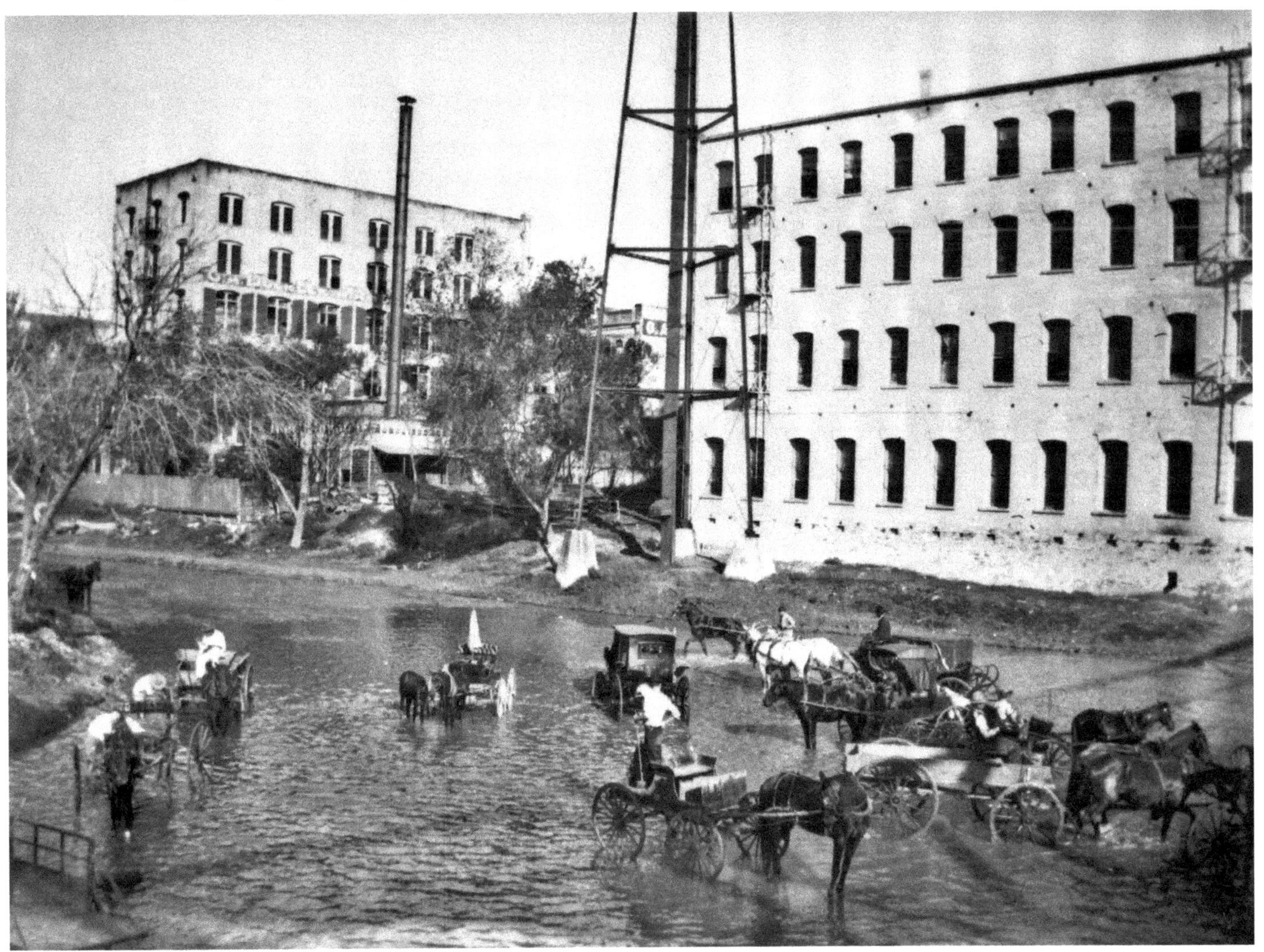

Around 1919 this Labor Day parade made its way down E. Houston Street. To the back is Graves Sunset Auto Livery.

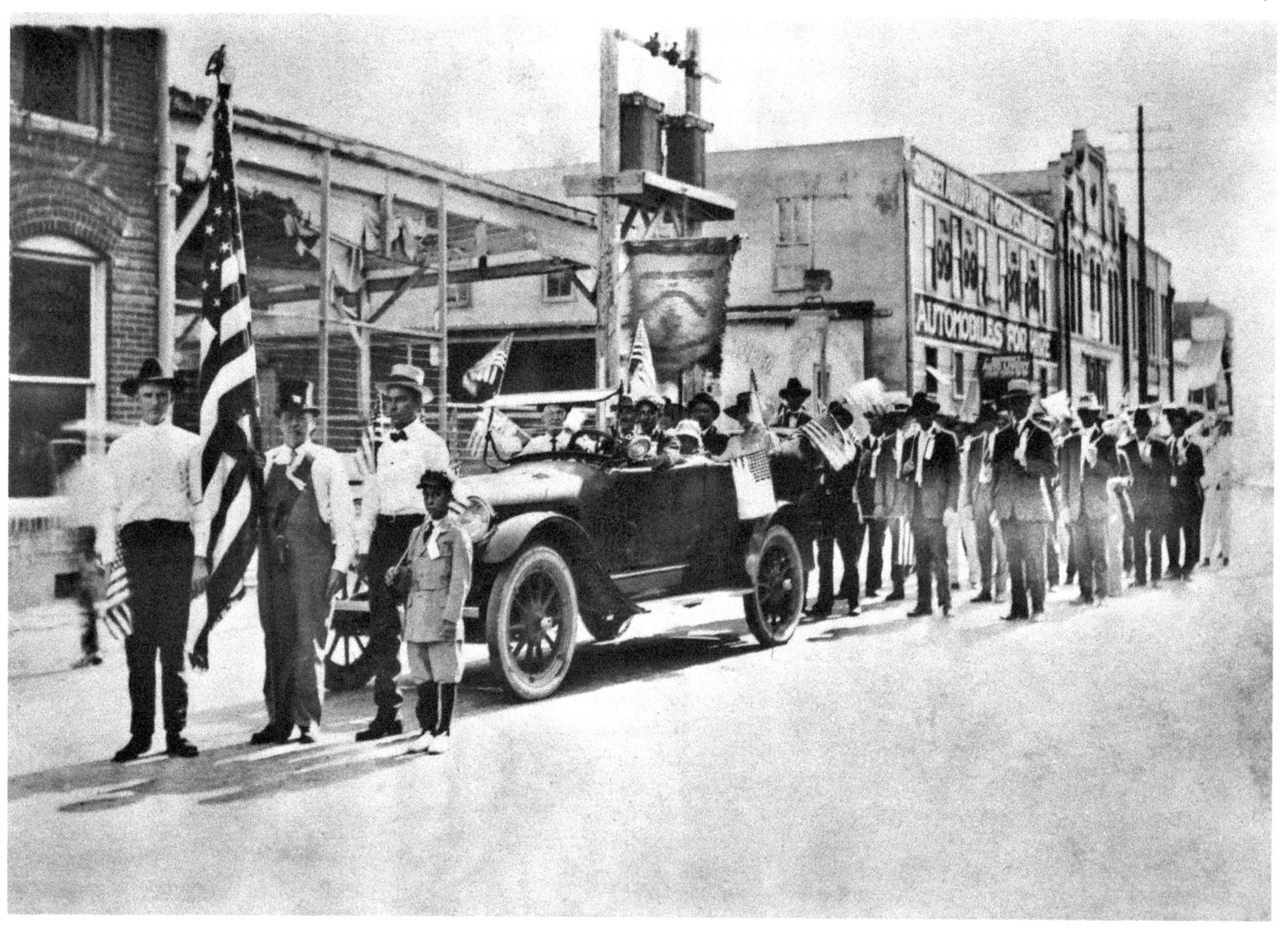

A group of students from Peacock Military Academy posed in theatrical costumes. School was obviously not all drill, athletics, and study.

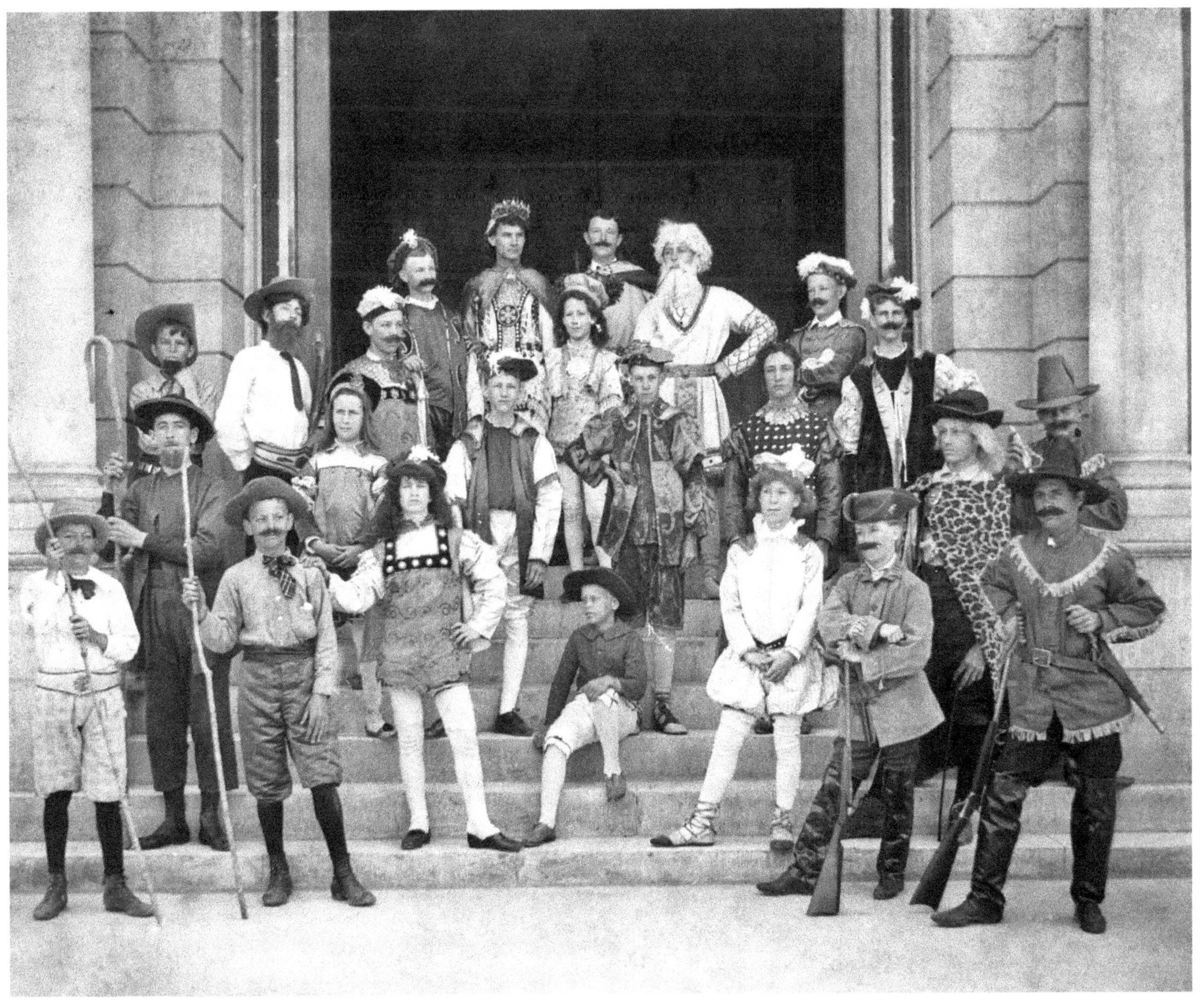

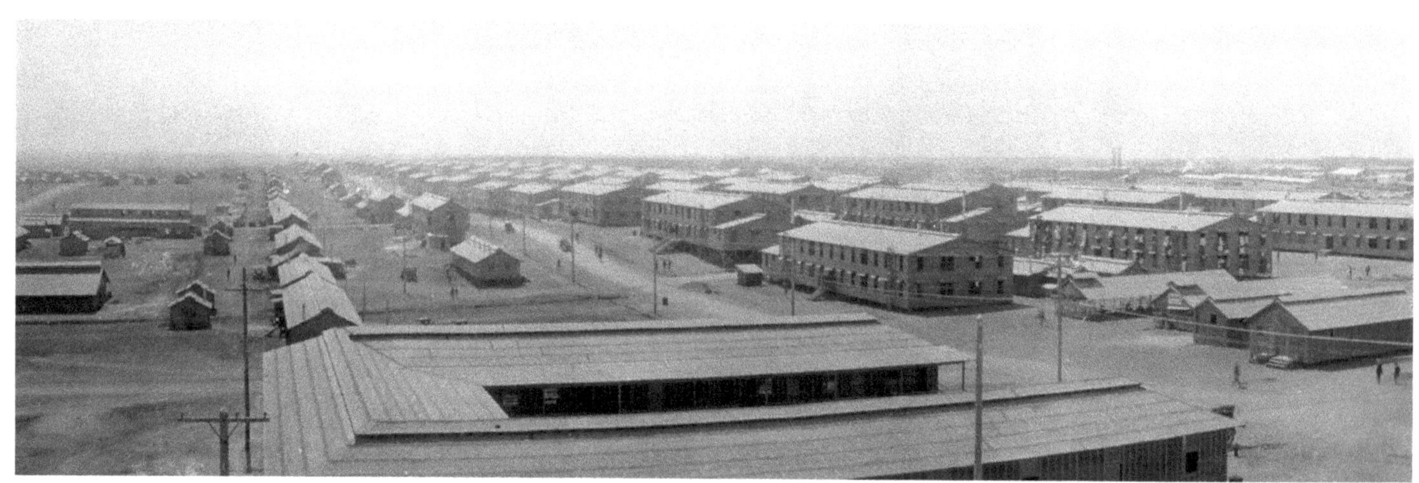

During World War I, the military presence in San Antonio greatly expanded. Here is a bird's-eye view of Camp Travis in October 1917. Camp Travis served as the training site of the 90th Division, made up of men from Texas and Oklahoma. By mid-October the division had over 31,000 men and officers.

On June 28, 1916, troops of the Illinois National Guard started for Texas by train. This photograph shows their arrival with the city decorated and people cheering. Company B, 3rd Illinois Infantry, National Guard marches northeast on Houston Street. Maverick Bank is the large building to the left, with the Wigwam Theatre No. 2 down the street at 512 ½ E. Houston.

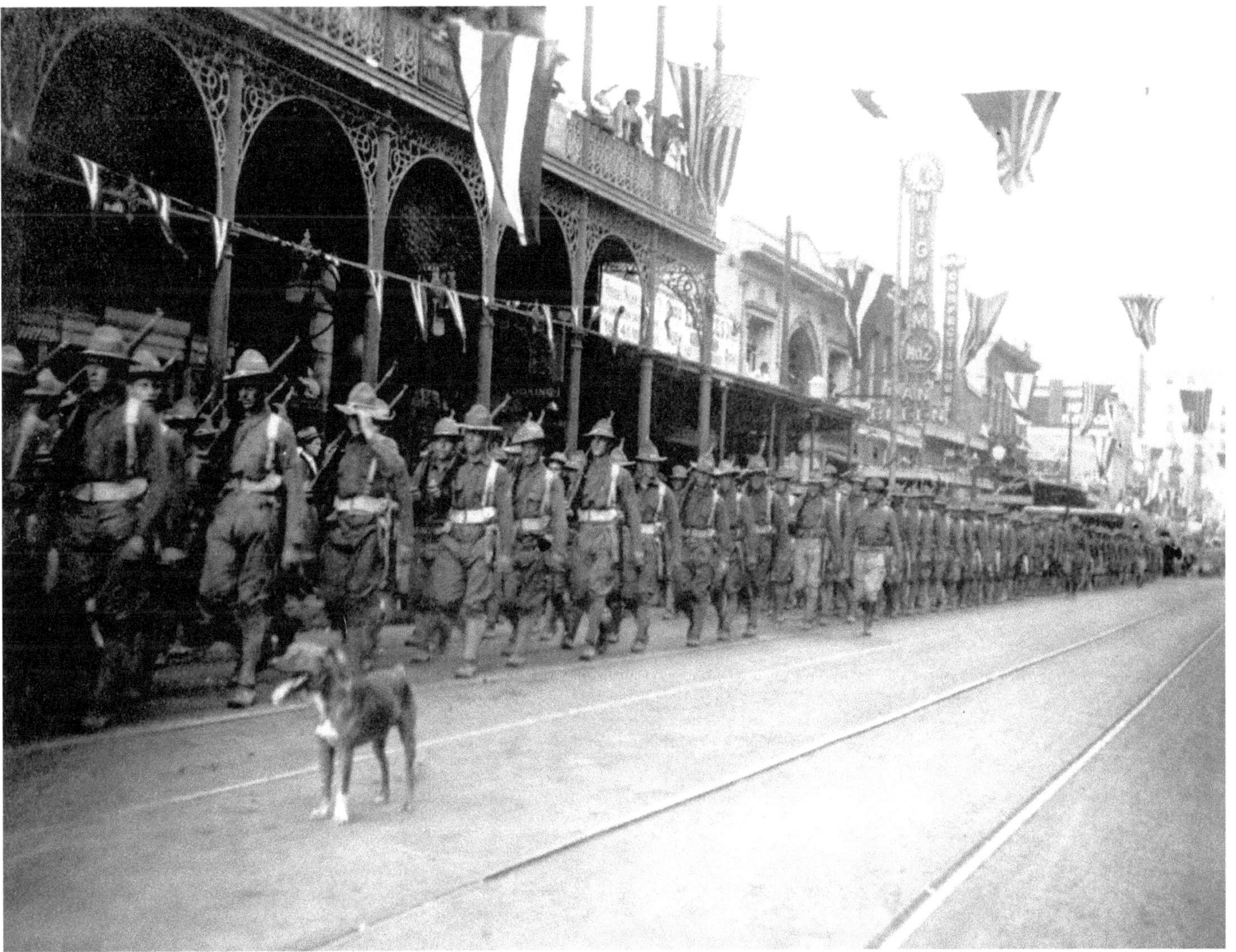

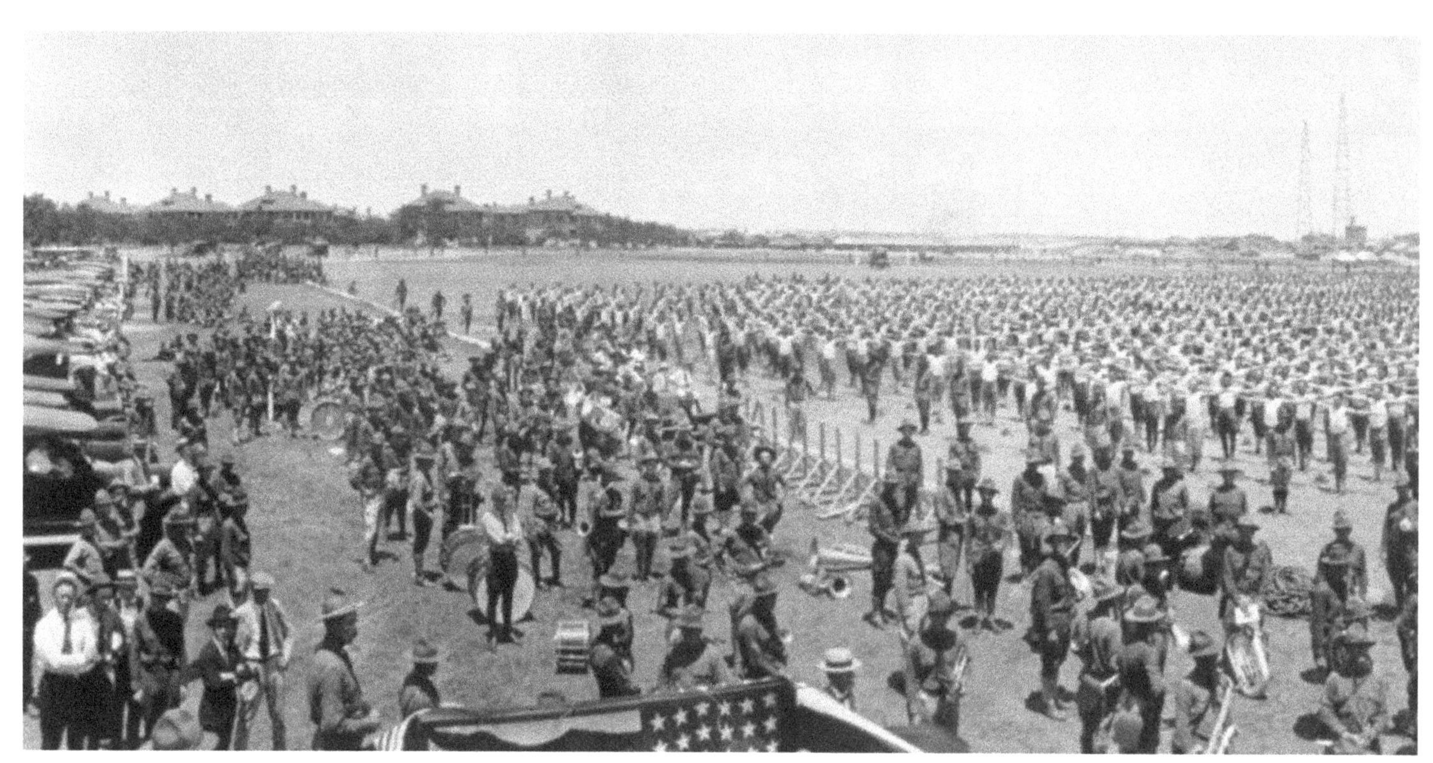

Troops ready for Flag Day ceremonies at Fort Sam Houston, June 14, 1918.

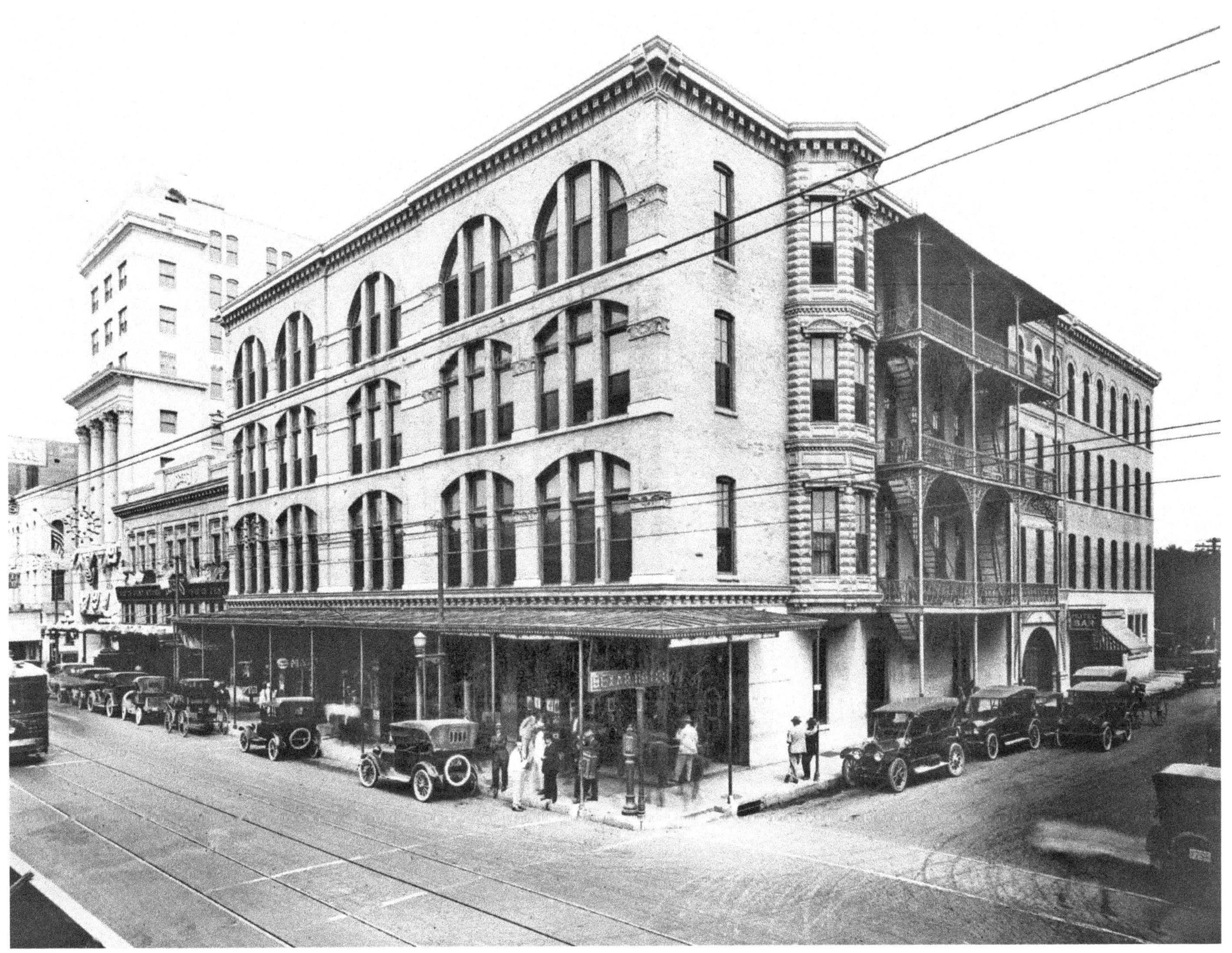

The Bexar Hotel at the corner of Jefferson and Houston streets, built about 1879, as it appeared around 1918. In 1923 it was remodeled as the Jefferson Hotel. After further renovations in 1929, it became the Guarantee State Bank. In 1946, all but the bottom floor was condemned, and in 1971, it was razed.

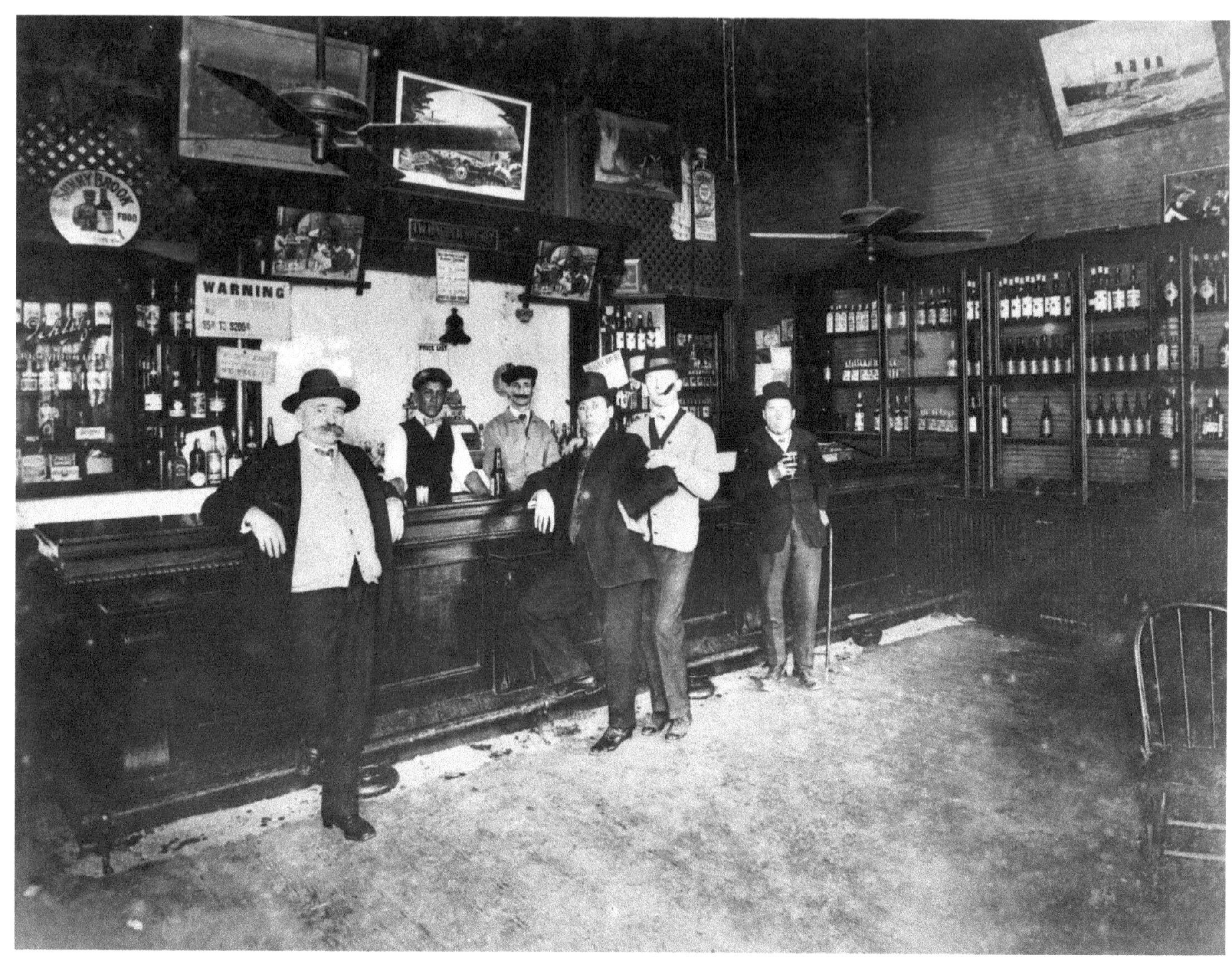

The Louis Bizy Saloon was not too busy on this day, around 1917. Located at 1008 W. Commerce then, it is now the area of Produce Row.

Maverick Bank building opened June 30, 1885, on the corner of Houston and Alamo streets. Known as the Workingmen's Bank, its five stories made it the tallest building in the city. It had eight fireproof vaults and a water-powered elevator. In 1893, it was sold to P. H. Swearingen. The elaborate ironwork set this building apart from all others.

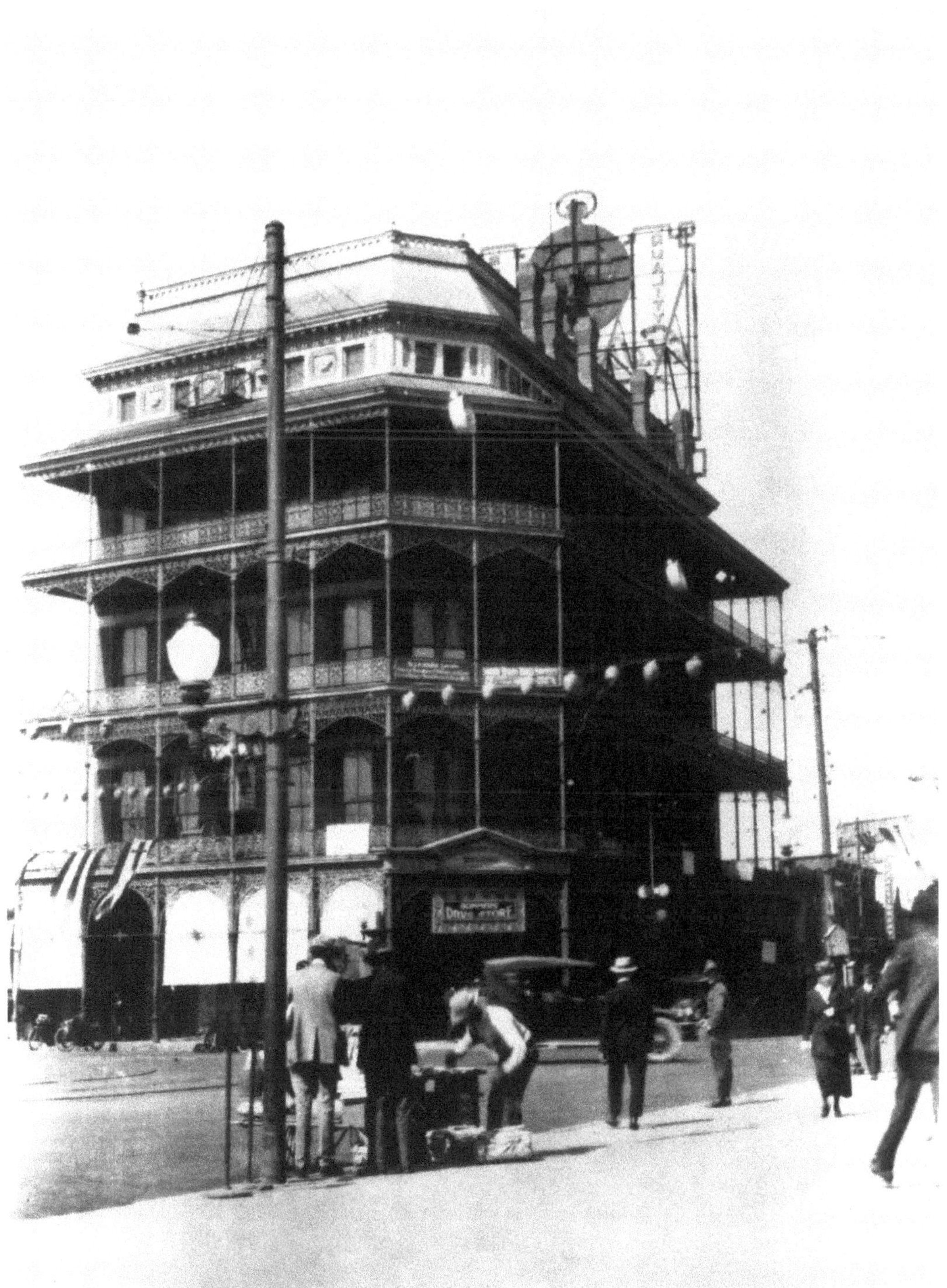

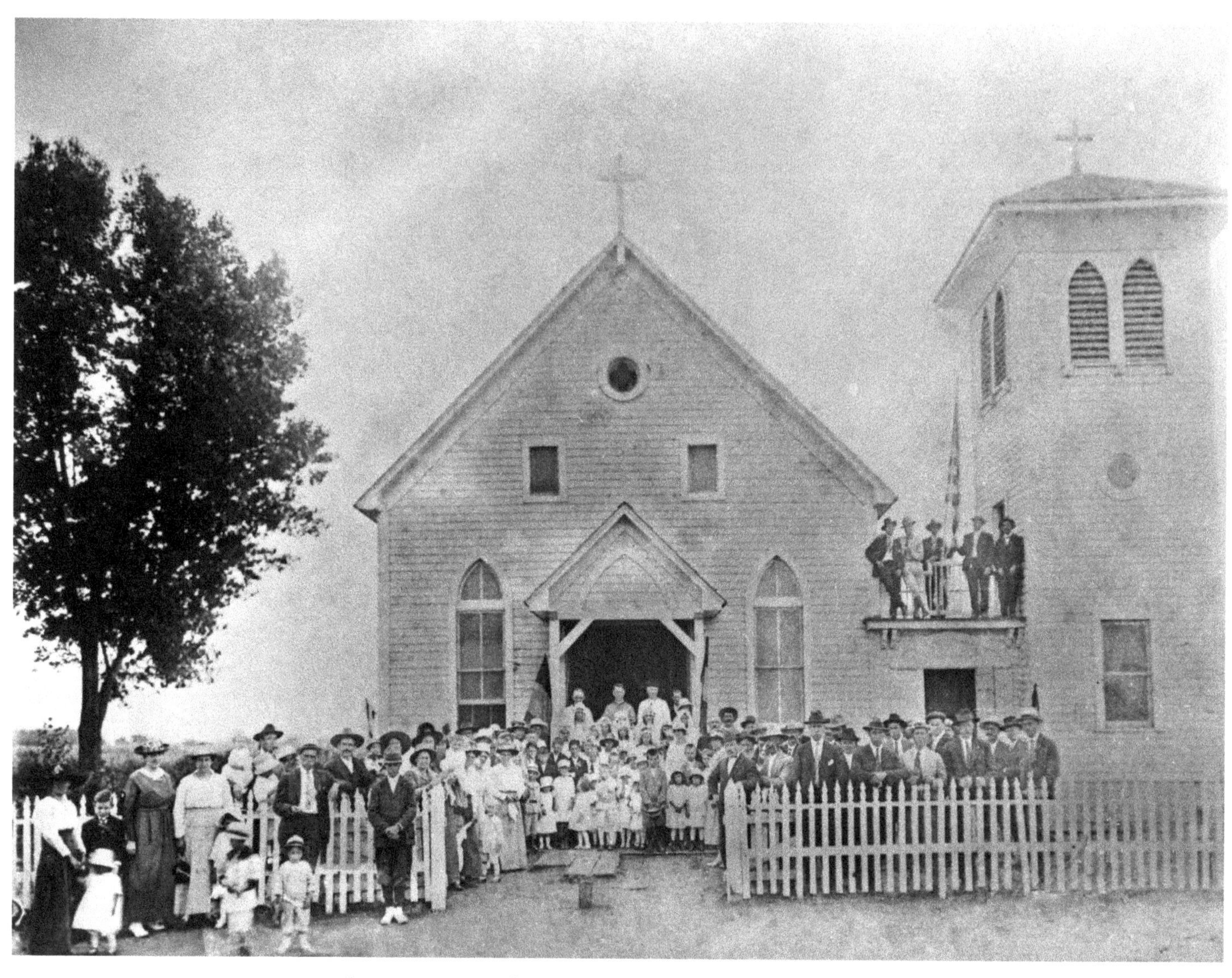

Congregation outside St. John Berchmans Church on Brady Boulevard. In the doorway is Archbishop Arthur J. Droessarts, standing between two priests and behind a confirmation class. Droessarts was the first archbishop of the Archdiocese of San Antonio, established in 1926, and was known for his charitable works and for building schools and churches.

From the Heights to the Depths

(1920–1939)

As the 1920s began, San Antonio was a rising star, with the largest population of any Texas city and still growing. Skyscrapers dotted the downtown landscape. Trolleys, and later buses, extended service routes.

In September 1921, the most devastating flood in the city's history filled downtown streets with water up to the second story of some buildings. That was enough. Over the next few years, Olmos Dam was built to help stabilize the river's water level. A channel was cut and locks installed to control water flow through the river downtown, keeping it a continuous level throughout the business district. Plans developed in the 1920s for the city's famous River Walk became a reality in the 1930s with help from federal assistance programs.

The real estate developments to the north supported the more affluent. The near west side was the opposite, a slum without running water or power. Between 1910–1930, refugees fleeing religious persecution and a revolution in Mexico found a home here. Health conditions in the neighborhoods where they settled became a great concern of city officials and civic groups. Beginning in 1939, approximately one thousand homes were replaced with the Alazan-Apache Courts, San Antonio's first public housing.

During the 1930s, about one-half of the nation's shelled pecans came from San Antonio. Most pecan shellers elsewhere in the country used machines but in San Antonio, thousands of Mexican laborers, refugees from the revolution or out of work because of the Great Depression, were paid $1 to $2 a week to shell pecans by hand. On January 31, 1938, a young Emma Tenayuca Brooks led 12,000 pecan shellers on a three-month strike. In the end, a twenty-five cent an hour minimum wage was federally mandated, but the shelling companies mechanized, throwing some 10,000 people out of work.

San Antonio's experiences during the depression were similar to those of the rest of the country. Banks and other businesses failed. Businesses cut staff and salaries for those who remained. Programs such as the National Youth Administration, Works Progress Administration, and Civilian Conservation Corps provided jobs for many. Workers for these organizations not only built the River Walk and restored La Villita and San Jose Mission, they also worked on schools, roads, and many other projects that benefitted the city.

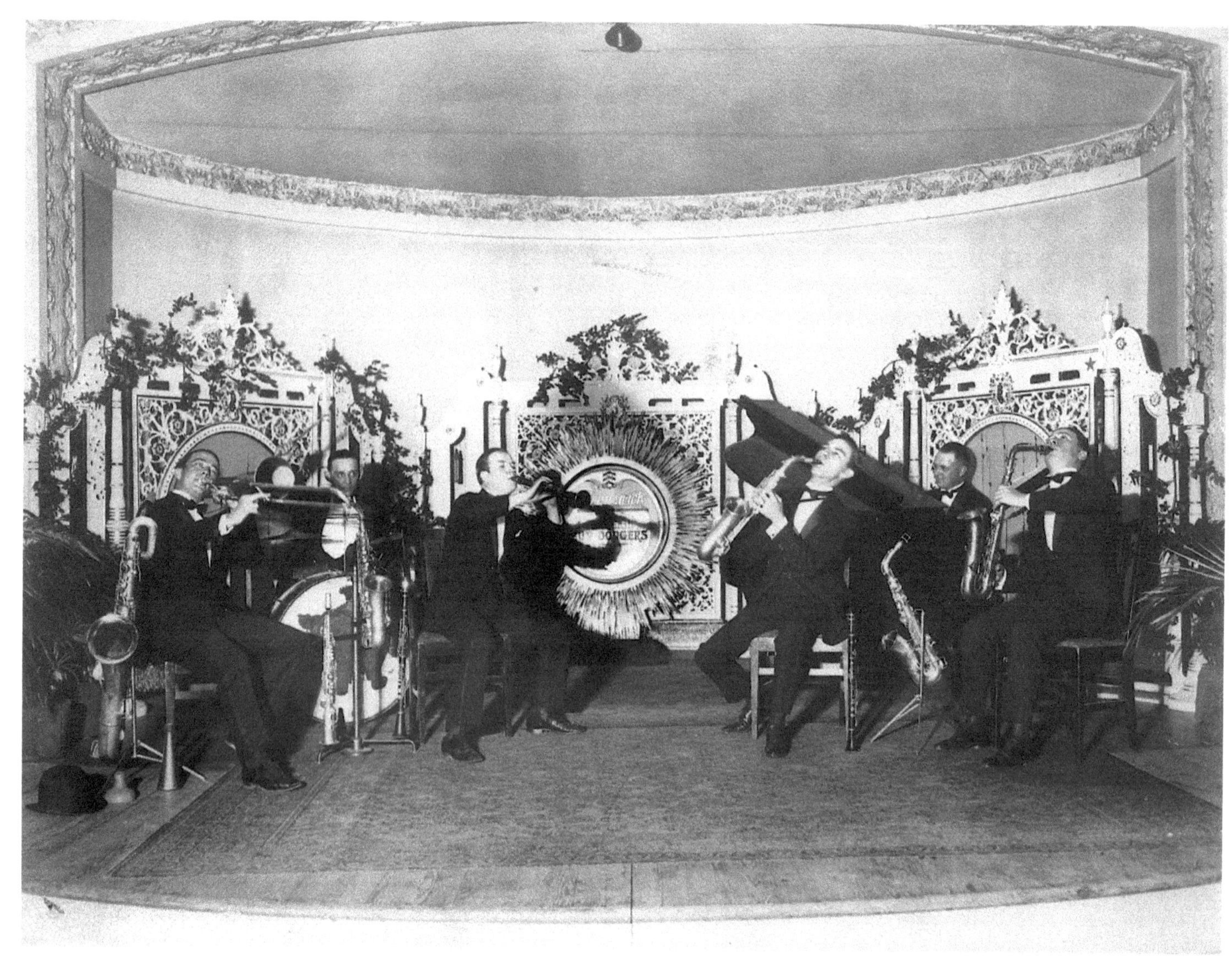

The Sun Dodgers orchestra plays in the early 1920s. Dick Post is the drummer.

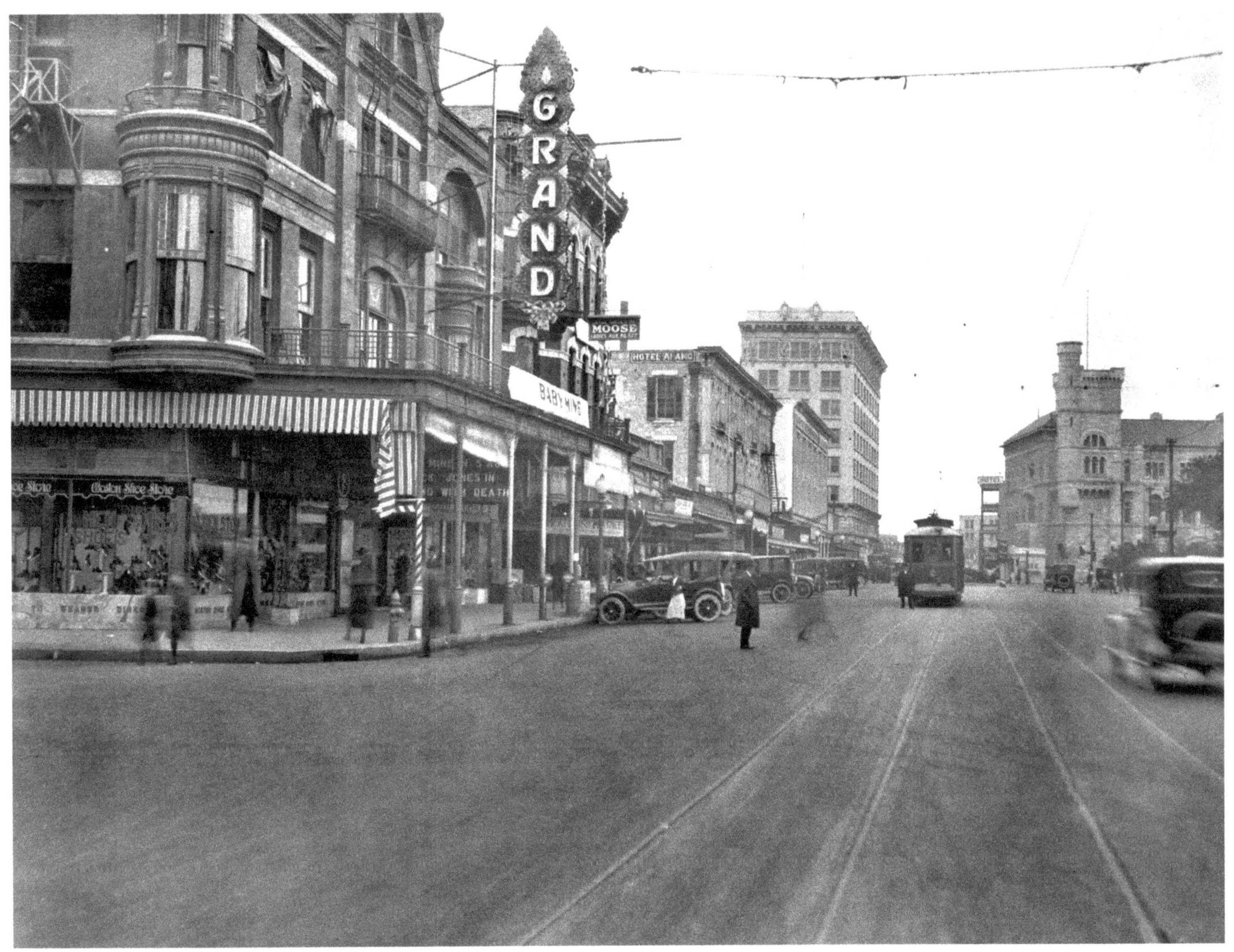

Looking north on Alamo Street on January 8, 1922. On the left is the Grand Opera House. In the back, at the right, is the Federal Building and Post Office, with the Maverick Bank building opposite.

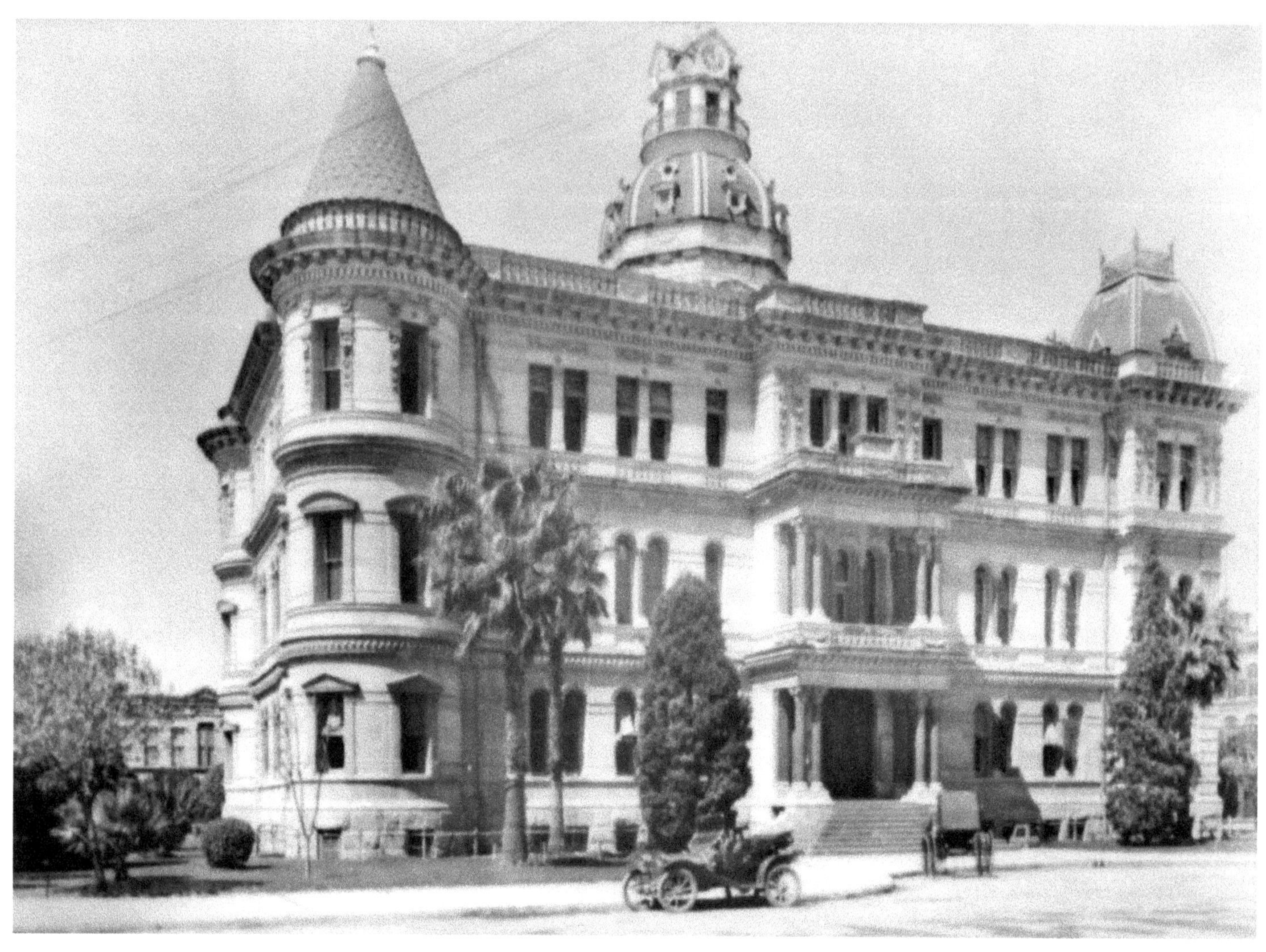

City hall completed in 1891 in the center of Military Plaza. In 1927, the clock tower and turrets were removed and a fourth floor added.

In September 1921 San Antonio suffered its worst flood. Here, we see the Alamo National Bank as floodwaters recede. Notice the dark horizontal flood line showing the high water level.

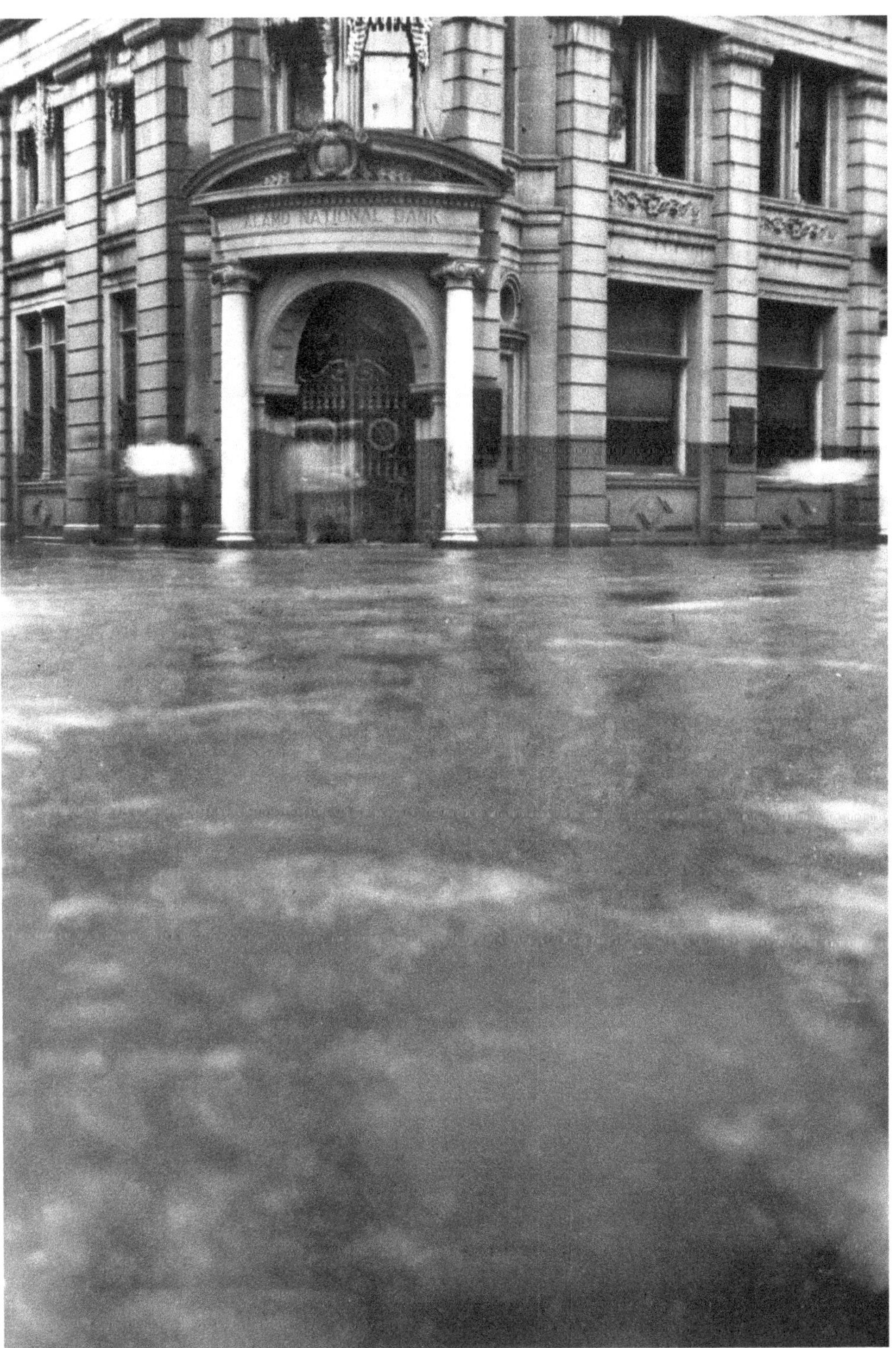

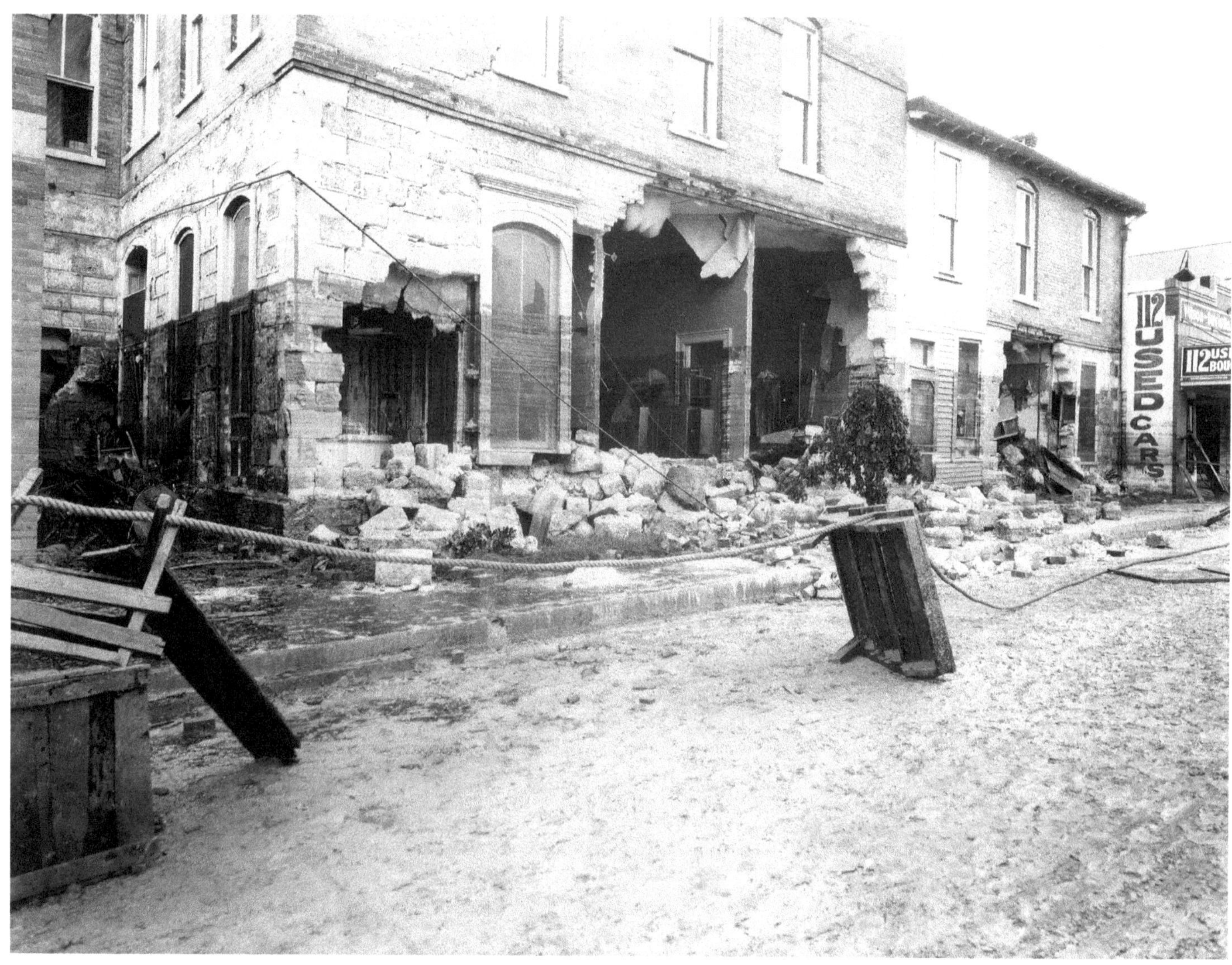

In some places, the damage done by the flood of 1921 was fairly extensive. Here, near the corner of Travis and St. Mary's, most of a wall collapsed and some stone began to wash down the street before the flood waters subsided. Notice the dark area on the inside and outside of the building showing the height to which the water rose.

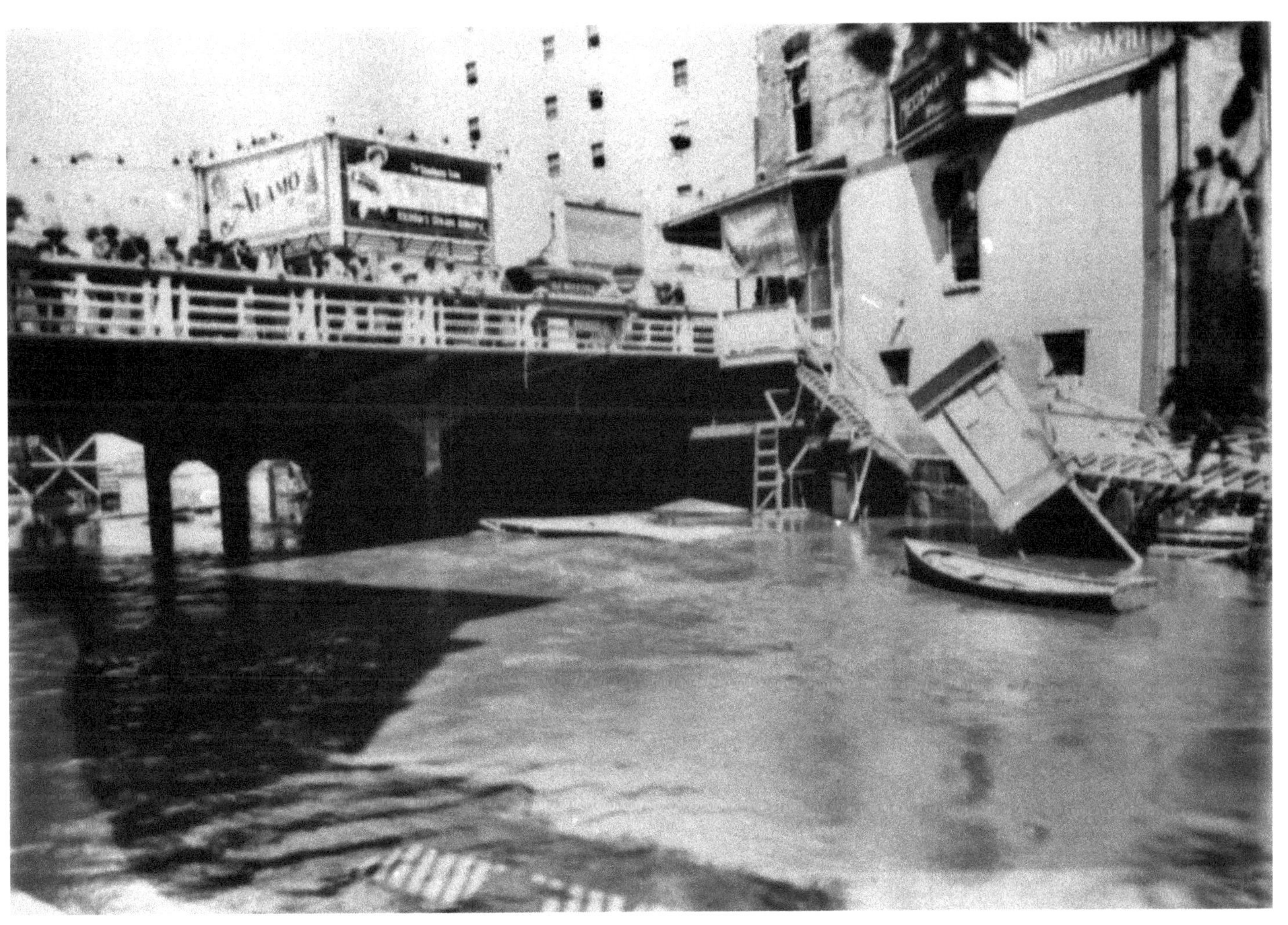

Another scene of the flood of 1921 showing destruction along the river. A rowboat drifts in the water, while men clean up debris. Such activity always brings a crowd, such as those watching from the bridge.

Olive Louise Martindale, Queen of the Court of the Sea, on her Fiesta San Jacinto float in April 1923. Each year, the Fiesta court has a theme that is reflected in costumes and floats.

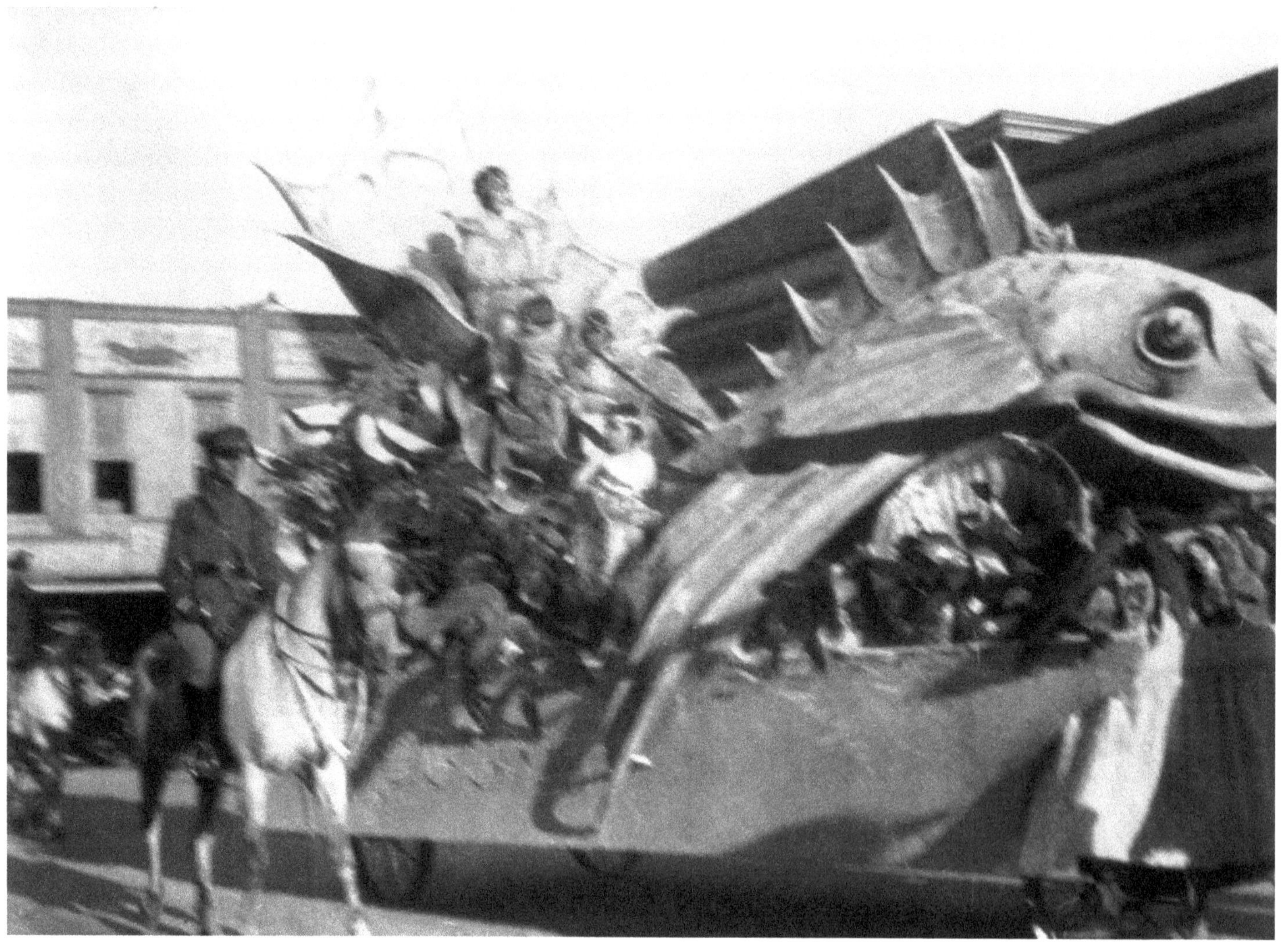

Dorothy Hillje, Dutchess of Abalone, Court of the Sea, on another 1923 Fiesta float.

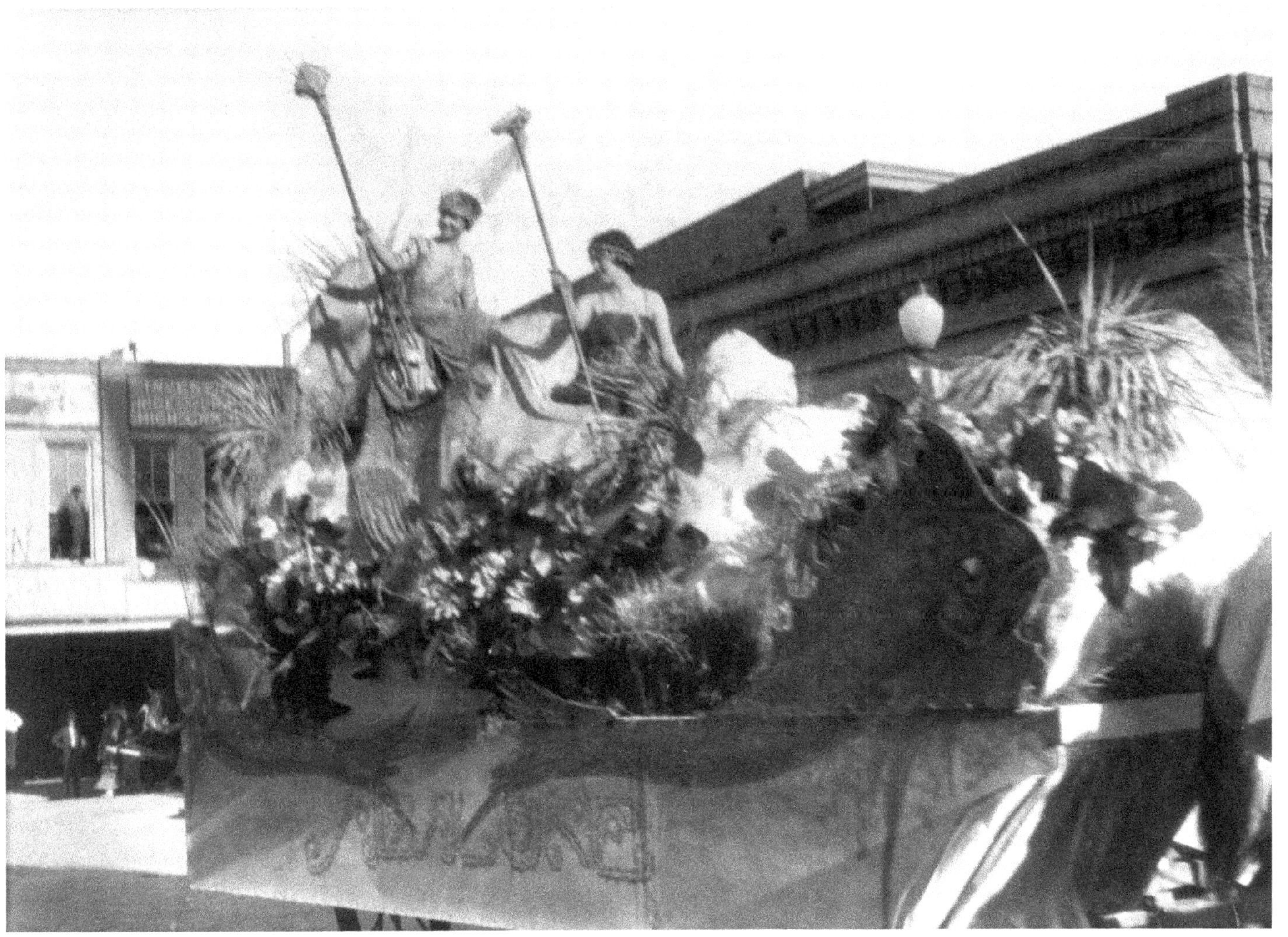

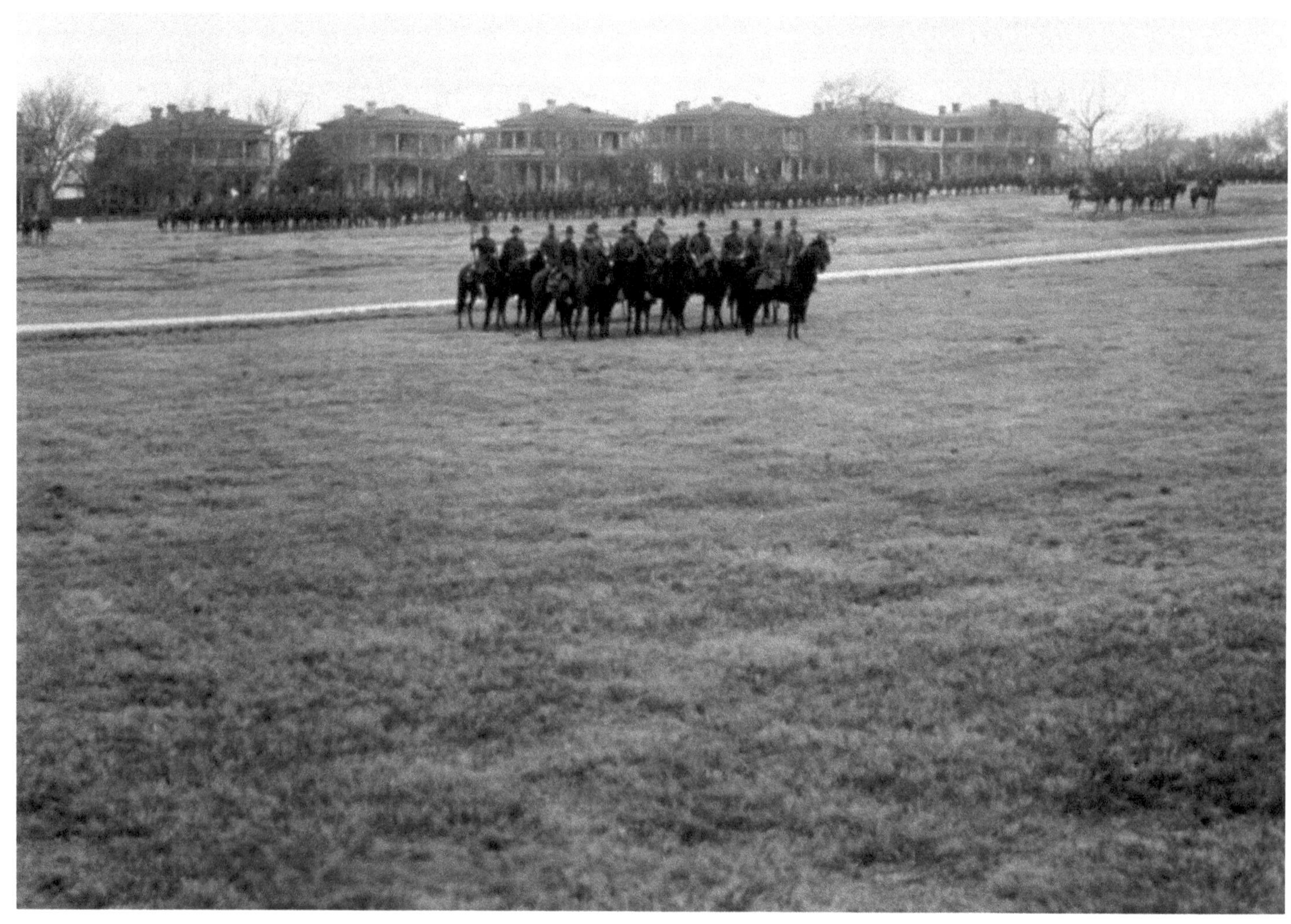

General John "Black Jack" Pershing, overall American commander in Europe during World War I and future Army chief of staff, reviewed troops at Fort Sam Houston on February 4, 1920.

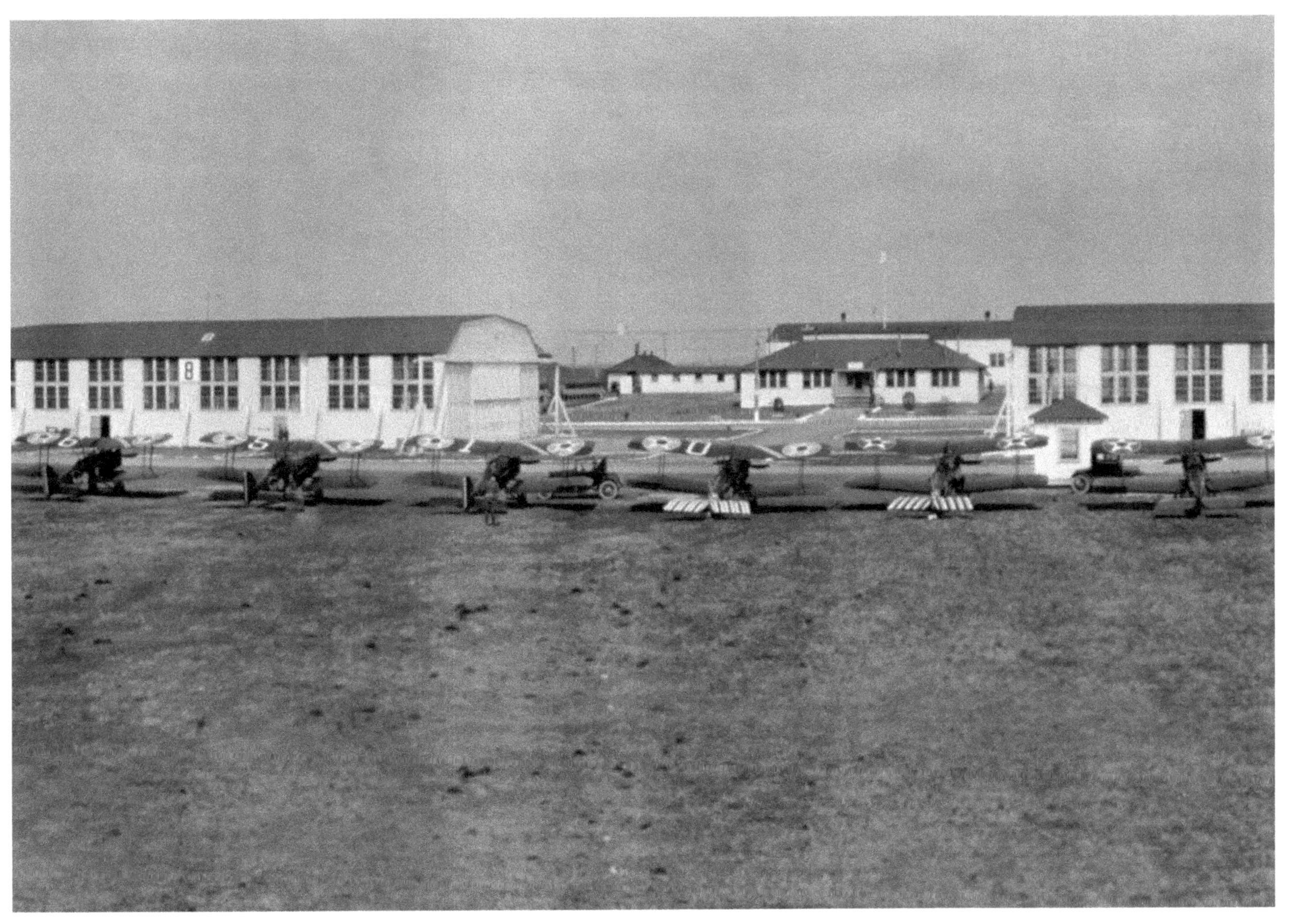

Kelly Field in the 1920s. Kelly began as an aviation depot and pilot training school in 1917. Most military pilots trained before World War II received their wings at Kelly Field.

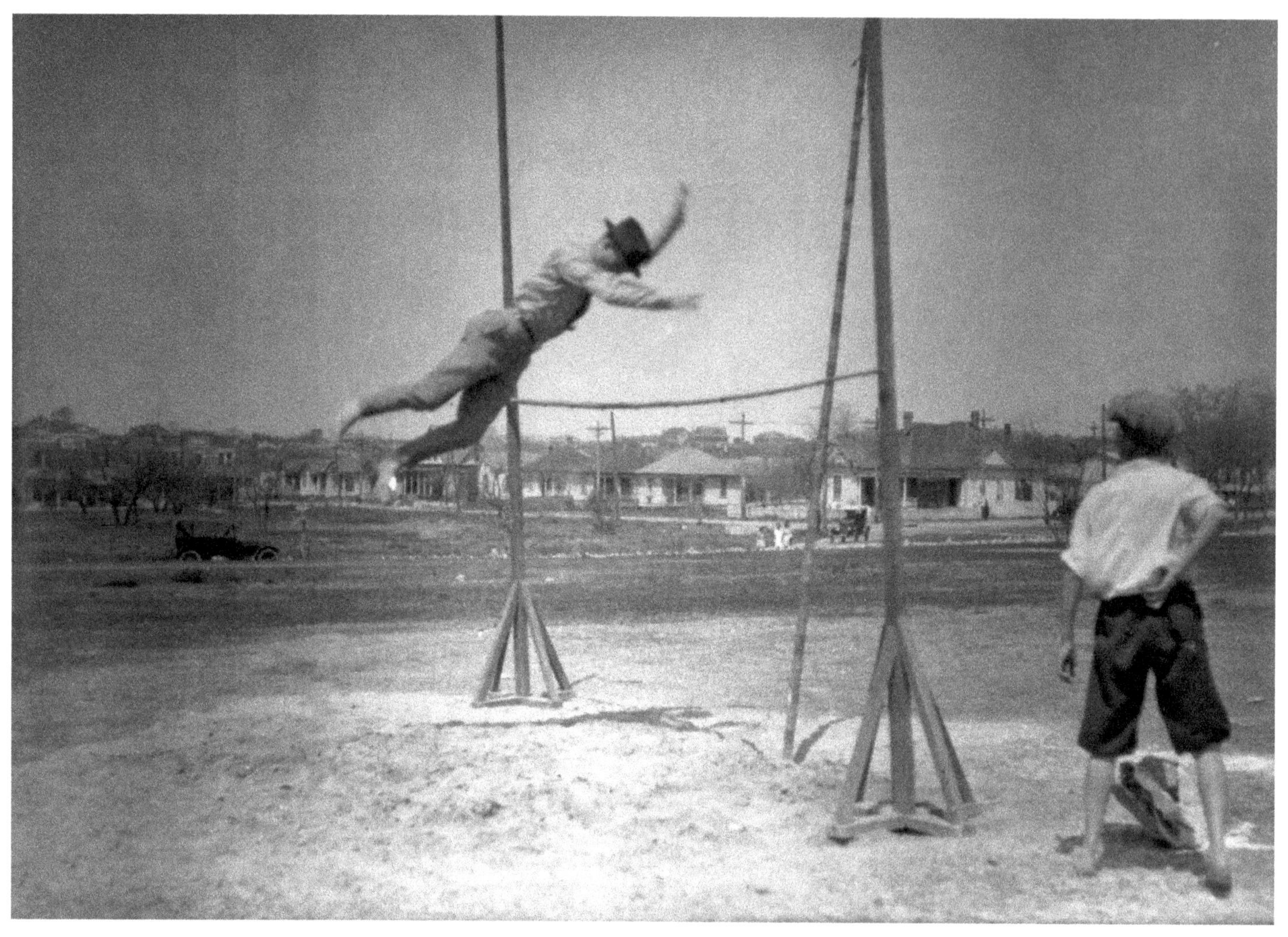

A man pole-vaulting in San Pedro Park in 1923. Houses in the background are on Ashby Street.

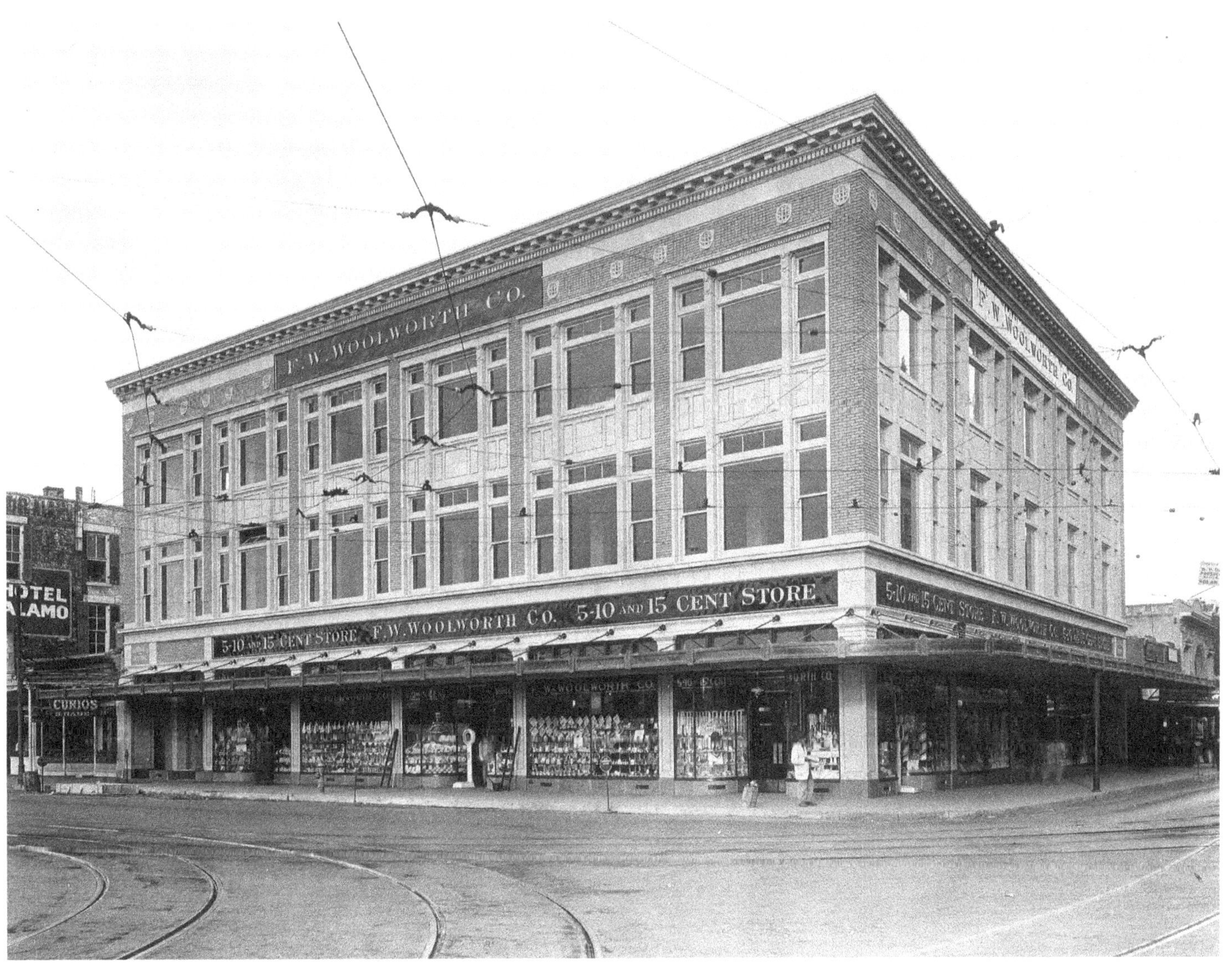

F. W. Woolworth opened its first San Antonio store in December 1912. This store at the corner of Houston and Alamo was one of 11,500 Woolworth stores when it opened on June 3, 1921. Pittsburgh Glass furnished all the display windows; H. Wagner, the interior woodwork; decorating and painting by Walter J. Daly; A. H. Shafer supplied all fixtures, heating, plumbing, and kitchen equipment; and tile and marble work was done by T. F. Phelan.

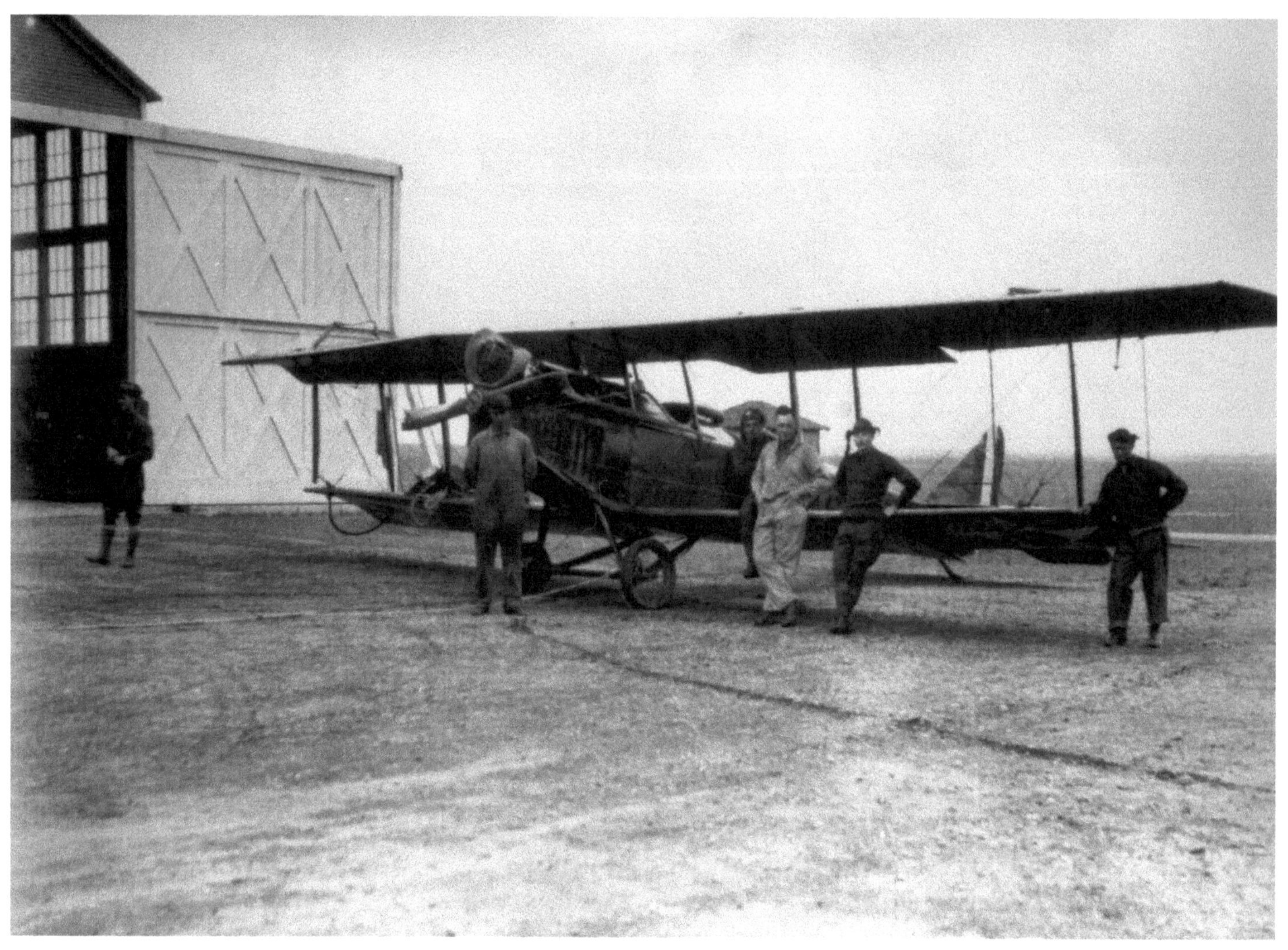

Five men pose around a biplane at Brooks Field in 1923.

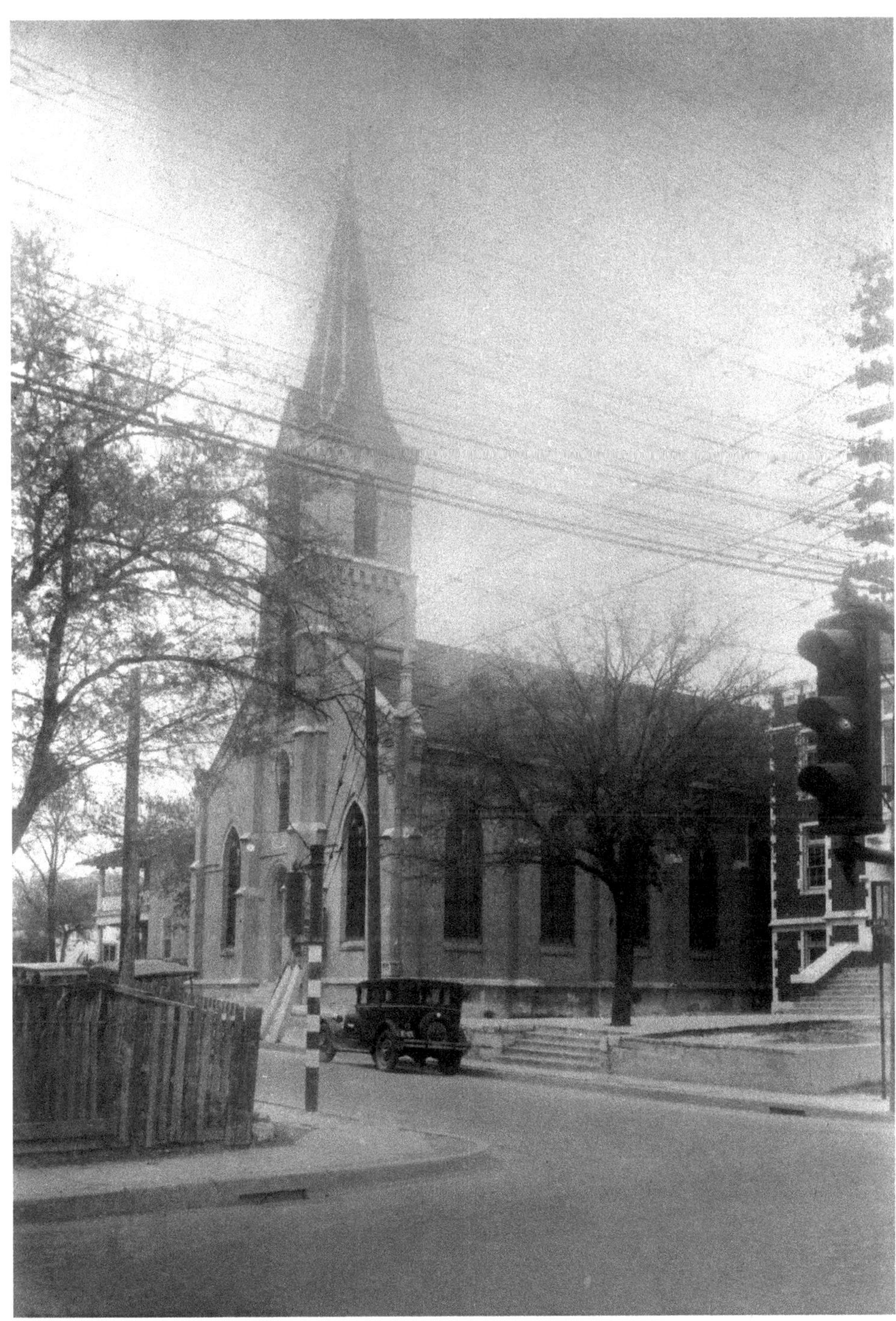

The second St. John's Lutheran Church was completed on January 12, 1886, at 306 E. Nueva Street. The recently constructed Parish Hall is visible on the right in this photo taken around 1922. The current church building was constructed in 1932.

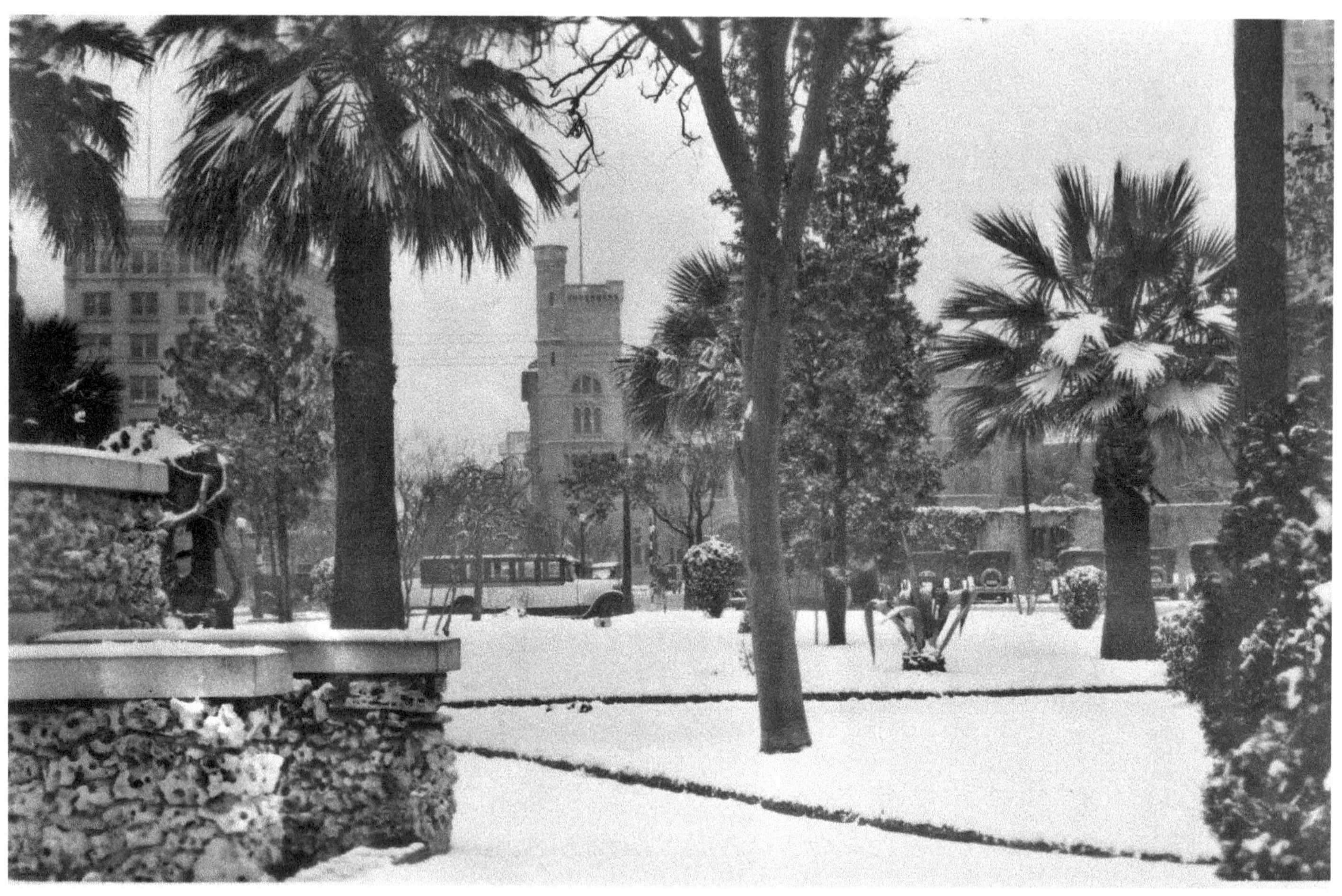

Alamo Plaza looking north after a rare snowfall in 1926. In the center rear is the Federal Building and Post Office.

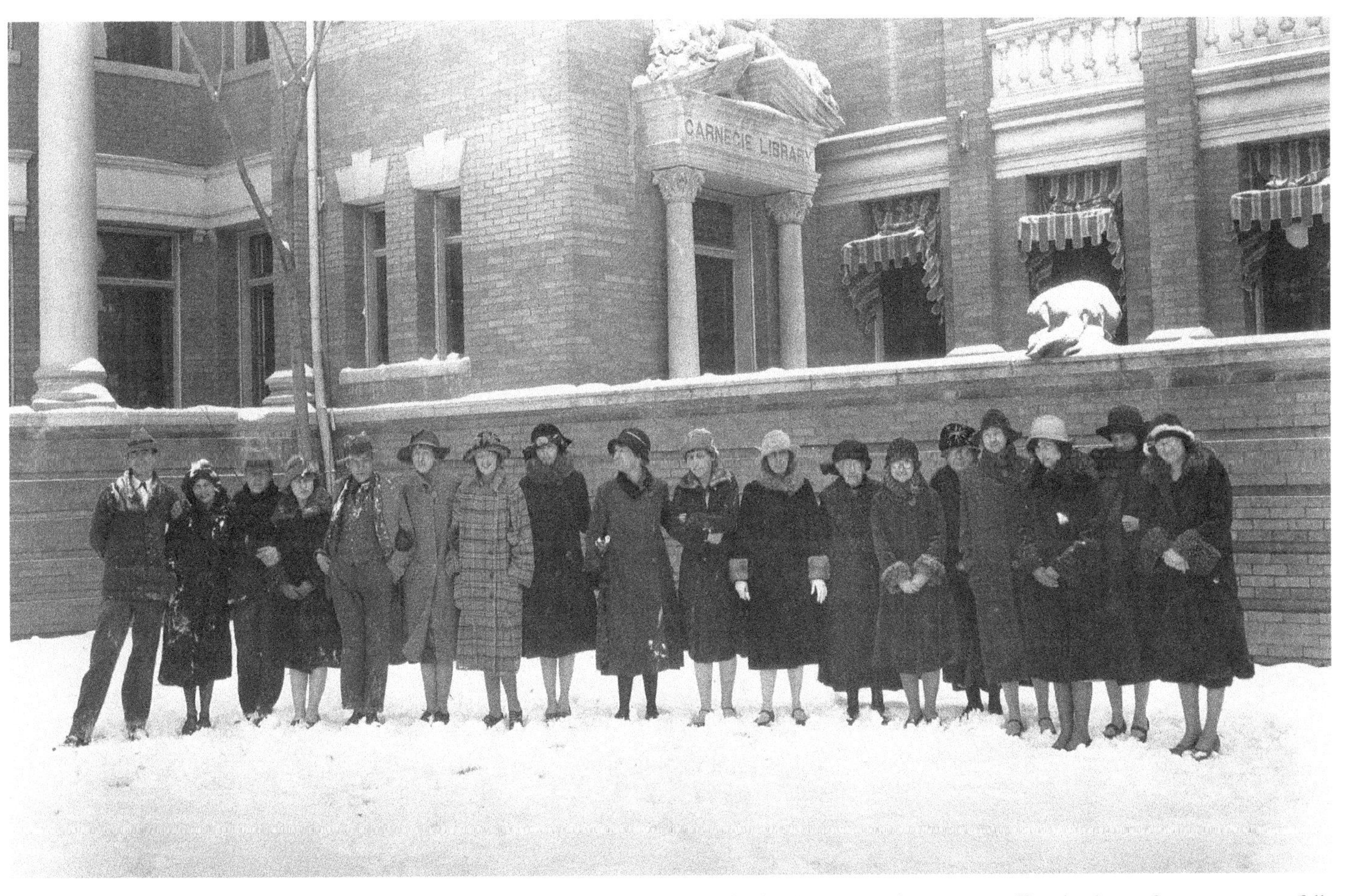

Standing outside the Carnegie Library are staff and others after a rare snowfall. Almost 6.5 inches of snow fell between January 23-24, 1926.

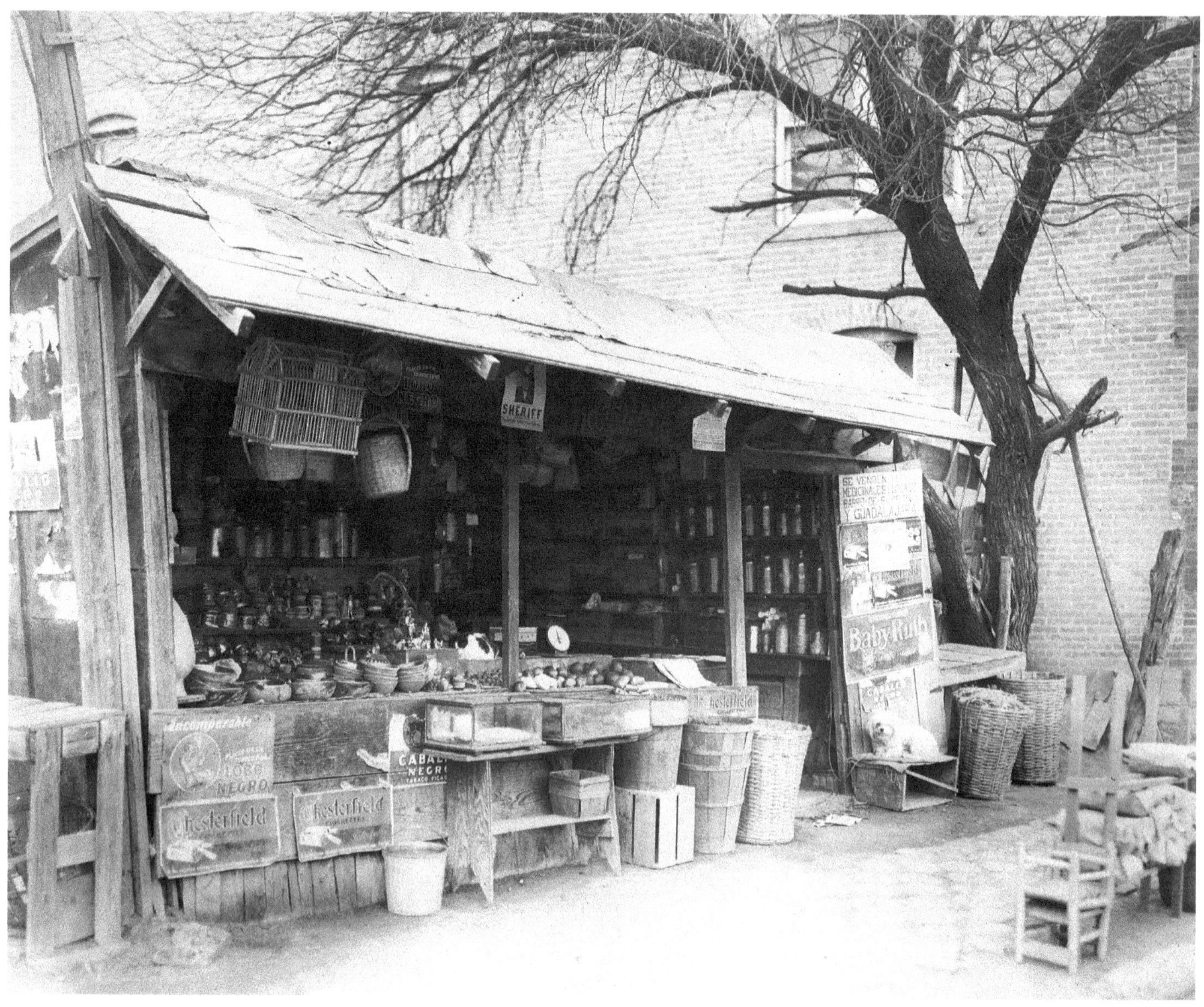

A "Mexican Shop" on S. Laredo Street in 1926. Advertising with broadsides was important even to a small shop like this one. The top sign on the door advertises herbs and medicines. The shelves were packed with all kinds of needed items, along with Baby Ruth candy bars and Chesterfield cigarettes. By the door, a small dog appears to be guarding the shop while the owner is away.

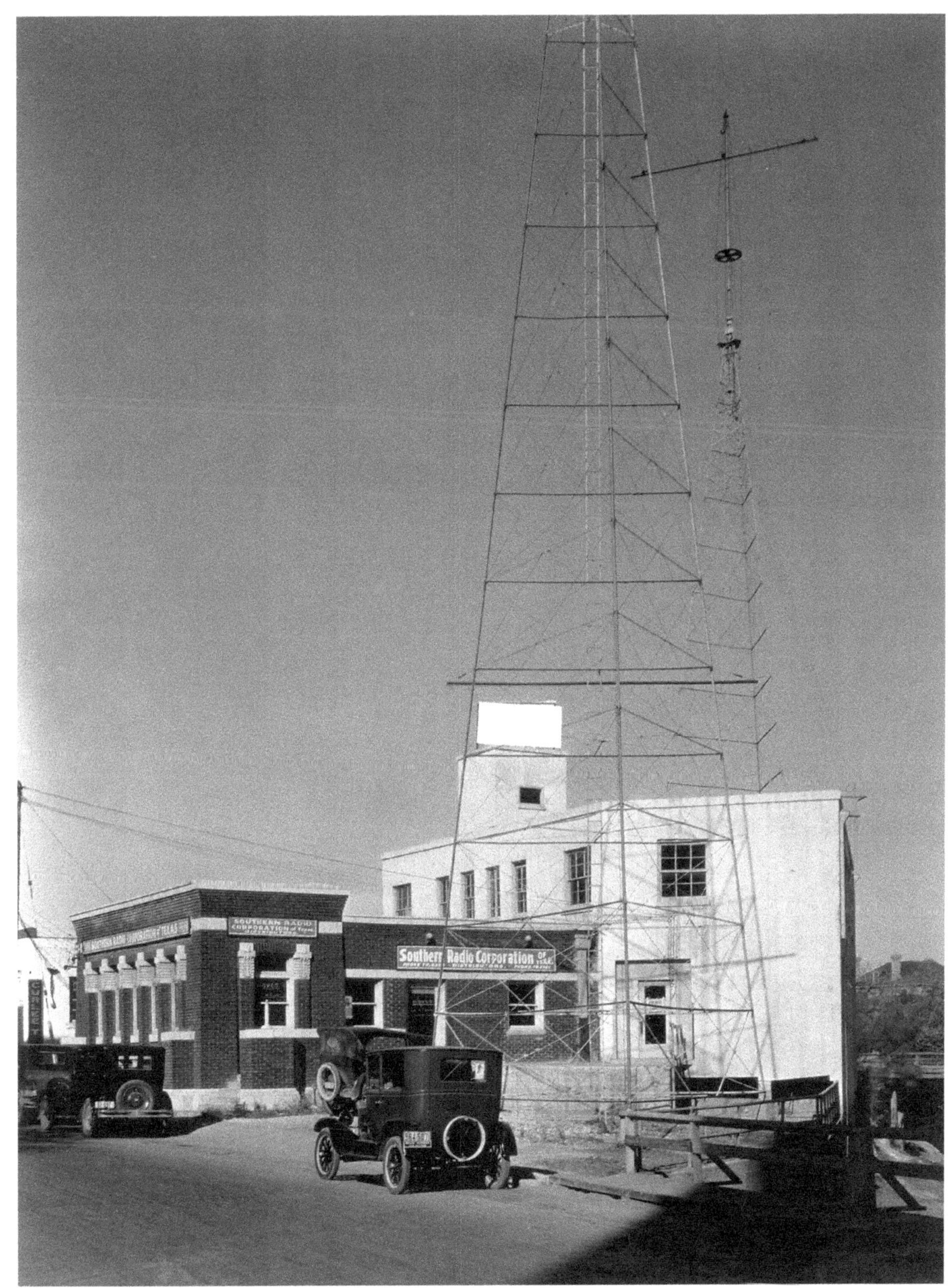

San Antonio's second radio station, WCAR, at 101 W. Pecan in 1926. WCAR, owned by John C. Rodriguez, began as Alamo Radio & Electric Company in 1921. By 1924, it was known as Southern Radio Corporation of Texas, transmitting on 1,140 kilocycles with 100 watts. In 1928, it became KTSA, which continues to broadcast today.

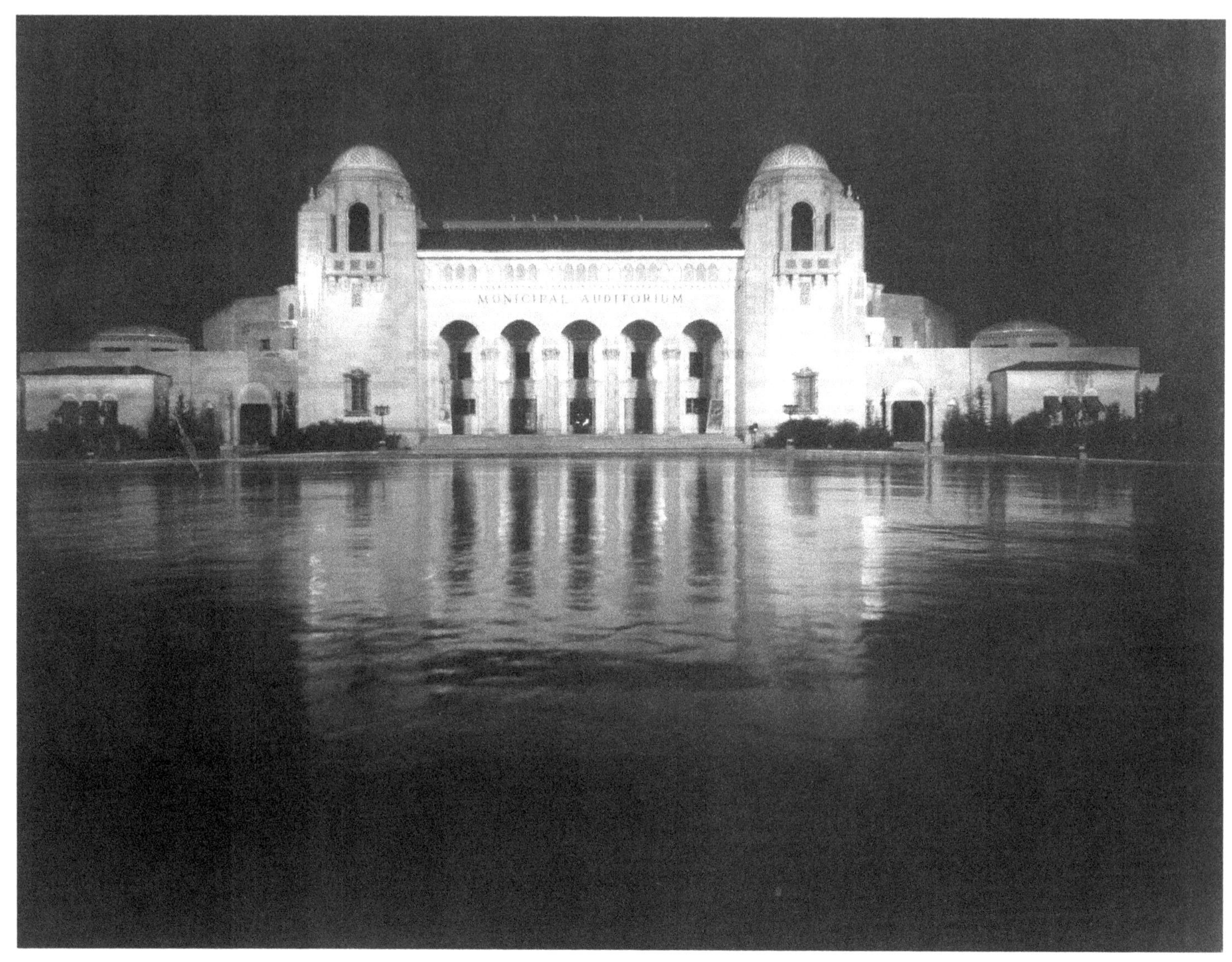

A beautiful night scene of the Municipal Auditorium. Opened in 1926, the auditorium was designed by Atlee B. Ayres, George Willis, and Emmett Jackson as a memorial to those who died in World War I.

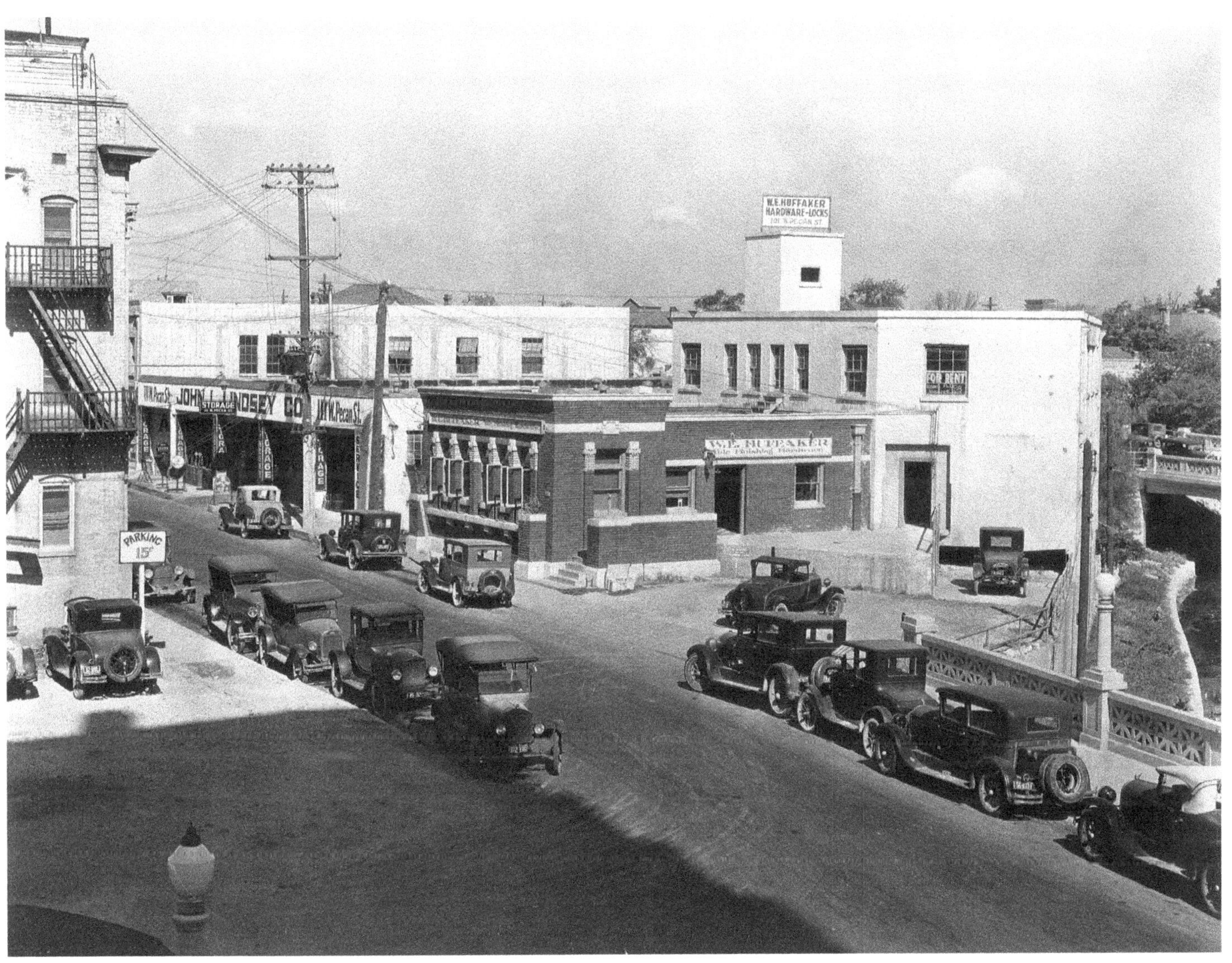

The beginning of the one hundred block of W. Pecan Street sits between the river and N. St. Mary's Street on the right and Soledad on the left. This photograph was taken between 1927–1933 when W. E. Huffaker was at 101 W. Pecan Street. John Lindsey Co. at 111 W. Pecan was a garage and storage operation. The building at the left with the fifteen-cent parking was the River View Apartments.

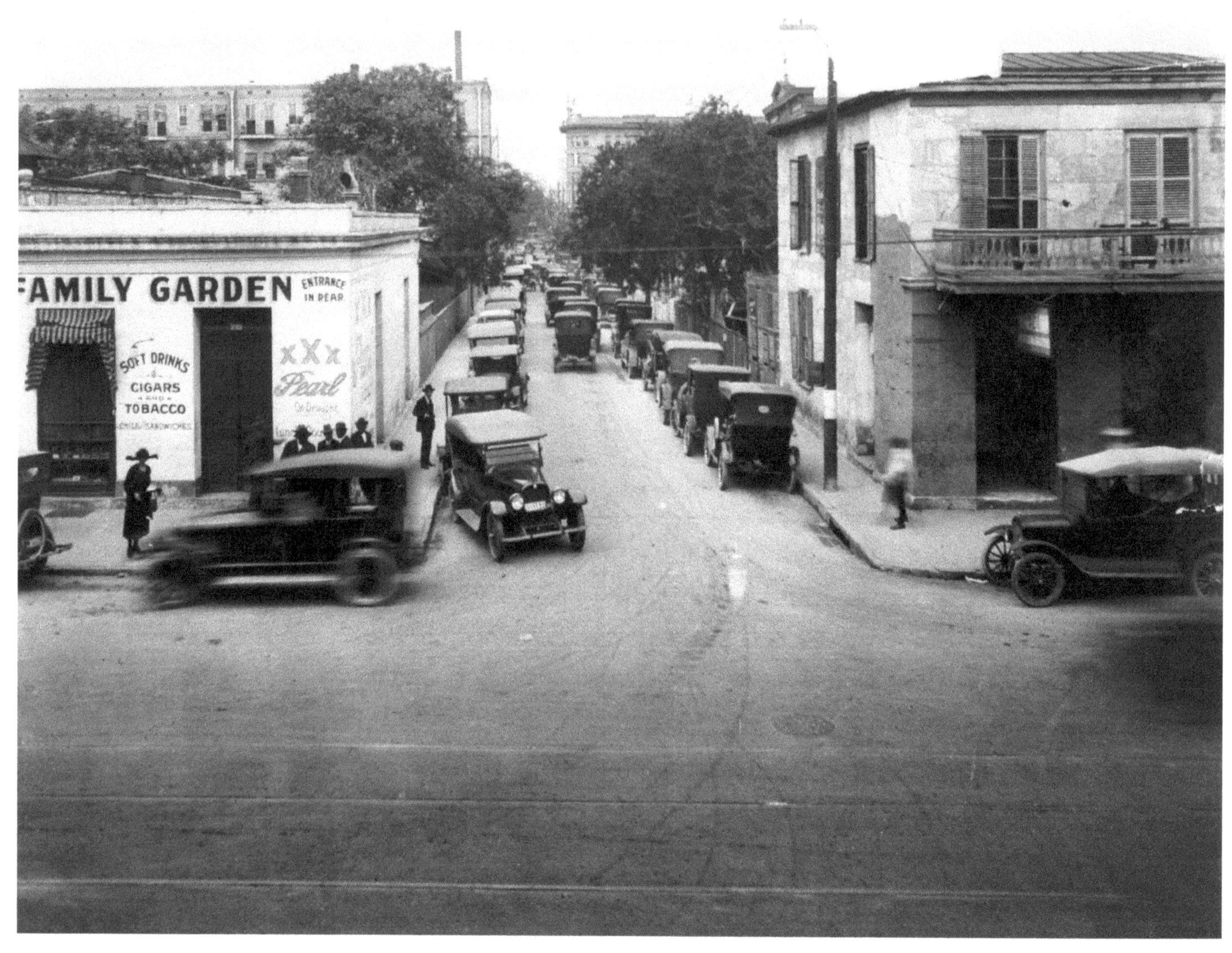

Bonham Street looking north. The Family Garden restaurant on the left served San Antonio-brewed Pearl beer. In the distance are the Menger and Crockett Hotels.

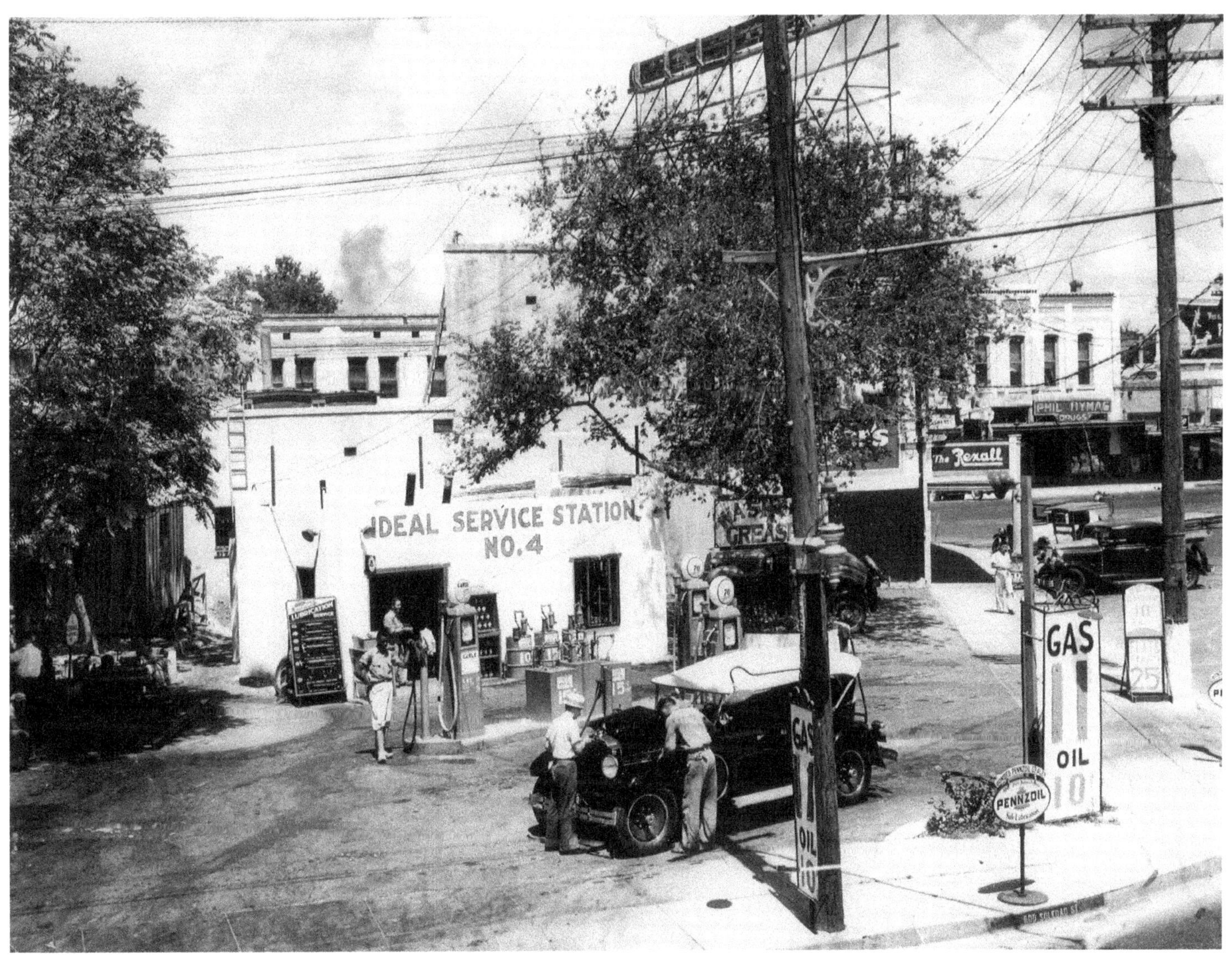

Remember when service stations were "full service," gas sold for 11 cents, oil for 10 cents, and you could get flats fixed for a quarter? The Phil Hymas Drug Store in the background was at 659 Main.

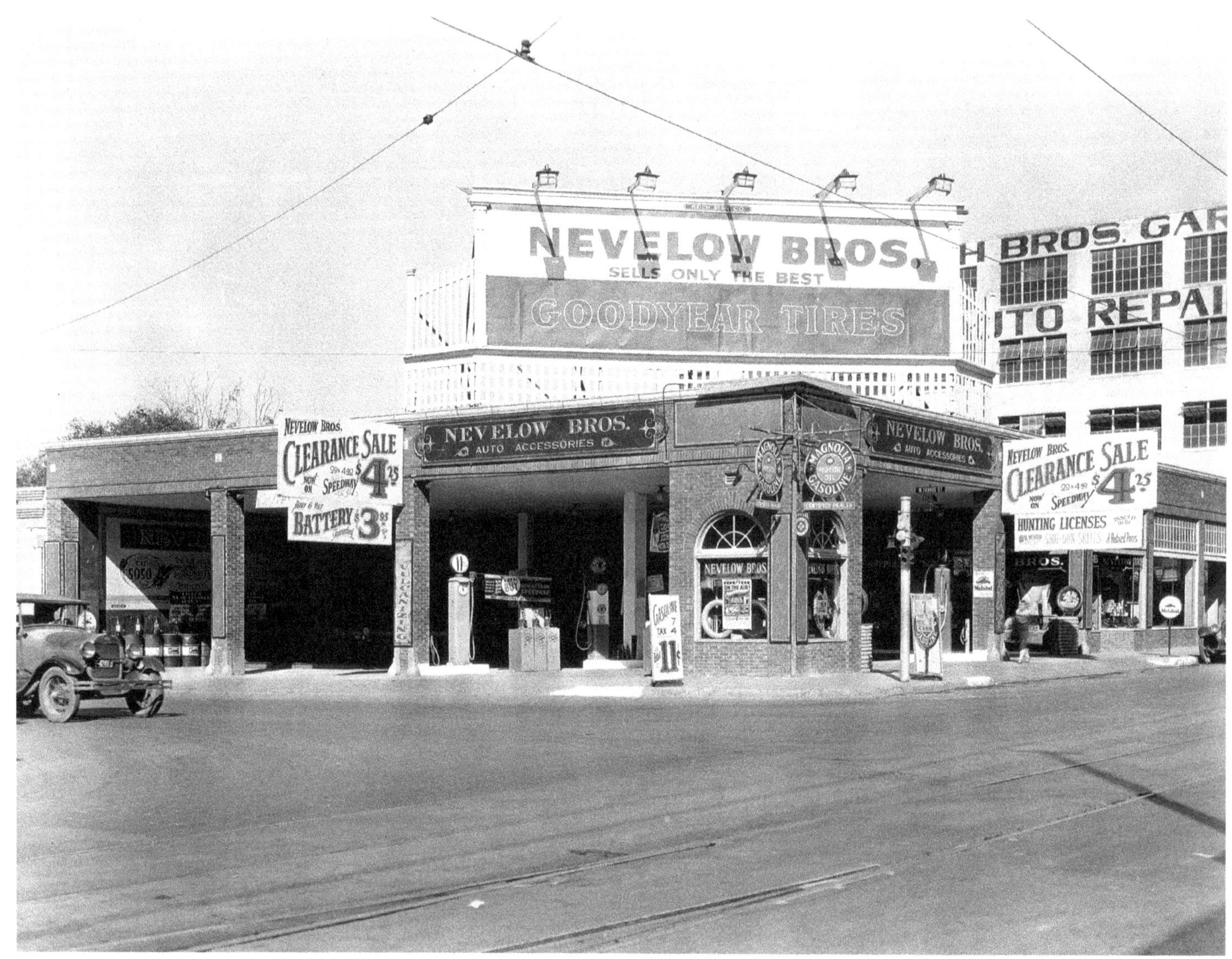

By the 1920s, the automobile required attention and grooming in much the same way as the horse did before it. About 1918, the Nevelow brothers—Jacob M., Samuel, Nathan, Leo, and Issy—opened this wholesale tire and accessories business at 512 E. Travis. Around 1930, they added other locations, but by 1936, each brother had gone out on his own in various ventures.

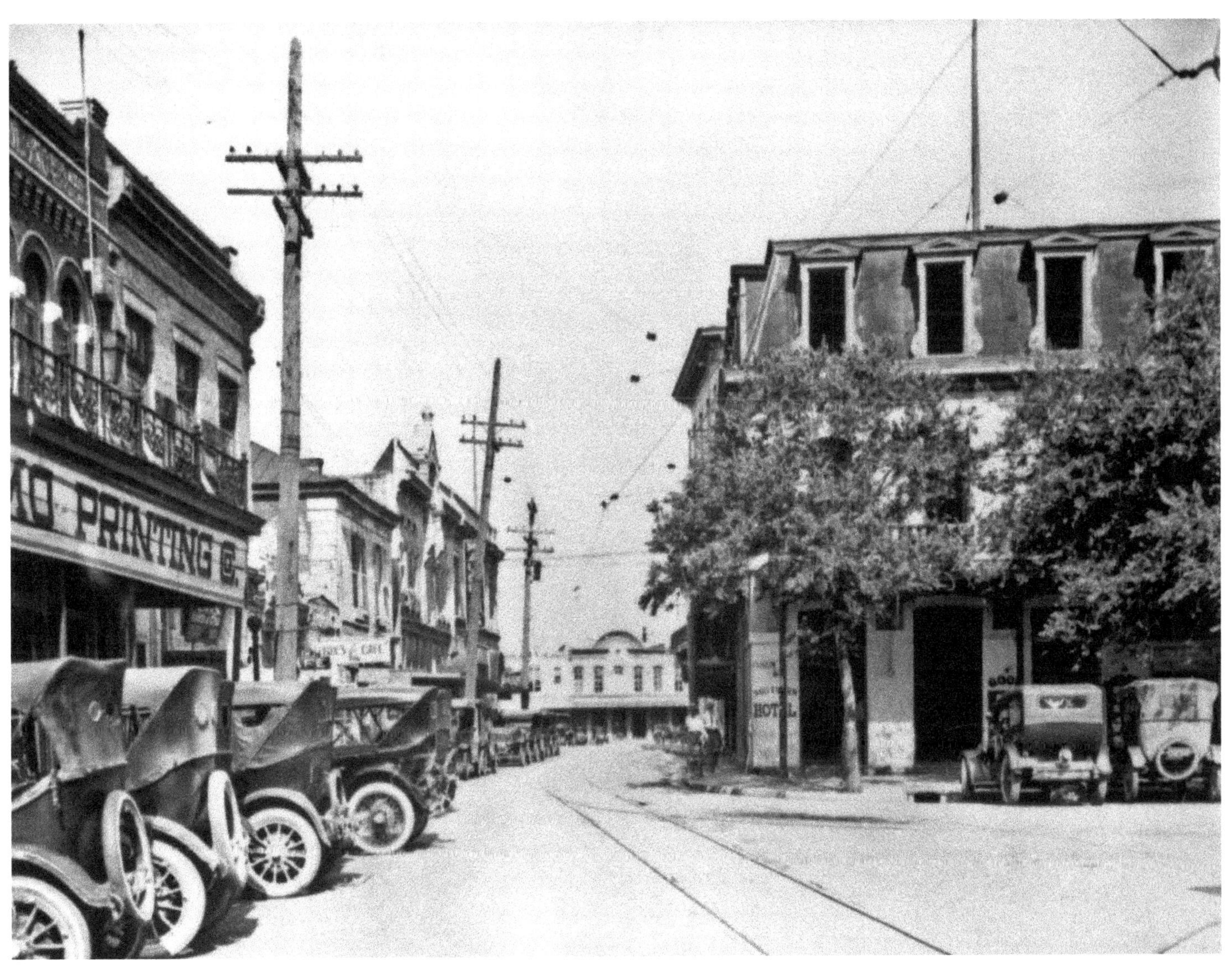

Dolorosa Street at Main Plaza, looking west, about 1925. On the right is the Southern Hotel. It appears to be a busy day with all the cars parked in front of the businesses along Dolorosa.

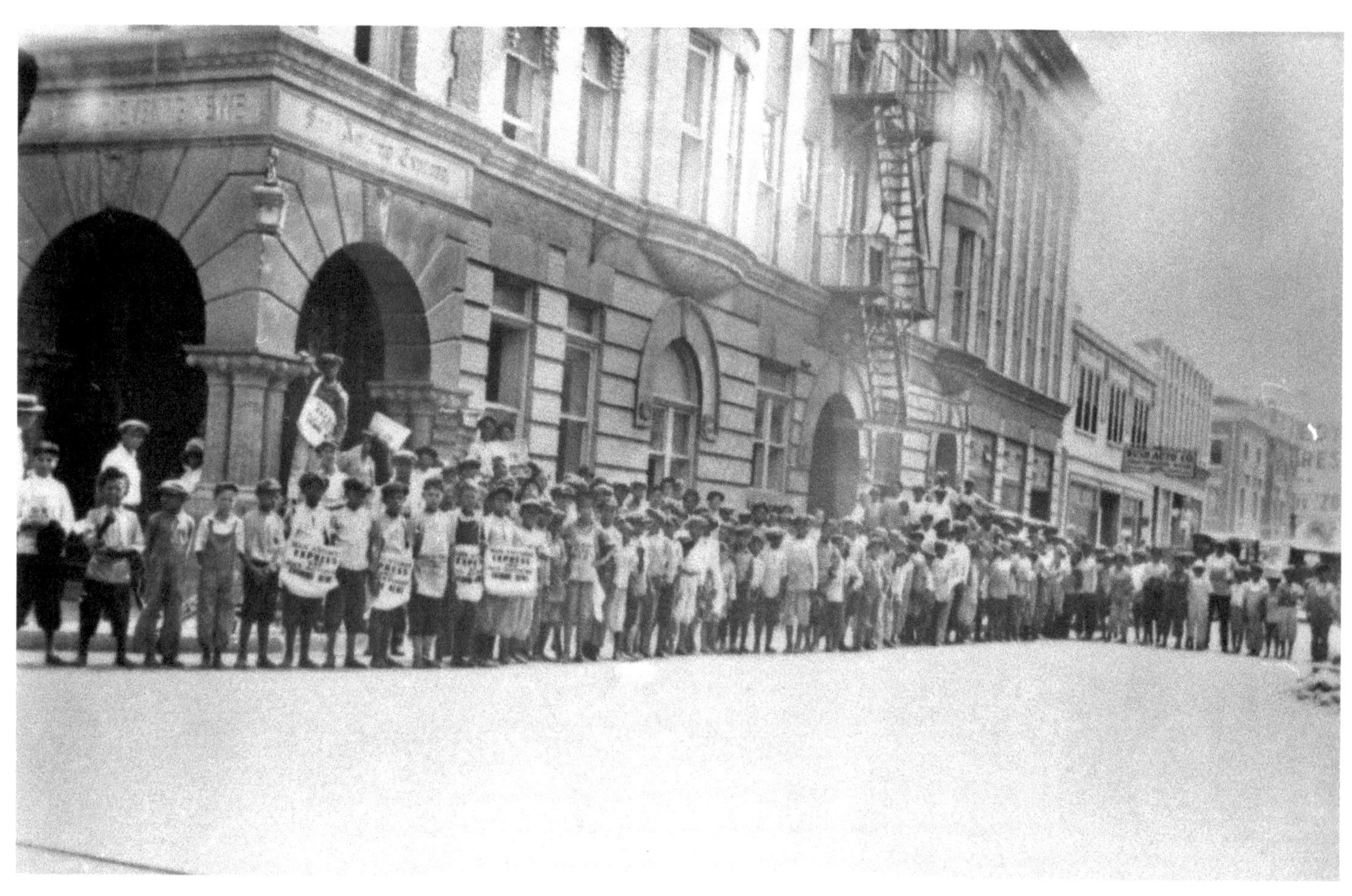

This gathering of mostly barefoot newspaper boys in front of the San Antonio Express-News building on Crockett Street was photographed around 1925.

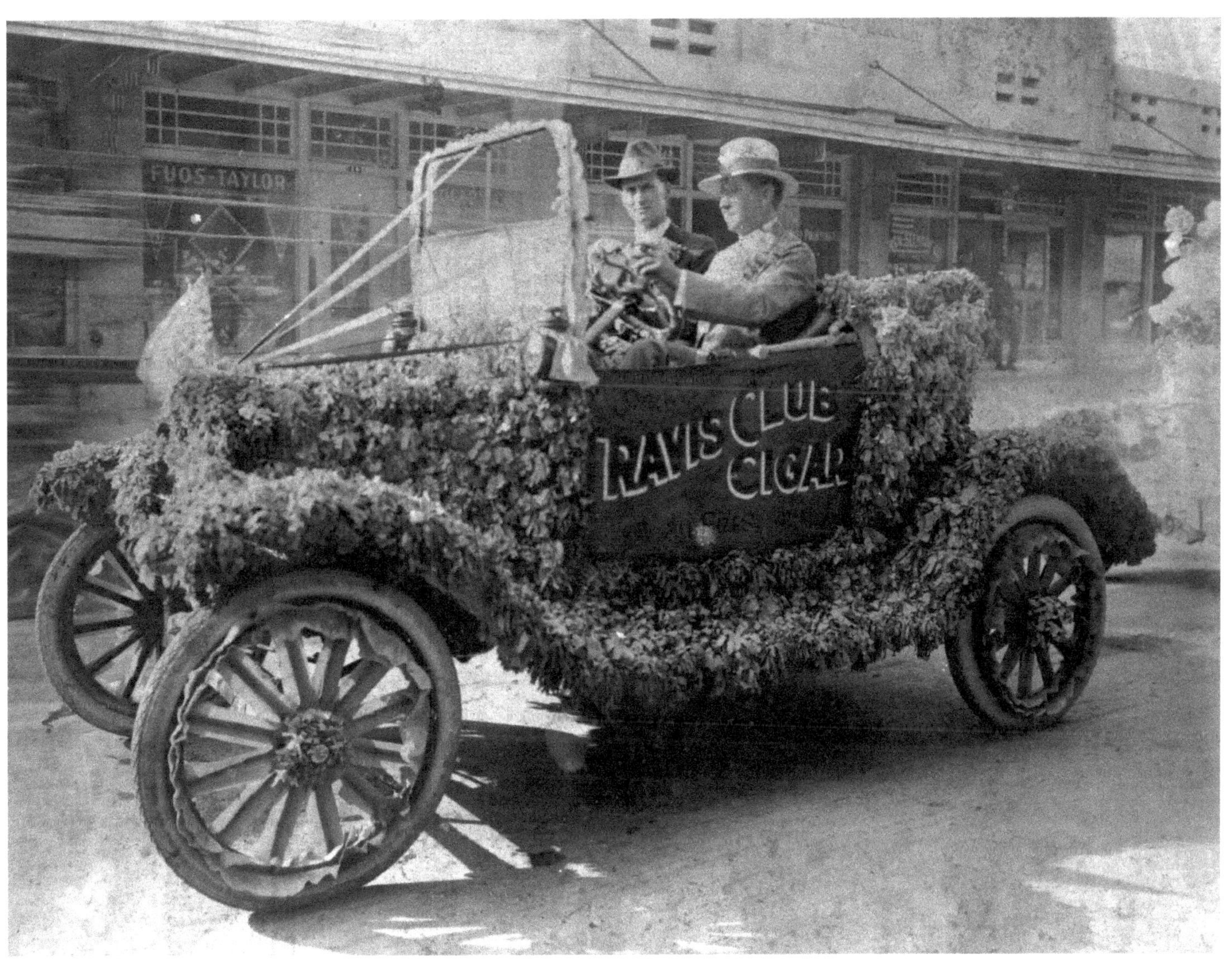

During an early 1920s Battle of Flowers parade, two unidentified men sit in the 400 block of N. Alamo Street in their automobile decorated with flowers and a sign for Travis Club Cigars, which were manufactured by the Finck Cigar Company, founded in 1893. In 1910, Finck began making this special cigar for members of the Travis Club, an exclusive social club.

A 1920s view of Travis Park Methodist Church. Travis Park is believed to have been the city's first Protestant congregation, organized in 1846. The first service in this building was held on September 26, 1886. In 1934, a prayer group began publishing a quarterly devotional for home use. That devotional, *The Upper Room,* is now read by nearly three million people worldwide. The tall building beyond housed the South Texas National Bank.

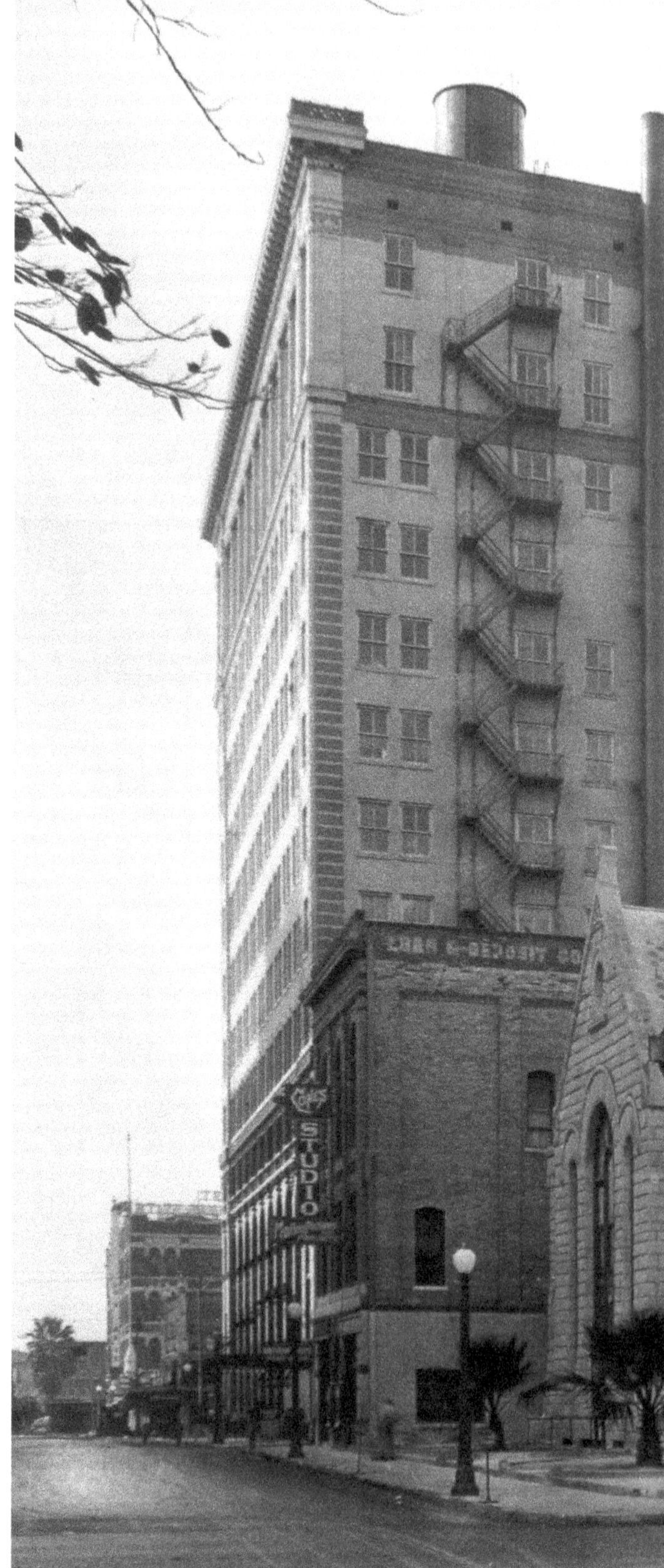

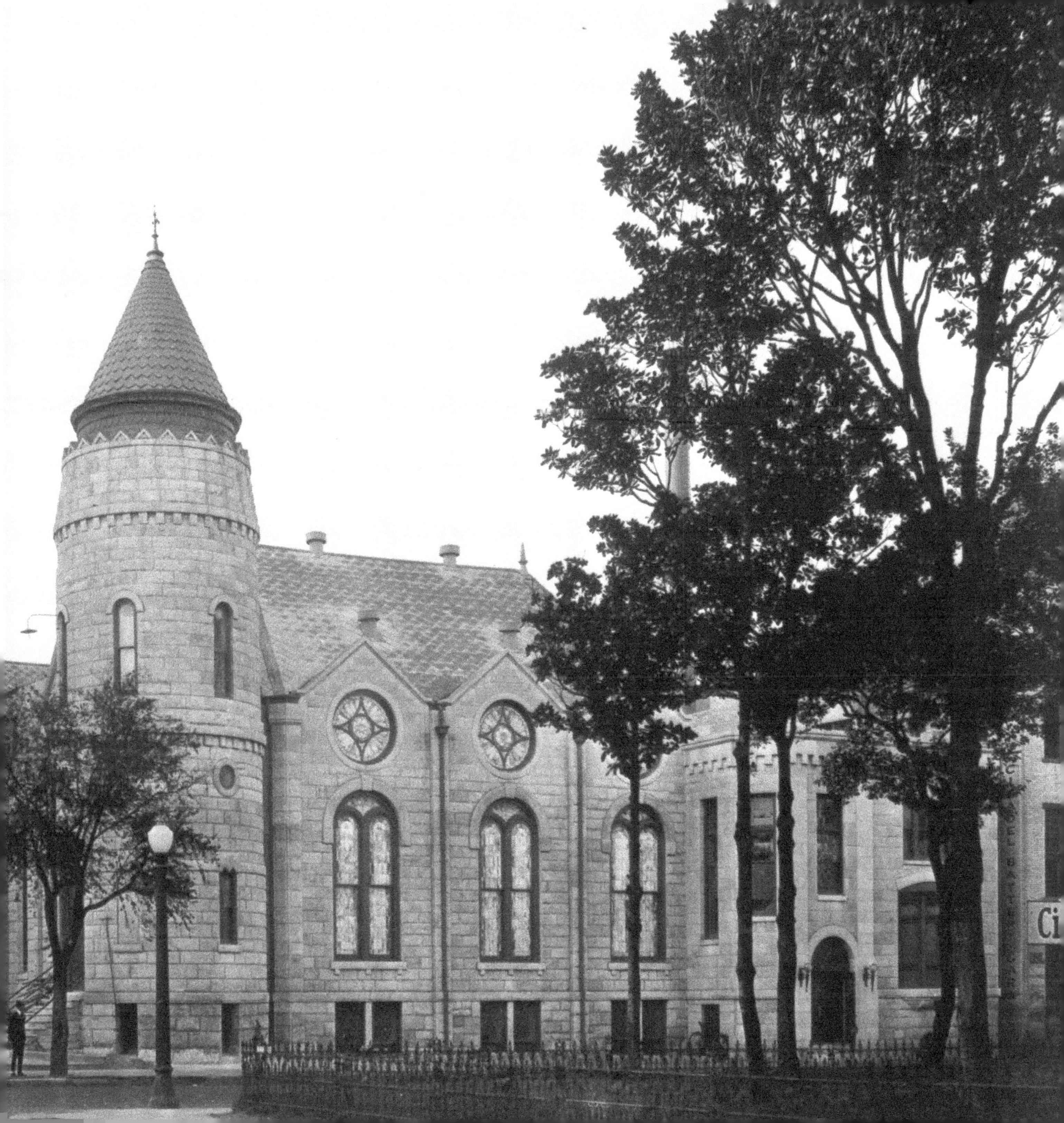

This 1923 Battle of Flowers parade float appears as a beautiful flower-covered locomotive with an elk head on the front.

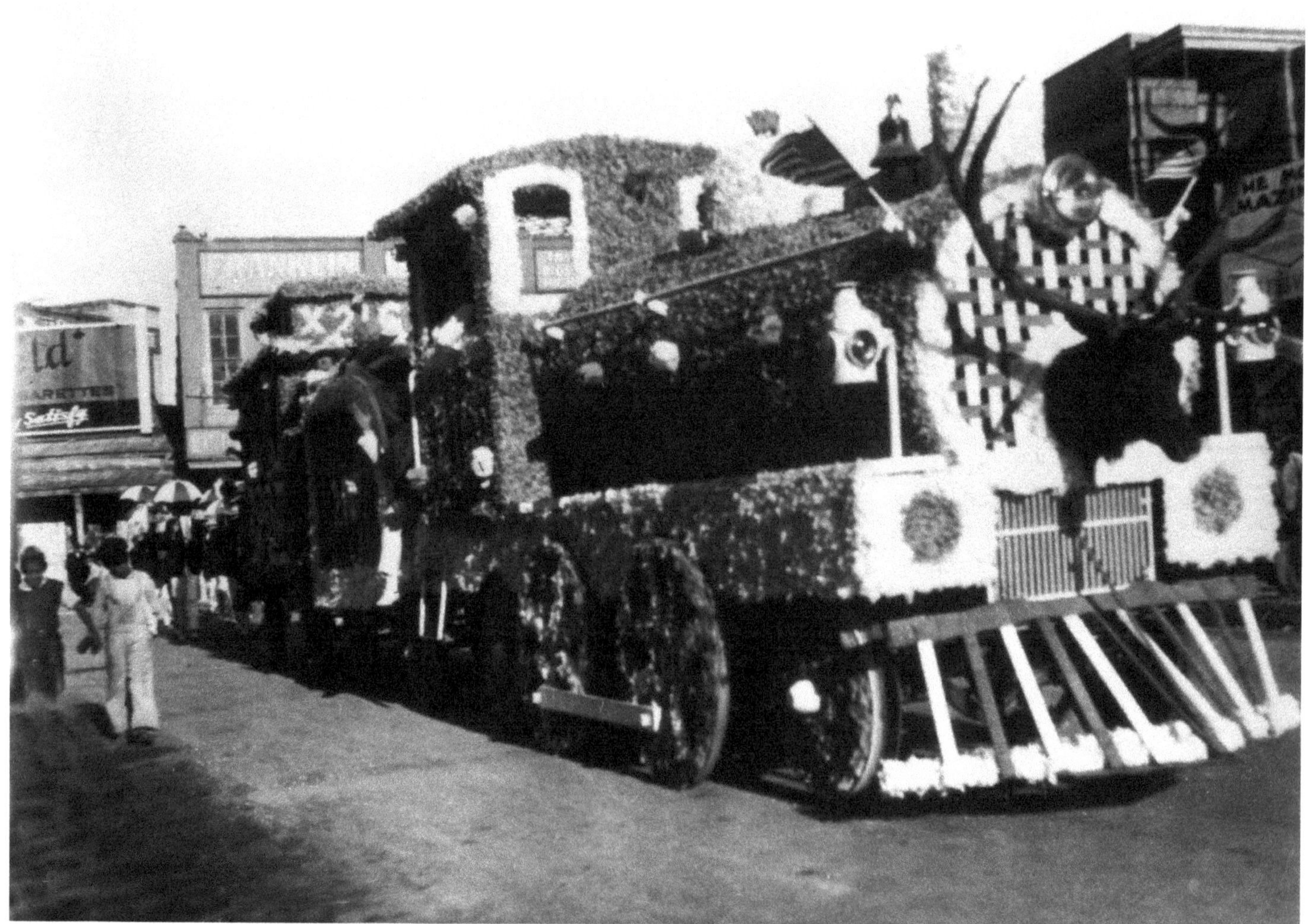

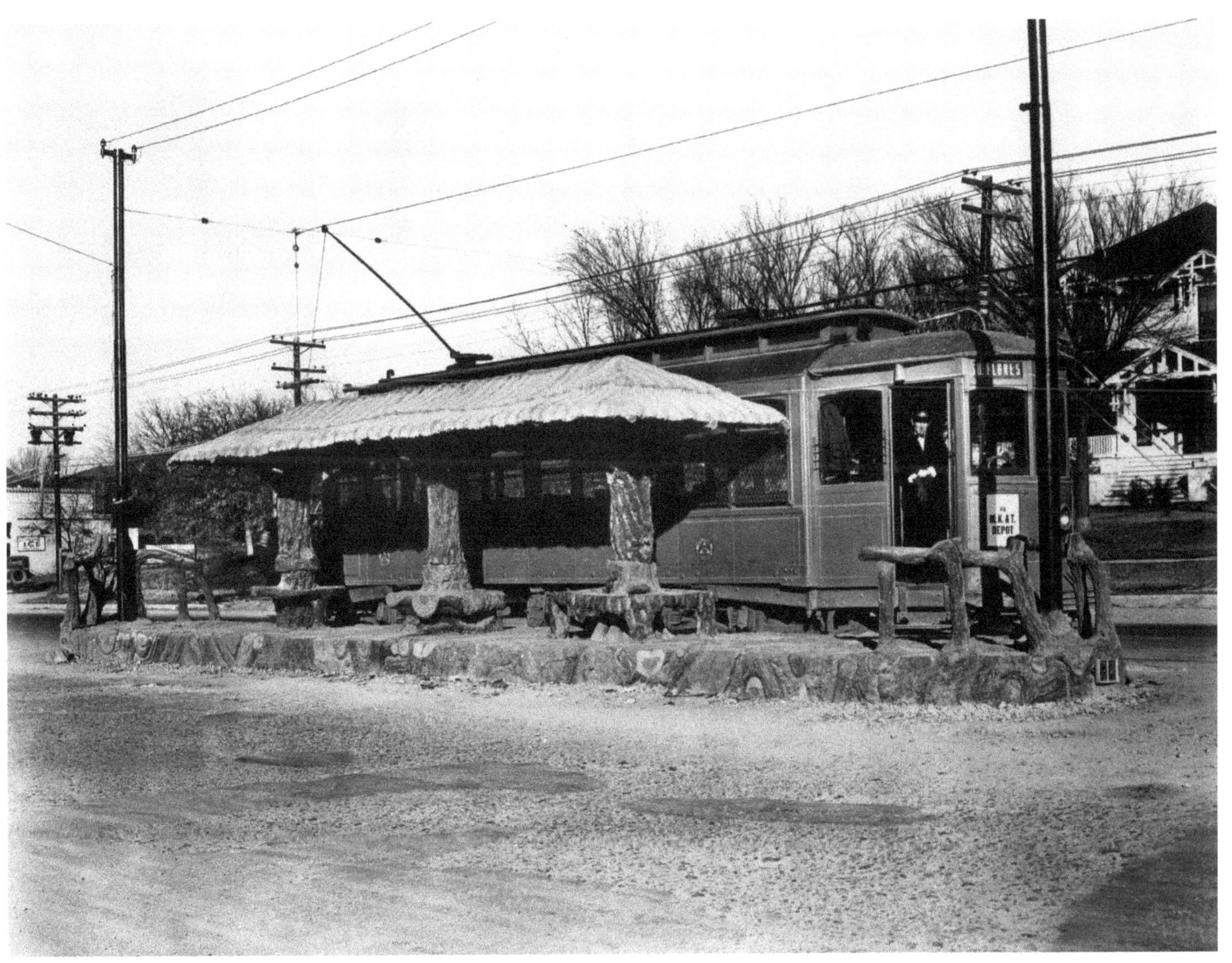

A trolley stop on Broadway at Patterson was created by Dionicio Rodriguez, a native of Toluca, Mexico. Rodriguez, who came to San Antonio in the 1920s, is noted for his rustic sculptures that appear to be made of wood but are actually a cement process. Other examples of his work can be seen at the Spanish Governor's Palace and Brackenridge Park. When he died some of his secret processes died with him.

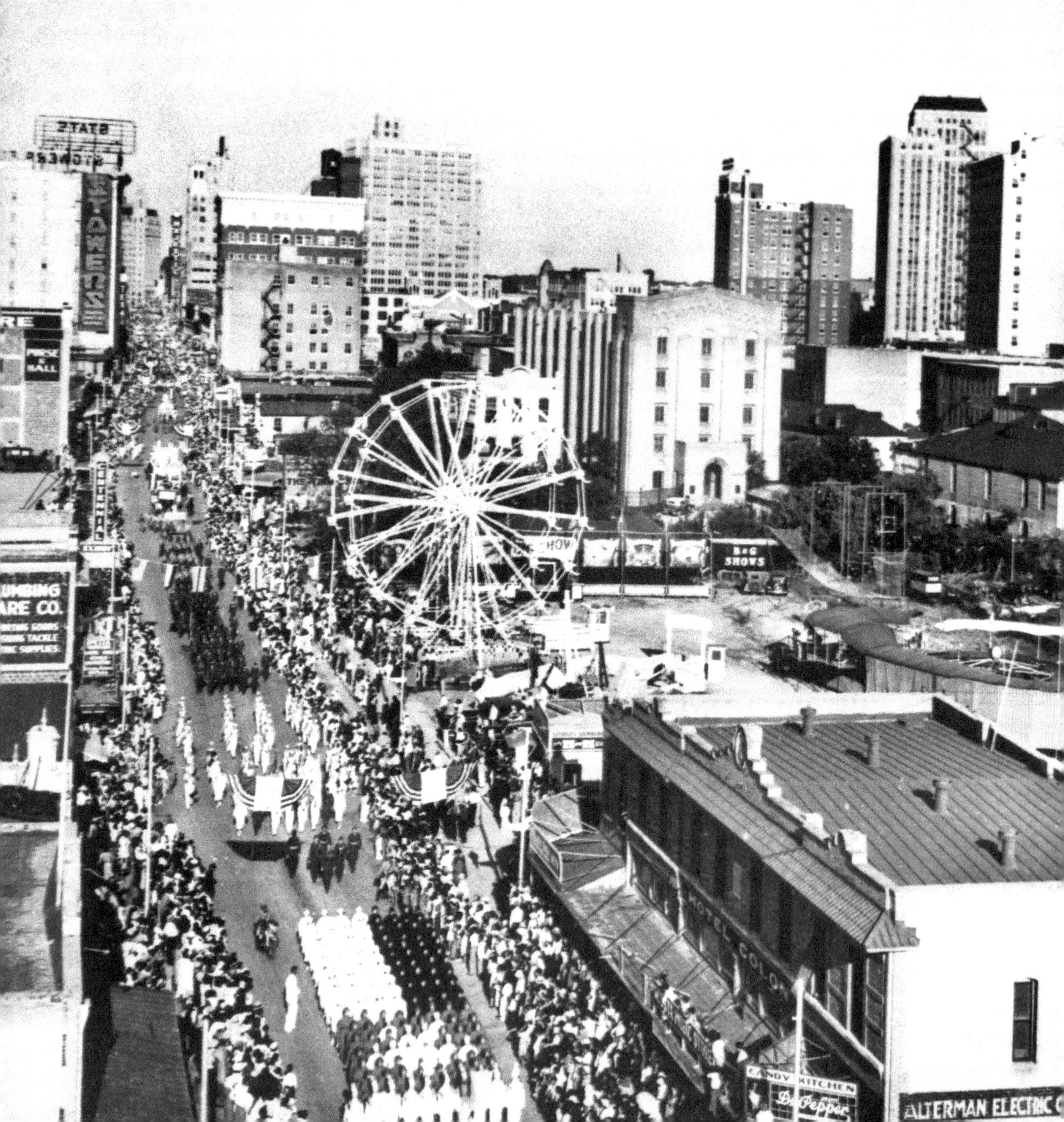

B&G SHOWS
CANDY KITCHEN
Dr Pepper
ALTERMAN ELECTRIC

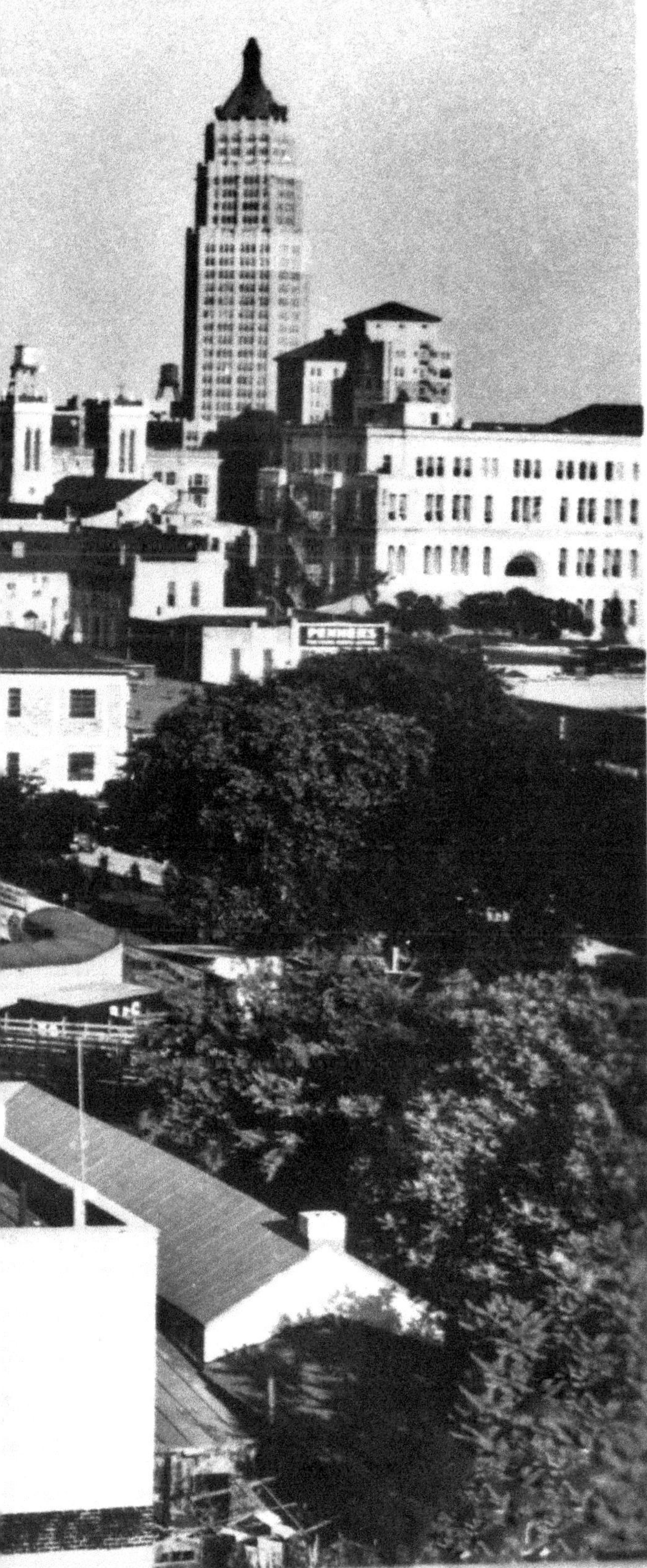

Fiesta parade down Houston Street as seen from Santa Rosa Hospital. The front center of the building housed the offices of the famous Dr. Aureliano Urrutia. Born to a poor Indian family, he became personal physician to Mexico's president Porfirio Diaz and was minister of the interior under Vitoriano Huerta. He fled to San Antonio in 1916 and became world-renowned for his surgical skills. In the right background is the Smith-Young Tower completed in 1929.

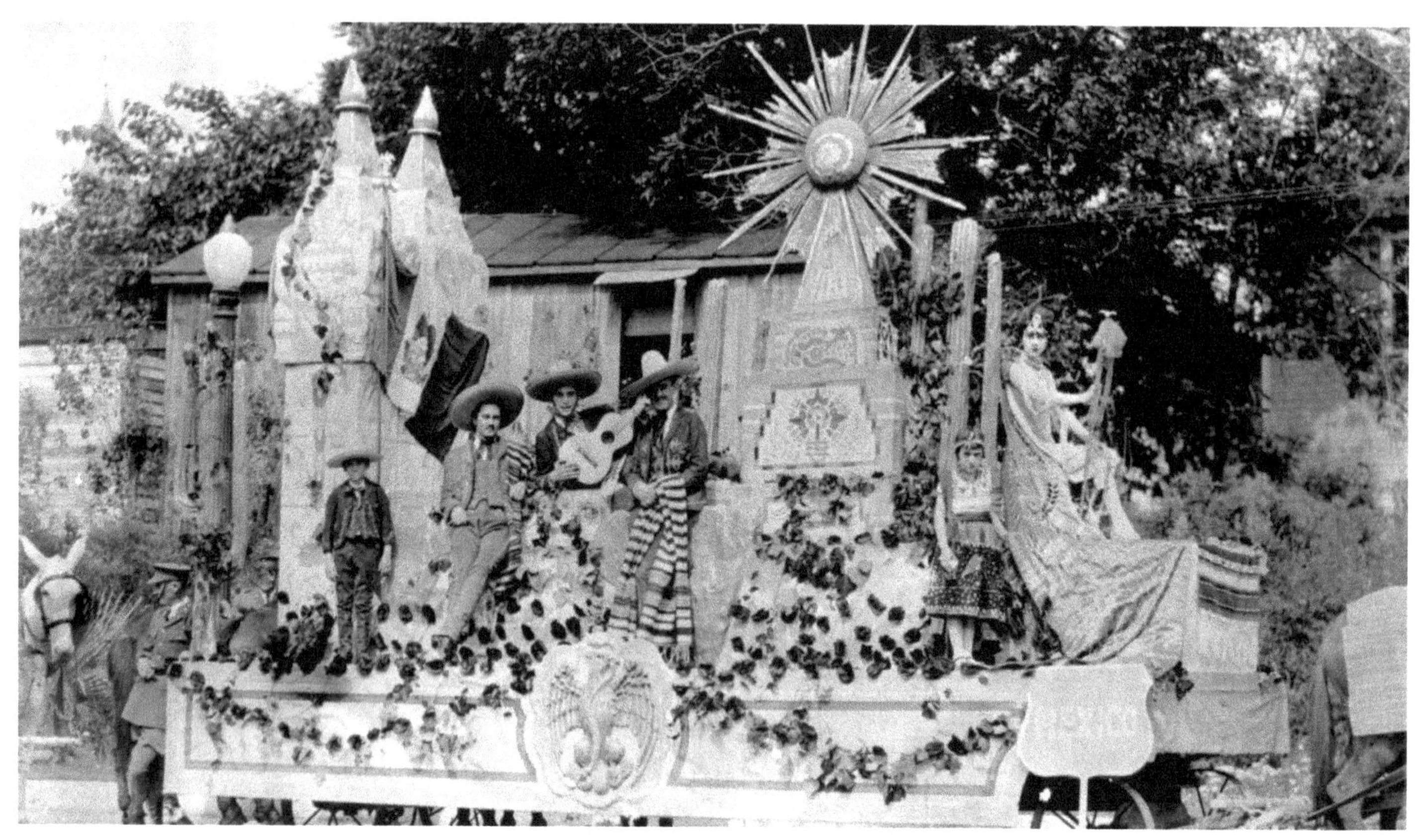

The float representing Mexico in the Parade of Nations around 1927. A beautifully flowered and costumed queen and her court are still pulled by horses.

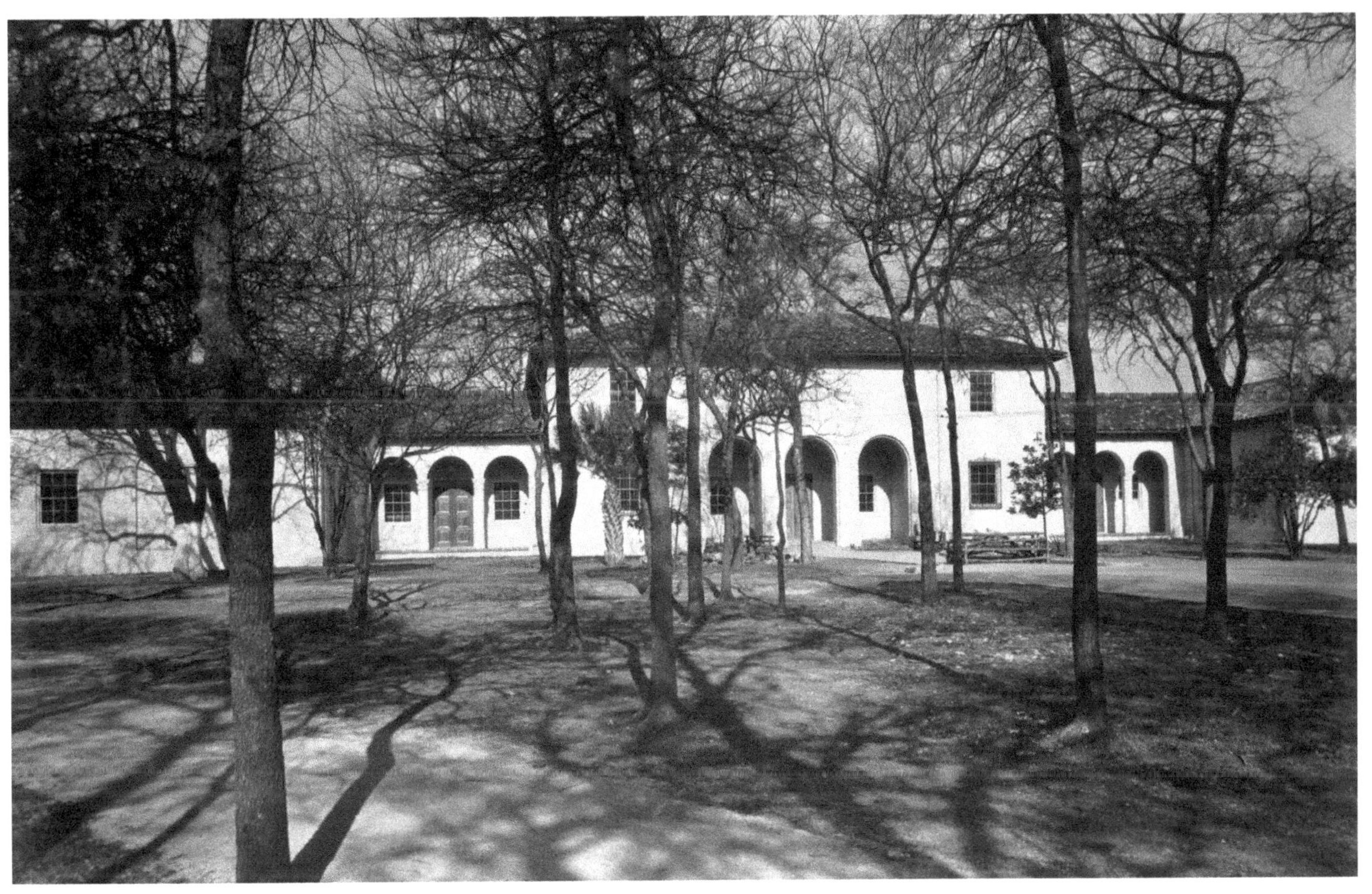

The exterior of the Witte Memorial Museum designed by Robert Moss Ayres. In 1925, Alfred G. Witte left $65,000 in his will to build a museum in Brackenridge Park. The city and the San Antonio Museum Association paid for the main building and Witte's gift paid for the wings. The grand opening came on the night of October 8, 1926.

Houston Street looking east, with the Gunter Hotel to the left and the Empire and Majestic theaters on the right. The Empire opened in December 1914 with *Neptune's Daughter*. A beautiful *Beaux Arts* interior, complete with orchestra, seated about 1,700. In the 1930s, staff would dress in the theme of each movie. It ceased to function in 1978, and in 1988, the city purchased both the Majestic and Empire for restoration.

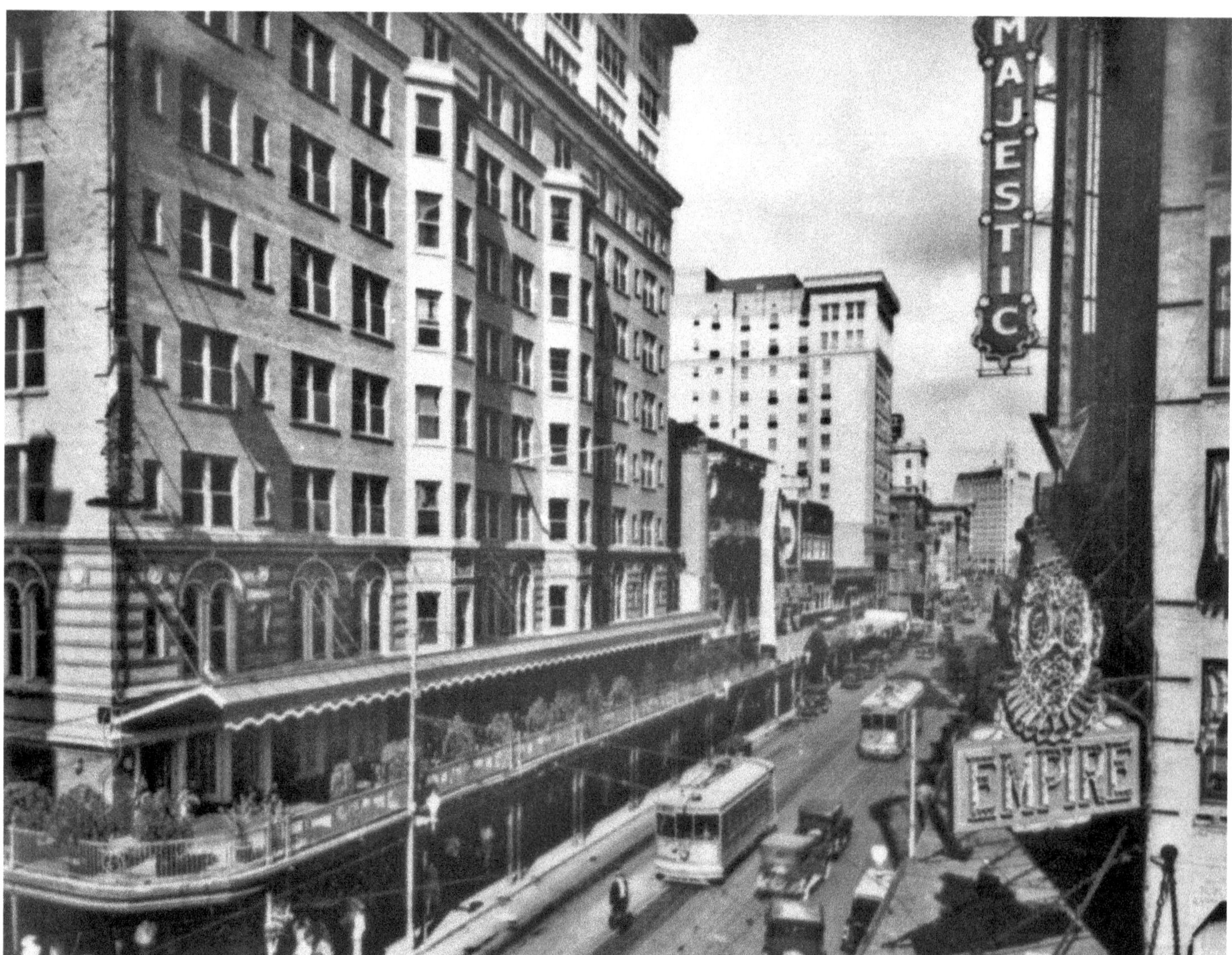

Two men standing on steel beam atop the Smith-Young Tower in 1928. The view is looking north with St. Mary's Street on the left. The Smith-Young Tower was designed by Atlee B. and Robert M. Ayres, a local father and son architectural firm. It sits on a former peninsula of the San Antonio River known as Bowen's Island. When finished, it would be thirty-one stories high and cost $2.5 million dollars.

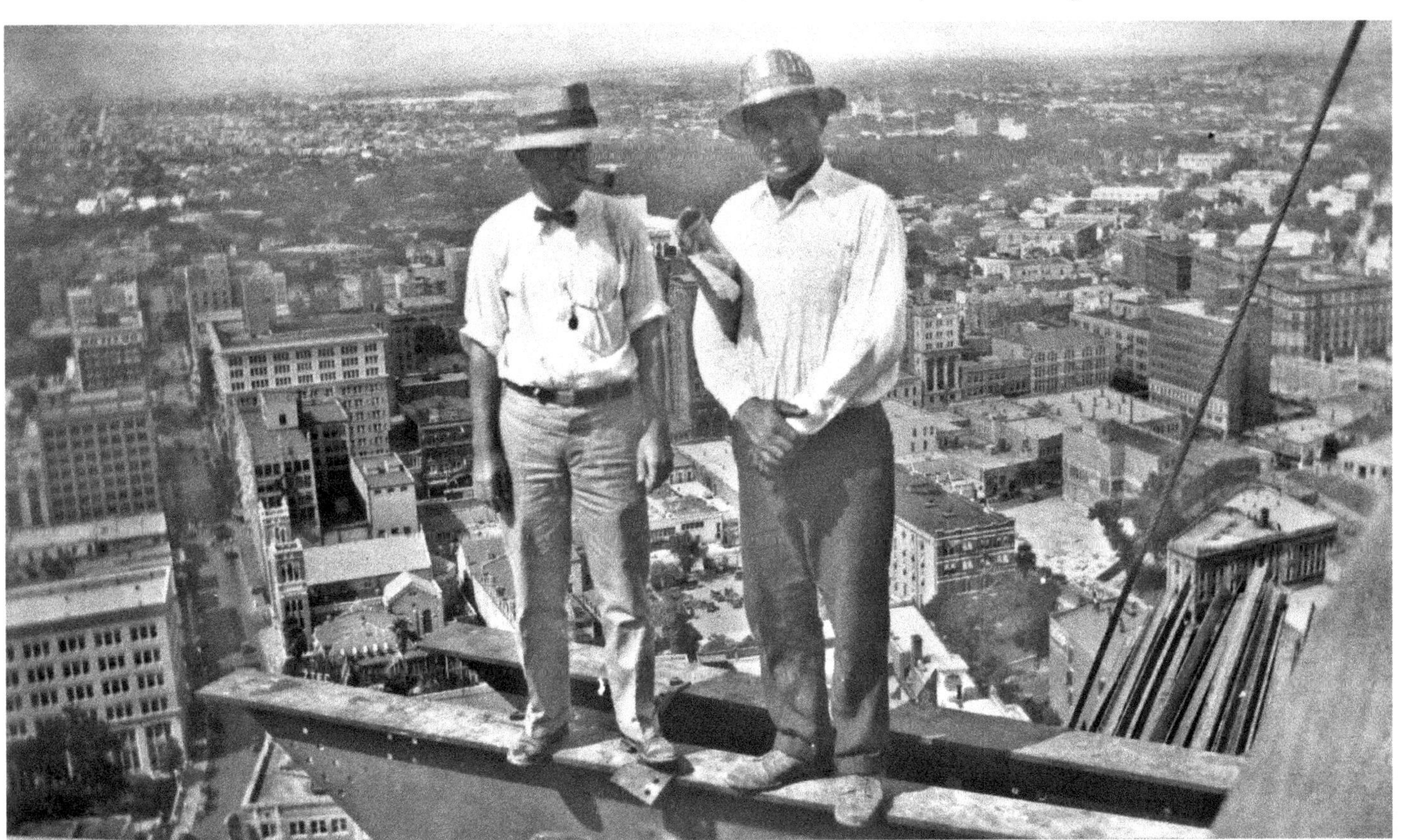

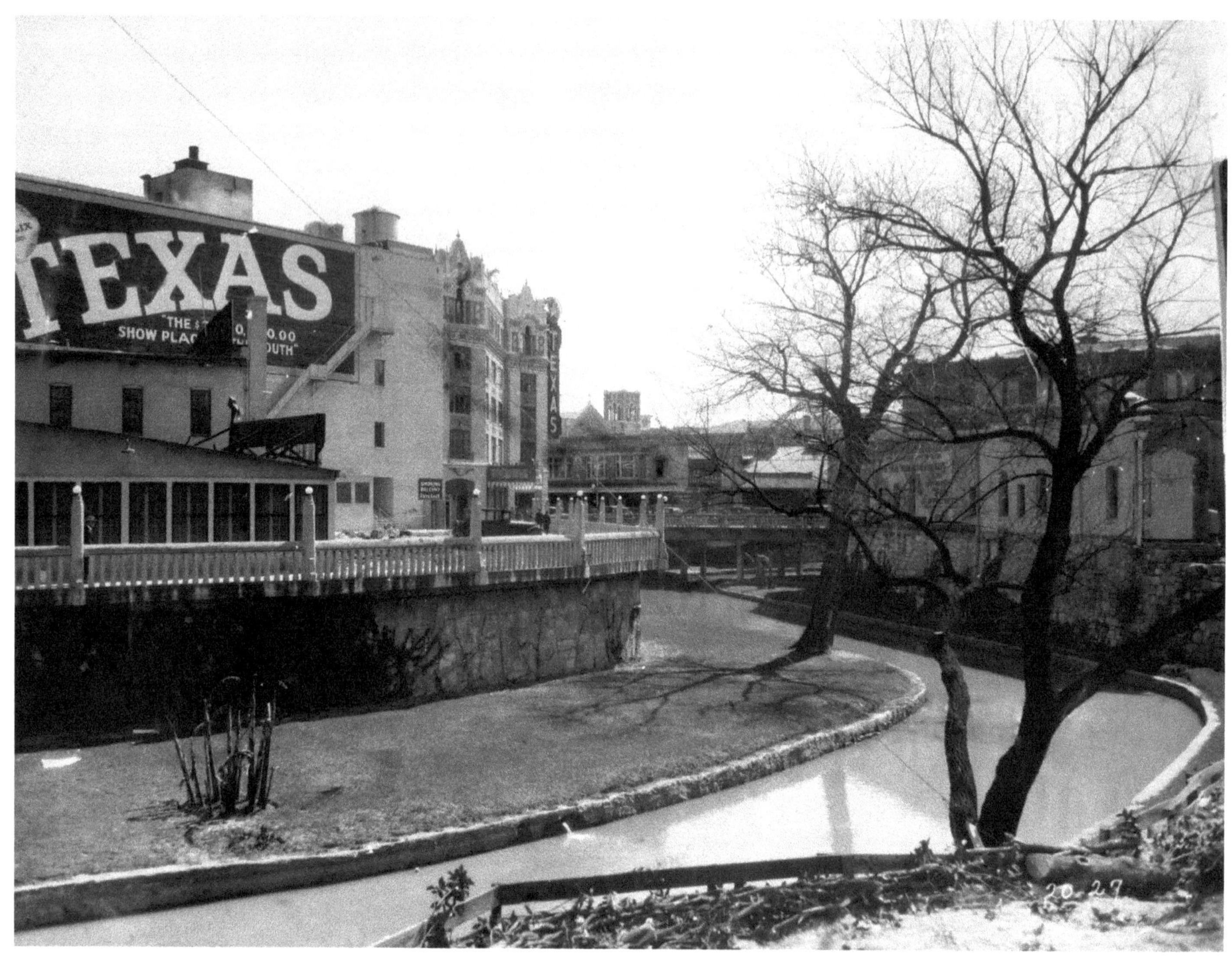

The San Antonio River looking downstream toward the Houston Street Bridge. The original span on this site, then Paseo Street, was the first iron bridge in San Antonio, erected in 1870. This iron bridge was moved to Grand (now Jones) Avenue in 1885, and in 1927, to Hildebrand near Carey Street. The present concrete bridge on Houston Street dates from 1914.

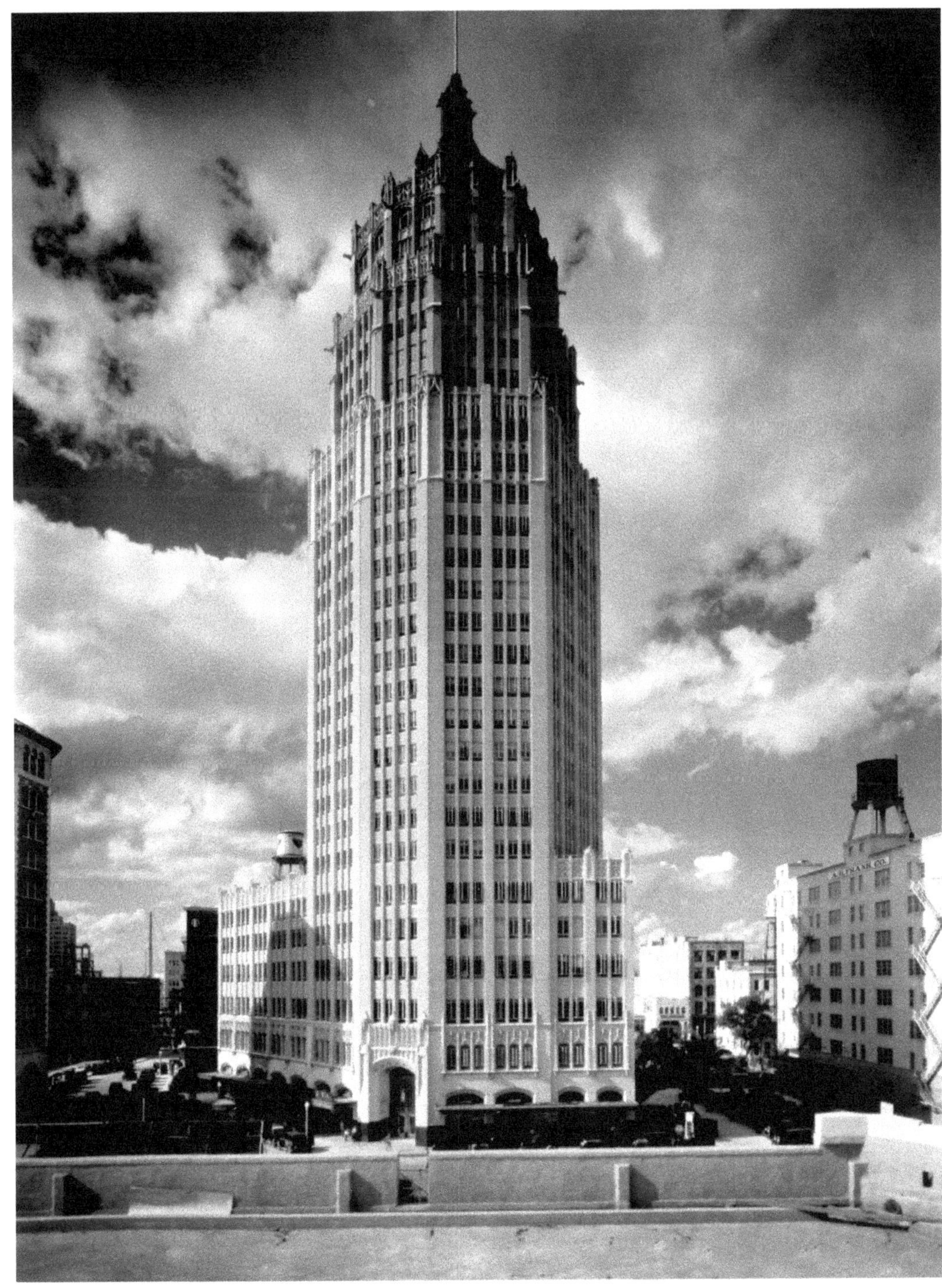

The completed Smith-Young Tower at 310 S. St. Mary's Street. Opened in 1929, it was the tallest building west of the Mississippi until the late 1950s. Originally, Sears, Roebuck & Company had their first San Antonio store on the first six floors. In 1938, the name was changed to the Pan American Building. In 1942, it was renamed the Transit Tower, and finally, in 1962, the Tower Life Building.

A great crowd welcomes the Old Gray Mare Band from Brownwood, Texas, as it marches down Houston Street on October 9, 1928. On the horse, Ruby Latham Ables waves to onlookers. The parade is in honor of the Tenth Annual National American Legion Convention.

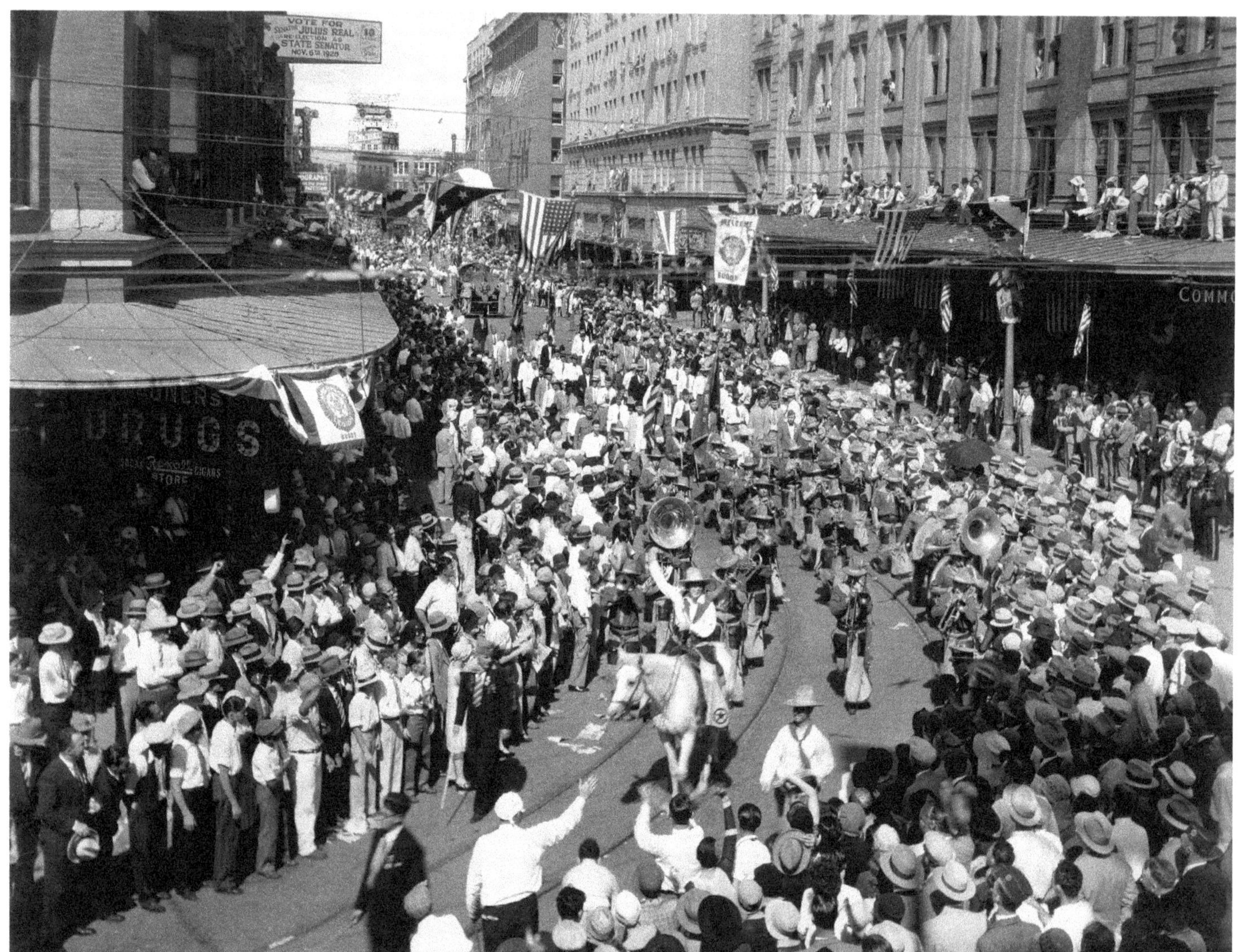

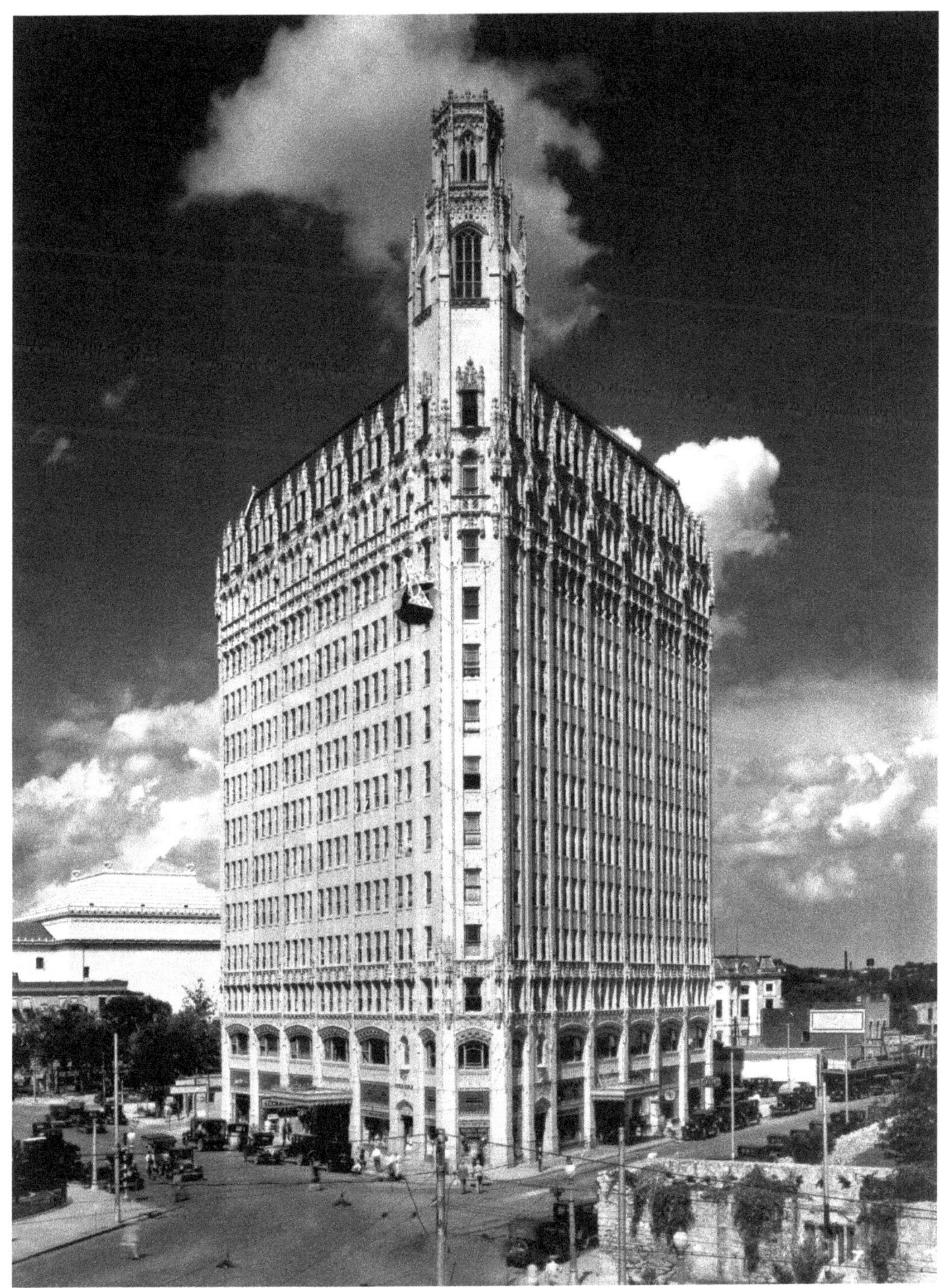

The thirteen-story Medical Arts Building opened to the public in April 1926 as the most modern medical facility in the area. The building with its Gothic Revival tower was designed by Ralph H. Cameron. In 1976, it became the Landmark Building. As of 1985, it has been known as the Emily Morgan Hotel.

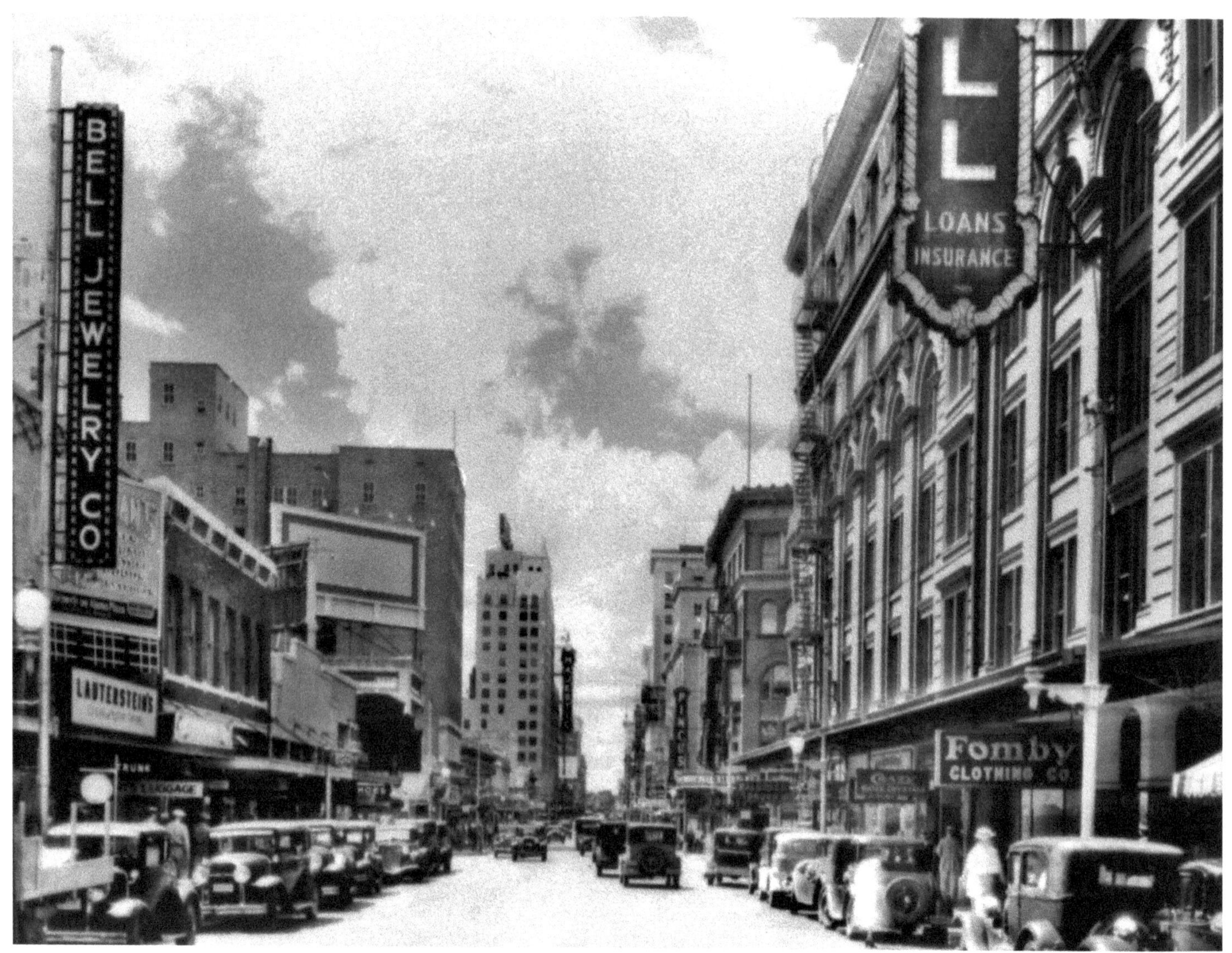

Houston Street looking west on a busy day. Bell Jewelry opened in the city in 1852 when David Bell arrived with his family from Pennsylvania. It has had various names and locations over the years. Near the center right of the picture is Pincus. This clothing store was opened by David L. Pincus in 1933 and closed in 1986.

The Spanish Governor's Palace, once the seat of government under Spain and Mexico, had deteriorated greatly by the 1920s–1930s. In the shadow of the large stone county courthouse and city hall, it was surrounded by poor adobe houses. It served several functions, including a second-hand clothing store and a "hamburger joint." Above the second door from the right, the Hapsburg crest is still visible.

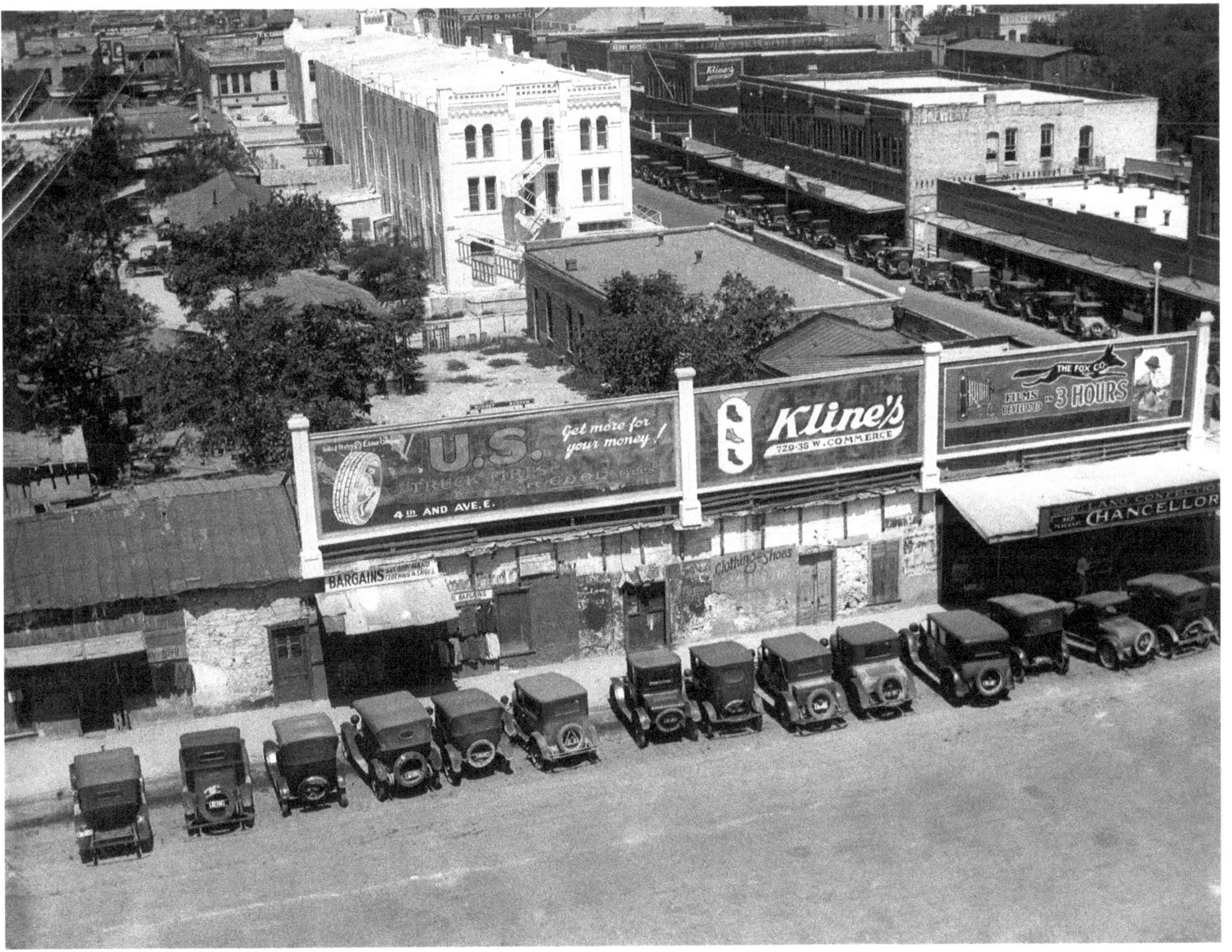

Mission San Jose y San Miguel de Aguayo, was founded in February 1720, on the east bank of the San Antonio River. Between 1724-1727, it was moved to the west bank and over the next seventy years a church, granary, friary, and Indian houses were constructed. In 1794 the missions were secularized, and several of the structures collapsed over the years. In 1933, the Civil Works Administration began reconstruction.

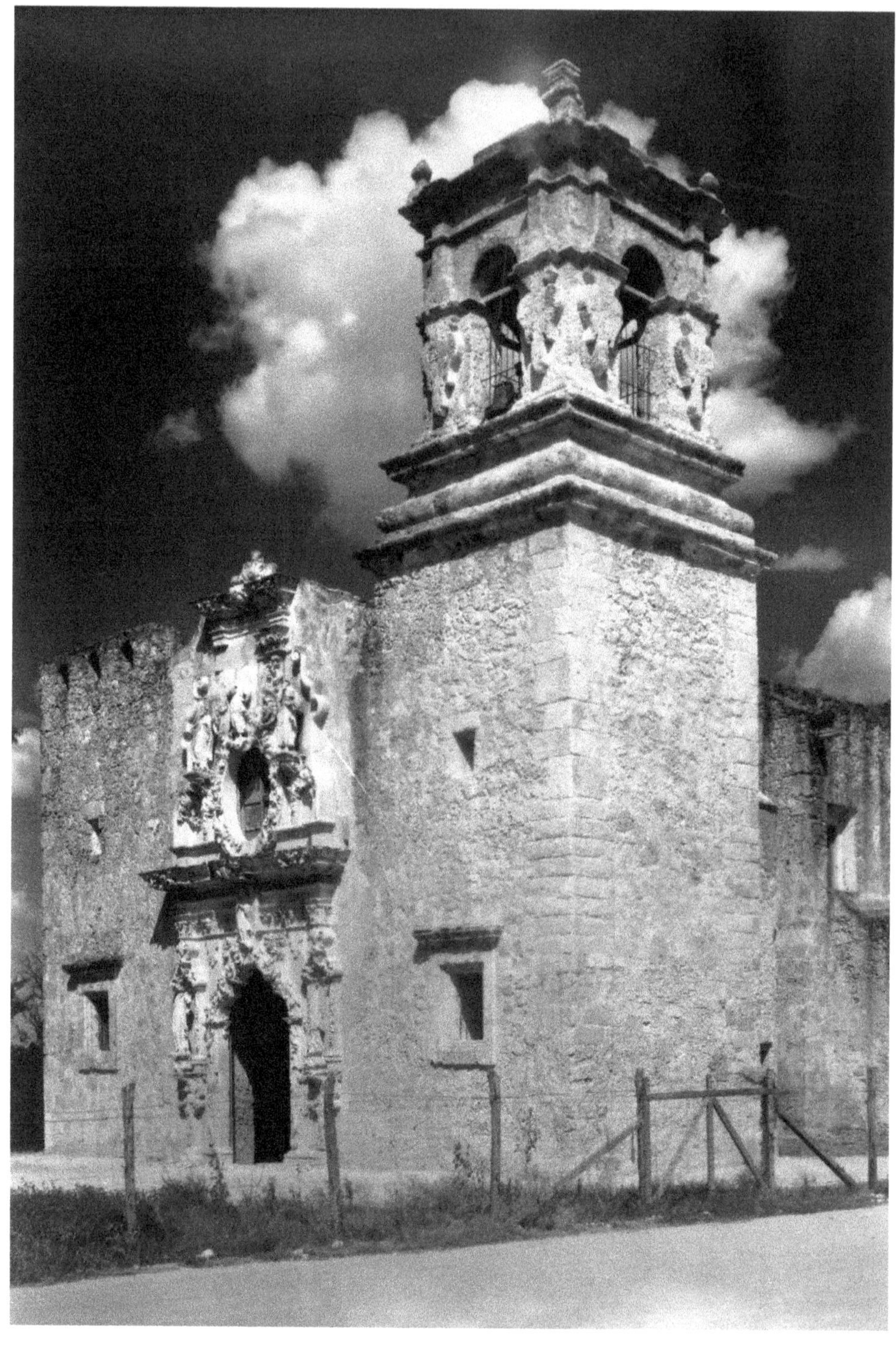

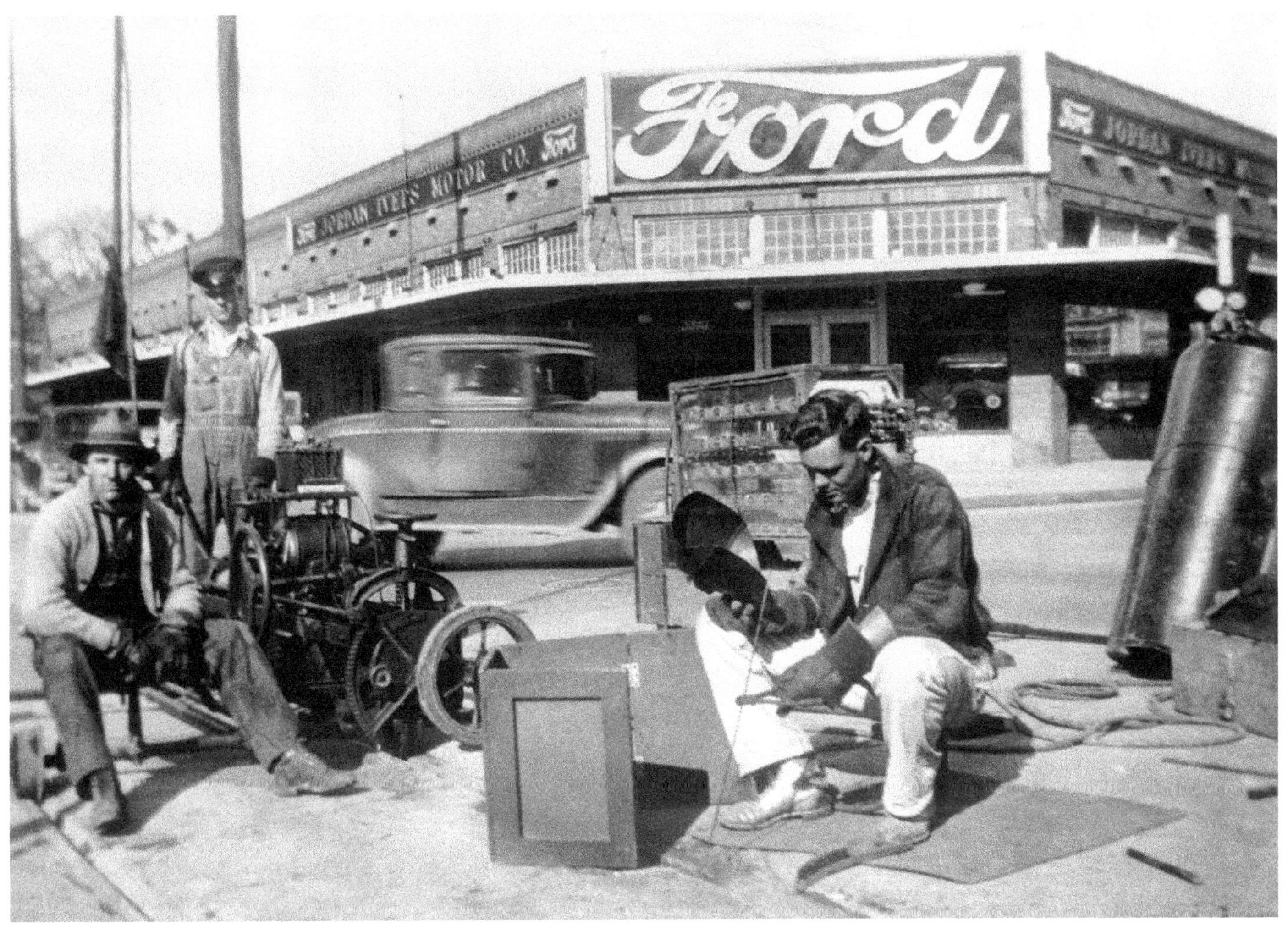

San Antonio Traction Company employees at Garden Street (now S. St. Mary's) and S. Alamo repair a broken rail joint on an old streetcar-track crossing. On the right is John Kellogg Kight, welder; the seated grinder is Arnold Yarbrough; and standing is flagman William B. Kight. The San Antonio Traction Company was a forerunner of the current city bus company, VIA.

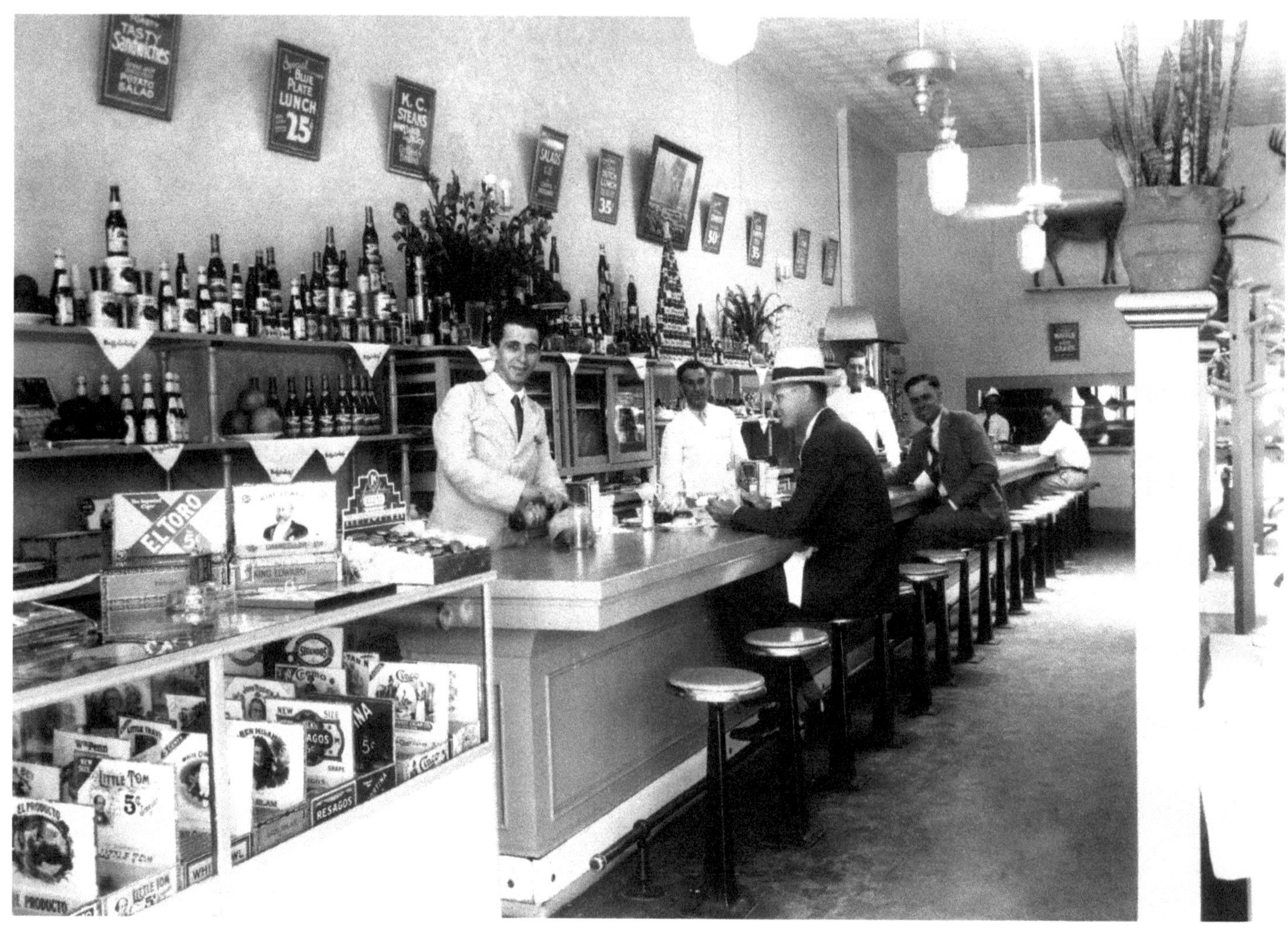

The interior of the Buffalo Cafe at 315 W. Commerce in 1933. The cafe existed from about 1926 to 1968. Shown here is Samuel Sockler, who owned the establishment for many years. The staff and customers are all neatly dressed. Menu boards on the wall offer "tasty, toasty sandwiches" with potato salad, a blue plate special for twenty-five cents, or "cold Dutch lunch" for thirty-five. Also, note the cigar counter with open display boxes.

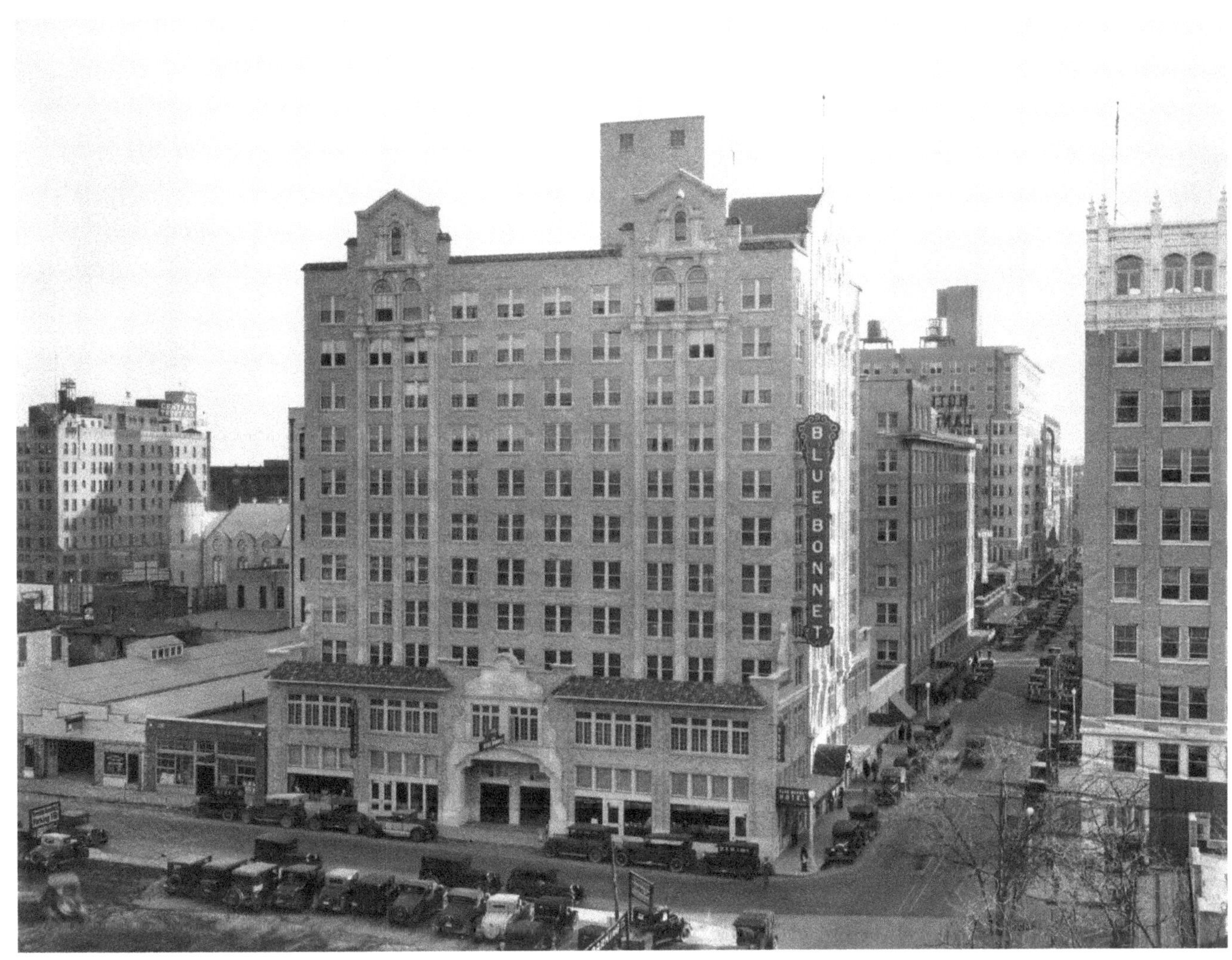

The twelve-story Blue Bonnet Hotel, built between 1927–1928, was a San Antonio landmark for many years before being razed in 1989. For several years during the 1930s, record companies would record local and regional artists in a studio in the hotel. Over the years, Don Albert, W. Lee O'Daniel & His Hillbilly Boys, Al Dexter, Eva Garza, and others made music history here, but not legendary bluesman Robert Johnson, as has often been erroneously claimed. His famous San Antonio recordings were made at the Gunter Hotel.

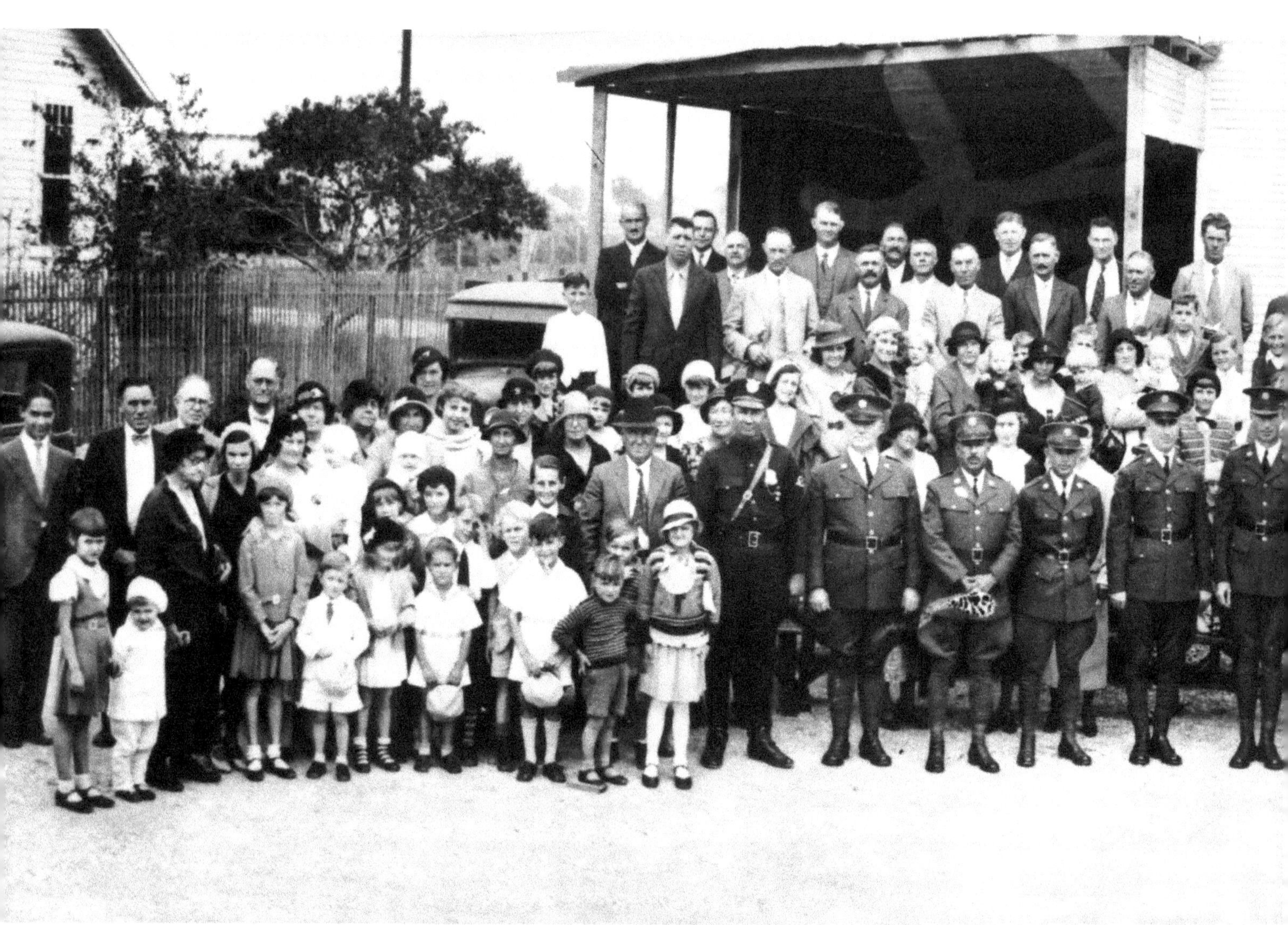

The congregation of St. John Berchmans Church celebrate Armistice Day, 1933, with Belgian and American veterans. Next to the flag is Reverend Father Richard Verschaffelt who served the parish from 1910 to 1912, and 1933 to 1942. St. John Berchmans Church was blessed in August 1910.

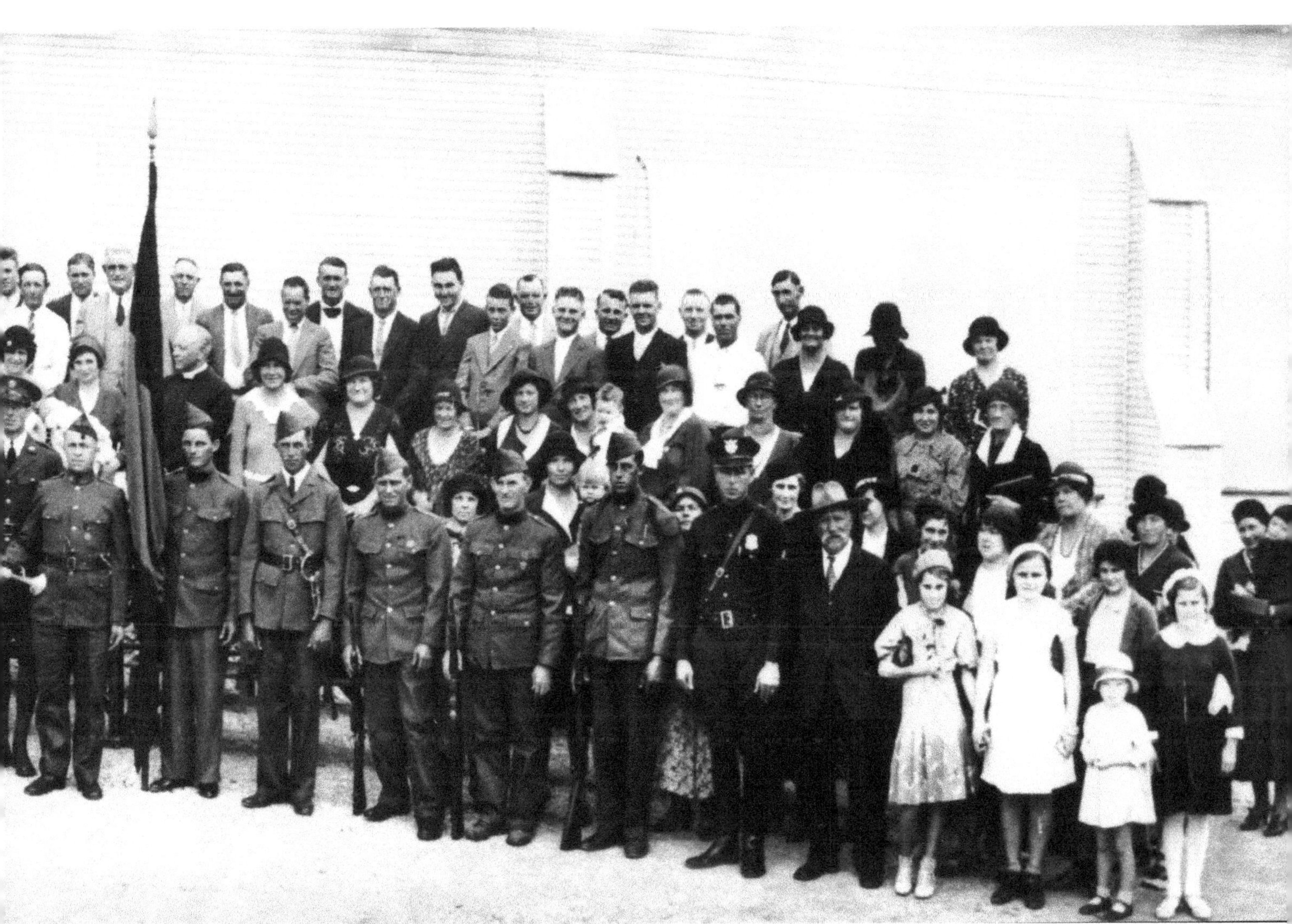

The Gunter Hotel opened on November 20, 1909. The Mahncke Hotel was purchased by the San Antonio Hotel Company in 1907, razed, and a new hotel built. It was named The Gunter for Jot Gunter, a primary backer of the project who had died in July 1907. KTSA radio had a broadcast studio there, and the roof terrace was a splendid entertaining area.

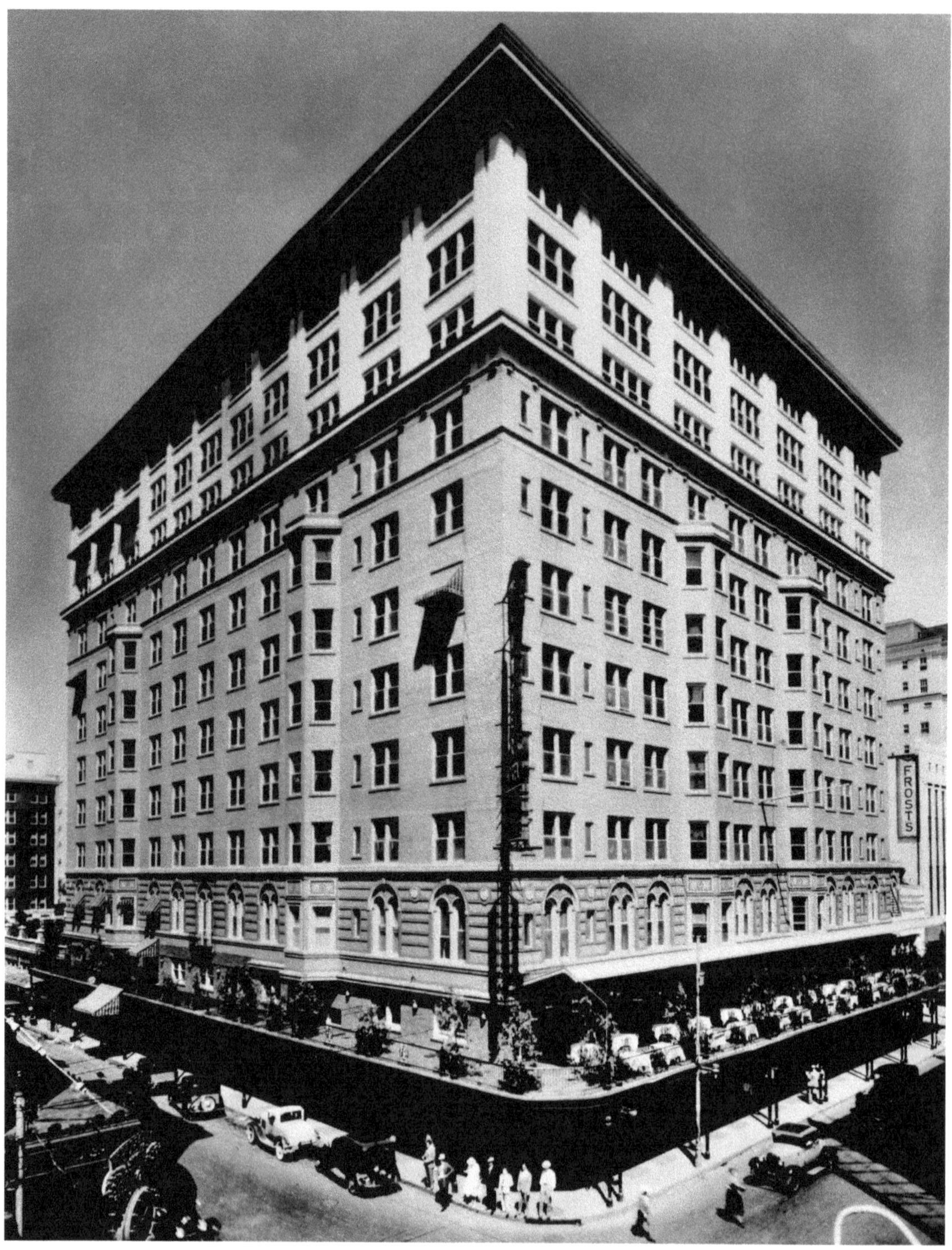

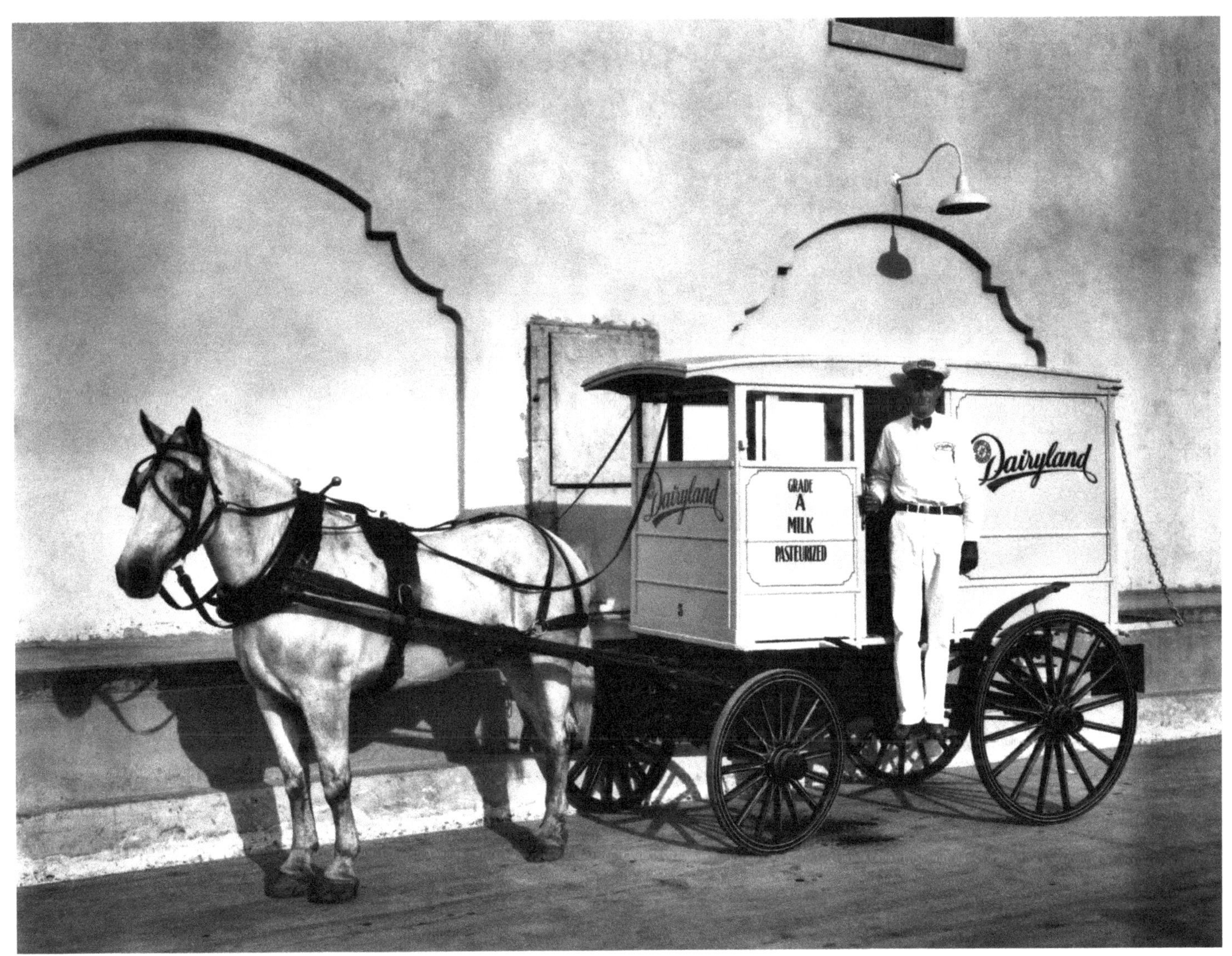

This unidentified milkman was photographed at the Dairyland headquarters, 102 E. Josephine. Dairyland was part of Southwest Dairy Products Company, which had several retail ice cream stores in the city. Around 1947, it became Foremost Dairy.

A view of the San Antonio River from ground level near the Navarro Street Bridge. The camera is looking west with the St. Mary's Street Bridge in the distance. After the devastation of the 1921 flood, the city built the Olmos Dam and dug an overflow channel, preserving the big bend in the river. During the 1930s, through the efforts of the Conservation Society, WPA, and the city, the river bend was turned into a park and tourist area.

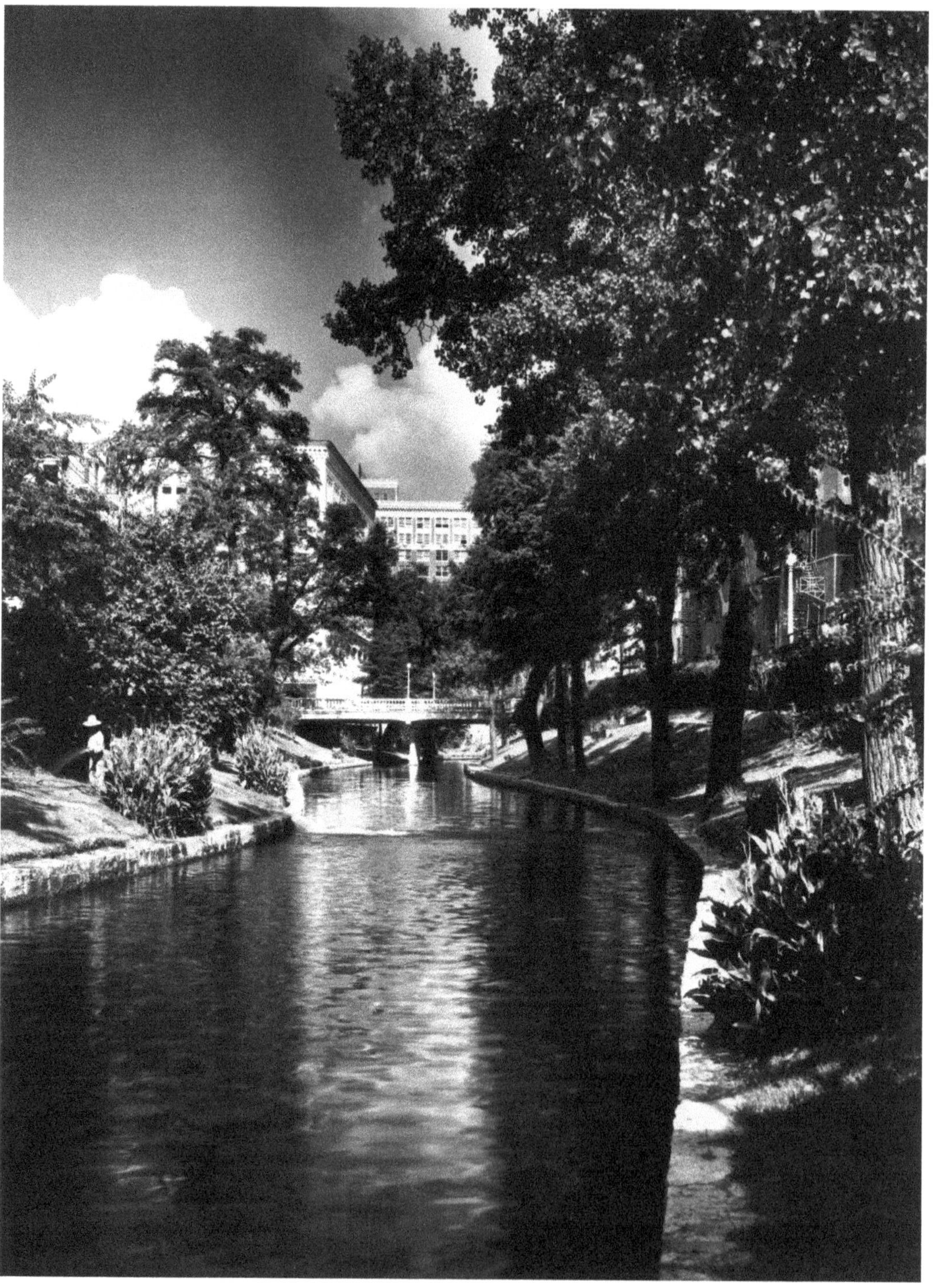

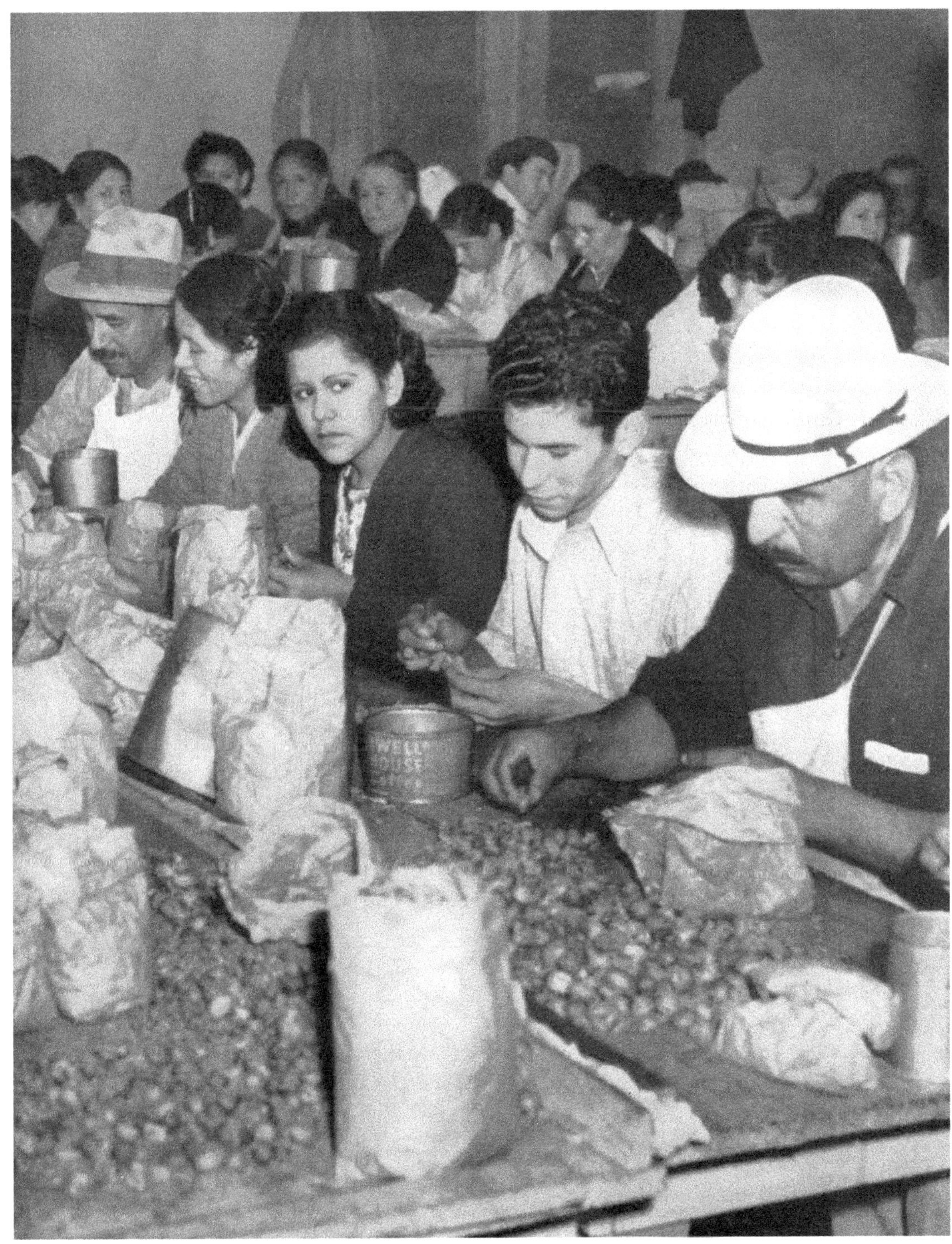

People shelling pecans by hand required little other than tables, benches, pecans, and containers. By January 1938 there were 12,000 pecan shellers employed in 110 different plants here. A National Recovery Administration report for December 1934 (based on fourteen plants) stated that workers received $1.29 a week for 34.8 hours. The shelling cost was about three-and-a-half cents per pound, and pecans sold for thirty-one to thirty-four cents a pound.

Almost 65,000 of San Antonio's Hispanic population lived in a four-square-mile area on the West Side. Houses rented for fifty cents to a dollar per week. Only nine percent had toilets and 39 percent had "privies." A mere 25 percent had electric lights. While most houses had only two rooms, the average family consisted of about five people. In 1938, 72 percent of tuberculosis deaths in San Antonio were on the West Side.

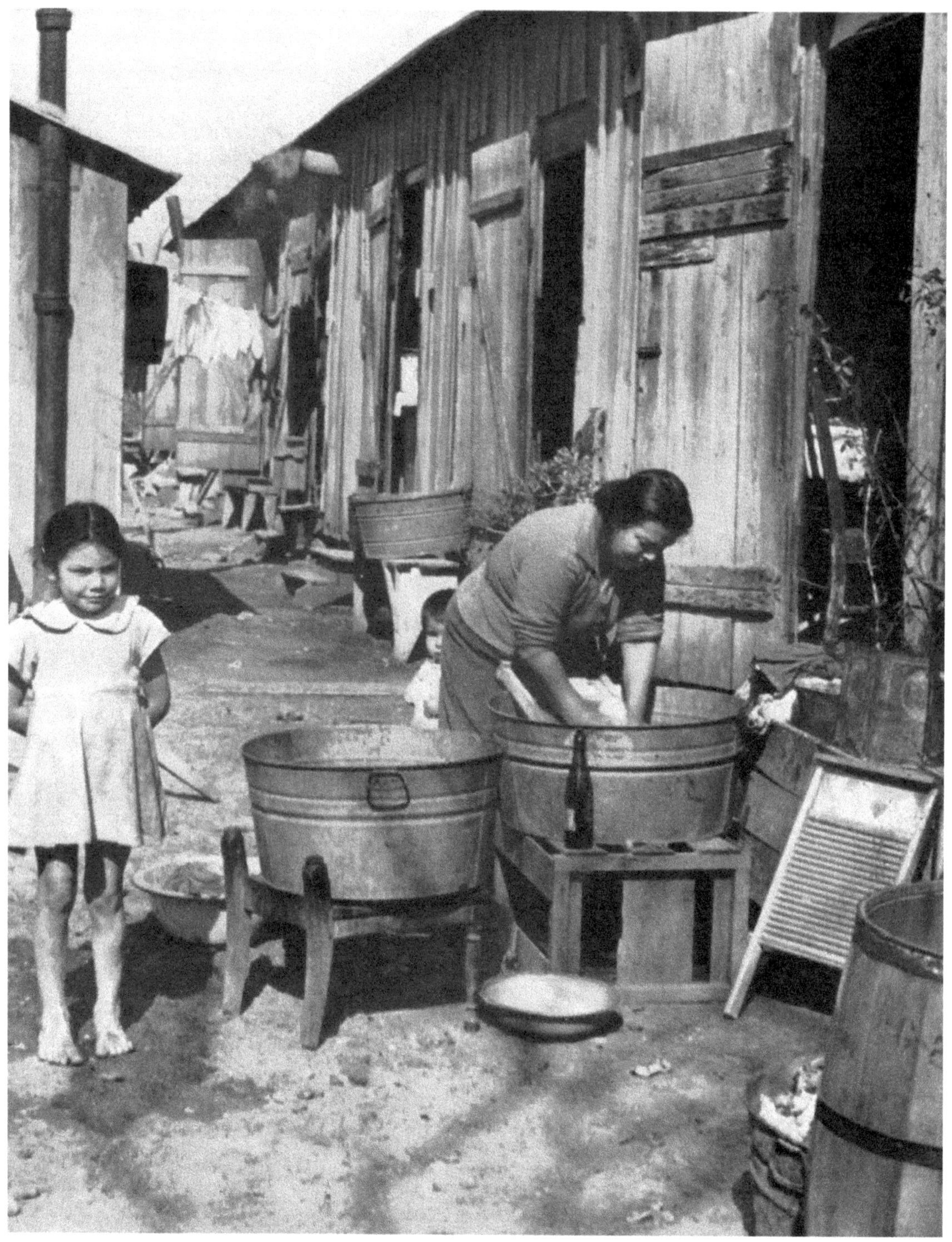

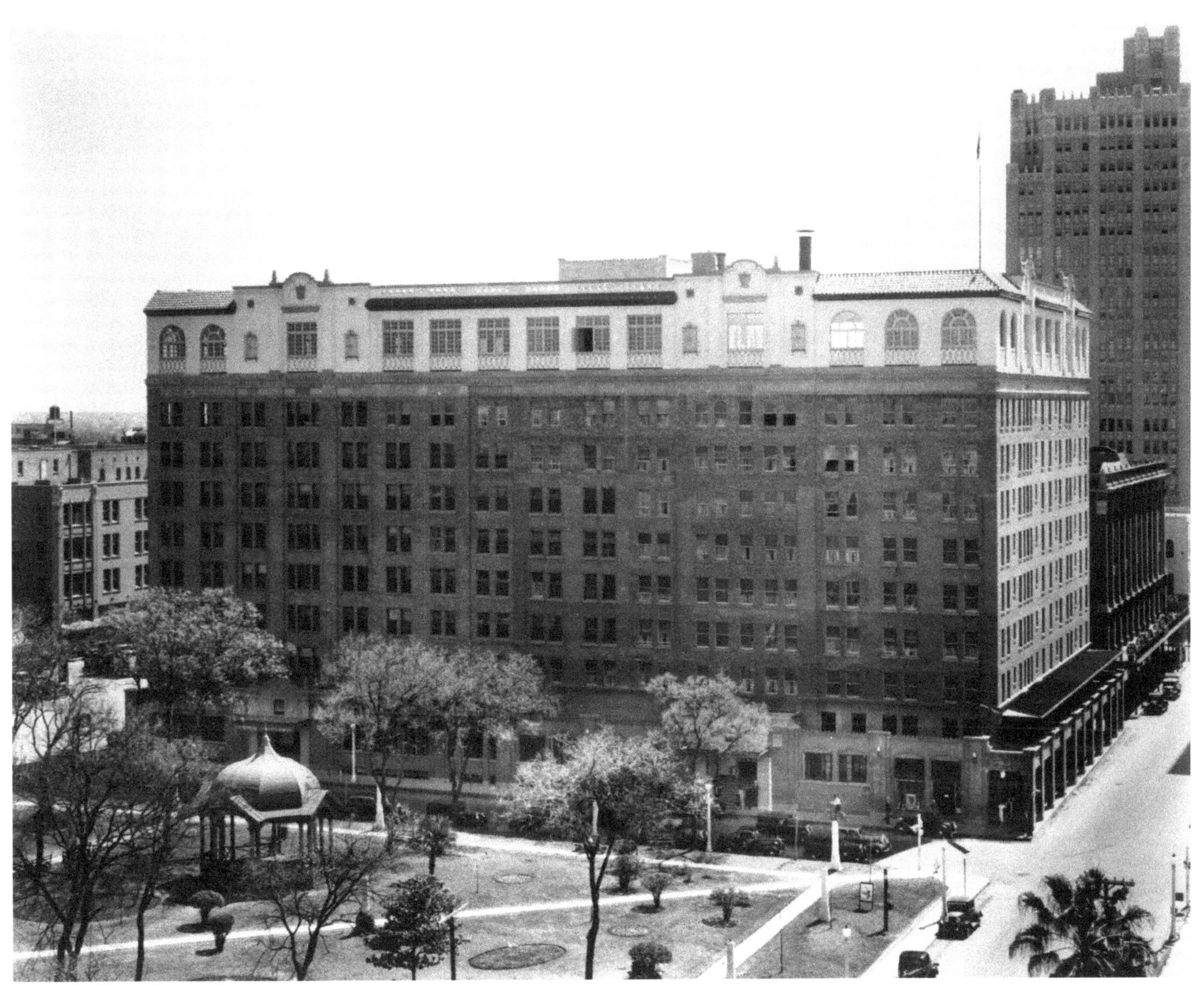

Looking southeast from the Elks Club is the St. Anthony Hotel at 304 E. Travis Street. To the left and front is Travis Park with its bandstand. Cattlemen A. H. Jones and B. L. Naylor constructed this modern first-class hotel that opened in 1909 with 210 rooms. Two years later, a wing was added. Bought in 1936 by R. W. Morrison, the St. Anthony was the first fully air-conditioned hotel in the world.

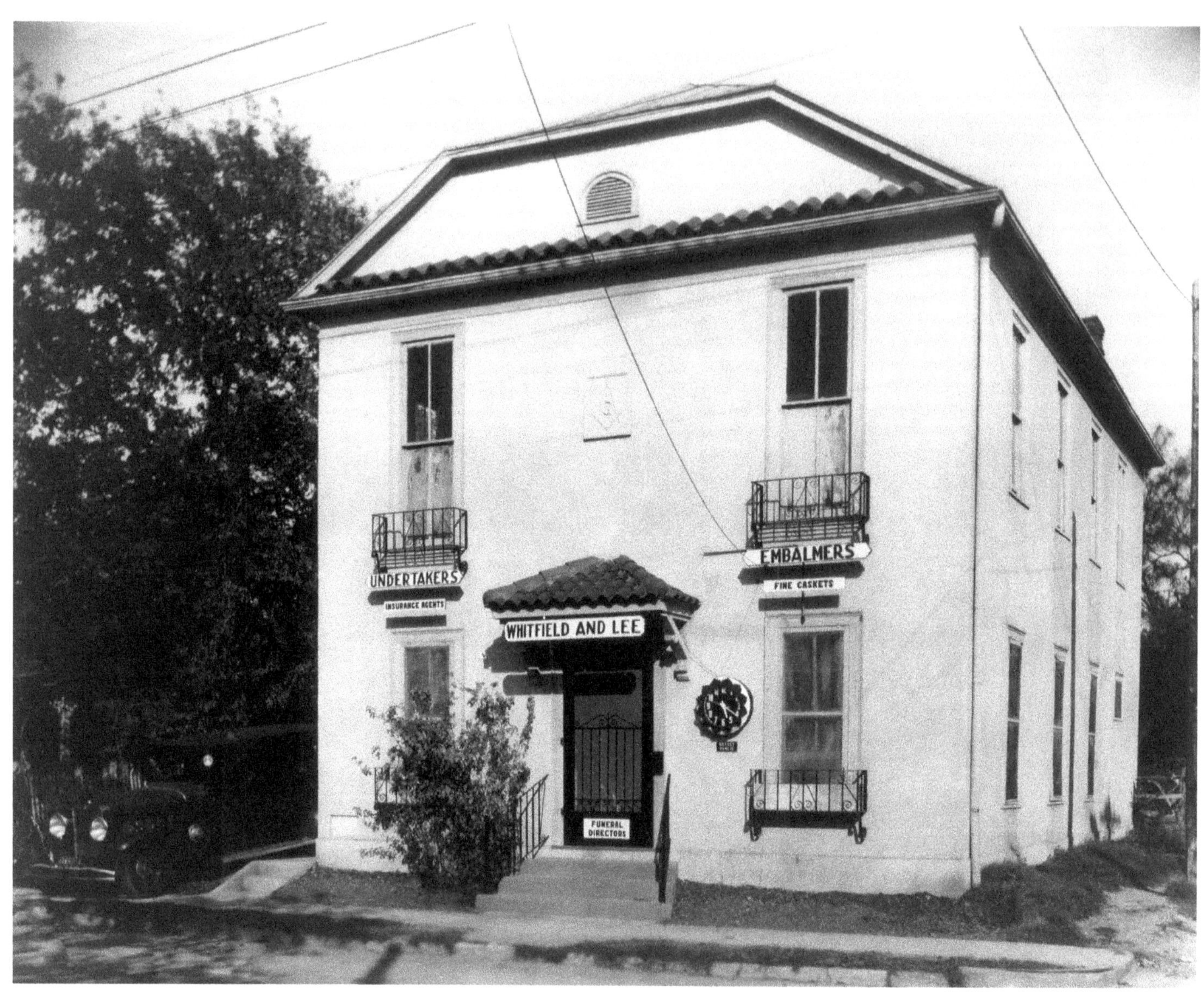

In the early 1900s, 220 Chestnut served as a residence. From about 1918 to 1923 it was the Carter & Sutton Funeral Home; some time in the 1930s it was Whitfield and Lee, funeral directors; and, in the late 1940s it was Citizens Funeral Home. In the late 1950s it was made into apartments, but throughout most of the twentieth century, the upstairs served as the Beacon Light Masonic Hall.

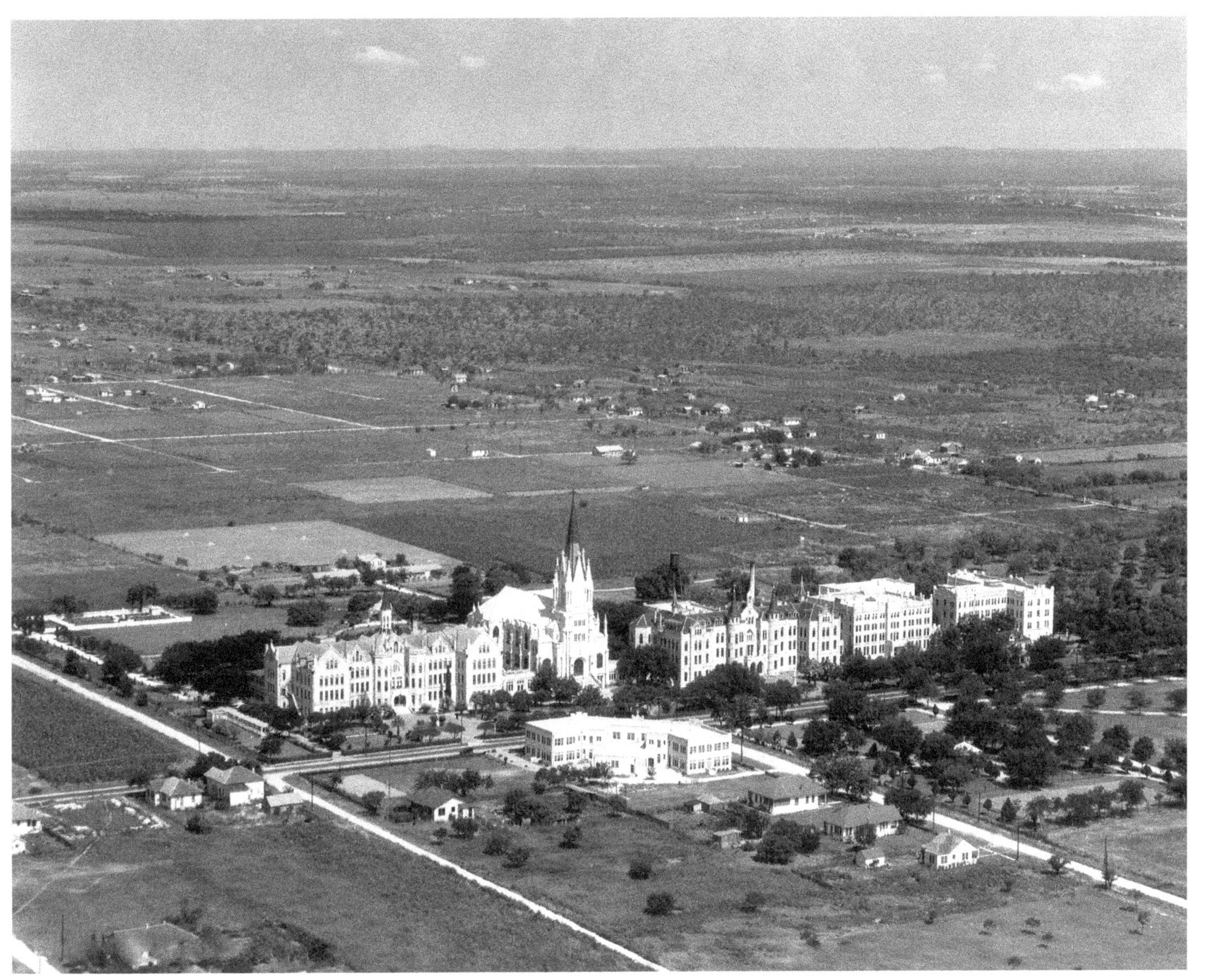

Our Lady of the Lake College (now University), in 1932, is the oldest regionally accredited institution of higher education in San Antonio. It was established in 1895 as an academy for girls on property donated by Henry Elmendorf. The tallest building is the Gothic Conventual Chapel designed by Leo Dielmann. The Gothic Revival building just to its right is "Old Main" which was designed by James Wahrenberger.

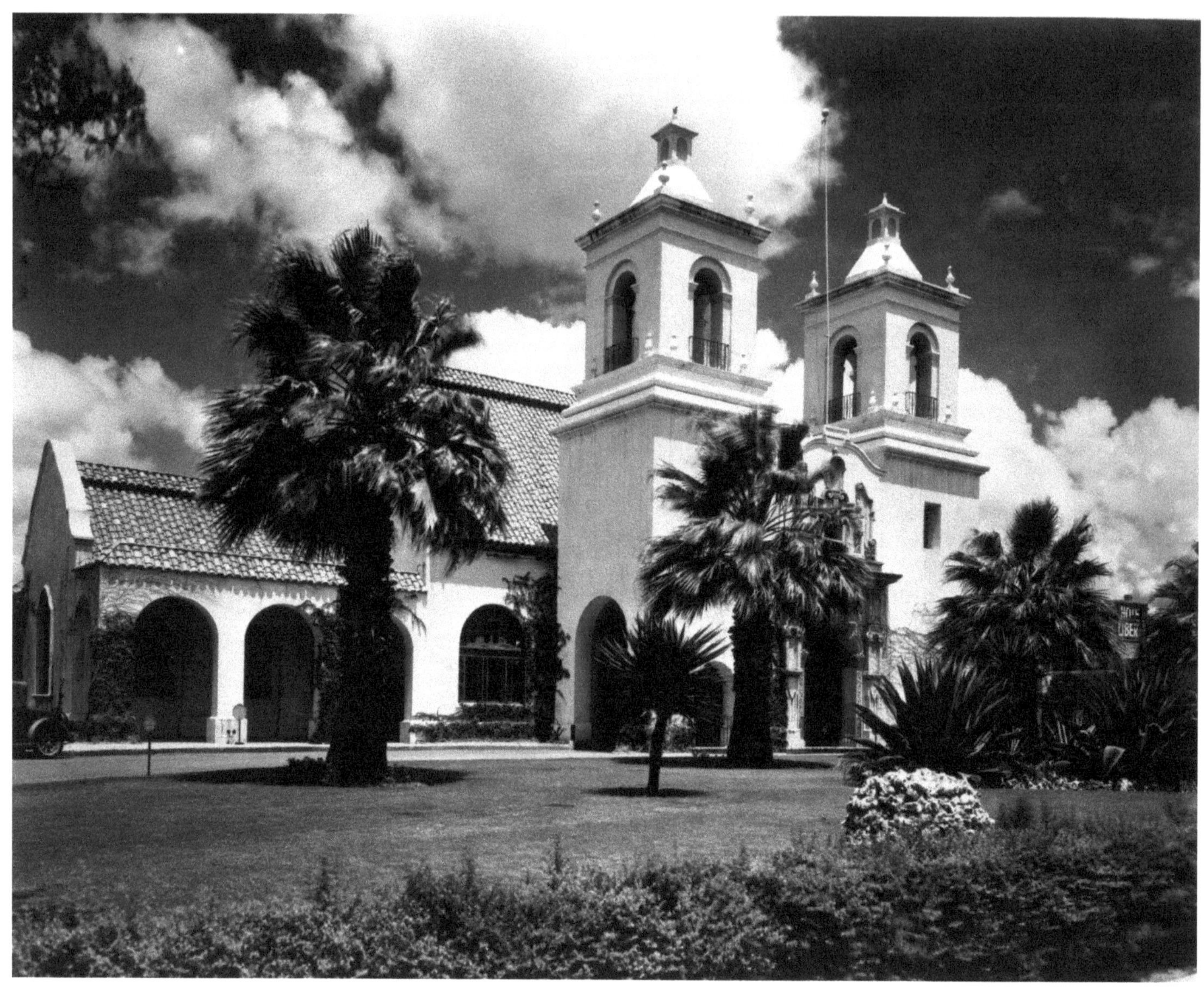

The Missouri-Kansas-Texas Railroad Station (M-K-T or Katy) at 415 S. Flores Street. The Spanish Colonial Revival structure was designed by New York architect Frederick Sterner, and built in 1917. The two towers replicate those at Mission Concepcion. The building was razed in 1968.

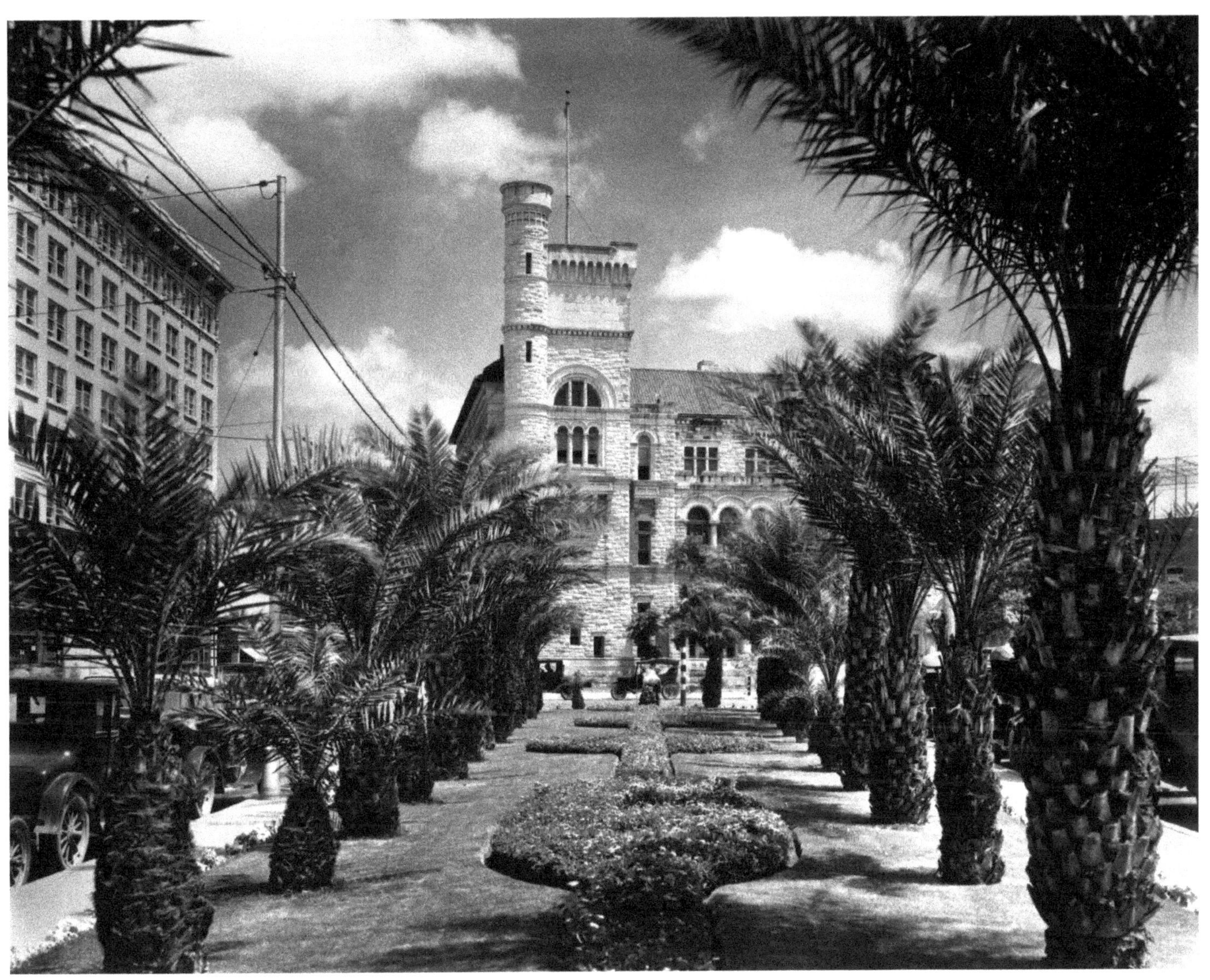

Seen through columns of palm trees in Alamo Plaza is the Federal Building and Post Office which served San Antonio from 1890 to 1935. Construction on the castle-like structure was begun in 1887 as four-mule-team wagons hauled huge stones that were cut and chiseled, each to fit its individual place.

Alamo Plaza looking north. The taller structures in the background from left to right are the Gibbs Building, Federal Building and Post Office, Medical Arts Building, and the Scottish Rite Cathedral. The Alamo is toward the right center.

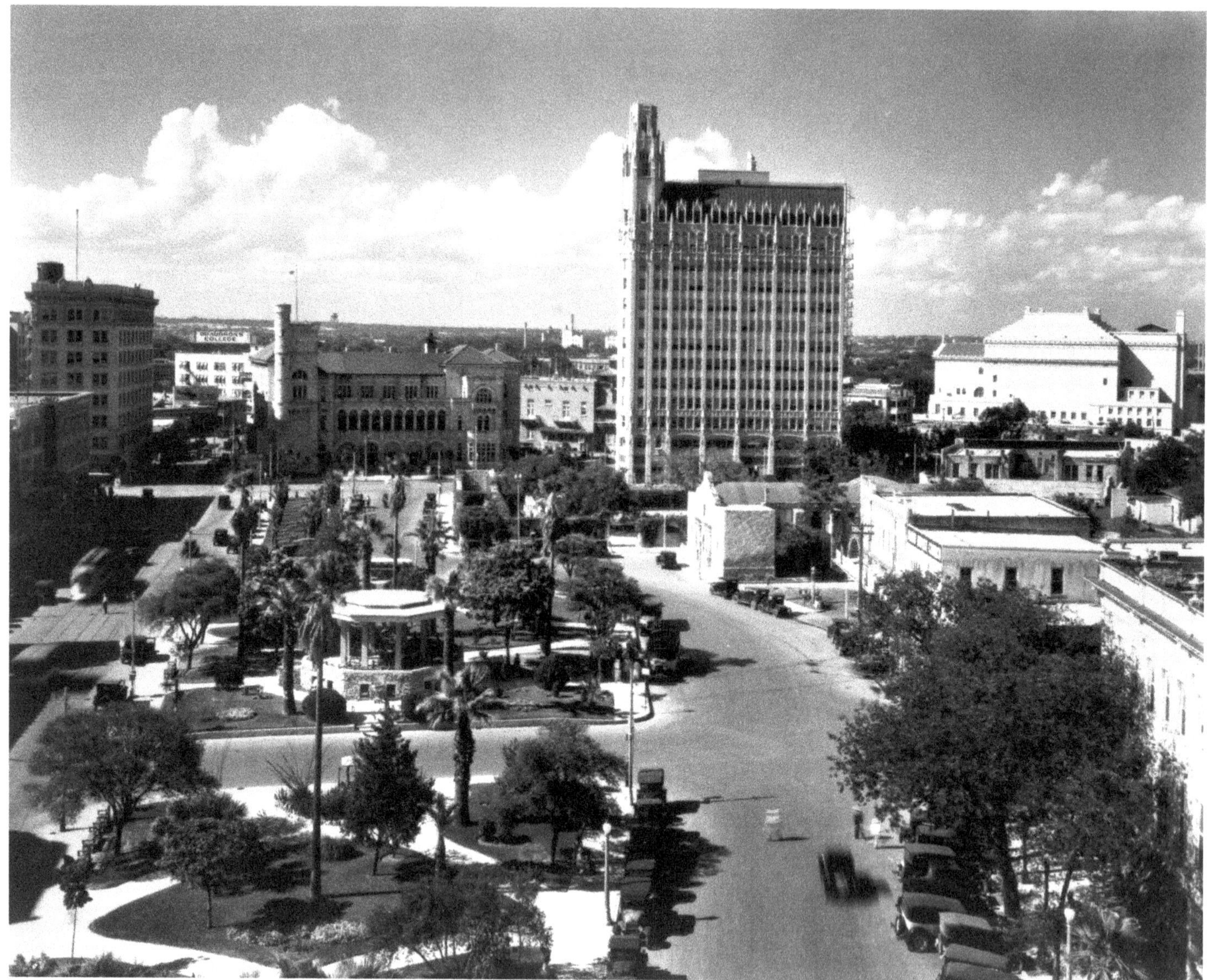

The Wagner Drug Store, at the corner of Houston and St. Mary's, was owned by Sommers Drug Stores by the 1930s. Sommers was founded by Carter F. Sommers in 1913 when he, then a bookkeeper, purchased part ownership in the Schwab-McElroy Drug Stores and was elected president. Carter ran the company until his death in 1951. On August 17, 1981, Eckerd Drug Co. purchased forty-one Sommers stores.

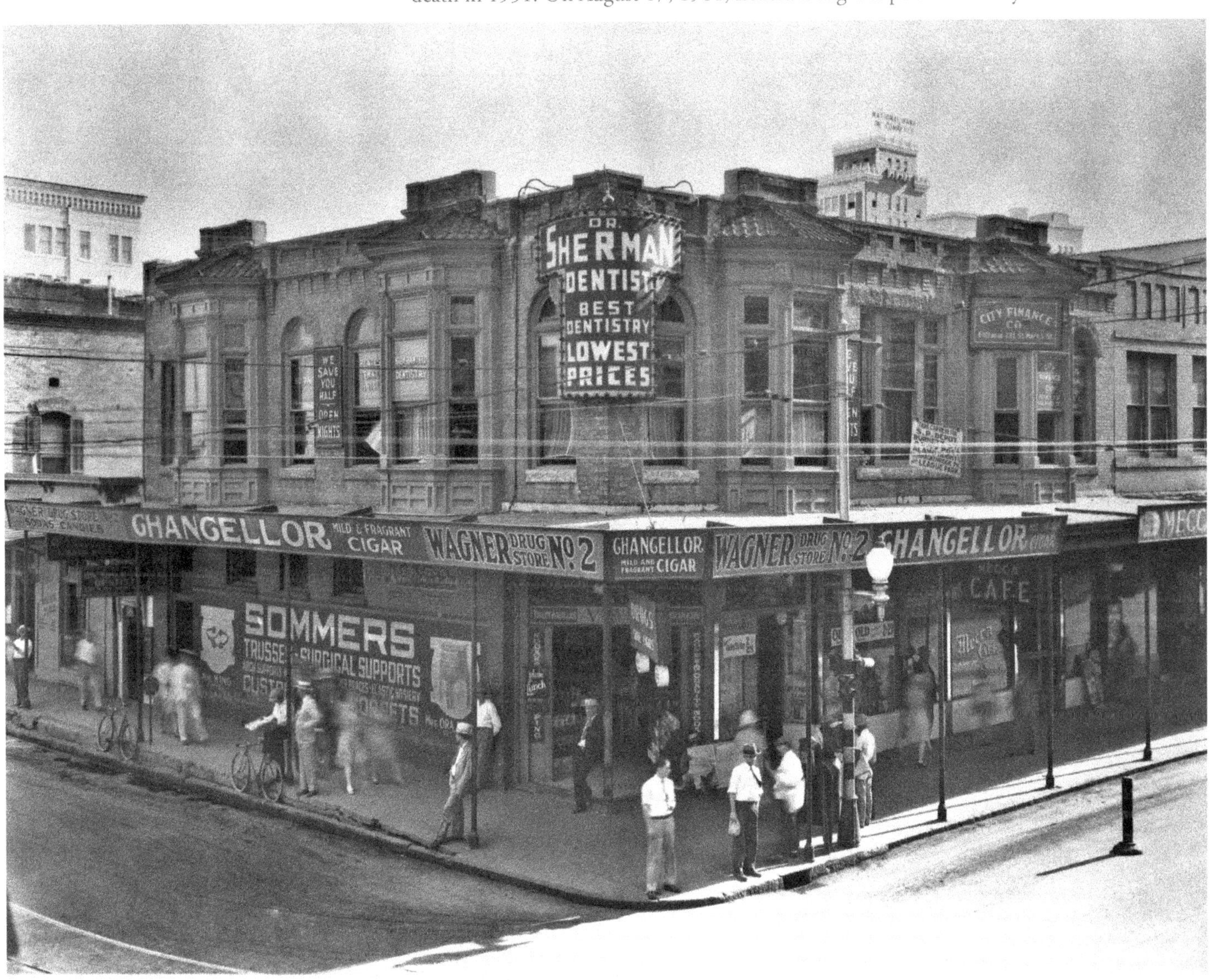

A view of La Villita on December 29, 1939, during its restoration. The site of a Coahuiltecan Indian village, the area became a Spanish settlement in the early 1700s. Over the years, it fell into ruin and in 1939, a two-year restoration began. The National Youth Administration trained 1,800 young people in arts and crafts during the process. The Smith-Young Tower rises in the background.

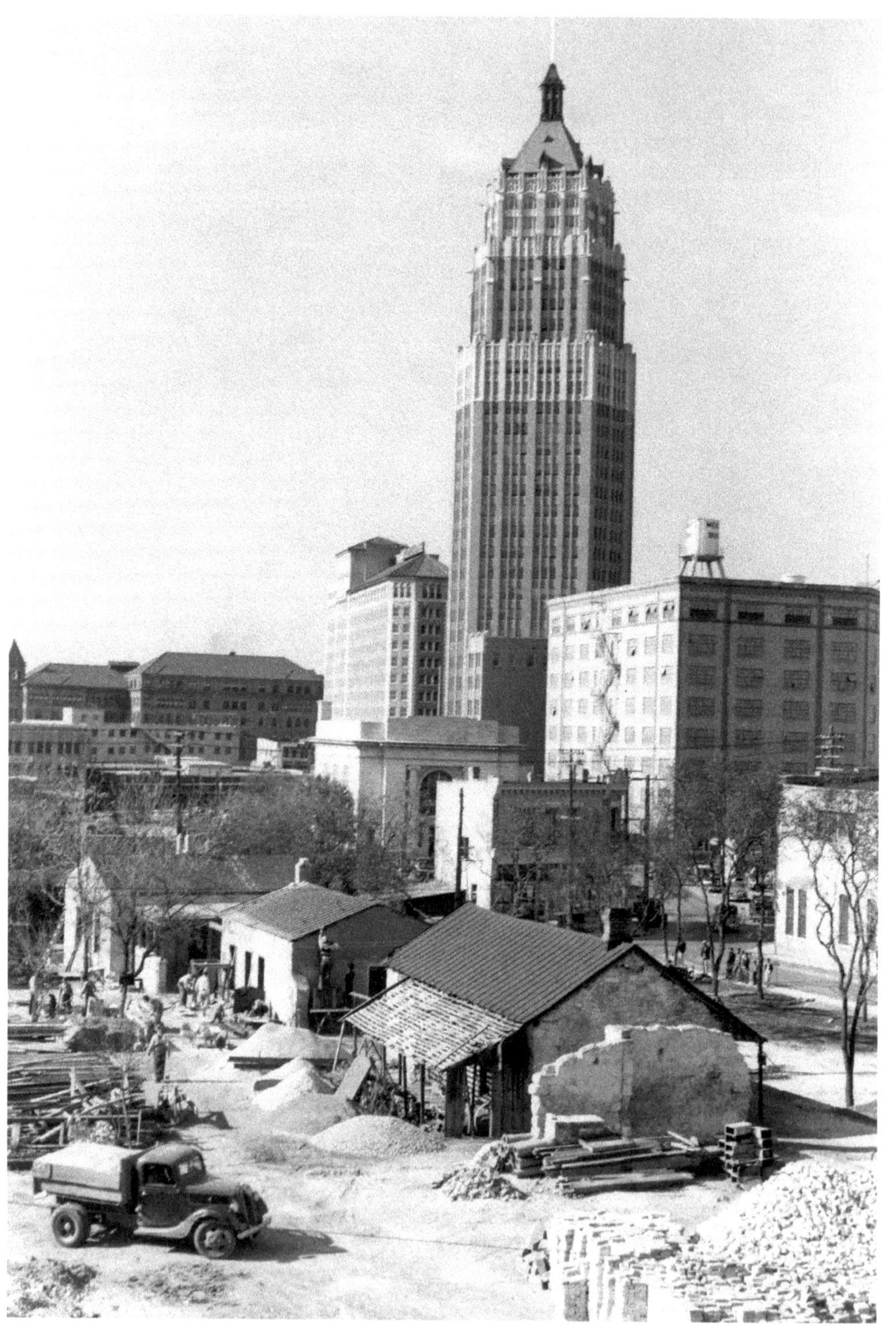

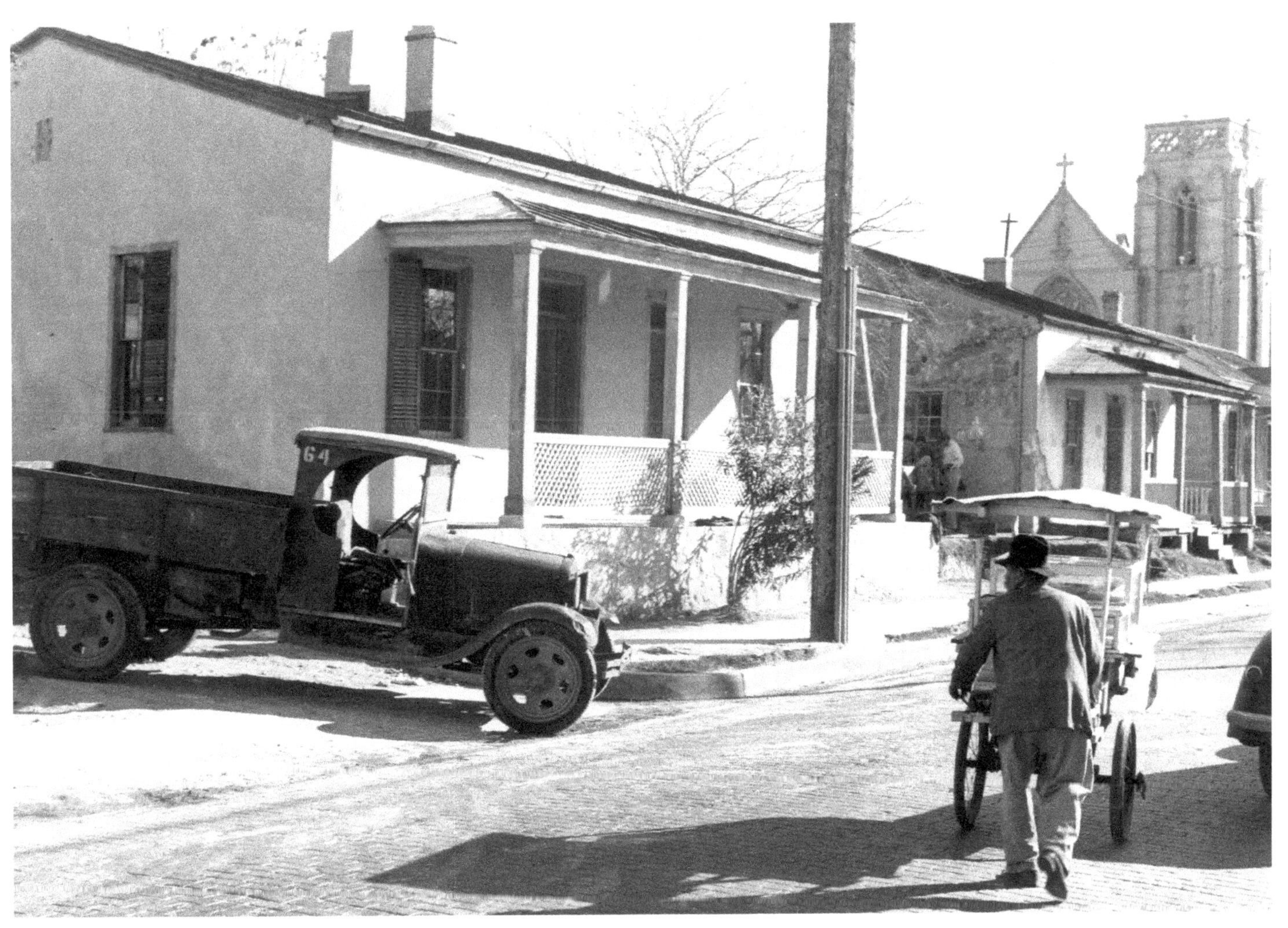

Two of the buildings being restored in La Villita, their north sides facing Presa Street. During World War II, the area was used as a Red Cross center. In 1972, the twenty-seven buildings were added to the National Register of Historic Places. The buildings are owned by the city and rented to artists and craftspeople.

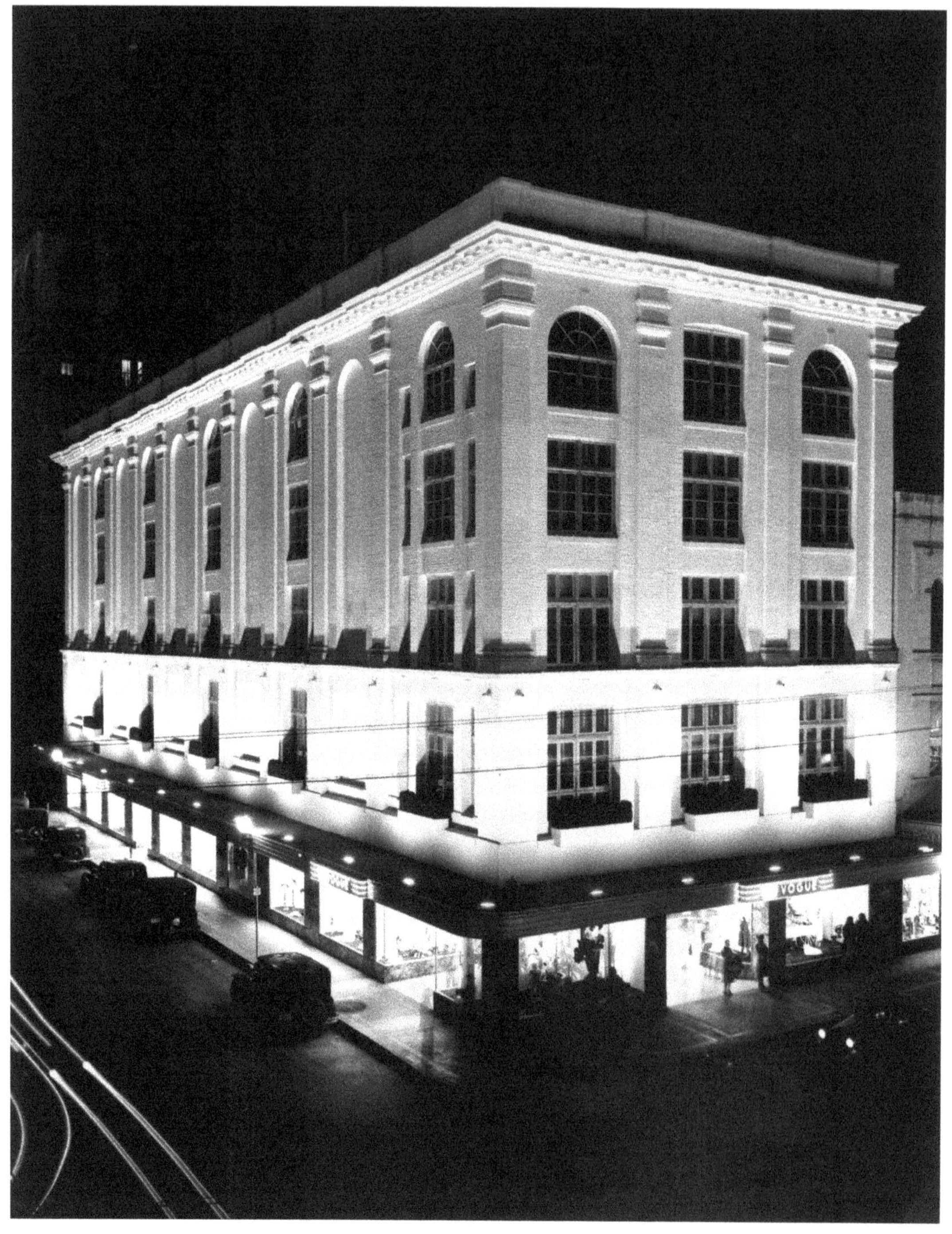

A nighttime view of the Vogue, a women's clothing store at 301 E. Houston Street (corner of Navarro Street). In 1965 the name became Margo's Vogue and was affiliated with Margo's La Mode of Dallas.

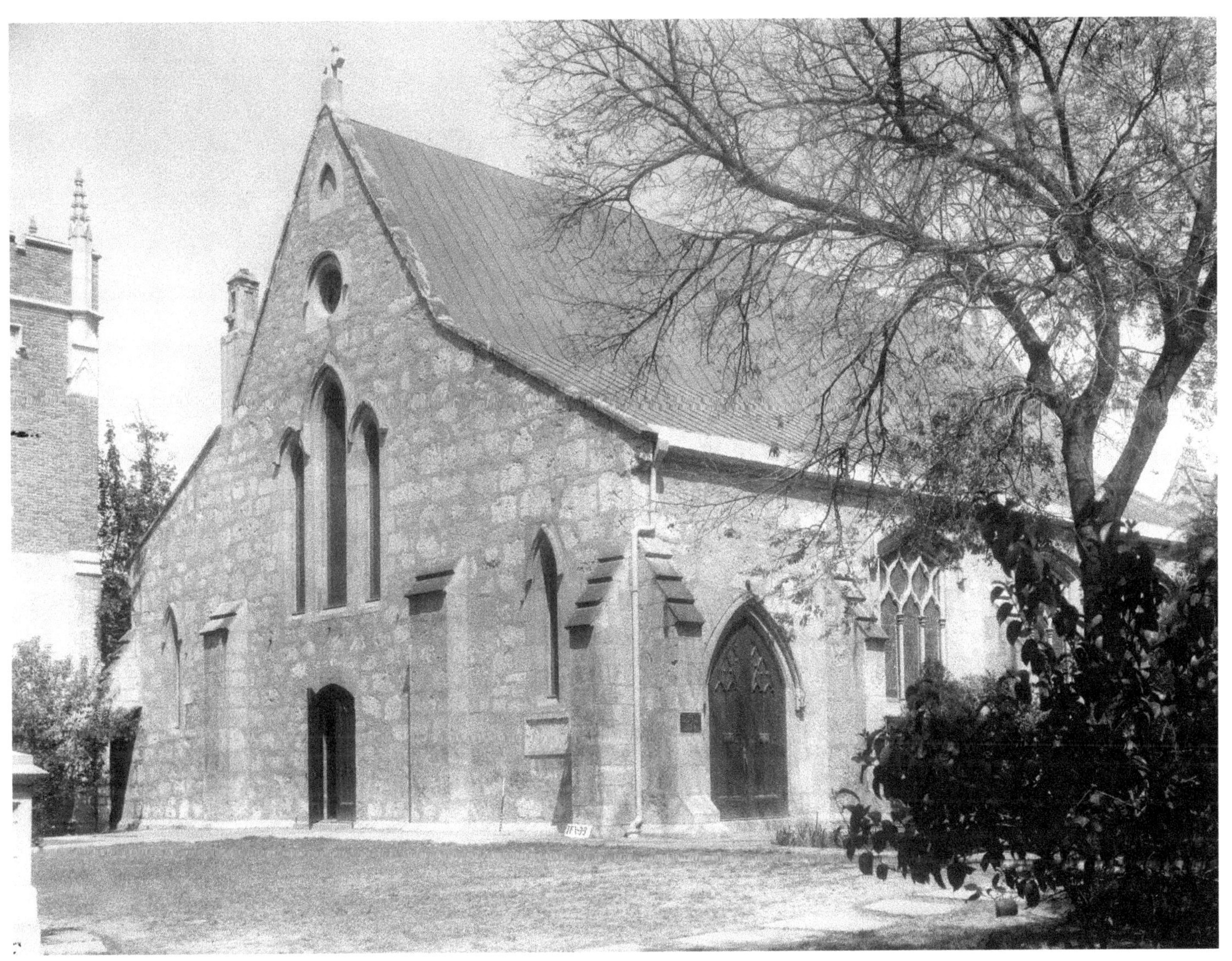

St. Mark's Episcopal Church was founded by an army chaplain in 1850 as Trinity Mission. In 1858, it reorganized into St. Mark's, and the cornerstone of the church was laid a year later. The Civil War stopped construction, which did not begin again until 1873. One of the bell cotes houses a bell cast from a cannon found buried on Alamo property.

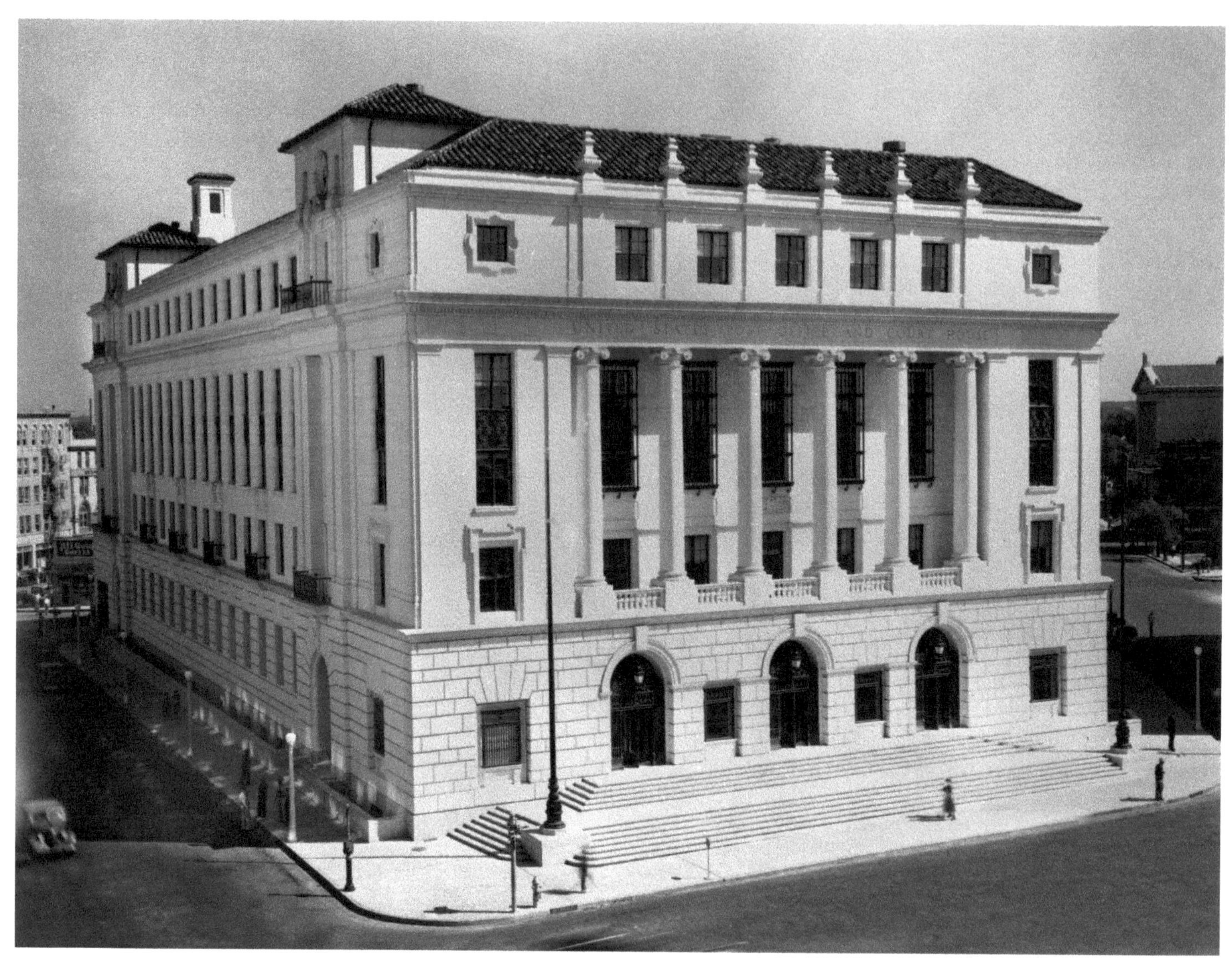

Architect Ralph H. Cameron designed this Federal Post Office and Courthouse which opened in 1937 on the site of the previous one at 615 E. Houston. While excavating and building the Post Office the remains of at least sixteen people were found. The site had served as a cemetery for the Valero Mission (Alamo) until about 1738.

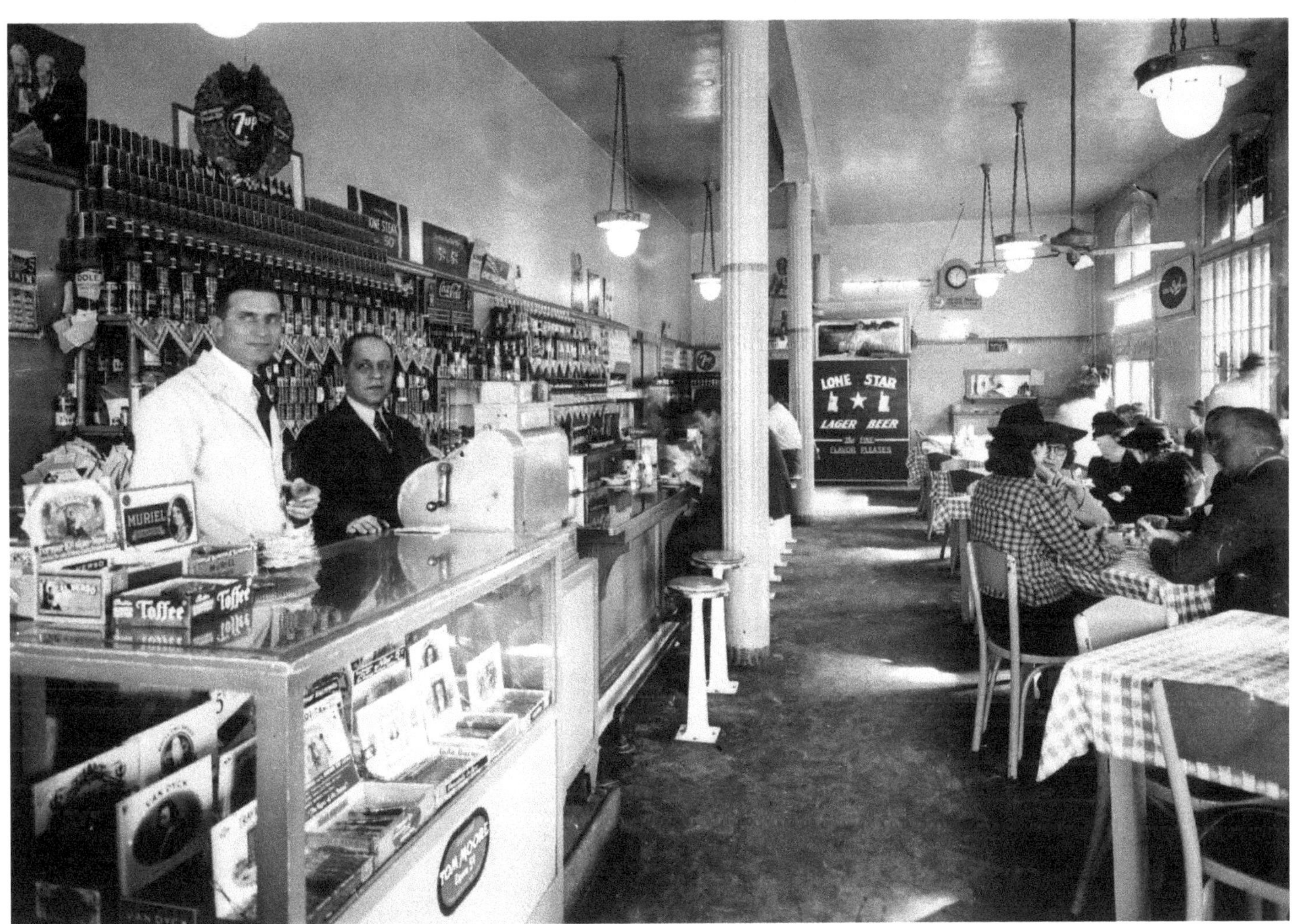

An interior photograph of the Prudential Cafe in the Prudential Life Insurance Building (Washer Building) around 1939. Arthur Sockler is second from the left, behind the cash register. Sockler was from Greece and arrived in the United States in 1890, first going to Chicago and coming to San Antonio in the 1930s. Note the Lone Star Beer banner on the rear wall.

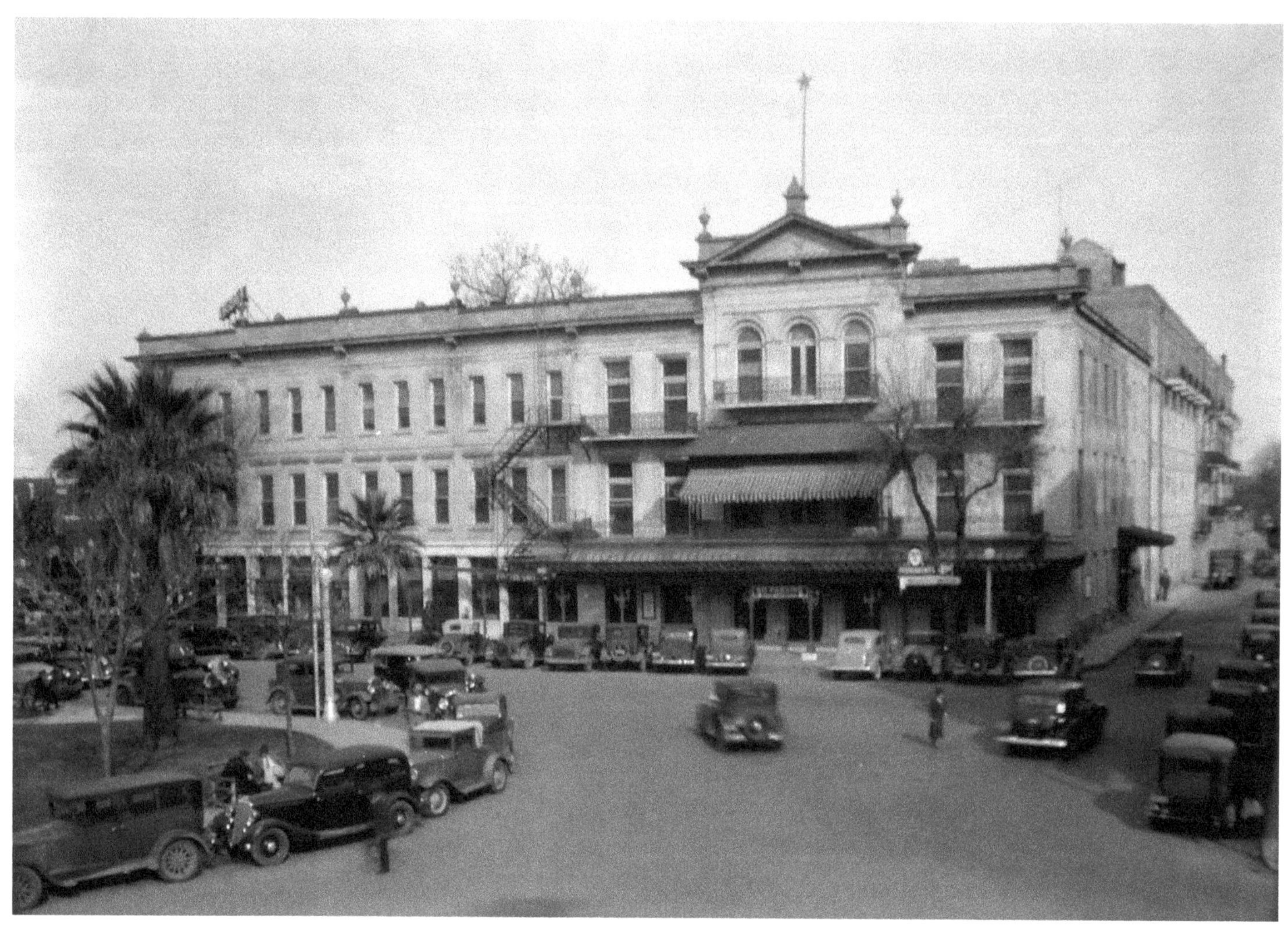

The Menger Hotel in the 1930s. The original fifty-room hotel has been expanded and now has 350 rooms. The Roosevelt Bar is said to be an exact replica of the one in the House of Lords in London. Theodore Roosevelt recruited his Rough Riders at the Menger in May 1898.

From Depression to Elation

(1940–1969)

These three decades were dominated by military and economic growth. During the first two years of the 1940s, San Antonio was still in the throes of the Depression. Once the United States became involved in World War II, the city was filled with troops training at Fort Sam Houston and Kelly and Randolph air fields. The city supported the war effort completely, with paper and scrap-metal drives and rationing. In 1943, San Antonio led all other cities in the nation in the number of tin cans it turned over to the government. It was also a major testing site for synthetic rubber tires.

The postwar period again saw San Antonio's population nearly triple, from 253,854 in 1940 to 654,153 in 1970. To support this growth, highway construction boomed. Development of suburbs expanded, some of which were designed for returning veterans. Downtown retail businesses declined, but malls, such as North Star (1960) and Wonderland (1961) attracted many. Kelly became a military-civilian complex for maintenance of aircraft. Lackland Air Force Base separated from Kelly, to become a training base for the newly created United States Air Force.

Politically, as of April 1, 1952, the city changed from a mayor-commissioner form of government to council-manager form. This became fully realized in 1955 when the Good Government League came into power. Throughout this period the city council annexed more and more land, increasing the geographical area and tax base. In the 1950s, McCarthyism arrived in San Antonio, with one group seeking to censor or remove books from the public library. The librarian, supported by the library board, stoutly refused.

The city and local civic groups made greater efforts to attack the problem of slums on the west side as urban renewal programs began.

The year 1968 was a pivotal one. From April to October of that year, San Antonio hosted HemisFair '68, the first officially designated international exposition in the southwestern United States. HemisFair spotlighted San Antonio on the world's stage. Efforts at increasing tourism and business in bio-tech, computer and light manufacturing have continued to this day.

San Antonio has come a long way from its days as a small village on the frontier's edge, becoming one of the nation's largest and most visited cities.

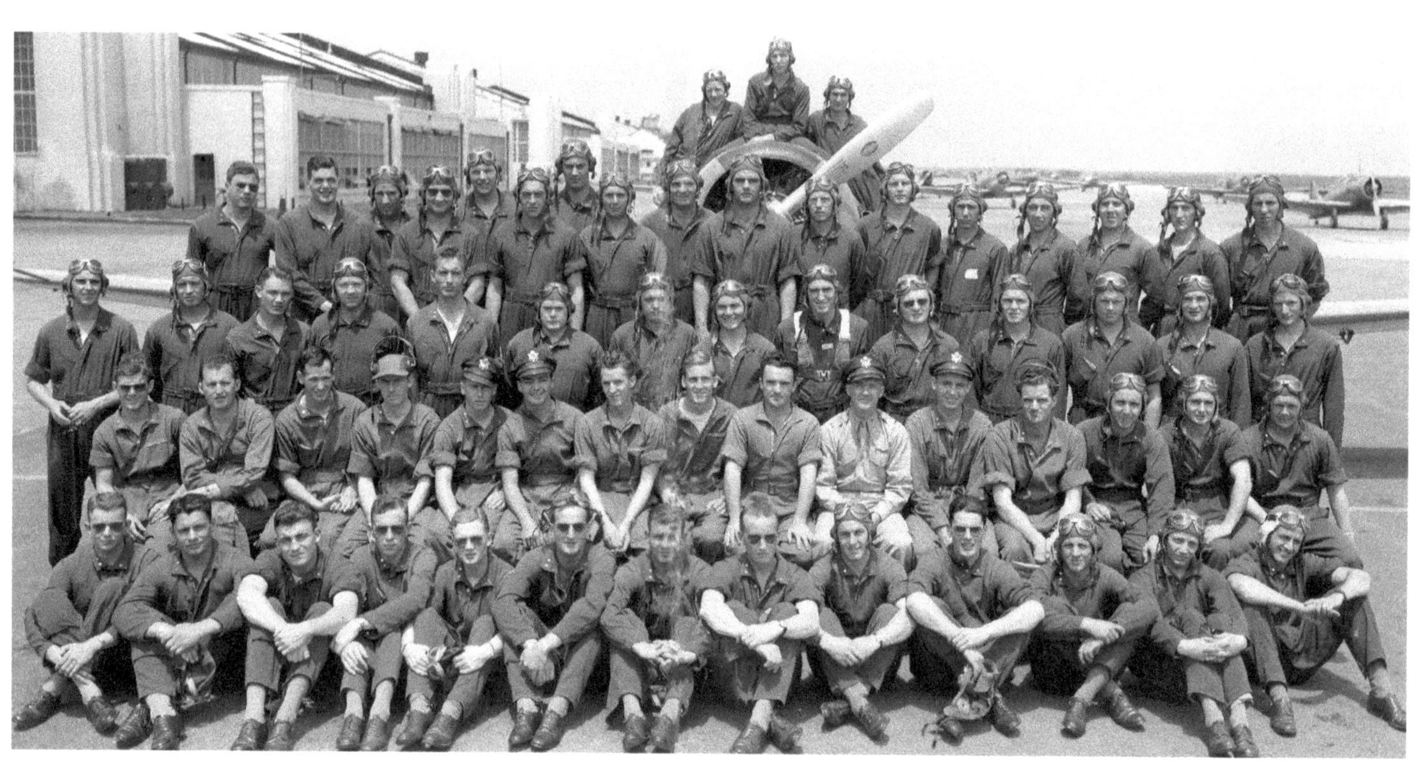

Class 42 F2, R-Squadron. World War II brought young men from all over the country to the temperate climate of San Antonio for military training. These soldiers were training as pilots at the United States Army Air Corps Training Center at Kelly Field. The photo was taken April 25, 1942.

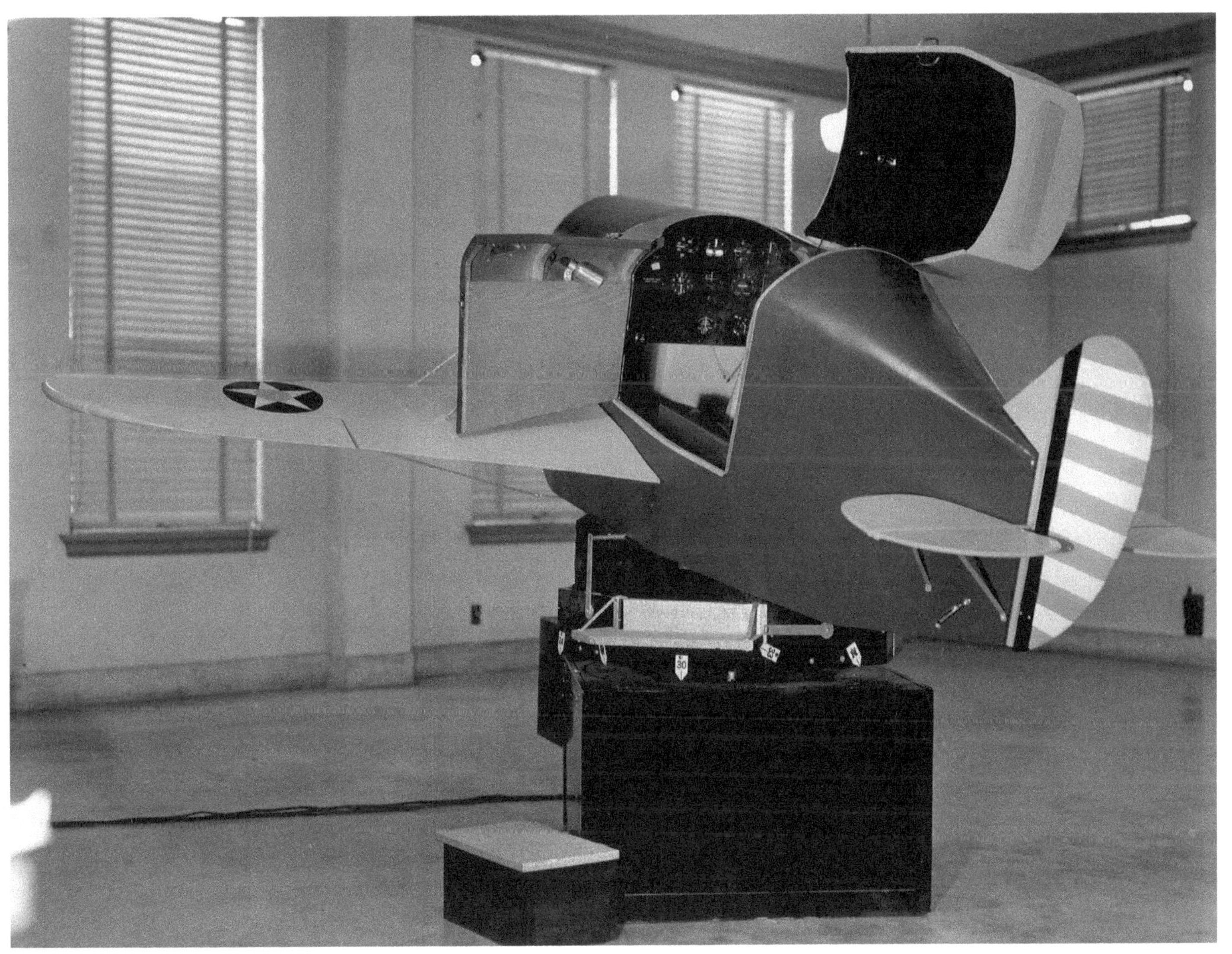

This training device was called "a Link." It taught how to maneuver and turn "like the real thing-only it's by instruments." Trainees would get fifteen or more hours in this before moving on to airplane training at Kelly.

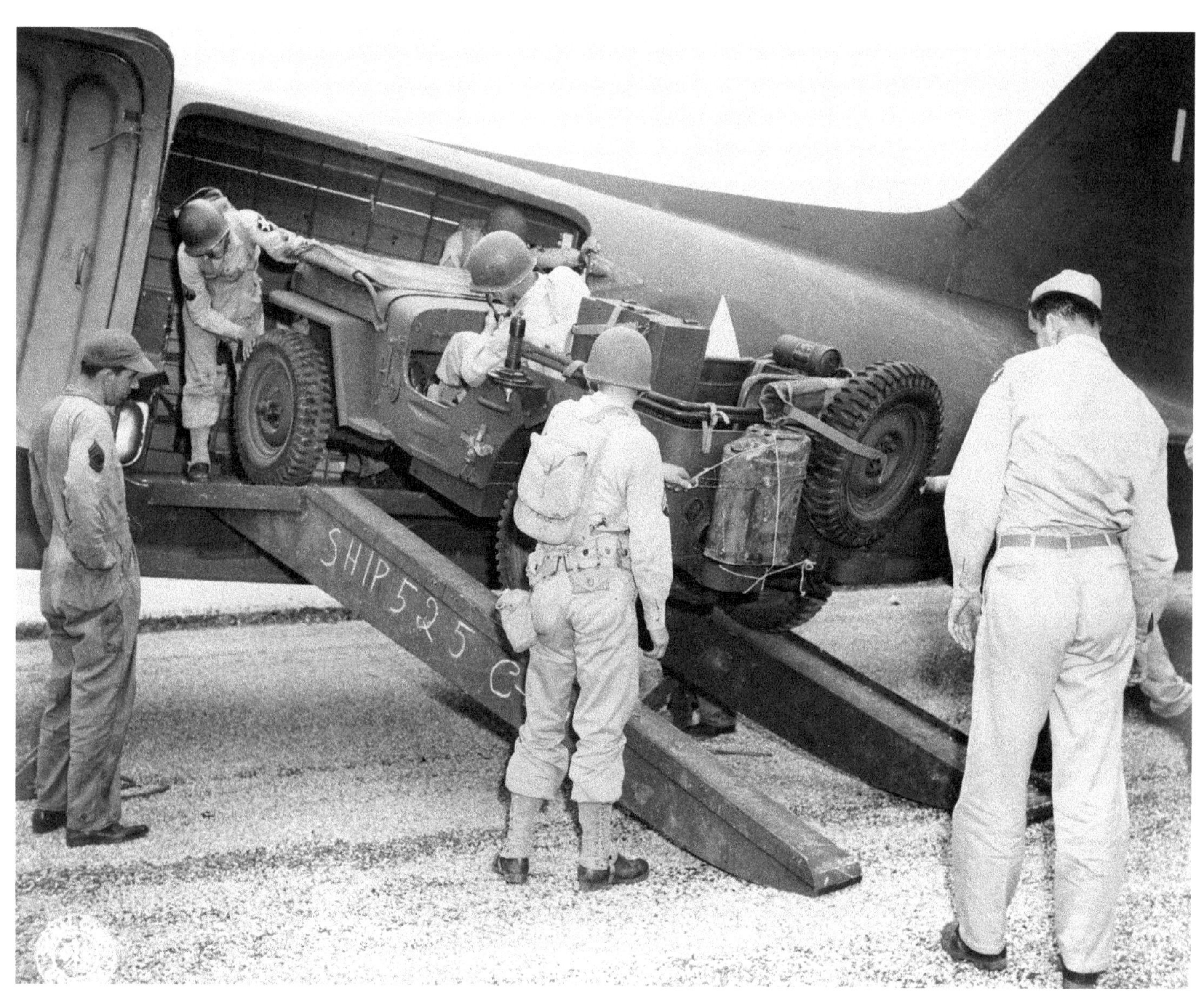

After the United States entered World War II, San Antonio became a beehive of activity to support the war effort, as in the previous World War. Fort Sam Houston, Kelly Field, and Randolph Field all boomed. Here, a jeep is being loaded for shipment.

This beautiful garden spot was once a quarry for the first Portland Cement Company west of the Mississippi (1880). Local prisoners were used to create the Japanese Garden in 1917–18. It is about 400 feet long, 300 feet wide and 60 feet high. Native plants abound, and fish swim in the pond. During World War II, the name was changed to Chinese Tea Garden. The original name was restored in 1984, and the gardens are being replenished.

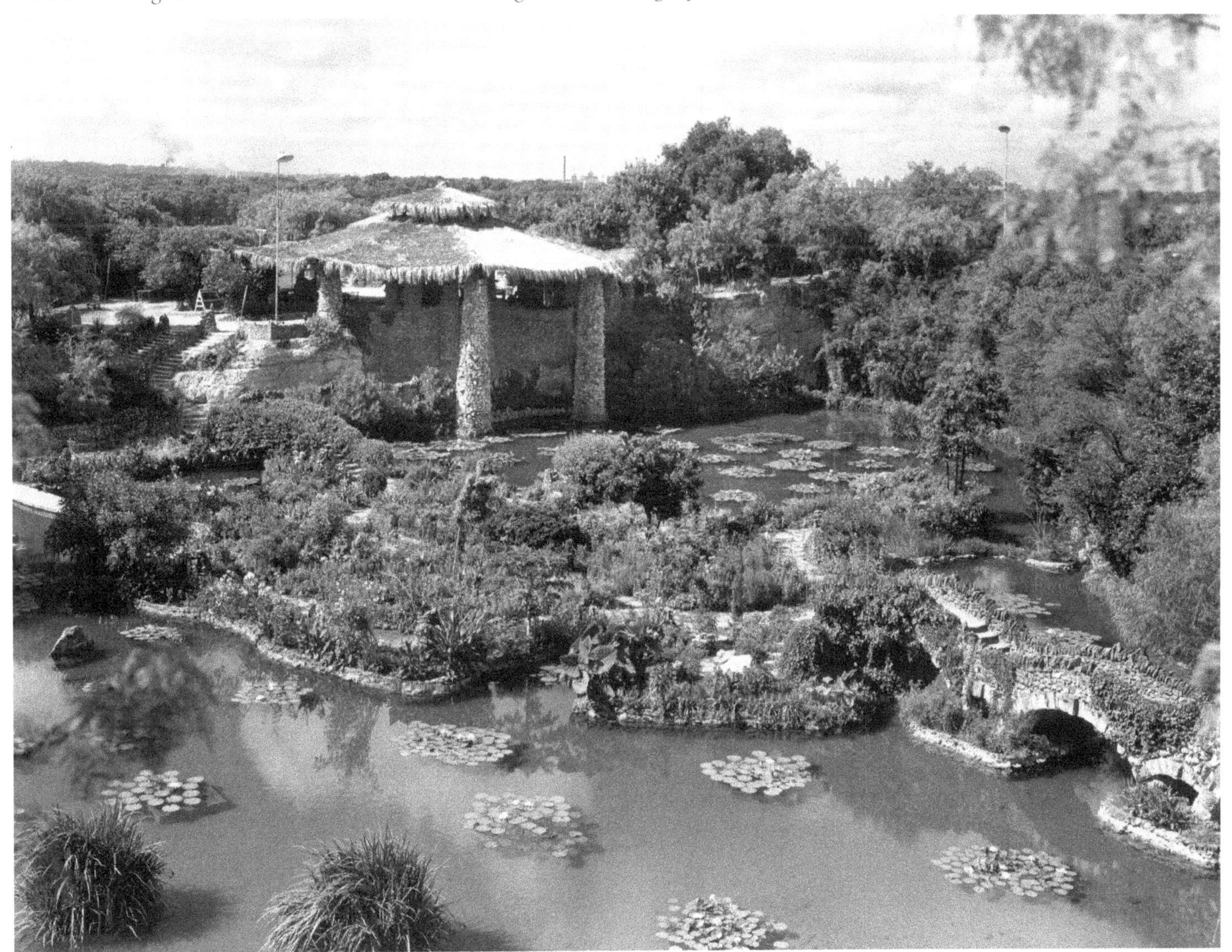

On September 30, 1897, a twenty-four year old nun, now known as Saint Therese of Lisieux, died at the Carmel Convent in France. The Basilica of the National Shrine of the Little Flower was built in 1931 in her honor and is staffed by Discalced Carmelite Friars. There are many artistic features to the Basilica but of special note is the eighteen-foot altar of Carrara marble, a creation of Louis Rodriguez.

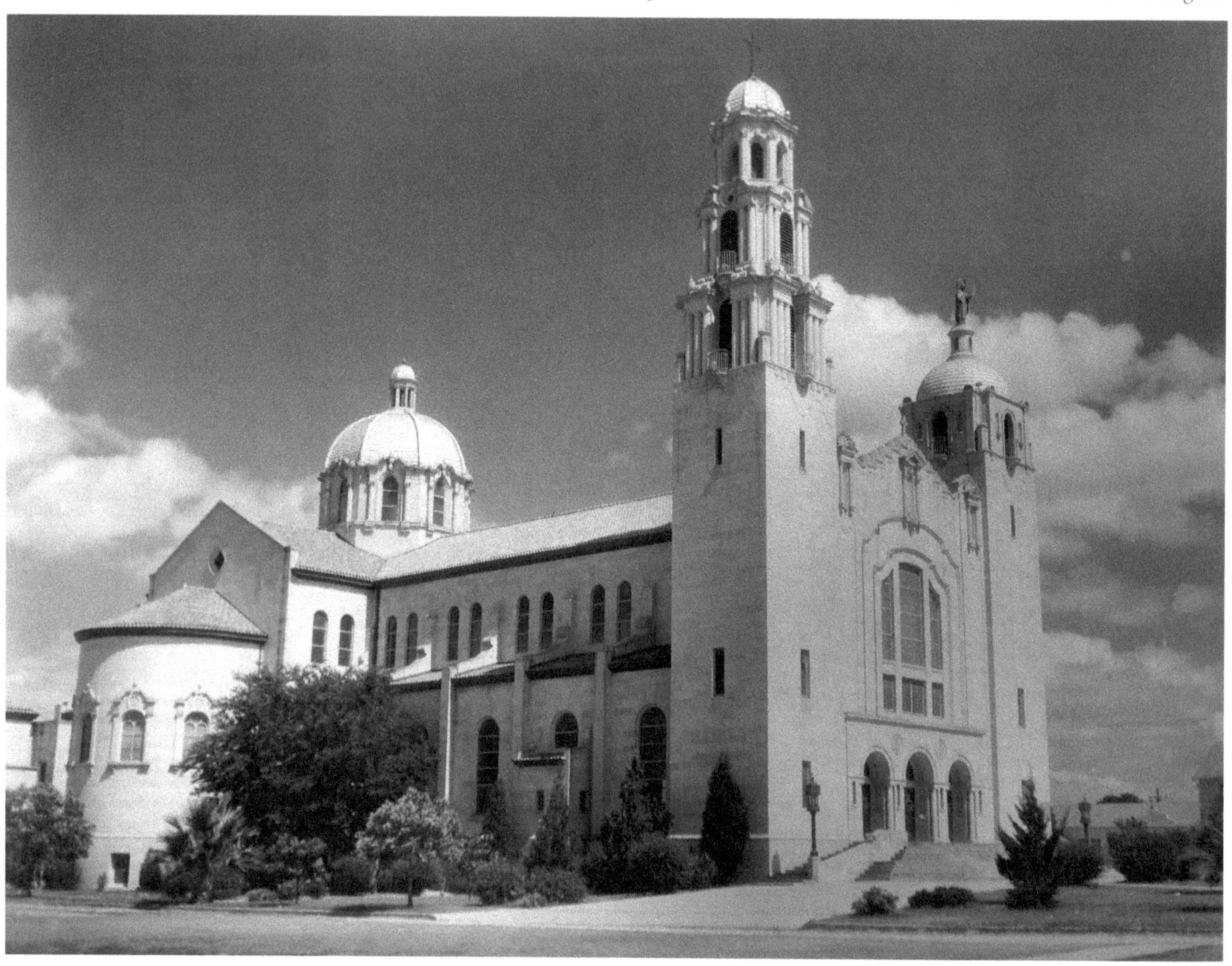

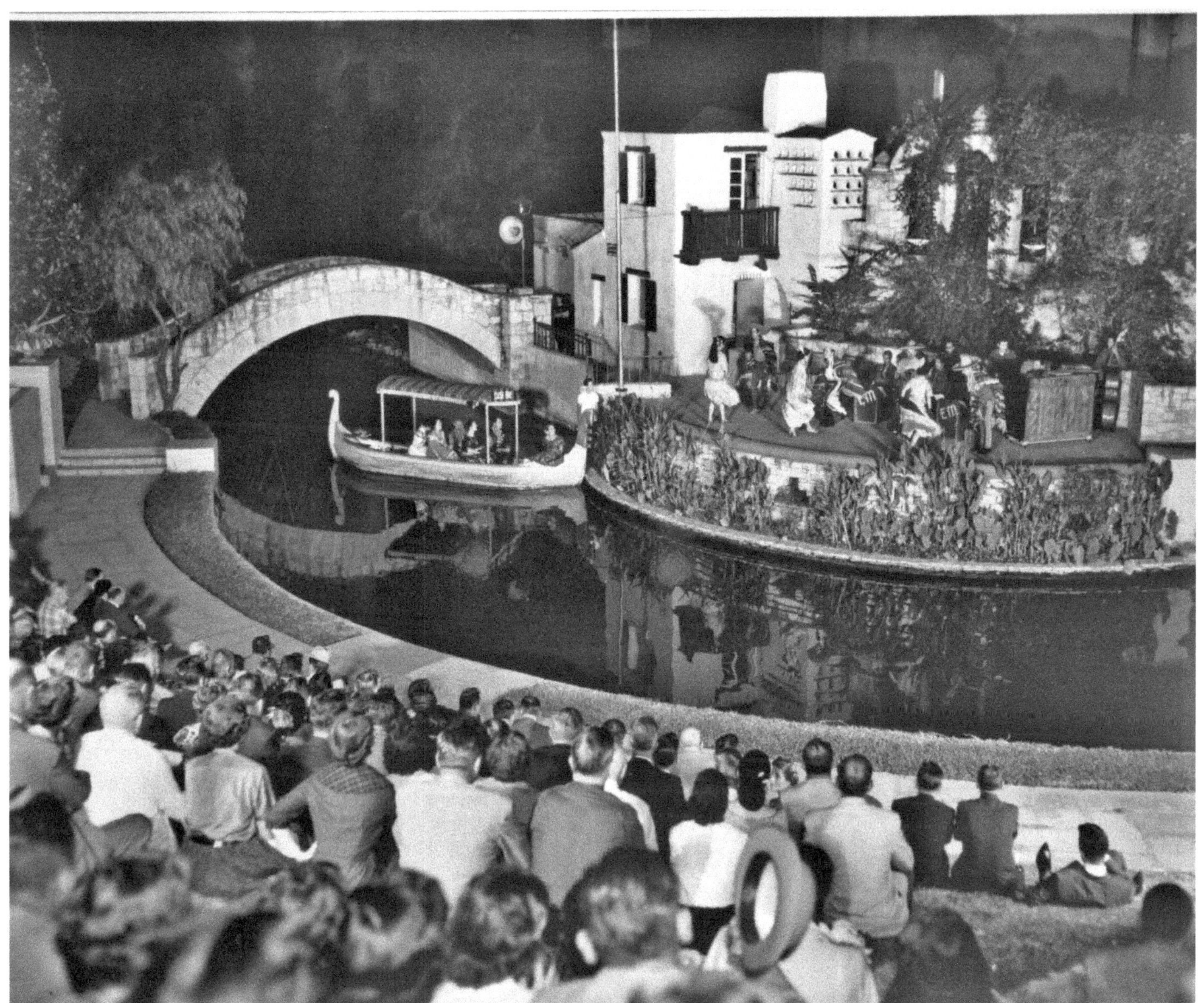

Spectators looking across the San Antonio River at performers on the stage of the Arneson River Theater. The open air theater, which seats about 500, was built in 1939 by the Works Projects Administration. During the summer, Fiesta Noche del Rio takes place. In the picture is a Casa Rio boat. Casa Rio has served Mexican food along the river since 1948.

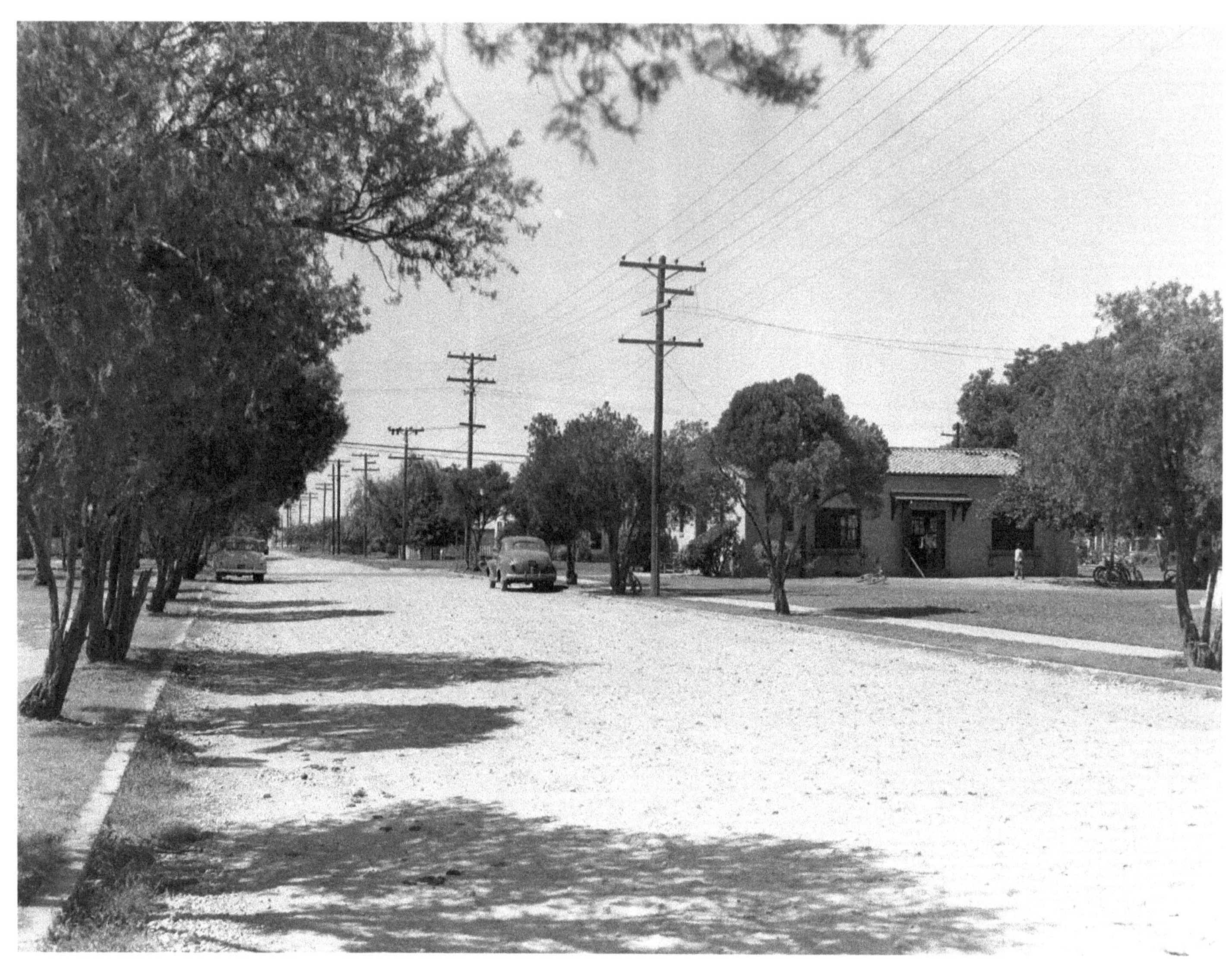

Marion Street in the Palm Heights subdivision on a bright, sunny day in 1952. Just south of downtown and not far from Kelly Field, this neighborhood really began to grow after World War II. In the 1950s and 1960s, there were Friday-night dances at the Palm Heights Community Center, 1201 W. Malone, and movies in the park during the summer.

Union Stockyards was founded in 1889 at 1716 S. San Marcos Street by a group of South Texas ranchers and trail drivers. When first built, it was on the far edge of town. Cattle, sheep, and hogs were bought and sold and shipped by train. By the time of this picture, trucks carried the livestock.

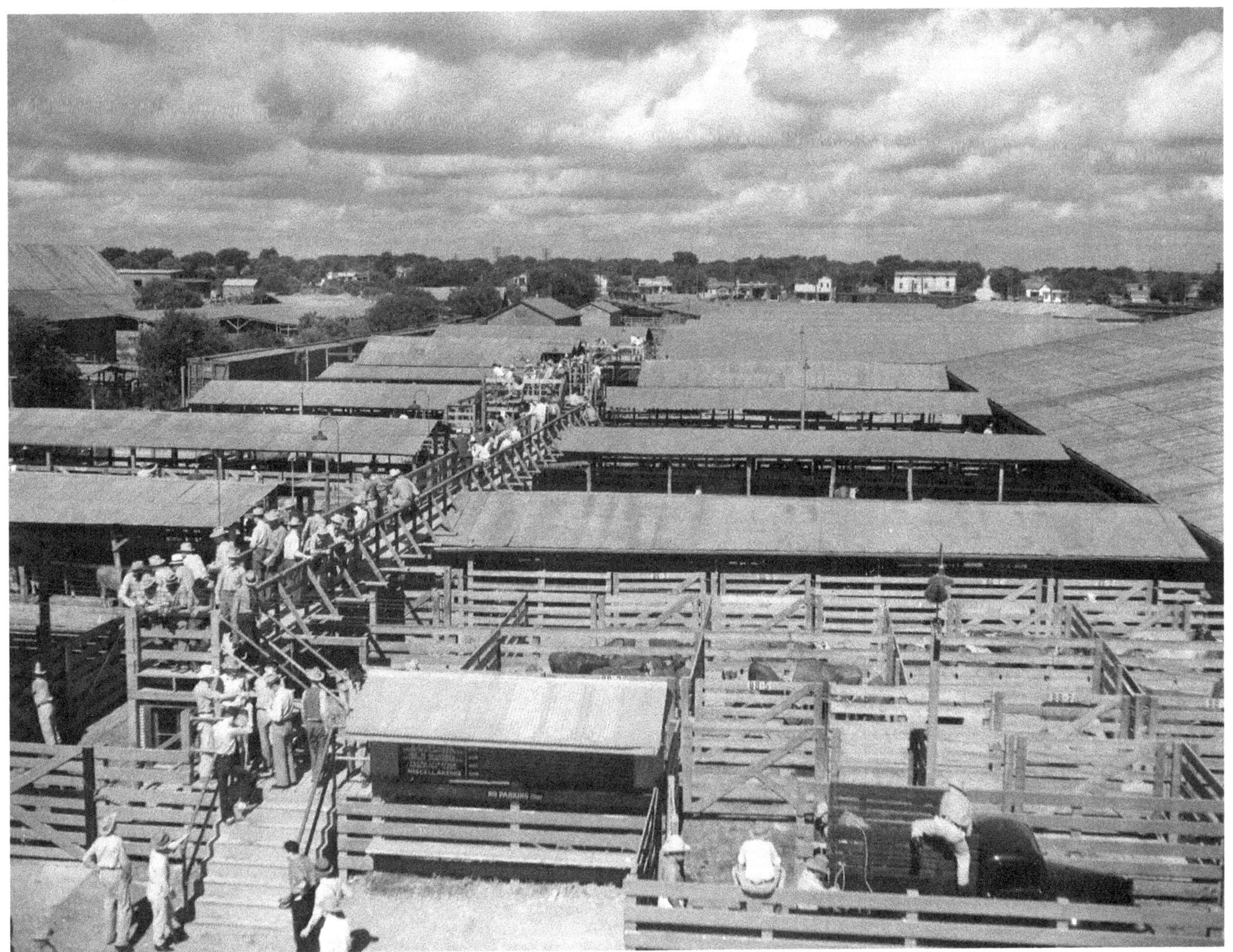

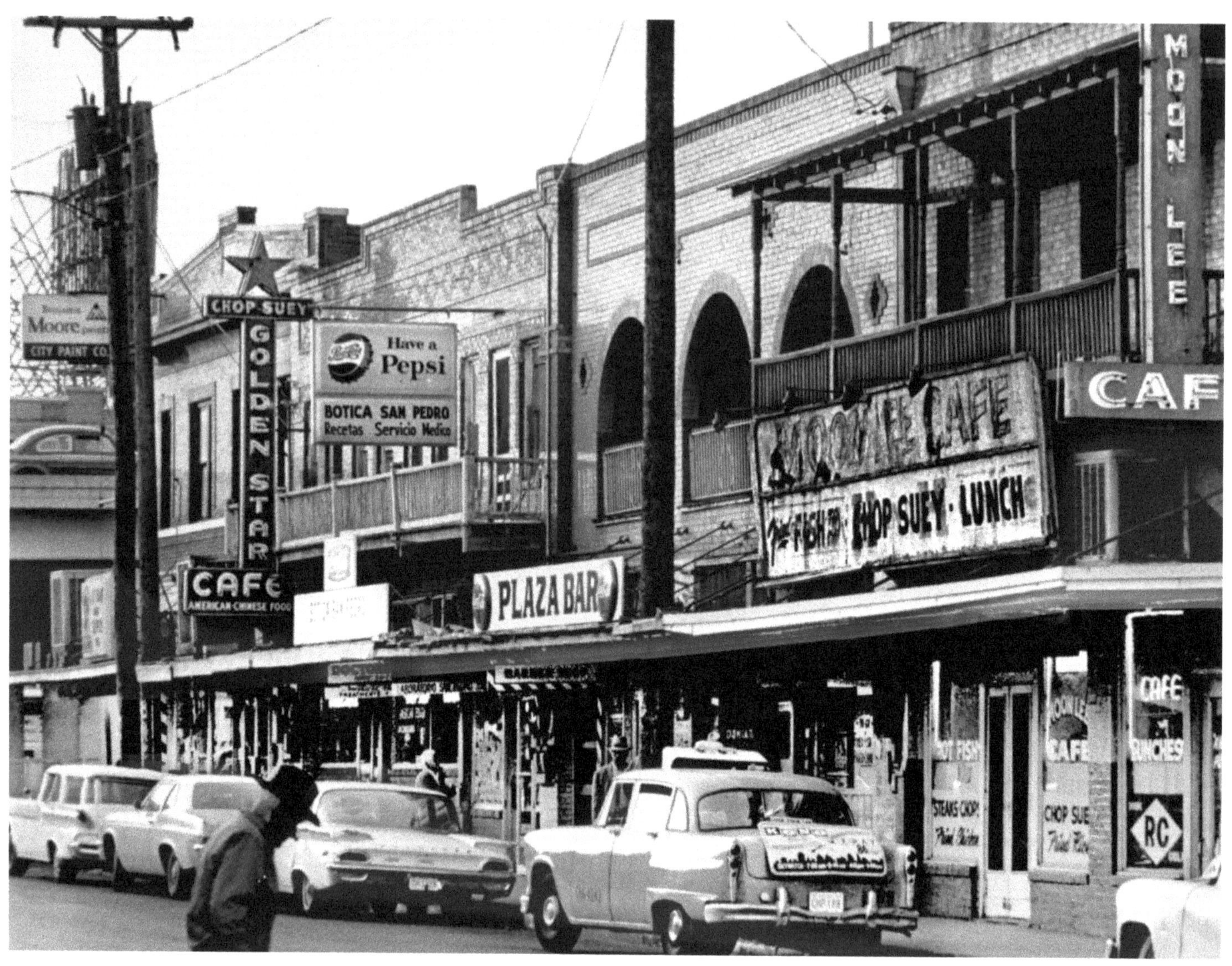

The north side of the 1100 block of W. Commerce was culturally diverse in the mid-1960s. From left to right are Back W. Jung's Golden Star Cafe, Maria Fernandez Botica San Pedro (Pharmacy), Victor Pizzini's Plaza Bar, and Lee Fook's Moon Lee Cafe.

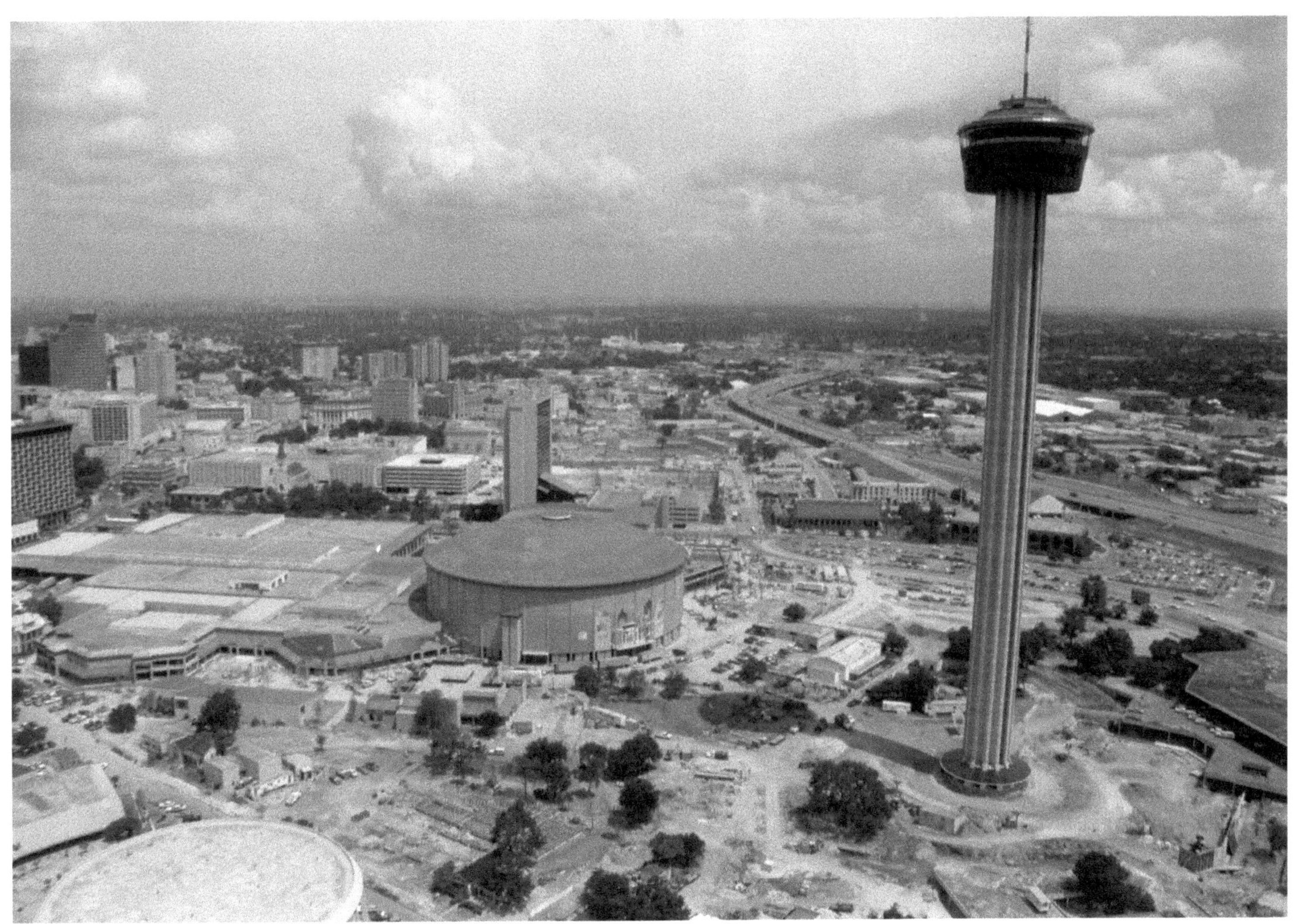

From April 6 to October 6, 1968, San Antonio was host to HemisFair '68. Homes and businesses on 92.6 acres of downtown were cleared to make room for the building of new structures and the relocation of historic buildings in order to showcase the cultures of the western world. This aerial photograph shows HemisFair still under construction. The Tower of the Americas stands to the right. The round building at the center is the Arena.

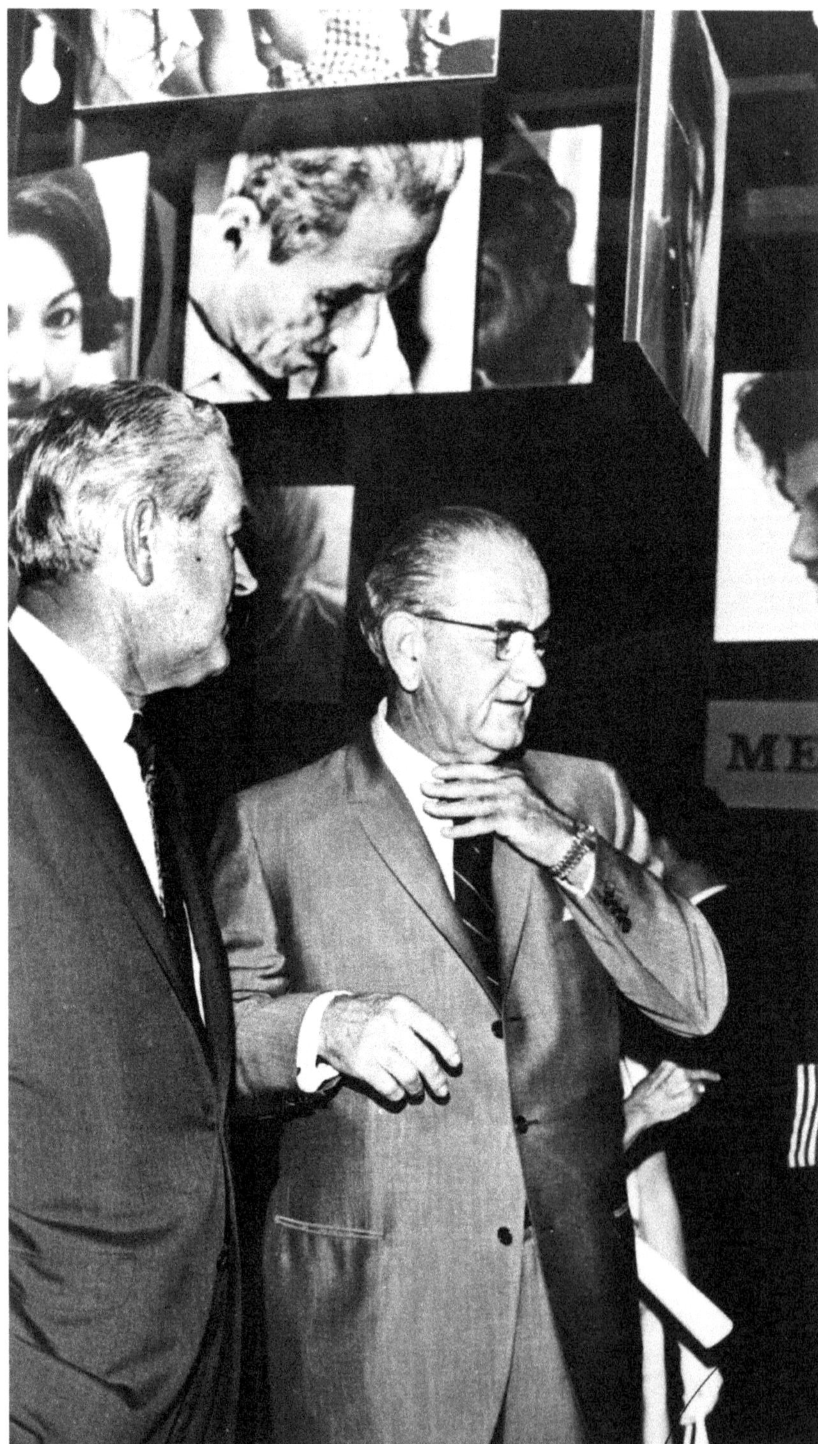

Governor John Connally and President Lyndon B. Johnson tour the Institute of Texan Cultures during HemisFair '68. The Institute helps preserve Texas ethnic heritage by making visible the contributions of the many diverse cultures that have created what it means to be a Texan.

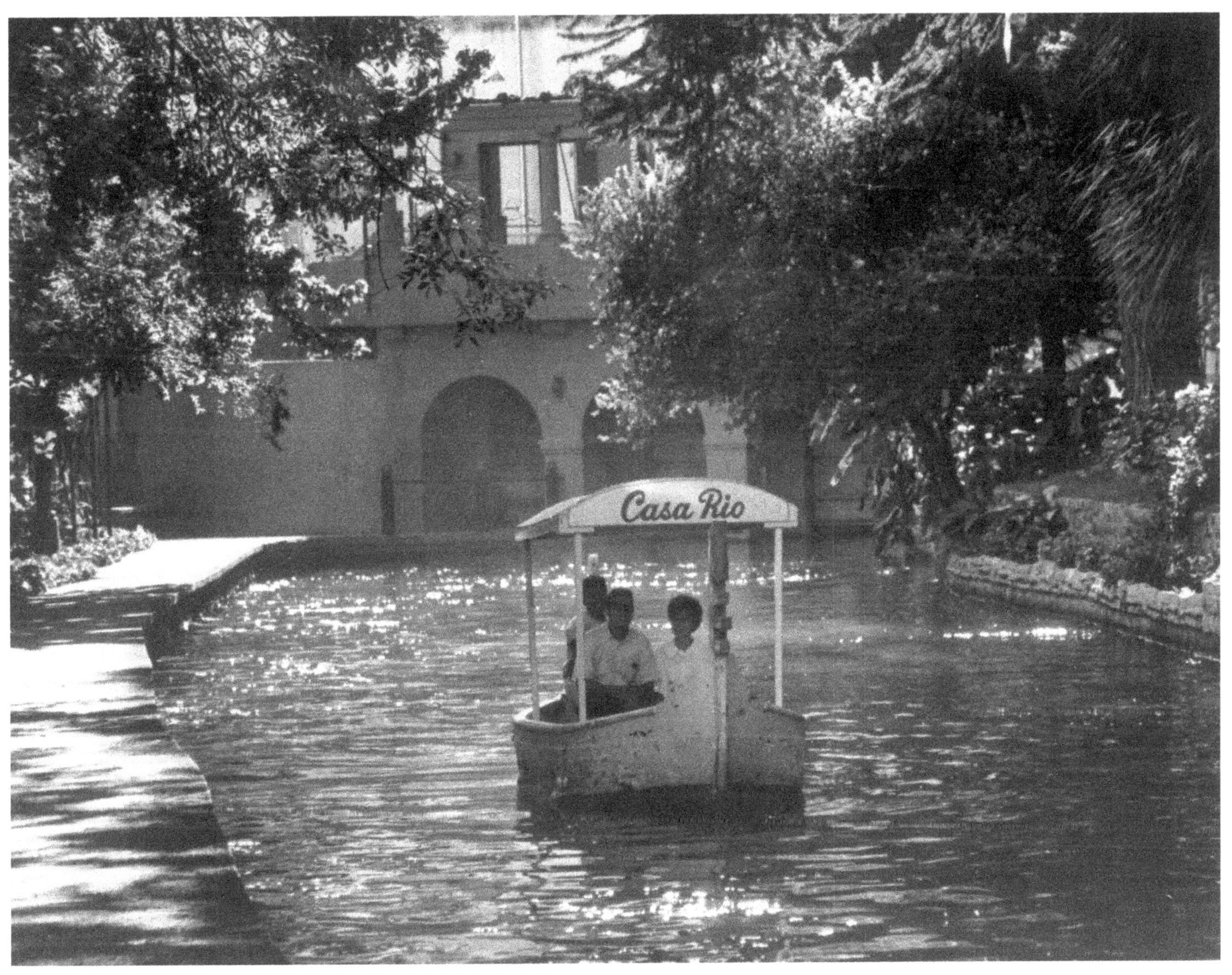

A Casa Rio pleasure boat cruising down the river. Casa Rio Mexican restaurant has been a staple for San Antonians and visitors since 1948.

Notes on the Photographs

These notes, listed by page number, attempt to include all aspects known of the photographs. Each of the photographs is identified by the page number, photograph's title or description, photographer and collection, archive, and call or box number when applicable. Although every attempt was made to collect all available data, in some cases complete data was unavailable due to the age and condition of some of the photographs and records.

II **Aerial of San Antonio**
University of Texas at San Antonio
Institute of Texan Cultures
083-0649

VI **Cadets from Peacock Military Academy**
University of Texas at San Antonio
Institute of Texan Cultures
089-0026

X **Haymarket Square or Plaza**
San Antonio Public Library
SAPL007-001

2 **The Vance Building**
University of Texas at San Antonio
Institute of Texan Cultures
101-0068

3 **South Side Alamo Plaza**
University of Texas at San Antonio
Institute of Texan Cultures
081-0477

4 **French Building and Post Office**
University of Texas at San Antonio
Institute of Texan Cultures
075-0330

5 **Commerce Street**
University of Texas at San Antonio
Institute of Texan Cultures
075-0332

6 **Zork & Griesenbeck**
University of Texas at San Antonio
Institute of Texan Cultures
75-1139

7 **Commerce Street, 1870**
University of Texas at San Antonio
Institute of Texan Cultures
L-2355-K

8 **Hay**
University of Texas at San Antonio
Institute of Texan Cultures
083-0087

9 **The Alamo**
University of Texas at San Antonio
Institute of Texan Cultures
083-0083

10 **Soledad**
University of Texas at San Antonio
Institute of Texan Cultures
101-0044

11 **Commerce Street, 1875**
University of Texas at San Antonio
Institute of Texan Cultures
075-1196

12 **The "Bat Cave"**
University of Texas at San Antonio Institute of Texan Cultures
081-0499

13 **Charles Hummel Shop and Residence**
University of Texas at San Antonio Institute of Texan Cultures
081-0494

14 **San Pedro Park**
University of Texas at San Antonio Institute of Texan Cultures
101-0075

16 **Hugo and Schmeltzer Wholesale Grocery Store**
University of Texas at San Antonio
Institute of Texan Cultures
081-0513

17 **Exterior of F. Groos and Company**
University of Texas at San Antonio Institute of Texan Cultures
081-493

18 **Military Plaza**
Library of Congress
LC-DIG-ppmsca-10494

19 **Mill Bridge Crossing**
University of Texas at San Antonio Institute of Texan Cultures
082-130

20 **Commerce Street Bridge**
University of Texas at San Antonio
Institute of Texan Cultures
075-1089

21 **Wagon Crossing at Old Mill Bridge**
San Antonio Public Library
SAPL077-027

22 **Menger Hotel**
University of Texas at San Antonio
Institute of Texan Cultures
081-0480

23 **Covered Wagon**
University of Texas at San Antonio
Institute of Texan Cultures
099-0184

24 **St. Joseph's Catholic Church**
University of Texas at San Antonio
Institute of Texan Cultures
088-0311

25 **East Side Main Plaza**
University of Texas at San Antonio
Institute of Texan Cultures
101-0045

26 **Temple Beth-El**
University of Texas at San Antonio
Institute of Texan Cultures
093-0384

27 **Duerler Confectionery**
University of Texas at San Antonio Institute of Texan Cultures
101-0114

28 **Military Plaza**
University of Texas at San Antonio Institute of Texan Cultures
079-0107

29 **Saint Mary's Hall**
University of Texas at San Antonio Institute of Texan Cultures
074-1249

30 **Commerce Street**
University of Texas at San Antonio Institute of Texan Cultures
083-0106

31 **Alamo Fire Company No. 2**
University of Texas at San Antonio Institute of Texan Cultures
086-0512

32 **Mission Concepcion**
University of Texas at San Antonio Institute of Texan Cultures
088-0323

33 **The Immigrants' Home**
San Antonio Public Library
SAPL007-029

34 **Vegetable Stands**
University of Texas at San Antonio Institute of Texan Cultures
101-0050

35 **Northeast Corner Main Plaza**
University of Texas at San Antonio Institute of Texan Cultures
075-1103

36 **Cowboy in San Antonio**
University of Texas at San Antonio Institute of Texan Cultures
070-0425

37 **Grand Opera House**
University of Texas at San Antonio Institute of Texan Cultures
073-1683

38 **Annual Reunion Terry's Texas Rangers**
University of Texas at San Antonio Institute of Texan Cultures
102-0193

39 **Central Grammar and High School**
University of Texas at San Antonio Institute of Texan Cultures
101-0072

40 **Old Veramendi Palace**
University of Texas at San Antonio Institute of Texan Cultures
075-1175

41 **Laying Courthouse Cornerstone**
University of Texas at San Antonio Institute of Texan Cultures
073-0203

42 **Farmer's Drug Store**
University of Texas at San Antonio Institute of Texan Cultures
081-0208

43 **D. Heye Carriage Trimming**
University of Texas at San Antonio Institute of Texan Cultures
091-0168

44 **Clifford Building**
University of Texas at San Antonio Institute of Texan Cultures
086-0404

45 **Early Celebration in Front of Alamo**
University of Texas at San Antonio Institute of Texan Cultures
076-0504

46 **Chili Stand**
University of Texas at San Antonio Institute of Texan Cultures
081-0509

47 **Military Plaza**
University of Texas at San Antonio Institute of Texan Cultures
z-2128-2

48 **Market House on Market Street**
University of Texas at San Antonio Institute of Texan Cultures
101-0103

49 **Men from Pearl Brewery**
University of Texas at San Antonio Institute of Texan Cultures
z-1822-c

50 **Original Pearl Brewery**
University of Texas at San Antonio Institute of Texan Cultures
z-1822-a

51 **The "Schooner Saloon"**
University of Texas at San Antonio Institute of Texan Cultures
z-2126-g-03

52 **F. Kalteyer and Sons**
University of Texas at San Antonio Institute of Texan Cultures
075-0822

53 **Cavalrymen**
Library of Congress
LC-B2-220-5

54 **Rische's Opera House**
University of Texas at San Antonio Institute of Texan Cultures
083-0487

55 **Ringling Bros Circus**
University of Texas at San Antonio Institute of Texan Cultures
075-1141

56 **Tramway Sprinkler no. 6**
University of Texas at San Antonio Institute of Texan Cultures
075-0856

58 **Federal Building**
University of Texas at San Antonio Institute of Texan Cultures
076-0525

59 **Frank Bros.**
University of Texas at San Antonio Institute of Texan Cultures
075-1182

60 **President McKinley**
University of Texas at San Antonio Institute of Texan Cultures
075-0199

61 **The Carnegie Library**
San Antonio Public Library
SAPL007-007

62 **Pioneer Flour Mills**
University of Texas at San Antonio Institute of Texan Cultures
082-642

63 **Woeltz Building**
University of Texas at San Antonio Institute of Texan Cultures
100-0273

64 **Fourth of July Parade, Houston St.**
University of Texas at San Antonio Institute of Texan Cultures
075-0853

65 **H. F. Wosnig and Company**
University of Texas at San Antonio Institute of Texan Cultures
087-0287

66 **St. John Berchmans Chapel**
University of Texas at San Antonio Institute of Texan Cultures
068-3193

67 **Circus Wagons**
University of Texas at San Antonio Institute of Texan Cultures
084-5496

68 **Floodwaters**
University of Texas at San Antonio Institute of Texan Cultures
091-0166

69 TROOPS ON REVIEW
Library of Congress
09011U

70 AEROPLANE USED FOR MESSAGES
Library of Congress
LC-B2-2229-2

71 LIEUTENANT FOULOIS
San Antonio Public Library
SAPL007-003

72 FORT SAM HOUSTON
Library of Congress
09382u

73 LONE STAR BREWING COMPANY'S FLOAT
University of Texas at San Antonio
Institute of Texan Cultures
074-1295

74 MOORE BUILDING
University of Texas at San Antonio
Institute of Texan Cultures
084-0639

75 MAN FEEDING SWANS
University of Texas at San Antonio
Institute of Texan Cultures
091-0011

76 SAN ANTONIO RIVER
University of Texas at San Antonio
Institute of Texan Cultures
091-0322

77 ALAMO PLAZA
University of Texas at San Antonio
Institute of Texan Cultures
069-8337

78 MOUNT ZION BAPTIST CHURCH
University of Texas at San Antonio
Institute of Texan Cultures
093-0013

79 CROWD GATHERED AT POST OFFICE
University of Texas at San Antonio
Institute of Texan Cultures
098-0283

80 HORSE-DRAWN FLOAT
University of Texas at San Antonio
Institute of Texan Cultures
z-1822-d-2

81 THEODORE ROOSEVELT
Library of Congress
3b43780u

82 THE CITY MARKET
Library of Congress
12807u

83 GREAT NORTHERN RAILROAD STATION
University of Texas at San Antonio
Institute of Texan Cultures
102-0609

84 GEORGE DULLNIG'S BUILDING
University of Texas at San Antonio
Institute of Texan Cultures
postcard

85 AUTO MEET
University of Texas at San Antonio
Institute of Texan Cultures
083-0593

86 MAHNCKE HOTEL
University of Texas at San Antonio
Institute of Texan Cultures
079-0376

87 ALAMO PLAZA
Library of Congress
3d01920u

88 THE ALAMO
Library of Congress
3a00197u

89 NIGHT SCENE
University of Texas at San Antonio
Institute of Texan Cultures
101-0102

90 U.S. ARMY MANEUVERS IN TEXAS
Library of Congress
3a03509u

91 HOT SULPHUR WELLS
University of Texas at San Antonio
Institute of Texan Cultures
093-0400

92 BLERIOT AIRPLANE
University of Texas at San Antonio
Institute of Texan Cultures
004-0559

93 MAIN PLAZA
University of Texas at San Antonio
Institute of Texan Cultures
069-8765

94 CHERRY STREET AND COMMERCE
University of Texas at San Antonio
Institute of Texan Cultures
z-774-1

95 BELGIAN GARDENERS FLOAT
University of Texas at San Antonio
Institute of Texan Cultures
074-1016

96 DITCH DIGGING
University of Texas at San Antonio
Institute of Texan Cultures
085-0417

97 FAIRMOUNT HOTEL
University of Texas at San Antonio
Institute of Texan Cultures
089-0616

98 LIONEL PERRY, NINE-YEAR-OLD NEWSBOY
Library of Congress
03871u

99 SAN ANTONIO MESSENGERS
Library of Congress
03874u

100 ALAMO NATIONAL BANK
University of Texas at San Antonio
Institute of Texan Cultures
069-8418

101 PEET PERSYN'S BARN
University of Texas at San Antonio
Institute of Texan Cultures
074-1082

102 PRINCESS THEATRE
University of Texas at San Antonio
Institute of Texan Cultures
084-0761

103 HOUSTON STREET
University of Texas at San Antonio
Institute of Texan Cultures
099-0977

104 FLASH FLOOD
University of Texas at San Antonio
Institute of Texan Cultures
069-8518

105 FLOODWATERS ON HOUSTON STREET
University of Texas at San Antonio
Institute of Texan Cultures
101-0001

106 HOUSTON AND NAVARRO AFTER FLOOD
University of Texas at San Antonio
Institute of Texan Cultures
099-0311

107 INTERIOR OF BULL BROTHERS
University of Texas at San Antonio
Institute of Texan Cultures
087-0455

108 SAN ANTONIO VOLUNTEER FIRE DEPARTMENT MEMBERS
University of Texas at San Antonio
Institute of Texan Cultures
079-0012

109 BIRD'S-EYE VIEW
University of Texas at San Antonio
Institute of Texan Cultures
099-0527

110 TURNVEREIN GIRLS
University of Texas at San Antonio
Institute of Texan Cultures
074-1244

111 BOYS WASHING BUGGIES
University of Texas at San Antonio
Institute of Texan Cultures
074-0141

112 EAST HOUSTON STREET
University of Texas at San Antonio
Institute of Texan Cultures
080-0238

113 **Peacock Military Academy**
University of Texas at San Antonio
Institute of Texan Cultures
073-1203

114 **Camp Travis**
Library of Congress
6a30665u

115 **Illinois National Guard**
University of Texas at San Antonio
Institute of Texan Cultures
099-0667

116 **Flag Day, Fort Sam Houston**
University of Texas at San Antonio
Institute of Texan Cultures
6a32409

117 **The Bexar Hotel**
University of Texas at San Antonio
Institute of Texan Cultures
100-0666

118 **The Louis Bizy Saloon**
University of Texas at San Antonio
Institute of Texan Cultures
079-0015

119 **Maverick Bank Building**
University of Texas at San Antonio
Institute of Texan Cultures
101-0069

120 **St. Berchmans Church**
University of Texas at San Antonio
Institute of Texan Cultures
074-1006

122 **The Sun Dodgers**
San Antonio Public Library
SAPL007-009

123 **Looking North on Alamo Street**
University of Texas at San Antonio
Institute of Texan Cultures
092-0043

124 **City Hall**
University of Texas at San Antonio
Institute of Texan Cultures
069-8468

125 **Alamo National Bank**
University of Texas at San Antonio
Institute of Texan Cultures
099-0511

126 **1921 Flood Damage**
San Antonio Public Library
SAPL007-025

127 **Aftermath of Flood**
University of Texas at San Antonio
Institute of Texan Cultures
069-8530

128 **Queen on Parade Float**
University of Texas at San Antonio
Institute of Texan Cultures
099-1028

129 **Fiesta Float**
University of Texas at San Antonio
Institute of Texan Cultures
099-1029

130 **General Pershing Reviewing Troops**
Library of Congress
6a35767u

131 **Kelly Field in the 1920s**
Library of Congress
6a35777u

132 **Man Pole-Vaulting in San Pedro Park**
University of Texas at San Antonio
Institute of Texan Cultures
099-1024

133 **F. W. Woolworth**
San Antonio Public Library
SAPL007-023

134 **Five Men at Brooks Field**
University of Texas at San Antonio
Institute of Texan Cultures
099-1035

135 **Saint John's Lutheran Church**
University of Texas at San Antonio
Institute of Texan Cultures
101-0064

136 **Snow, 1926**
University of Texas at San Antonio
Institute of Texan Cultures
084-0005

137 **After Snowfall**
San Antonio Public Library
SAPL007-008

138 **"Mexican Shop"**
San Antonio Public Library
SAPL007-021

139 **Second Radio Station**
San Antonio Public Library
SAPL007-032

140 **Night at Municipal Auditorium**
San Antonio Public Library
SAPL007-006

141 **West Pecan Street**
San Antonio Public Library
SAPL007-026

142 **Bonham Street**
University of Texas at San Antonio
Institute of Texan Cultures
079-0373

143 **Ideal Service Station & Hymas Drug Store**
San Antonio Public Library
SAPL007-017

144 **Nevelow Brothers**
San Antonio Public Library
SAPL007-018

145 **Dolorosa Street**
University of Texas at San Antonio
Institute of Texan Cultures
069-8771

146 **Newspaper Boys**
University of Texas at San Antonio
Institute of Texan Cultures
069-8474

147 **Travis Club Cigar**
University of Texas at San Antonio
Institute of Texan Cultures
100-0282

148 **Travis Park Methodist**
University of Texas at San Antonio
Institute of Texan Cultures
092-0048

150 **Battle of Flowers Parade**
University of Texas at San Antonio
Institute of Texan Cultures
099-1027

151 **Trolley Stop**
University of Texas at San Antonio
Institute of Texan Cultures
086-0097

152 **Fiesta Parade from Santa Rosa Hospital**
University of Texas at San Antonio
Institute of Texan Cultures
096-0872

154 **Parade of Nations**
University of Texas at San Antonio
Institute of Texan Cultures
099-0207

155 **Witte Museum**
University of Texas at San Antonio
Institute of Texan Cultures
084-0765

156 **Houston Street Looking East**
University of Texas at San Antonio
Institute of Texan Cultures
069-8953

157 **Two Men on Smith-Young Tower**
University of Texas at San Antonio
Institute of Texan Cultures
099-0483

158 **San Antonio River**
University of Texas at San Antonio
Institute of Texan Cultures
083-0518

159 **Smith-Young Tower**
University of Texas at San Antonio
Institute of Texan Cultures
101-0145

160 **Great Crowd**
University of Texas at San Antonio
Institute of Texan Cultures
104-0116

161 **Medical Arts Building**
University of Texas at San Antonio
Institute of Texan Cultures
101-0139

162 **Houston Street**
University of Texas at San Antonio
Institute of Texan Cultures
069-8958

163 **The Spanish Governor's Palace**
San Antonio Public Library
SAPL007-028

164 **San Jose Mission**
University of Texas at San Antonio
Institute of Texan Cultures
101-0124

165 **San Antonio Traction Company**
University of Texas at San Antonio
Institute of Texan Cultures
086-0145

166 **Interior of Buffalo Cafe**
University of Texas at San Antonio
Institute of Texan Cultures
073-0440

167 **Bluebonnet Hotel**
University of Texas at San Antonio
Institute of Texan Cultures
101-0152

168 **Belgian and American**
University of Texas at San Antonio
Institute of Texan Cultures
074-1004

170 **Gunter Hotel**
University of Texas at San Antonio
Institute of Texan Cultures
101-0151

171 **Dairyland Milk Wagon**
University of Texas at San Antonio
Institute of Texan Cultures
101-0159

172 **San Antonio River Near Navarro Street**
University of Texas at San Antonio
Institute of Texan Cultures
101-0133

173 **Shelling Pecans**
San Antonio Public Library
SAPL007-030

174 **West Side**
San Antonio Public Library
SAPL007-031

175 **St. Anthony Hotel**
University of Texas at San Antonio
Institute of Texan Cultures
101-0153

176 **220 Chestnut**
San Antonio Public Library
SAPL007-020

177 **Our Lady of the Lake College**
San Antonio Public Library
SAPL007-016

178 **Missouri-Kansas-Texas Railroad**
University of Texas at San Antonio
Institute of Texan Cultures
101-0128

179 **Palm Trees on Alamo Plaza**
University of Texas at San Antonio
Institute of Texan Cultures
101-0141

180 **Alamo Plaza**
University of Texas at San Antonio
Institute of Texan Cultures
101-0140

181 **Wagner Drug Store**
University of Texas at San Antonio
Institute of Texan Cultures
092-0011

182 **La Villita**
San Antonio Public Library
SAPL007-004

183 **Presa Street**
San Antonio Public Library
SAPL007-005

184 **The Vogue**
University of Texas at San Antonio
Institute of Texan Cultures
101-0147

185 **St. Mark's Episcopal Church**
Library of Congress
155337pu

186 **Post Office and Courthouse**
University of Texas at San Antonio
Institute of Texan Cultures
101-0143

187 **Prudential Cafe**
University of Texas at San Antonio
Institute of Texan Cultures
073-0441

188 **The Menger Hotel**
Library of Congress
154864pu

190 **Class 42 F2, R-Squadron**
San Antonio Public Library
SAPL007-012

191 **"A Link" Trainer**
San Antonio Public Library
SAPL007-013

192 **Loading Jeep into Plane**
Library of Congress
8e00130u

193 **Japanese Garden**
San Antonio Public Library
SAPL007-022

194 **Basilica of the National Shrine of the Little Flower**
San Antonio Public Library
SAPL007-019

195 **Arneson River Theater**
University of Texas at San Antonio
Institute of Texan Cultures
092-0143

196 **Marion Street**
San Antonio Public Library
SAPL007-015

197 **Union Stockyards**
San Antonio Public Library
SAPL007-010

198 **1100 Block of West Commerce**
University of Texas at San Antonio
Institute of Texan Cultures
082-0537

199 **HemisFair Aerial**
San Antonio Public Library
SAPL007-002

200 **Governor John Connally and President Lyndon B. Johnson**
University of Texas at San Antonio
Institute of Texan Cultures
070-0069

201 **Casa Rio Boat**
University of Texas at San Antonio
Institute of Texan Cultures
082-0524

HISTORIC PHOTOS OF SAN ANTONIO

San Antonio is an American city quintessentially founded upon change. From its beginnings as the mission Villa de Bejar to the present, San Antonio has consistently built and reshaped its appearance, ideals, and industry. Through changing fortunes, it has continued to grow and prosper by overcoming adversity and maintaining the strong, independent culture of its citizens and its distinctive identity.

Historic Photos of San Antonio captures this journey through still photography selected from the finest archives. Beginning in Civil War days and continuing through HemisFair 68, *Historic Photos of San Antonio* follows life, government, education, and events that shaped the city's history during those times.

This volume captures unique and rare scenes as depicted in nearly 200 historic photographs. Published in striking black and white, these images communicate historic events and everyday life of people working together to build a unique and prosperous city.

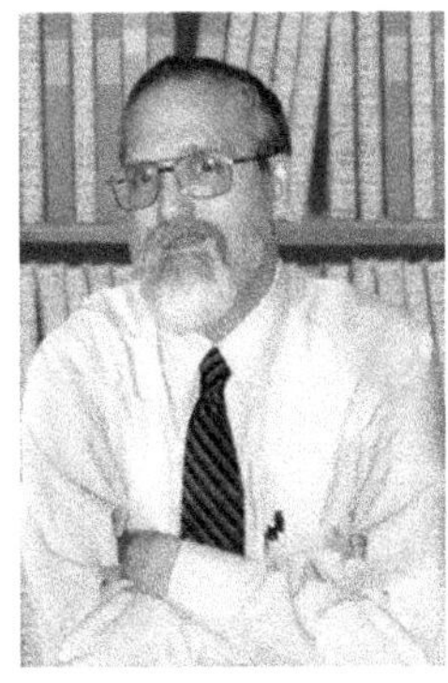

Frank S. Faulkner, Jr., was raised in South Texas. He attended Texas A&M University, earning a Bachelor of Arts in English. His Master of Science in Library Science is from Our Lady of the Lake University. He also has a Master of Theological Studies from Oblate Graduate School of Theology.

He has taught school, worked in retail sales, and served in the United States Army.

Mr. Faulkner has been with the San Antonio Public Library for over twenty-five years, working at Landa Branch Library; the Information and Ready Reference Department; the History, Social Science, and General Reference Department; and finally the Texana/Genealogy Department since its creation in 1995. In 2002, he was named Public Services Manager of the Texana/Genealogy Department.

Mr. Faulkner and his wife are involved in archaeology, church, and reading, as well as their family.

WWW.TURNERPUBLISHING.COM

www.ingramcontent.com/pod-product-compliance
Lightning Source LLC
LaVergne TN
LVHW060613110826
845154LV00003B/79

* 9 7 8 1 6 8 3 3 6 9 6 5 3 *